Iona Opie was born in 1923. During the ~~war she worked in the~~ meteorological section. Since then she has engaged in research ~~and~~ is an honorary member of the Folklore Society.

Peter Opie was born in 1918. During the war he served in the Royal Fusiliers (1939), was commissioned into the Royal Sussex Regiment (1940) and was invalided in 1941. He was President of the Anthropology Section of the British Association, 1962–63, and President of the Folklore Society, 1963–64. Peter Opie died in 1982.

The Opies began their research together in 1944. Specializing in the literature and traditions of childhood, they became, to quote Brian Jackson in *The Guardian*, 'superb archivists of the folklore movement'. They were jointly awarded the Coote-Lake Medal in 1960. Their joint publications include *The Oxford Dictionary of Nursery Rhymes*, *The Puffin Book of Nursery Rhymes*, *Children's Games in Street and Playground* (which was awarded the Chicago Folklore Prize), *The Oxford Book of Children's Verse* and *The Classic Fairy Tales* (also in Paladin).

1 Whereabouts of Chief Contributing Schools

IONA AND PETER OPIE

The Lore and Language
of Schoolchildren

A PALADIN BOOK

GRANADA
London Toronto Sydney New York

Published by Granada Publishing Limited in 1977
Reprinted 1982

ISBN 0 586 08311 1

First published in Great Britain by
Oxford University Press Ltd 1959
Copyright © Iona and Peter Opie 1959

Granada Publishing Limited
Frogmore, St Albans, Herts AL2 2NF
and
36 Golden Square, London W1R 4AH
515 Madison Avenue, New York, NY 10022, USA
117 York Street, Sydney, NSW 2000, Australia
100 Skyway Avenue, Rexdale, Ontario, M9W 3A6, Canada
61 Beach Road, Auckland, New Zealand

Made and printed in Great Britain by
Hazell Watson & Viney Ltd, Aylesbury, Bucks
Set in Linotype Ehrhardt

Preface

MORE than 200 years ago Queen Anne's physician John Arbuthnot, friend of Swift and Pope, observed that nowhere was tradition preserved pure and uncorrupt 'but amongst School-boys, whose Games and Plays are delivered down invariably from one generation to another'. If Dr Arbuthnot made any notes on his discovery they have not been found (he let his children make kites of his papers); and none of his eminent contemporaries, nor, indeed, many people since have given much further thought to the subject. The curious lore passing between children aged about 6–14, which today holds in its spell some 7 million inhabitants of this island, continues to be almost unnoticed by the other six-sevenths of the population. In fact one of the difficulties in making the present study has been that, since this work has no true predecessor, we had first to find out what there was to find out, before we knew whether there existed a subject to study. The generally held opinion, both inside and outside academic circles, was that children no longer cherished their traditional lore. We were told that the young had lost the power of entertaining themselves; that first the cinema, and now television had become the focus of their attention; and that we had started our investigation fifty years too late.

The study which comes nearest to being a predecessor to the present work is Norman Douglas's 'breathless catalogue' of *London Street Games* published in 1916. This pioneer work and social document of first importance is, however, something of a curiosity. Written by a fastidious literary craftsman, and based on genuine research amongst young cockneys, it records the secret joys of the gutter in a finely printed limited edition for the bibliophile. Even so, the book might have been a success if it had not been almost incomprehensible to anyone but a street arab. It is a skilful prose-poem fashioned out of the sayings and terminology of Douglas's urchin friends; and we must admit that it was only after several years, when we ourselves had become familiar with the argot which the kids still speak in London's alleyways and tenement courts, that we appreciated the book's finer points. Douglas was not interested in glossing the terms, and giving details of the games and pranks he listed, because he was under the impression that the street lore was largely impromptu, and therefore transient and merely local. Although he afterwards admitted (*Late Harvest*, 1946) that the words of one of the games he had witnessed, 'Buck, buck, how many fingers have I got up?', had survived from the time of Nero, he continued to believe, as he had done when he collected the games (mostly in 1913), that they were rapidly disappearing. The reason he made his catalogue, he said, was to see whether the next lot of children knew even the names of the street sports he recorded. So it may be as well to report straight away that, of the 137 child-chants and fragments of chants which Norman Douglas heard in the streets the other side of two world wars, more than 78 per cent (108 verses to be precise) are still being chanted by youngsters today.

Douglas had, indeed, a healthy mistrust of pedants who claim to discern a relic of marriage by capture in a simple singing game, and find a meaning 'not quite nice' in every underived child word like 'obobé' and 'a-lairy'. In *London Street Games* he characterizes this kind of person as 'Aunt Eliza'. Very possibly he had in mind Lady (Alice Bertha) Gomme whose 964-page, two-volume *Traditional Games of England, Scotland and Ireland* had appeared in 1894–8. This monumental compilation has remained the standard work on children's games (it does not, unfortunately, include children's customs and language) for the past sixty years. Yet in one sense, as Norman Douglas's book sharply revealed, it was out of date before ever it was published. It presented, anyway, only a partial picture. Lady Gomme, it is true, conscientiously secured correspondents all over Britain, but two features about her records have to be borne in mind: firstly, that the games with which she was supplied were largely recollections of what her correspondents had played when they were young, probably forty or fifty years earlier (i.e. around 1850), or were re-collections;[1] and secondly, that almost all her correspondents were country dwellers, and tended to be well-to-do. The great warren of city backstreets where the mass of the nation's children are bred and brought up remained *terra incognita*; and there is a slightly unreal feeling about most of the games Lady Gomme describes, as if the children had had to wash their hands and faces before playing them.

It is noticeable that in almost all books and articles on children's play (and there has been a continuous flow of them ever since Strutt's *Sports and Pastimes of the People of England* in 1801), the regular source of information has been the author's or other adult's childhood reminiscences;

1. That is to say, when they did collect from children, they asked for games which they remembered playing themselves.

and the *cri de cœur* has been nostalgia for the 'good old days'. The inevitable result has been that while the highlights of children's play, the dramatic and haunting 'Wally, wally, wallflower growing up so high', and the spectacular scrimmage of 'Hi Jimmy Knacker', have been documented over and over again, the everyday games have usually been overlooked. And the verbal lore, the amusing quips and jeers, the significant calls and superstitions, which mean so much in the life of a ten-year-old at the time, have been too ordinary to be filed in memory's archive.

The present study is based on the contributions of some 5,000 children attending, in the 1950s, seventy local authority schools, in different parts of England, Scotland, and Wales, and one school in Dublin. The schools included small village schools in remote rural districts, such as one where squirrels stole from the pockets of children's coats hanging in the porch; and they included the grim barrack-like buildings to be seen in nearly every city. They included central secondary schools like the one in mountainous Radnorshire, where, since the population averages 39 to the square mile, the children have to travel to school each day from widely separated homesteads; and they included schools where children rush in across the road from a single great tenement block. They included schools with long histories, and records of academic distinction, such as Kirkcaldy High School, where Carlyle was once a master; and a modern slum-clearance school where it was believed no traditional lore existed, and the girls were found to possess more than almost anywhere in Britain. They included a bilingual school, in which the first language of many of the contributing children was Welsh (the Welsh speakers pick up English rhymes almost before they know the meaning of the words, when they begin to mix with the E stream children). [1] And they included schools as far apart as Pendeen in the toe of Cornwall, and Golspie on the east coast of Sutherland, where the children were asked exactly the same questions about their lore that their predecessors had been asked sixty years earlier. [2]

Broadly speaking we believe that our contributing schools, and the

1. For a parallel situation: Russian, Polish, and Galician Jew immigrant children learning old English games in a Missouri playground, see L. R. C. Yoffie, 'Three Generations of Children's Singing Games in St. Louis', *Journal of American Folklore*, vol. lx, 1947, pp. 1–51.
2. In 1892 Bodley's librarian, E. W. B. Nicholson, gave the headmaster of Golspie School a questionnaire on children's games, rhymes, sayings, local customs, tales, and beliefs, and offered a prize to the pupil submitting the best essay. From the entries he received he wrote his book *Golspie: Contributions to its Folklore* published in 1897. (The actual children's papers are preserved in the Bodleian Library, MS. Eng. misc. c. 58.) In 1952, through the courtesy of the Sutherland Director of Education, 38 pupils at Golspie Senior Secondary School tackled the same questionnaire; and in 1953 a further group of 51 children answered a series of special questions covering item by item the traditions written down by their Victorian counterparts.

children in them, are representative of the child population as a whole. The study does not, however, except incidentally, include the lore current among children in the private, fee-charging establishments. And it does not, despite the sections on tortures and pranks after nightfall, set out to include the lore and language of the delinquent. We are concerned here merely with the fun-loving but father-fearing specimen who is typical of the vast majority. It seems necessary to say this because there continues to be such a spate of books about children who are mentally handicapped, or socially deprived, or who are in trouble with the police, that a book about the ordinary child is rather extraordinary. Indeed the picture which emerges is a happy one. It contains some tears but much laughter, some hard knocks but no whining; and the warm feeling the children have for their homes, and the pleasant relationships they evidently enjoy with their parents (revealed, for instance, in their descriptions of special days in the year), should gladden the heart of the most confirmed pessimist.

The present work is solely concerned with the contemporary school-child, and wherever possible his story is told in his own words. All rhymes, riddles, jokes, records of strange beliefs, descriptions of rites and customs, and other curiosities of juvenile lore and language for which no source is given may be taken as coming *direct from oral tradition*, collected by us or on our behalf from the children themselves. The only exception to this is the use we have occasionally made of some manuscript collections, acknowledged hereafter, which had already been compiled by various interested persons when we began work, and which were generously placed at our disposal. Historical annotation and comparative material has largely been relegated to the footnotes, or to paragraphs following the sign *⁎*. When we do not give a locality to a particular item it may be taken to have been fairly generally known; and even when we do name the place or places where a piece of lore was current, it does not, of course, necessarily mean that it was known only in those places, but that those were the places, or some of them, where we collected it. When we say that a rhyme or other item is known 'all over Britain' we mean, literally, that we had recordings of it from north, south, east, and west, perhaps from children in twenty or more different schools.

This is the first time, we believe, that oral lore has been studied in a number of widely separated places at the same time. And if our modest, unsponsored, and wholly voluntary survey has turned out to be the most comprehensive folklore collecting scheme which has yet been undertaken in Britain, it is, firstly, a tribute to our devoted band of collectors; and it is, secondly, a sad illustration of the way Britain's rich oral heritage, so often beautiful as well as scientifically interesting, continues to be neglected by those who otherwise care for the good things of this country.[1]

It may be, of course, that the information recorded here will seem trifling to some. But to us the unexpected quantity and variety of the traditions which have been collected, and of the street and playground games which are being described in companion volumes, do seem to show that children today are storing up for themselves just as lively memories as any of those with which we are now regaled by the old folk. In a way, this book contains information which would not ordinarily have been written down for another fifty years, for it is made up of what will be the childhood recollections of the older generation after A.D. 2000. Having now spent some length of time watching the rising generation, the first in the nuclear age, we cannot but feel that it is a virile generation. The modern school-child, when out of sight and on his own, appears to be rich in language, well-versed in custom, a respecter of the details of his own code, and a practising authority on traditional self-amusements. And a generation which cares for the traditions and entertainments which have been passed down to it is not one which is less good than its predecessors.

I. O. & P. O.

WEST LISS,
HAMPSHIRE

---

1. Unfortunately most academic and governmental people are not aware that English traditional lore exists to be collected. See, if interested, our two papers: 'The Collection of Folklore in England', *Journal of the Royal Society of Arts*, vol. ci, 21 August 1953, pp. 697–714; and 'England, the Great Undiscovered', *Folk-Lore*, vol. lxv, December 1954, pp. 149–64.

Acknowledgements

We are deeply indebted to the many talented people who have given their time and energy to gathering material for this volume. We do trust that they have always realized how appreciative we have been; and we can only hope that the finished work does not fall too far below their apparently high expectations.

The chief contributing schools, and the teachers responsible, have been as follows:

ABERDEEN	Powis Junior Secondary School (Mr James Thomson, lately Head Teacher)
ABERYSTWYTH	Dinas Secondary Modern School (Ysgol Eilradd Dinas) (Mr Hywel Watkins, Head Master, and Mr D. P. Hughes)
ALTON	Alton County Primary School (Mr Nicholas J. Wickham)
ANNESLEY	Annesley County Primary School (Mr L. Spolton)
BIRMINGHAM 11	Golden Hillock Road Primary School (Miss Freda Tomlinson)
BIRMINGHAM 27	Acocks Green Junior Mixed School (Miss Gladys Watson, Head Mistress)
BISHOP AUCKLAND	Cockton Hill School (Mr Harold Guthrie)
BLACKBURN	Intack School (Mrs E. H. Higham, Head Teacher)
CAERLEON	Caerleon Junior Mixed School (Miss P. Hockey, J.P., Head Mistress)
CAISTOR	The Grammar School (Mr R. Capper, Head Master)
CLEETHORPES	The Grammar School for Girls (Miss Iris Sawbridge)
CROYDON	Selhurst Grammar School for Boys (Mr Hugh Hughes)
DOVENBY	The Controlled School (Miss Isabelle Benson, Head Mistress)
DUBLIN	St Catherine's School, Meath Street (through the Rev. John Maher)
DUNDEE	Dens Road School (Miss Jane Tosh)

ECCLESFIELD	The Grammar School (Mr Linden Huddlestone)
EDINBURGH	Moray House School (Miss Maureen R. C. Laing)
ENFIELD	Suffolks Secondary Modern School (Mr A. H. Sellick)
ETTON	Etton Church of England Primary School (Mrs J. M. Johnson, Head Mistress)
FORFAR	Forfar Academy (Mr Douglas J. McMillan)
GLASGOW E.	Newlands School (Miss F. L. S. Begg)
GLASGOW E. 2	Shettleston School (Miss F. L. S. Begg)
GOLSPIE	Golspie Senior Secondary School (through Mr T. E. M. Landsborough, Sutherland Director of Education)
HELENSBURGH	Hermitage Senior Secondary School (Dr Ian J. Simpson)
IPSWICH	The School of Commerce and Social Studies (Miss Yvonne K. Rodwell)
KIRKCALDY	Kirkcaldy High School (Miss J. B. T. Christie, lately Woman Adviser)
KNIGHTON	Knighton Secondary Modern School (Mr Frank Noble)
LANGHOLM	Langholm Academy (Miss Eva Smart)
LAVERSTOCK	St Andrew's Junior School (Miss D. Belfield, Head Mistress)
LINCOLN	Spring Hill Secondary Modern School (Miss M. M. Fenton, Head Mistress)
LIVERPOOL (BOOTLE)	Balliol Modern Secondary School (Mr W. Stewart Elliott)
LONDON E. 8	Wilton Way County Secondary School (Miss Betty Gould)
LONDON S.E. 5	Wilson's Grammar School (Mr Linden Huddlestone)
LONDON S.E. 7	Maryon Park Secondary Modern School (Miss Dorothy King)
LUNCARTY	Redgorton School, near Luncarty (Mr A. K. Lunan, Head Master)
LYDNEY	Lydney Grammar School (Miss Alice Higgs)
MANCHESTER (SALE)	Sale County Grammar School for Boys (Mr G. G. Urwin)
MARKET RASEN	The Modern School (Mr S. B. Vickers, Head Master, together with Mr Fox and Mr Houlton)
NEWBRIDGE	Greenfield Secondary School (Mr Gordon Groves, J.P., Head Master)
NEWCASTLE UPON TYNE	Wingrove Road Junior School (Miss E. T. Kerr, Head Mistress)

OUNDLE	Oundle Church of England Primary School (through Mr H. Caudwell)
OXFORD	Headington Church of England School (Mrs E. Skwierczynska)
	Headington Secondary School (Miss Margaret Hornsey)
PENDEEN	Pendeen Primary School (Miss Ida Bennetts, Head Mistress)
PENRITH	The Boys' National School (through Mr John Jackson)
	The Girls' County School (through Mr John Jackson)
	Queen Elizabeth Grammar School (through Mr John Jackson)
	Tynefield Secondary Modern School (through Mr John Jackson)
PERTH	Kinnoull School (Mr J. S. Soane, Head Master)
PETERBOROUGH	Eastholm Secondary Modern School (through Mr R. W. Cowe)
PONTEFRACT	The King's School (Mr J. S. Golland)
PONTYPOOL	The County School for Girls (Miss A. Francis, Head Mistress)
PORTSMOUTH	Southern Grammar School for Girls (Miss Peggy Samways)
RUTHIN	Brynhyfryd Grammar School (Miss Una Williams)
SCARBOROUGH	Hinderwell Primary School (Miss R. Horsman)
SHREWSBURY	Monkmoor Secondary Modern School for Girls (Mrs Waddington)
SOUTH ELMSALL	Broad Lane Girls' School (Miss Blanche Eyre)
SOUTH MOLTON	The Secondary School (Mr Derek Stewart)
SPENNYMOOR	The Spennymoor Grammar Technical School (Mr William Sumner, Head Master; Mr Matthew Walton)
STOKE-ON-TRENT	(Through student teachers from the County of Stafford Training College, under the direction of Mr Norman Culpan)
	Meir Secondary Modern School, Longton
	Northwood County Primary School, Hanley
	Penkhull County Secondary School
	St Gregory's Roman Catholic Secondary Modern School, Longton
	Summerbank County Modern Girls' School, Tunstall
STREET	Street County Mixed (Senior) School (Mr R. R. Tomlin)

SWANSEA	Glanmor Secondary School for Girls (Miss Joyce A. Terrett)
THIRSK	Thirsk Grammar and Modern School (Miss M. S. Burton)
WELSHPOOL	The High School for Boys and Girls (Miss Dorothy Dyson)
WELWYN	St Mary's Secondary School (Mr Gwilym I. James)
WOOTTON BASSETT	The Church School (Mr John C. Harvey-Webb)
YORK	Tang Hall Junior School (Miss Theodora Ross)

In addition Miss W. I. Gilchrist and the students at St Katharine's College, near Ormskirk, and Miss A. E. Osmond and the students at the Training College, Bedford, have been to much trouble on our behalf, particularly in connection with the distribution maps; so has Miss H. A. Beecham of Florence Nightingale Hall, Nottingham University, and Mr Alex Helm of Congleton, who have both made careful specialized surveys for us; and Mr John Marsden of Exeter School, and Mr P. C. Sheppard of Brentwood School, who have each supplied us with quantities of information relative to certain lines of inquiry.

Further we have had valuable assistance from individual collectors and contributors, amongst them: Mr Gareth Adamson (Liverpool); Miss D. I. Barrow (Radcliffe County Secondary School); Miss D. M. Batchelor (Mundham, Norfolk); Mrs Anne Baxter (Edinburgh); Miss W. Berry (Sowerby); Mr Colin V. Brindley (Holmfirth County Primary School); Mr H. J. Brooks; Miss Emily Chisholm (Loughton); Miss E. G. M. Coles, a life-long folklore collector in Huntingdonshire (Spaldwick County Primary School); Mrs D. M. Cornish (Chudleigh); Mrs R. T. Coxon (Plympton St Mary); Mrs G. Davies (Great Staughton County Primary School); Mrs Jane Dawson; Miss Olive Delvino (London); Mr Ian Dunmur (Sheffield); Mr Roy Dunstan (Lincoln); Mr T. E. Easterfield (London N. W. 11); Miss Gillian Edwards (Cambridge); Mrs M. E. Elders (High Laver C. of E. School); Mr John L. Gilbert (Peterborough); Mr E. D. Glover (Hayes and Brimington); Mr Wilfred Granville; Mr Robert Graves; Mr Roger Lancelyn Green; Mr Geoffrey Handley-Taylor; Miss Winifred Hart (Oxted); Mr J. L. Hobbs, Borough Librarian, Shrewsbury; Mr W. Howard (Plympton St Mary C. of E. Primary School, Devon); Mr Daniel Howison (London); Miss Carrol Jenkins, who has contributed to every stage in the development of this work (Bath); Mrs G. I. Jones (Anglesey); Mr Roland Knaster; Miss Erica Kurz; Miss B. A. Kneller (Redhill); Mr David Lockhart (Ballingry); Miss Deirdre Le Faye (London and Reading); Miss H. Mackereth (Ashford); Mrs M. M. Mawson (Lancashire); Mr Geoffrey Potter (Worcester); Miss S. C. Priest (Durham); Mr James Reeves; Mr W. S. Reilly (Ulverston); Mr T. Scott (Gedney Drove End County Primary School, Spalding); Mrs L. Sewell (Knutsford); Miss J. M. Shelmerdine; Mr P. L. H. Smith (County Secondary Boys' School, Shoreham-by-Sea); Mr Morris A. Snellgrove (London and Dorking); Miss K. I. Stevenson (Ulverston); Mrs Phyllis Tatlow (Eckington, Derbyshire); Mrs D. G. Thomson and Miss Lesley Thomson (Castle Eden); Mr T. Todd; Miss Ruth L. Tongue, a life-long collector of folklore in Somerset (Harrow and Somerset); Miss G. E. Toyer (Luton); Mr Frank Turner (Liverpool); Mr R. C. Warner; and Mrs W. Wells (Farnham, Surrey). Some of the above have been continuous contributors throughout the eight years it has taken to prepare this volume, and in this connection we would like to mention that Miss J. B. T. Christie (Kirkcaldy), Mr John C. Harvey-Webb (Wiltshire), Mr Frank Noble (Knighton), Miss Yvonne K. Rodwell (Ipswich), Mr J. S. Soane (Perth), Mr G. G. Urwin (Sale, Manchester), and Mr S. B. Vickers (Market Rasen) have, similarly, been constant friends to this work, doing very much more than organize the collection of material within their schools as already acknowledged; while Miss Joyce A. Terrett of Swansea, as well as giving much other assistance, has for seven years sent us a monthly packet of material, and has collected not only in Swansea and Glamorgan but in several parts of Europe.

We have also had the benefit of some excellent manuscript collections, made independently of our survey: Mr L. R. England, Director of Mass-Observation Ltd, kindly made available to us reports prepared by Mass-Observation's panel of voluntary observers; Mr F. Grice lent us his collection of children's rhymes collected in County Durham; Miss Brigid Maxwell, Editor, Home Section, *Farmers Weekly*, lent us the 105 readers' essays on children's play entered for a competition; Mr H. W. Harwood, formerly chief reporter of the Halifax *Courier and Guardian*, presented us with a life-time's collections in and around Halifax, and has given much other assistance; Miss Jean C. Rodger, compiler of *Lang Strang*, gave us the long loan of a life-time's collectings in and around Forfar, and gathered further material specially for us; Mr W. J. A. Hahn, late Chief Librarian and Curator, Camberwell Public Libraries, placed in our keeping 1,052 children's essays on juvenile interests and activities entered (1954) for the stimulating competition which is sponsored annually by the Libraries Committee, and Miss G. Johnson, Mr Hahn's successor, sent us a similar number of essays the following year.

Our acknowledgements should also reveal the generosity traditionally shown by one folklorist to another in their respective fields, and demonstrate the usefulness of the Folk-Lore Society's meetings. Thus we would mention that we have had material or information from: Miss Violet Alford, author of *Introduction to English Folklore*; Dr Wilfred Bonser, Hon. Librarian of the Folk-Lore Society's library, the most valuable of its kind in the country; Col. P. W. F. Brown; Mrs Mary Danielli; the late Mr Allan Gomme, M.B.E.; Miss Christina Hole, editor of *Folklore*; Dr Margaret Murray; Mr L. F. Newman, F.S.A.; Mr M. M. Rix; and Professor E. M. Wilson. Also, Miss Theo Brown, Folklore Recorder, The Devonshire Association; Mrs Katharine M. Harris, Committee on Ulster Folk Life and Traditions; and Miss Sara Jackson, Librarian, The English Folk Dance and Song Society.

For behind-the-scenes work on our behalf, arranging introductions, and other kindnesses, we are indebted to: Mrs H. A. Lake Barnett, until recently Hon. Secretary of the Folk-Lore Society; Mr Norman Culpan, Hon. Secretary of the Society for Teachers of English; Mr Geoffrey Dando, when Secretary to The Standing Conference for Local History; Professor J. H. Delargy, Hon. Director of the Irish Folklore Commission, and Mr Sean O'Sullivan, Archivist; Miss F. A. R. Murray, Hon. Secretary of the Lincolnshire Local History Society, who never failed to obtain for us whatever we asked for; Mr E. J. Nicol, Regional Officer of the National Council of Social Service, Birmingham; Lord Raglan, F.S.A.; and Mrs Bertha Walton who was one of the corner-stones in the early organization of the survey. We are also grateful for the good offices of *The Scottish Educational Journal*, *The Sunday Times* (would readers please note that the history of 'Pop goes the weasel' has had to be left to a later volume), and *The Times Educational Supplement*.

It is a pleasure, too, to acknowledge the friendly help we have received from scholars and collectors in other countries who have made possible the comparison of the lore in the British Isles with that current overseas. We are grateful to: Mrs Patricia Evans, for sending her booklets on children's play in San Francisco; Professore and Signora V. Gargiulo (Capri); Mr W. B. Hughes (Sydney); Mr G Legman (New York); The Rev. J. T. Munday (Broken Hill, Northern Rhodesia); Miss Kerstin Munck [Mrs Edgar Osborne] (Stockholm); Professeur Roger Pinon, for the parts as they appeared of his *La nouvelle Lyre Malmédienne*; Dr Elfriede Rath (Museum für Volkskunde, Vienna); Miss Cecily Raysor (Chicago); Mrs Grace Partridge Smith, the veteran American folklore collector (Carbondale, Illinois); Dr Brian Sutton-Smith (Wellington, New Zealand); Mr Ian Turner (Victoria, Australia); Professor Francis Lee Utley, past President of the American Folklore Society (Columbus, Ohio); and Mr Carl Withers, author of *A Rocket in my Pocket*, etc. (New York). Most of all, we are indebted to Dr Dorothy Howard of the State Teacher's College, Frostburg, Maryland, one of the originators of this field of study, who not only sent us her great thesis 'Folk Jingles of American Children', the fruit of seven years' collecting in the 1930s, but a quantity of her subsequent collectings both in Maryland and in Australia.

Nearer home, we wish to thank Mrs Jean Fullerton, who put in three months' intensive work reorganizing our files; Mr Robert Lusty, when a Director of Michael Joseph Ltd, for originally inciting us to undertake this work; Miss Joan Ford, who came to us in 1950 after leaving school, and has remained a kind of resident technical adviser ever since; and we should mention that it has been no disadvantage to us having three schoolchildren living in the house, especially when they have been as tolerant of our interests as have been James, Robert, and Letitia.

Finally we wish to express our heartfelt gratitude to Miss F. Doreen Gullen of Scarborough, formerly of *The Scottish Educational Journal*, and editor of *Traditional Number Rhymes and Games* (1950), who, from the commencement of the work to its final editing and typing, has been a source of strength and wisdom without which we do not think we could have brought this undertaking to its conclusion.

Contents

Distribution Maps

1 Introductory

THE scraps of lore which children learn from each other are at once more real, more immediately serviceable, and more vastly entertaining to them than anything which they learn from grown-ups. To a child it can be a 'known fact' that the Lord's Prayer said backwards raises the devil, that a small knife-wound between the thumb and forefinger gives a person lock-jaw, that a hair from the head placed on the palm will split the master's cane. It can be a useful piece of knowledge that the reply to 'A pinch and a punch for the first of the month' is 'A pinch and a kick for being so quick'. And a verse a child hears the others saying,

> Mister Fatty Belly, how is your wife?
> Very ill, very ill, up all night,
> Can't eat a bit of fish
> Nor a bit of liquorice.
> O-U-T spells out and out you must go
> With a jolly good clout upon your ear hole spout,

may seem the most exciting piece of poetry in the language.

Such a verse, recited by 8-year-olds in Birmingham, can be as traditional and as well known to children as a nursery rhyme; yet no one would mistake it for one of Mother Goose's compositions. It is not merely that there is a difference in cadence and subject-matter, the manner of its transmission is different. While a nursery rhyme passes from a mother or other adult to the small child on her knee, the school rhyme circulates simply from child to child, usually outside the home, and beyond the influence of the family circle. By its nature a nursery rhyme is a jingle preserved and propagated not by children but by adults, and in this sense it is an 'adult' rhyme. It is a rhyme which is adult approved. The school-child's verses are not intended for adult ears. In fact part of their fun is the thought, usually correct, that adults know nothing about them. Grown-ups have outgrown the schoolchild's lore. If made aware of it they tend to deride it; and they actively seek to suppress its livelier manifestations.

Certainly they do nothing to encourage it. And the folklorist and anthropologist can, without travelling a mile from his door, examine a thriving unselfconscious culture (the word 'culture' is used here deliberately) which is as unnoticed by the sophisticated world, and quite as little affected by it, as is the culture of some dwindling aboriginal tribe living out its helpless existence in the hinterland of a native reserve. Perhaps, indeed, the subject is worthy of a more formidable study than is accorded it here. As Douglas Newton has pointed out: 'The world-wide fraternity of children is the greatest of savage tribes, and the only one which shows no sign of dying out.'

Continuity

No matter how uncouth schoolchildren may outwardly appear, they remain tradition's warmest friends. Like the savage, they are respecters, even venerators, of custom; and in their self-contained community their basic lore and language seems scarcely to alter from generation to generation. Boys continue to crack jokes that Swift collected from his friends in Queen Anne's time; they play tricks which lads used to play on each other in the heyday of Beau Brummel; they ask riddles which were posed when Henry VIII was a boy. Young girls continue to perform a magic feat (levitation) of which Pepys heard tell ('One of the strangest things I ever heard'); they hoard bus tickets and milk-bottle tops in distant memory of a love-lorn girl held to ransom by a tyrannical father; they learn to cure warts (and are successful in curing them) after the manner which Francis Bacon learnt when he was young. They call after the tearful the same jeer Charles Lamb recollected; they cry 'Halves!' for something found as Stuart children were accustomed to do; and they rebuke one of their number who seeks back a gift with a couplet used in Shakespeare's day. They attempt, too, to learn their fortune from snails, nuts, and apple-parings – divinations which the poet Gay described nearly two and a half centuries ago; they span wrists to know if someone loves them in the way that Southey used at school to tell if a boy was a bastard; and when they confide to each other that the Lord's Prayer said backwards will make Lucifer appear, they are perpetuating a story which was gossip in Elizabethan times.[1]

1. Witches were supposed to say their prayers backwards, with awful effect, as is noted in Robert Greene's *A Qvip for an Vpstart Courtier*, 1592, sig. D3, and this method of raising the devil is also mentioned by Defoe in his *System of Magick*, 1727, pp. 259–60. Refer-

The same continuity obtains in their games and play songs. When the Birmingham 8-year-olds chant about 'Mister Fatty Belly' they are perpetuating a verse with a lineage going back to schooldays under the Regency, for P. H. Gosse (the father of Sir Edmund) recorded that when he was at school, 1818–23: 'One boy meeting another would address him with these queries; the other giving the replies:

> Doctor! Doctor! how's your wife?
> Very bad, upon my life.
> Can she eat a bit of pie?
> Yes, she can, as well as I.'[1]

Today, sets of these responses, usually repeated for counting-out or skipping, have been collected from schoolchildren in Aberdeen, Bath, Manchester, Market Rasen, Scarborough, Spennymoor, Tunstall, and York City; and some of the versions are all but identical with the rhyme as it was known more than 130 years ago. Thus a 12-year-old Spennymoor girl reports:

'When I get home from school there is usually some little girls out of the infants school playing in the street, and their special little rhyme is:

> Little fatty doctor, how's your wife?
> Very well, thank you, she's alright.
> Can she eat a twopenny pie?
> Yes sir, yes sir, and so can I.

The older girls think that rhyme is silly for them, so they play faster games.'

Apparent Uniformity of the Lore

The fact that schoolchild lore continues to thrive in a natural manner amongst unselfconscious adherents, and that we have been able to watch it functioning in a number of widely separated communities, has allowed us to carry our study a step further than we thought possible at the outset; it has enabled us to obtain a picture of the state of traditional lore over the country as a whole. Thus it has shown that traditional lore exists

---

ences to schoolboys' possession of the secret occur in *Notes and Queries*, 1st ser., vol. iv, 1851, p. 53, and 3rd ser., vol. iv, 1863, p. 492; and we knew it ourselves in our schooldays, but never dared test it. For accounts of boys who did, see William Henderson, *Folk Lore of the Northern Counties*, 1866, p. 19, and *The Listener*, 3 January 1957, p. 10. A 13-year-old Tredegar, Monmouthshire girl tells us it is believed there that if one runs round the church three times the devil will appear.
1. 'A Country Day-School Seventy Years Ago', *Longman's Magazine*, vol. xiii 1889, p. 518.

everywhere; that as many, if not more, traditional games are known to city children as to country children; and that children with homes and backgrounds as different from each other as mining community and garden suburb share jokes, rhymes, and songs, which are basically identical.[1] Conscious as we were of the economy of human invention, and the tenacity of oral tradition (the two elements without which there would be no folklore), we were not prepared for quite the identity of ritual and phraseology which has been revealed throughout the land in children's everyday witticisms, and in the newer of their self-organized amusements.

The faithfulness with which one child after another sticks to the same formulas even of the most trivial nature is remarkable. A meaningless counting-out phrase such as 'Pig snout, walk out', sometimes adapted to 'Boy Scout, walk out', or a tag for two-balls like 'Shirley Temple is a star, s-t-a-r', is apparently in use throughout England, Scotland, and Wales. If, in the vicinity of Westminster, a visitor hears for the first time children skipping to the simple chant,

> Big Ben strikes one,
> Big Ben strikes two,
> Big Ben strikes three,

he may well suppose that the words are the just-for-the-minute invention of a particularly unimaginative local child. Yet this formula is repeated all over London, down side-streets behind the Victorian mansions of Kensington, in the bustle of Hackney, in Manor Park, and outside London in Croydon, Enfield, and Welwyn. Travelling farther afield it will be found in use at Scunthorpe in Lincolnshire, at Cwmbran in Monmouthshire, in Edinburgh, in Glasgow, and, in fact, apparently everywhere. Nor is it a passing fad of the juvenile fancy, for it will be found that Norman Douglas quotes it in *London Street Games* (p. 49); and the fact has to be faced that since 1916 some 30 million children have dashed through the nation's playgrounds, respecters neither of persons nor property, yet preserving the silly chant as carefully as if it was a magic incantation. Similarly 'Pig snout, walk out' is known to have been current in the Island of Bute in 1911.[2] And although 'Shirley Temple is a star'

1. The city child usually knows more games than the country child, for he has more time to play them. The real country child, living in a village or on a small-holding, is generally expected to do jobs around the home when he returns from school, and once he has passed the singing-game stage, his play tends to be limited to whatever free time there is at school. However, his knowledge of traditional wisdom – proverbs, dark sayings, and seasonal customs – is correspondingly greater.

2. *Miscellanea of the Rymour Club*, vol. ii, pt. ii, 1913, p. 69.

cannot be so old, children have carried it to Australia and Canada and have planted it in those countries, or, perhaps, have brought it here from across the sea.

Even when it seems certain that a rhyme must be purely local, such as the song little girls skip to in Manchester,

> Manchester Guardian, Evening News,
> I sell Evening News,

it may be no more than a variation on an established theme. In Radcliffe, Lancashire, one girl skips while two others turn the rope chanting,

> Manchester, Bolton Evening News,
> I sell evening one . . .

In Wellington, Shropshire, the girls skip to,

> Wellington Journal, Evening News,
> Ever see a cat in a pair of shoes?

In Shrewsbury,

> London, Liverpool, Weekly Post,
> I say number one, two, three.

In Swansea, amongst several variants,

> South Wales Evening Post,
> Un, dau, tri [*one*, *two*, *three*].

And our own correspondents, and correspondents to the *Manchester Guardian* (23 and 28 April 1955), recall skipping to versions of this chant in north-west England as far back as the nineties.[1]

Speed of Oral Transmission

Since, through our collaborators, it has been possible to keep an eye on several widely separated places simultaneously, we have, on occasion,

---

1. Children, it seems, are no more inventive than the ridiculed old country-folk with their ancient multi-adaptable weather proverbs, e.g.:

> When Roseberry Topping puts on a hat,
> Let Cleveland then beware of that.
> > *North Riding of Yorkshire.*

> When Traprain puts on his hat,
> The Lothian lads may look at that.
> > *East Lothian.*

> When Bredon Hill puts on his hat.
> Ye men of the vale, beware of that.
> > *Worcestershire.*

been afforded glimpses of oral transmission in actual operation. The speed with which a newly made-up rhyme can travel the length and breadth of the country by the schoolchild grapevine seems to be little short of miraculous. Some idea of the efficiency of oral transmission can be obtained by following verses which are topical, or which are parodies of newly published songs, and can consequently be dated, although for test purposes it is, unfortunately, best to study specimens which are of a scurrilous or indelicate nature for with these there is, in general, less likelihood of dissemination by means other than word-of-mouth.

A notorious instance of the transmission of scurrilous verses occurred in 1936 at the time of the Abdication. The word-of-mouth rhymes which then gained currency were of a kind which could not possibly, at that time, have been printed, broadcast, or even repeated in the music halls. One verse, in particular, made up one can only wonder by whom,

> Hark the Herald Angels sing,
> Mrs Simpson's pinched our king,

was on juvenile lips not only in London, but as far away as Chichester in the south, and Liverpool and Oldham in the north. News that there was a constitutional crisis did not become public property until around 25 November of that year, and the king abdicated on 10 December. Yet at a school Christmas party in Swansea given before the end of term, Christmas 1936, when the tune played happened to be 'Hark the Herald Angels Sing', a mistress found herself having to restrain her small children from singing this lyric, known to all of them, which cannot have been composed much more than three weeks previously. Many an advertising executive with a six-figure budget at his disposal might envy such crowd penetration. Similarly, the ultra juvenile verse,

> Temptation, temptation, temptation,
> Dick Barton went down to the station,
> Blondie was there
> All naked and bare,
> Temptation, temptation, temptation,

wherever it may have originated, was reported to us in quick succession as rife among children in Kirkcaldy in January 1952, as known to children in Swansea in January 1952, and it reached children in Alton in February 1952. These three places are up to 400 miles apart; yet an instance of even more distant transmission can be cited. At the beginning of 1956 'The Ballad of Davy Crockett' was launched on the radio. It was especially intended to appeal to children, and quickly reached the top of the adult hit parade. (For a note on the Crockett craze see pages 138–40.) But the official words of the ballad, beginning,

> Born on a mountain top in Tennessee,
> Greenest state in the Land of the Free,

were very small beer compared with the word-of-mouth stanzas which rapidly won approval in juvenile society. One composition, beginning 'The Yellow Rose of Texas', was collected in Perth in April 1956, in Alton, Battersea, Great Bookham, Reading, and Scarborough in July 1956, in Kent in August 1956, and in Swansea in September 1956. Another parody, sung by schoolgirls in Swansea in September 1956, appeared to have local associations:

> Born on a table top in Joe's Café,
> Dirtiest place in the U.S.A.
> Polished off his father when he was only three,
> Polished off his mother with D.D.T.
>> Davy, Davy Crockett,
>> King of the Wild Frontier.

The teacher who sent this verse remarked that Joe's Café was a popular Swansea establishment near the beach. Subsequently, however, we had news of the verse being current in Brentwood, Hornchurch, Reading, Upminster, and Woolwich, all naming 'Joe's Café'. But unknown to any of our home observers, and before the official Davy Crockett song had reached Britain, an Australian correspondent, writing 3 January 1956, had reported that the following ditty was 'sweeping the schools' in Sydney:

> Reared on a paddle, pop in Joe's café,
> The dirtiest dump in the U.S.A.,
> Poisoned his mother with D.D.T.
> And shot his father with a .303.
>> Davy, Davy Crockett,
>> The man who is no good.

It seems that the schoolchild underground also employs trans-world couriers.

Wear and Repair during Transmission

The previous section has shown how quickly a rhyme passes from one schoolchild to the next, and illustrates a further difference between school lore and nursery lore. In nursery lore a verse or tradition, learnt in early childhood, is not usually passed on again until the little listener has grown up, and has children of his own, or even grandchildren. The period between learning a nursery rhyme and transmitting it may be anything from twenty to seventy years. With the playground lore, however, a rhyme may be excitedly passed on within the very hour it is learnt; and, in general, it passes between children who are the same age, or nearly so, since it is uncommon for the difference in age between playmates to be more than five years. If, therefore, a playground rhyme can be shown to have been current for a hundred years, or even just for fifty, it follows that it has been retransmitted over and over again; very possibly it has passed along a chain of two or three hundred young hearers and tellers, and the wonder is that it remains alive after so much handling, let alone that it bears resemblance to the original wording.

In most schools there is a wholly new generation of children every six years; and when a rhyme such as 'Little fatty doctor, how's your wife?' can be shown to be more than 130 years old it may be seen that it has passed through the keeping of not less than twenty successive generations of schoolchildren, and been exposed to the same stresses that nursery lore would meet only after 500 years of oral conveyance. This, in itself, makes schoolchild lore of peculiar value to the student or oral communication, for the behaviour and defects of oral transmission can be seen in operation during a relatively short period, much as if the phenomenon had been placed in a mechanical stresser to speed up the wear and tear.

Thus we find that variations, even apparently creative ones, occur more often by accident than by design. Usually they come about through mishearing or misunderstanding, as in the well-known hymnal misapprehension:

> Can a woman's tender care
> Cease towards the child she-bear?

A line in the song 'I'm a knock-kneed sparrow' quickly becomes 'I'm a cockney sparrow'. 'Calico breeches', no longer familiar to youth today, become 'comical breeches'. 'Elecampane' becomes 'elegant pain'. 'Green gravel, green gravel' becomes by association 'Greengages, greengages'. And the unmeaning 'Alligoshee, alligoshee', in the marching game, is rationalized to 'Adam and Eve went out to tea'. At one school the pledges 'Die on oath', 'Dianothe', and 'Diamond oath' were all found to be current at the same time. The common tendency to speed up a ritual or abridge a formula also produces surprising results. At a Surrey school the pledge 'Cub's honour' became, by jest, 'Cub's-on-a-car', which was presently abridged, so that the standard pledge became 'Car'. Indeed the corruptive influence of the pun on language and custom is more considerable than might be supposed. When a child, as a sign of derision, expels air through his compressed lips, the stock retort is 'We have them with custard'. The chain here is that breaking wind was, at one time, by the process of rhyming slang, known as a 'raspberry tart', hence 'raspberry'. Subsequently this became the name for the imitative noise made with the mouth; and this term is still retained, although it has disappeared as a name for the original exhalation.

Again, a fool is very generally called a 'blockhead', his head being likened to the denseness of wood. Consequently, as a joke, when somebody says 'touch wood' he is liable on occasion to touch the head of a notorious dunce, or of a child whom he wishes to make out to be a dunce, or, in self-deprecation, his own head. This joke has in fact become so commonplace that many children are already forgetting that touching the head is a joke, and state seriously: 'If you say that something nice is going to happen you must either touch wood or your head', or, without qualification, 'To avert ill-luck it is the custom to touch your head'. So it is that the time is upon us when, in a prefabricated classroom with desks and fittings manufactured entirely out of plastic and chromium, it will not be possible for children to touch wood, only their heads; and when these children grow up it may become normal with the adult population, too, to put a finger to their brow as a superstitious act of self-protection.

Thus, it may be seen, oral lore is subject to a continual process of wear and repair, for folklore, like everything else in nature, must adapt itself to new conditions if it is to survive. An old rustic prognostication about magpies, for instance, is now commonly repeated by city children (who probably would not recognize a magpie even if they saw one) when telling fortunes with bus tickets. The lyrics of certain obsolescent singing games have obtained a new lease of life by being speeded up and sung while skipping. Cigarette cards, which have become scarce, are being replaced in flicking games by milk-bottle tops, known as 'flying saucers'. The bonfires of Hallowe'en have been postponed five days to become part of the effigy burning on Guy Fawkes Night. And a ribald rhyme of sixty years ago such as 'Lottie Collins has no drawers' is now chanted in honour of a modern idol, Miss Diana Dors.

To illustrate this mutation it may be interesting to set out some recordings of a playground rhyme at different stages in its history to show how, over the course of 200 years, it has been remoulded and brought up to date. In 1725 a song about a cup-shot grenadier, probably dating from the previous century, had already, according to Henry Carey, become proverbial as a children's play-rhyme. Grenadiers, however, are no longer objects of popular derision, and, although the grenadier still survives as the disgraceful hero of the rhyme in nursery lore where change is slower,[1] in the playground the rhyme has developed along more contemporary lines.

Development of a Playground Rhyme

1725

> Now he acts the *Grenadier*,
> Calling for *a Pot of Beer*:
> *Where's his Money? He's forgot*:
> *Get him gone, a Drunken Sot.*
>
> Lines from Henry Carey's ballad 'Namby Pamby' (1726 edn., E3–4).

1774

> Whoes there
>   A Granidier
> What dye want
>   A Pint of Beer.
> Whoes there
>   A Granidier
> What dye want
>   A Pint of Beer.
>
> 'Catch, The Soldier and the Ale House Man' as noted down, with tune, by Samuel Wesley when 8 years old (British Museum, MS. Adds. 34998, f. 34).

1780

> Who comes here?
>   A Grenadier.
> What do you want?
>   A Pot of Beer.
> Where is your Money?
>   I've forgot.
> Get you gone
>   You drunken Sot.
>
> 'Mother Goose's Melody' (1795 edn., p. 42).

c. 1907

> Eenty, teenty, tuppenny bun,
> Pitching tatties doon the lum;
> Who's there? John Blair.
> What does he want? A bottle of beer.
> Where's your money? I forgot.
> Go downstairs, you drunken sot.
>
> Collected from schoolchildren in Edinburgh. Used for counting-out. Rymour Club, 'Miscellanea', vol. 1, 1911, p. 104.

c. 1910

> Far are ye gaein'?
> Across the gutter.
> Fat for?
> A pund o' butter.
> Far's yer money?
> In my pocket.
> Far's yer pocket?
> Clean forgot it!
>
> Current among children in Forfar, c. 1910. Jean C. Rodger, 'Lang Strang', 1948.

1916

> Rat a tat tat, who is that?
> Only grandma's pussy-cat.
> What do you want?
> A pint of milk.
> Where's your money?
> In my pocket.
> Where is your pocket?
> I forgot it.
> O you silly pussy-cat.
>
> Used for skipping, 'London Street Games', 1916, p. 64.

1. See *The Oxford Dictionary of Nursery Rhymes*, 1951, p. 195.

1939

A frog walked into a public house
And asked for a pint of beer.
Where's your money?
In my pocket.
Where's your pocket?
I forgot it.
Well, please walk out.

Used for counting-out in Swansea.

1952

A monkey came to my shop
I asked him what he wanted.
A loaf, sir. A loaf, sir.
Where's your money?
In my pocket.
Where's your pocket?
I ain't got it.
Well, out you bunk.

Skipping for two'. Girl, 12, Market Rasen.

1943

Rat tat tat, who is that?
Only Mrs Pussy Cat.
What do you want?
A pint of milk.
Where's your penny?
In my pocket.
Where's your pocket?
I forgot it.
Please walk out.

Used for skipping at Castle Eden, Co. Durham.

1952

A pig walked into a public house
And asked for a drink of beer.
Where's your money, sir?
In my pocket, sir.
Where's your pocket, sir?
In my jacket, sir.
Where's your jacket, sir?
I forgot it, sir.
Please walk out.

Used for counting-out. Girl, 12, Cleethorpes.

1950

Mickey Mouse
In a public house
Drinking pints of beer.
Where's your money?
In my pocket.
Where's your pocket?
I forgot it.
Please walk out.

Used for counting-out in Alton.

1954

I had a little beer shop
A man walked in.
I asked him what he wanted.
A bottle of gin.
Where's your money?
In my pocket.
Where's your pocket?
I forgot it.
Please walk out.

Used for skipping in York City.

In illustrating the variations which have occurred in this rhyme over the years (most of them due to contact with newer verses), we should repeat that to us the remarkable feature of schoolchild lore is how comparatively little it alters considering the usage it receives.

Sources of the Rhymes

The children themselves often have a touching faith in the novelty of their oral acquisitions. Of the rhyme,

> House to let, apply within,
> Lady turned out for drinking gin,

which we have collected from twenty-four places in the British Isles, also from South Africa, Australia, and the United States, and which was recorded as traditional in 1892 (G. F. Northall, *English Folk-Rhymes*, p. 306), an Alton girl remarked: 'Here's one you won't know because it's only just made up.' Of the couplet,

> Mrs Mason broke a basin
> How much did it cost?

lines which are the recollection of a counting-out formula recorded in 1883 (G. F. Jackson, *Shropshire Folk-lore*, p. 573), a Birmingham child vouched the newness because it was 'named after a teacher's wife'. Children are, in fact, prone to claim the authorship of a verse when they have done no more than alter a word in it, for instance substitute a familiar name for a name unknown to them; and they tend to be passionately loyal to the presumed genius of a classmate, or of a child who has just left their school, who is credited with the invention of each newly heard composition. The unromantic truth, however, is that children do not 'go on inventing games out of their heads all the time', as Norman Douglas believed; for the type of person who is a preserver is rarely also creative, and the street child is every bit as conservative as was George VI with his lifelong preference for the hymns he sang in the choir at Dartmouth. The nearest the normal child gets to creativeness is when he stumbles on a rhyme, as we have overheard: an 8-year-old, playing in some mud, suddenly chanted 'Stuck in the muck, stuck in the muck', whereupon his playmates took up the refrain, 'Stuck in the muck, stuck in the muck'. A 10-year-old added:

> It's a duck, it's a duck,
> Stuck in the muck, stuck in the muck,

and the group echoed this too, and went on chanting it, spasmodically with apparent satisfaction, for above an hour, so that it seemed certain that we were in at the birth of a new oral rhyme. But when we asked them about it a week later they did not know what we were talking about. The fact is that even a nonsense verse must have some art and rhythm in it if it is to obtain a hold on a child's mind, although exactly what the quality is which gives some verses immortality is difficult to discover.

Where, then, do the rhymes come from? The origins of only a few can be traced, but these few may be indicative. The popular verse,

> Sam, Sam, the dirty man,
> Washed his face in a frying pan;
> He combed his hair with a donkey's tail,
> And scratched his belly with a big toe nail,

known throughout Britain in a multitude of versions (this one is from a 13-year-old boy in Pontefract) is a relic of a once famous song 'Old Dan Tucker' composed by the black-faced minstrel Daniel Decatur Emmett, of 'Dixie' fame, and printed in 1843. Similarly Nellie Bligh who 'shuts her eye' ('because she cannot shut her ears'), or who catches a fly and ties it to a pin, was the heroine of a mid-nineteenth-century nigger minstrel song by Stephen Foster; while a further 'Ethiopian' legacy is the little tongue-tripping verse,

> I saw Esau sawing wood,
> And Esau saw I saw him;
> Though Esau saw I saw him saw
> Still Esau went on sawing,

sometimes sung by children when skipping (this version from an 8-year-old Alton girl), which is descended from the lyric 'I saw Esau kissing Kate' written by Harry Hunter for the Mohawk Minstrels sometime about 1875.[1] Again, the child rhyme,

> Johnny Morgan played the organ,
> Jimmy played the drum,
> His sister played the tambourine
> Till father smacked her bum,

is a perverted recollection of the chorus of John Read's music-hall song 'Johnny Morgan' published in 1877; and the little *jeu d'esprit*, known to children from one end of Britain to the other,

> Tiddly Wink the barber
> Went to shave his father,
> The razor slip
> And cut his lip,
> Tiddly Wink the barber,

1. The song was revived as a comedy item in 1956, though not before we had collected versions from children who had received it from the nineteenth century, apparently by oral conveyance.

33

is further living testimony to Read's genius. In 1878 the original chorus of 'Tiddle-a-Wink the Barber, The Popular Comic Song, Written, Composed & Sung with Immense Success by John Read', went:

> Tiddle-a-Wink, Tiddle-a-Wink, Tiddle-a-Wink the Barber,
> Tiddle-a-Wink, Tiddle-a-Wink, went to shave his father
> But he made a slip and cut his lip,
> Which made his father roar,
> The father knock'd poor Tiddle-a-Wink
> Bang upon the floor.

This process of children adopting or adapting popular songs for use in their games continues, of course, in the present day. Songs such as 'The more we are together', 'Show me the way to go home', 'Horsie, horsie, don't you stop', and 'The Lambeth Walk' (now sometimes 'Lambert's Walk') have a playground existence today far removed from their dance-band origins. Likewise, the post-war song 'Music! Music! Music!' ('Put another nickel in') written by Stephan Weiss and Bernie Baum, and published in 1950, seems assured of immortality, for both the original lyric, and juvenile extemporizations of it extolling film stars or denigrating teachers, are still to be heard in the playground, although in radio terms the composition has become a museum piece. It is, perhaps, only to be expected that the most memorable verses should turn out to be the work of professional humorists and song-writers.

Regional Variation

If the uniformity of schoolchild lore, to which we have so far been witness, was the whole story it would of course only be necessary to study one locality to know what goes on in every locality; and no matter how comprehensive and virile the lore was found to be, if it was the same everywhere, it would confirm the apprehensions of those who suppose that standardized education, mass entertainment, and national periodical literature have already subverted local traditions and characteristics. Happily our tale is not yet complete. Two distinct streams of oral lore flow into the unending river of schoolchild chant and chatter, and these two streams are as different from each other as slang and dialect. The slangy superficial lore of comic songs, jokes, catch phrases, fashionable adjectives, slick nicknames, and crazes, in short that noise which is usually the first that is encountered in playground and street, spreads everywhere but, generally speaking, is transitory. The dialectal lore flows more quietly but deeper; it is the language of the children's darker doings: playing truant, giving warning, sneaking, swearing, snivelling, tormenting, and fighting. It belongs to all time, but is limited in locality. It is so time-worn indeed that it cannot be dated, and words of which Shakespeare would have known the meaning, as 'cog', 'lag', and 'miching', are, in their particular districts, still common parlance; while the language which children use to regulate their relationships with each other, such as their terms for claiming, securing precedence, and making a truce, vary from one part of the country to another, and can in some instances be shown to have belonged to their present localities not merely for the past two or three generations, but for centuries.

Conflicting as are the characteristics of these two types of lore, the one rapidly spreading from place to place and having a brief existence, the other having a prolonged existence but rarely spreading, it is not impossible to see how they subsist together. When a child newly arrives in a district any slang expression he knows, any jokes or tricks, or any new skipping or 'two-ball' rhymes he brings with him, are eagerly listened to, and if found amusing, are added to the local repertoire, and may eventually supplant similar pieces of lore already known. But the local children, while willing to enlarge their store of jokes and rhymes, will not consciously brook any alteration to what they already know. The new child must learn, and very quickly does so, the 'legislative' language of his new playmates (see Chapter 8). He must learn the local names for the playground games, and the expressions used while playing them. Unless he does this, he will not merely be thought peculiar, he will not be understood. A child who moves from Lincoln and cries 'Screams' for mercy in Leicester will find that he receives no sympathy, since the accepted truce term in Leicester is 'Croggies'. Similarly a 12-year-old Spennymoor girl who says,

'When the rope is turning away from the nobby-ender it is lupey-dyke. When the nobby-ender is out he takes the laggy-ender's place and the laggy-ender takes the foggy-ender's place so that the foggy-ender becomes the nobby-ender',

will be thought out of her mind if she says this in the hearing of a Spital-fields girl, although both children in fact adhere to this practice while skipping, and both may skip to the same rhymes.

This regional variation in the children's dialectal lore has been as unexpected as the slavish uniformity of their slang lore; and when the children's customs and superstitious practices are examined, in particular their calendar customs, the regional differences are remarkable. While some children roll eggs at Easter, or nettle the legs of classmates on the twenty-ninth of May, or leave little gifts on people's doorsteps on St Valentine's Day, or act under the delusion that they are above the law on the night of 4 November, other children, sometimes living only the other side of a hill, will have no knowledge of these activities. It is not perhaps of much consequence that in different parts of England children have different ritual ways of disposing of their milk teeth, that there are more than sixty names for the illegal pursuit of knocking at doors and running away, that in some places walking under a ladder can be lucky and seeing a black cat can be unlucky, and that some children make fools on the first of May with more zeal than on the first of April; but the children's loyalty to local customs and forms of speech is at least evidence that the young in Britain do not take as their authority only what they hear and see on the radio and television and in the national press.

2 Just for Fun

THE oral rhymes which children inherit, almost automatically, after about seven years' residence in this island, may be divided into two classes. There are those which are essential to the regulation of their games and their relationships with each other; and there are those, seemingly almost as necessary to them, which are mere expressions of exuberance: a discordant symphony of jingles, slogans, nonsense verses, tongue-twisters, macabre rhymes, popular songs, parodies, joke rhymes, and improper verses, epitomized in the nonsensical couplet,

> Oh my finger, oh my thumb,
> Oh my belly, oh my bum,

which is repeated for no more reason than that they heard someone else say it, that they like the sound of the rhyme *thumb* and *bum*, that it is a bit naughty, and that for the time being, in the playground or in the gang, it is considered the latest and smartest thing to say – for they are not to know that the couplet was already old when their parents were youngsters.[1]

Rhyme seems to appeal to a child as something funny and remarkable in itself, there need be neither wit nor reason to support it.

> Mrs White had a fright
> In the middle of the night,
> She saw a ghost eating toast
> Half-way up the lamp post.

'I think what's so clever about this,' says a 9-year-old, 'is the way it all rhymes.' Hence, apparently, the popularity of the rather horrid and otherwise pointless jests they have: 'Do you want an apple?' 'Yes.' 'Wipe your nose and go to chapel.' 'Do you want a sweet?' 'Yes.' 'Suck your feet.' 'Do you want jelly?' – 'Rub your belly.' 'Do you want treacle?' – 'You're a big fat beetle.' And hence the way lines of current dance songs become catch phrases: 'O Nicholas, don't be so ridiculous', and 'See you later, alligator' – 'In a while, crocodile', repeated *ad nauseam* in 1956.

1. A correspondent hailing from Faversham informs us that the couplet was current in her childhood around 1910.

37

Listening to children as they 'tumble and rhyme' out of school (as Dylan Thomas described them) they seem to have a chant on their lips as constantly as they have a comic in their hands, or a sweet in their mouth. A group of small, round-faced toughs come step-hopping out of school, chanting over and over again, 'Roly poly barley sugar; roly poly barley sugar', and laughing at the littlest one who cannot get his step-hop in time with the rest. A party of girls sauntering along the pavement, arms intertwined in friendship, croon a happy song of little meaning:

> I'm a knock-kneed chicken, I'm a bow-legged sparrow,
> Missed my bus so I went by barrow.
> I went to the café for my dinner and my tea,
> Too many radishes – Hick! Pardon me.

And in the school forecourt twenty or thirty children, those who live in the outlying villages, are killing time, while they wait for the school bus 'which is always late', chorusing at the full extent of their voices:

> Never let your braces dangle,
> Never let your braces dangle.
> Poor old sport
> He got caught
> And went right through the mangle;
> Went through the mangle he did, by gum,
> Came out like linoleum,
> Now he sings in kingdom-come:
> Never let your braces dangle, chum.

These rhymes are more than playthings to children. They seem to be one of their means of communication with each other. Language is still new to them, and they find difficulty in expressing themselves. When on their own they burst into rhyme, of no recognizable relevancy, as a cover in unexpected situations, to pass off an awkward meeting, to fill a silence, to hide a deeply felt emotion, or in a gasp of excitement. And through these quaint ready-made formulas the ridiculousness of life is underlined, the absurdity of the adult world and their teachers proclaimed, danger and death mocked, and the curiosity of language itself is savoured.

Satirical Rhymes

The following doggerels are examples of the trivial verse which children most frequently learn from each other. Sometimes such rhymes are employed for skipping, ball-bouncing, or 'dipping' (as they call counting-out), but the particular rhymes given here are usually repeated just for fun, for the fun of the versification, and perhaps because, in the crude images evoked, adults are made to look undignified.

Masculine, Feminine, Neuter,
I went for a ride on my scooter,
I bumped into the Queen
And said, Sorry old bean,
I forgot to toot-toot on my tooter.

Boy, 9, Hindhead.

Mother made a seedy cake,
Gave us all the belly ache;
Father bought a pint of beer,
Gave us all the diarrhoea.

Girl, 12, Farnham, Surrey.[1]

Quick, quick,
The cat's been sick.
Where? Where?
Under the chair.
Hasten, hasten,
Fetch the basin.
No, no,
Fetch the po.
Kate, Kate, you're far too late,
The carpet's in a dreadful state.

Boy, 11, London.

The king had a chair,
The queen had a throne,
What's the matter with the prince?
He's all skin and bone.

Children, Newcastle upon Tyne.

In fourteen hundred and ninety-two
Columbus sailed the ocean blue;
He lost his yacht, the clumsy clot,
That was a good one, was it not?

Girl, 13, Aberdeen. An extension of a history mnemonic.

Red, white, and blue,
My mother is a Jew,
My father is a Scotsman,
And I'm a kangaroo.

Girl, 11, Perth.

One, two, three,
Mother caught a flea,
Put it in the tea-pot
And made a cup of tea.
The flea jumped out,
Mother gave a shout,
In came father
With his shirt hanging out.

Boy, 11, Enfield.

Have you seen Pa
Smoking a cigar
Riding on a bicycle?
Ha! ha! ha!

Girl, 12, Tunstall.

I had an Auntie Nellie
Who had a wooden belly,
And when I touched it
Out popped jelly.

Boy, 12, Manchester.

A bug and a flea
Went out to sea
Upon a reel of cotton;
The flea was drowned
But the bug was found
Biting a lady's bottom.

Girl, 11, Farnham, Surrey.

1. According to a correspondent this verse was in existence over half a century ago in Portsmouth. Compare also the following, heard sung by little girls at Water Row, near Wiveliscombe, July 1897:

> Mother, mother, Nelly, Nelly,
> Make a cake to fill my belly.
> Mother made a seedy cake
> Which gave me the belly ache.

Folk-Lore, vol. xxvi, 1915, p. 160.

As in the old ballads and proverbial jingles assonance often takes the place of rhyme. On occasion *bursted* is paired with *nurse it*, *fork* with *short*, *belly* with *penny*, and *bananas* with *pyjamas*. In the following *nature* is rhymed with *tater* (potato), and *cute* is clearly intended to be a rhyme for *Luke*.

Adam and Eve in the garden
Studying the beauty of nature;
The devil jumped out of a Brussel
　　sprout
And hit Eve in the eye with a tater.
Girl, 10, Oxford.

Old Uncle Luke thinks he's cute
But Grandpa's even cuter,
He's ninety-eight and stays out
　　late
With Grandma on her scooter.
Girls, 11, Swansea.

Very commonly the key rhyme-word is a proper name; and such verses come nearest to the nursery rhyme pattern.

Queenie, Queenie Caroline,
Dipped her hair in turpentine,
Turpentine to make it shine,
Queenie, Queenie Caroline.
Girl, 9, Annesley.

Old Daddy Dacon
Bought a bit of bacon,
Put it on a chimney top
For fear it would be taken.
Boy, 10, Newcastle upon Tyne.

Harry Brown went to town
To buy a pair of breeches;
Every time he tumbled down
He bursted all his stitches.
Girl, 12, Lincoln.

Julius Caesar,
The Roman geezer,
Squashed his wife with a
　　lemon squeezer.
Boy, 9, Birmingham.

Eaver Weaver, chimney sweeper,
Had a wife and couldn't keep her,
Had another, didn't love her,
Up the chimney he did shove her.
Girl, c. 11, Welshpool.

Dear old Mr Fox,
He needs a Christmas box,
A hat and a coat
And a pair of khaki socks.
Boy, 10, Oundle.[1]

I'm Dirty Bill from Vinegar Hill,
Never had a bath and never will.
Children, Peterborough.

I see Dinah Price
Sliding on the ice,
I think slides are nice,
So does Dinah Price.
Girl, 13, Alton.

Mary Jane went to Spain
In a chocolate aeroplane;
The door fell in and she fell out
And landed on a chimney spout.
Girl, 10, Penrith.

Mr Ross, he thinks he's boss,
Because he's the owner of the
　　H.P. Sauce.
Girl, 12, Aberdeen.

1. Compare:

　　　Mr Knox keeps his socks
　　　In a pale pink chocolate box,

from 8-year-olds in Broken Hill, Northern Rhodesia.

Good King Wenceslas
Knocked a bobby senseless,
Right in the middle of
Marks and Spencer's.

Girl, c. 12, Swansea.

Matthew, Mark, Luke, and John,
Went to bed with their trousers on.
Mark cried out in the middle of the
night,
Oh, my trousers are too tight!

Boy, 11, London.

As with all oral rhymes the histories of these pieces vary considerably. While verses like 'Mr Ross', 'Good King Wenceslas', 'Mary Jane', and 'Masculine, Feminine, Neuter', are presumably of fairly recent composition, 'I'm Dirty Bill from Vinegar Hill' appears to be related to a negro folk-chant about a runaway slave, which begins:

> I'se wild Nigger Bill, frum Redpepper Hill.
> I never did wo'k, an' I never will.[1]

'Eaver Weaver, chimney sweeper', very popular today both in England and Wales, goes back anyway to 1877, when it was recorded as a counting-out rhyme in the *Mill Hill School Magazine*. A version of 'Queenie, Queenie Caroline' was known to Flora Thompson in her Oxfordshire childhood,

> Queen, Queen Caroline,
> Dipped her head in turpentine.
> Why did she look so fine?
> Because she wore a crinoline,

an echo, she suggests, of th coronation scene of George IV.[2] And the joke verse 'Matthew, Mark, Luke, and John' has almost certainly evolved, under the influence of the eighteenth-century nursery rhyme, 'Hey diddle dumpling, my son John, he went to bed with his Breeches on', from the White Paternoster, recorded in 1656:

> Matthew, Mark, Luke, and John,
> The bed be blest that I lye on.[3]

A similar Scottish puerility, given by a 13-year-old Kirkcaldy schoolboy,

> Matthew, Mark, Luke, John,
> Haud the cuddy till I get on.
> When I'm on gie's a scone,
> Matthew, Mark, Luke, John,

1. Thomas W. Talley, *Negro Folk Rhymes*, 1922, p. 94.
2. Flora Thompson, *Lark Rise*, 1939, p. 167. The rhyme is also recorded, from Edinburgh, by H. C. Bolton, *The Counting-Out Rhymes of Children*, 1888, p. 116.
3. Thomas Ady, *A Candle in the Dark*, 1656 (edition 1661, p. 59).

is known to have been in circulation amongst boys in Scotland for at least four generations.[1]

Nonsense Rhymes

It is only fitting that in the land which nurtured Lear and Lewis Carroll, and counts them national heroes, the young should carry a certain archive of nonsense verse in their heads.

The sausage is a cunning bird
With feathers long and wavy;
It swims about the frying pan
And makes its nest in gravy.

Boy, 12, Newcastle upon Tyne.

The elephant is a pretty bird,
It flits from bough to bough.
It builds its nest in a rhubarb tree
And whistles like a cow.

Girl, 12, Caistor.[2]

One day a pig went out to dig
For buttered buns for tea;
He took a spade and pick
And dug beside a tree.

Children, Hayes, Middlesex.

Once upon a time when birds ate lime
And monkeys chewed tobacco,
The pigs took snuff to make them tough
And that's the end of the matter.

Girl, 10, London.[3]

Birds and beasts figure prominently in such verses, but when really stirring adventures are narrated it is noticeable that there is no aversion to the first person singular being the centre of the nonsense.

As I was going to school one day to learn my A.B.C.,
I fell into a washing tub and sailed the ocean sea.
There came by a Chinaman who said I was a spy
And if I did not talk to him he'd poke me in the eye.
He tied me to a cabbage stalk
And cut my head with a knife and fork,
I grew so fat that I could not walk

---

1. A version, said to be repeated by boys 'in the course of their rollicking sports', is quoted by Robert Chambers, *Popular Rhymes of Scotland*, 1842, p. 59:

Matthew, Mark, Luke, John,
Haud the horse till I loup on;
Haud it fast, and haud it sure,
Till I get ower the misty muir.

For further references see *The Oxford Dictionary of Nursery Rhymes*, 1951, pp. 245–6, 303, 305.

2. Also from Adelaide, South Australia, where elephants nest in 'rubber trees'.

3. This rhyme, one of several variants, stems from the traditional opening to some of our native fairy tales. See, e.g., the opening to *The History of Four Kings, Their Queens and Daughters*, printed c. 1750; Robert Chambers, *Popular Rhymes of Scotland*, 1869, pp. 57 and 85; and Joseph Jacobs, *English Fairy Tales*, 1890, pp. 68 and 195.

I joined the Chinese army.
The captain's name was Bango,
Bango was his name,
And he played upon his whiskers
Till the clouds rolled by.

Versions from Enfield, Farnham, and Hayes.

The circulation which some of these extravagances can gain may be judged by the following:

Not last night but the night before,
Two tom cats came knocking at my door;
I went downstairs to let them in,
They knocked me down with a rolling pin.
The rolling pin was made of brass,
They turned me up and smacked my arse.

*Portsmouth, 1953. Very similar versions from Bath,
Bettws-y-Coed, Farnham, and Swansea.*

No last nicht but the nicht afore,
Three black cats cam' roarin' at the door;
Ane gat whisky, ane gat rum,
An' ane gat the dish-clout o'er his bum.

Dundee, 1956, and similar from Forfar.

Last night, the night before,
A lemon and a pickle came knocking at my door;
I went down to let them in
They hit me on the head with a rolling pin.

*Maryland, 1948. Similar from New Jersey, c. 1935,
and Los Angeles, 1954.*

And this 'vulgar street song', as Baring-Gould termed it in 1895, seems to have been known to children for over a century.[1] Lewis Carroll himself, though he may not have sung it in the street, seems to have been familiar with it. 'That reminds me,' he wrote to Arthur Hughes's little daughter Agnes, about 1866, 'of a very curious thing that happened to me at half-past four yesterday. Three visitors came knocking at my door, begging me to let them in. And when I opened the door, who do you think they were? You'll never guess. Why, they were three cats! Wasn't it curious? However, they all looked so cross and disagreeable that I took up the first thing I could lay my hand on (which happened to be the

1. The Rev. S. Baring-Gould in *A Garland of Country Songs*, 1895, says it was sung to an old air 'One night at ten o'clock'. A correspondent to *Notes and Queries*, 10th ser., vol. xii, 1909, p. 518, and 11th ser., vol. i, 1910, p. 55, recalled that the following was repeated to him by his mother some sixty years earlier:

It warn't last night, bu' th' night before,
Three big beggars knockt at the door;
I made haste to let them in,
An' was knockt down wi' a rowlin' pin.

rolling-pin) and knocked them all down as flat as pan-cakes! "If *you* come knocking at *my* door," I said, "*I* shall come knocking at *your* heads." That was fair, wasn't it?"[1]

Tangletalk

There is a difference between 'nonsense' and 'utter nonsense', and, curiously, 'utter nonsense' often seems to be more laboured and self-conscious, although it is just as traditional.

'As I walked down to the wayrail station, I met a bark and it dogged at me. I pulled a hedge out of a stake and necked its knock out.'

'You can say this when you are skipping if you like,' says a 12-year-old Market Rasen girl; and this fun of the transposed word is, in point of fact, straight from the traditional mummers' play of her forefathers.[2]

The deliberate juxtaposition of incongruities, the 'got the toothache in his toe' type of humour, is another genuine characteristic of native English wit, and examples of both types of tangletalk have been found amongst children in different parts of Britain, only minor differences existing between the rhymes in one place and another:

One midsummer's night in winter	It was a summer's day in winter,
The snow was raining fast,	The snow was raining down,
A bare-footed girl with clogs on	A bare-footed girl with clogs on
Stood sitting on the grass.	Stood sitting on the ground.
Market Rasen.	*Newcastle upon Tyne.*

These versions are so similar that they undoubtedly emanate from the same source. Likewise:

'Twas in the month of Liverpool	The flowers were gaily singing,
In the city of July,	The birds were in full bloom,
The snow was raining heavily,	When I went to the cellar
The streets were very dry.	To look for an upstairs room.
The flowers were sweetly singing,	I saw two thousand miles away
The birds were in full bloom,	A house just out of sight,
As I went down the cellar	It stood between two more,
To sweep an upstairs room.	Its walls were black-washed white.
London.	*Forfar.*

1. S. D. Collingwood, *The Life and Letters of Lewis Carroll*, 1898, p. 420.
2. Thus in the text recorded at Weston-sub-Edge, Gloucestershire, about 1864, Beelzebub says: 'I went up a straight crooked lane. I met a bark and he dogged at me. I went to the stick and cut a hedge, gave him a rallier over the yud jud . . .' – R. J. E. Tiddy, *The Mummers' Play*, 1923, p. 167. This piece of nonsense has also been collected recently from children in Forfar: 'As I went doon a ferm road a bark cam oot and dogged at me, I took a tree frae a stick and made it watter e'e.'

A popular recitation of this type (versions from ten schools) may not be as modern as first appears, since it may have been a theatre not a cinema that the original hero visited:

I went to the pictures tomorrow
I took a front seat at the back,
I fell from the pit to the gallery
And broke a front bone in my back.
A lady she gave me some chocolate,
I ate it and gave it her back.
I phoned for a taxi and walked it,
And that's why I never came back.

Kirkcaldy.

I went to the pictures next Tuesday
And took a front seat at the back.
I said to the lady behind me,
I cannot see over your hat.
She gave me some well-broken bis-
cuits,
I ate them and gave her them back;
I fell from the pit to the gallery
And broke my front bone at the back.

Enfield.

Sometimes the absurdity of these recitations is enhanced by a formal style of delivery. In Bath they proclaim:

'LOST, STOLEN, OR STRAYED

'A little man walking about barefooted with his grandfather's boots on, carrying on his back an empty sack full of cheese. Anyone finding the same, will they please return to Mr Green, door painted red, and they will be handsomely rewarded with a yard of wood to make themselves a flannel shirt.'

Quite commonly children make mock announcements: 'Ladies and Gentlemen – The next song will be a dance sung by the female gentleman sitting at the corner of the round table.' Or they ape the flustered lecturer, not unknown in their school halls:

> Ladies and Jellyspoons,
> I stand upon this speech to make a platform,
> The train I arrived in has not yet come,
> So I took a bus and walked.
> I come before you
> To stand behind you
> And tell you something
> I know nothing about.

The best known of these travesties is also probably the oldest:

> One fine day in the middle of the night,
> Two dead men got up to fight,
> Back to back they faced each other,
> Drew their swords and shot each other.
> A paralysed donkey passing by
> Kicked a blind man in the eye,
> Knocked him through a nine inch wall
> Into a dry ditch and drowned them all.

This has been collected in twelve different schools; and fifty years ago the rhyme was much the same except that usually there were present at the combat:

> One blind man to see fair play,
> And two dumb men to shout hurray.

In William IV's time the verse children knew, according to an edition of *Ditties for the Nursery* printed about 1830, was:

> Two dead horses ran a race,
> Two blind to see all fair,
> Two dead horses ran so fast
> The blind began to stare.

Just on five centuries ago, about 1480, a professional minstrel noted down in his pocket book (now Bodleian M.S. Eng. poet. e. 1) the crude rhyme:

> I saw iij hedles playen at a ball,
> an hanlas man served hem all,
> Whyll iij movthles men lay & low,
> iij legles a-way hem drow.

Rhymes and Songs in Scotland

Scottish children seem to be in a happy position. They know most of the English child's rhymes – although it is interesting to find that the versions they know are often nearer to Irish and American versions than to those found south of the Tweed [1] – and they also have their own hamely clinky rarely known to children outside Scotland.

> Oh ye cannae shove yer grannie aff the bus,
> Oh ye cannae shove yer grannie aff the bus,
> Ye cannae shove yer grannie
> For she's yer mammie's mammie,
> Ye cannae shove yer grannie aff the bus.
>
> *Edinburgh.*

> The candy man was guid tae me,
> He took me up an' gied me tea,
> Tea and toast an' a wee bit ham,
> 'Twas afa guid o' the candy man.
>
> *Aberdeen.*

> Oh for six a' clock, oh for seven I weary,
> Oh for eight a'clock, for then I see my dearie.

1. Another demarcation line is the Tees. Versions of rhymes belonging to Northumberland and Durham are frequently distinct from those circulating in the rest of England.

> Oh he's a bonnie lad, oh he's a bonnie fella,
> Oh he's a bonnie lad, wi' ribbons blue and yella.
> My mither says he's deed, oh isen that a peety?
> He'll come back again, ridin on a sheepie.
>
> *Forfar.*

Such verses are rarely exportable. The following oft-repeated lines (collected in Aberdeen, Forfar, and Kirkcaldy) would not rhyme if attempted in English:

> Me an' ma mither an' a great lot mair
> Kickit up a row on the wash-house stair.
> Along cam' a Bobbie and says, Who's there?
> Me an' ma mither an' a great lot mair.

And Glaswegian poetry such as the following is not likely to be appreciated by children south of the Humber:

> Annie get your gun,   Skitter up a lamp post
> Stick it up the lum [chimney].   Skitter up a tree,
> If you cannae get your granny   If you see a Bobbie man
> Annie get your gun.   Skitter in his e'e.

The street songs of Scottish children often possess a lyric quality rarely met on the lips of English urchins. In Forfar, for instance, toddlers have the poetic piece,

> Hey, bonnie lassie, can ye milk a coo?
> Just tak it be the titties and pu', pu' pu',

a couplet which would surely have delighted Burns as much as anything he seized upon in David Herd's collectings. In Edinburgh, and elsewhere, the boys go in for evocative dialogue verses:

> Last nicht I got an awful hammerin'.
>   Wha frae?
> Little Johnnie Cameron.
>   What fer?
> Ca'in's faither 'Greasy beard'.

And in Auld Reekie, also, orphanage kids have a song for 'two ballie' that one feels might have inspired the Bard to a merry tale:

> Ma wee man's a miner,
> He works at Abbeyhill,[1]
> He gets his pey on Setterday
> And buys a half a gill.
> He goes to church on Sunday
> A half an hoor late
> He pulls the buttons aff his shirt
> And puts them in the plate.

1. In Aberdeen children say he lives at Ferryhill.

Pluckings like these from the Scottish wool-bag of oral song seem to be as numerous as they were in the eighteenth century, and to be awaiting a new Burns to spin them into fine thread.

Nonsense Verse in Wales

The following rhymes were collected in Ruthin, and are popular with Welsh-speaking children. The first, 'Bachgen bach o Felin-y-wig', is a particular favourite throughout the Principality.

Bachgen bach o Felin-y-wig,	*A little boy from Melin-y-wig,*
Welodd o 'rioed damaid o gig,	*He never saw a bit of meat,*
Fe welodd falwen ar y bwrdd,	*He saw a snail upon the table*
Fe gipiodd ei gap a rhedodd i ffwrdd.	*And snatched his cap and ran away.*

Iâr fach wen	*Little white hen*
Â phoen yn ei phen,	*With a pain in her head,*
Iâr fach ddu	*Little black hen*
Â phoen yn ei phlu.	*With a pain in her feathers.*

Ar y ffordd wrth fynd i Ruthin	*On the way to Ruthin*
Gwelais ddyn yn gwerthu brethyn,	*I saw a man selling Welsh wool,*
Gofynnais iddo faint y llath,	*I asked him how much a yard,*
Mod i eisiau siwt i'r gath.	*I wanted to make a suit for the cat.*

As in England, verses about bugs are not absent from the repertoire. In one rhyme they see a louse on the sleeve of a happy tailor (*deiliwr llawen*). In another they cry:

Lluen, lluen, lluen,	*Louse, louse, louse,*
P'le welsoch chwi'r fath luen,	*Where did you see such a louse,*
Â llathen o dafod yn ei phen,	*With a yard of tongue in her head*
P'le welsoch fath anifel?	*Where did you see such an animal?*

There are two versions of the following. In one, Grandfather and Grandmother run around the house and a haystack, and when Grandmother falls over a stool so does Grandfather (*A dyna taid yn disgyn ar ei hôl*); in the other Grandad is more successful:

Taid a nain yn rhedeg râs	*Grandfather and grandmother running a race*
I fyny'r ffordd fain ac at y plâs,	*Up the narrow road and to the big house,*
Syrthiodd nain ar draws y stôl,	*Grandmother fell over a stool,*
Ha! Ha! ebe taid, Mae nain ar ôl.	*Ha! Ha! cried Grandfather, Grandmother is behind.*

Several versions of the old joke *paid a deud* are still popular, the tale varying according to where the narrator is going. A 12-year-old girl's favourite is:

Ar y ffordd wrth fynd i'r Bettws	*On the way to Bettws*
Gwelais ddyn yn plannu tatws;	*I saw a man planting potatoes;*
Gof'nais iddo beth o'n wneud,	*I asked him what he was doing,*
Plannu tatws, paid a deud.	*Planting potatoes, but tell no one.*

Other versions go 'On the way to Ruthin I saw a man driving a pig' (*mochyn*), and 'On the way to Liverpool (*Lerpwl*) I saw a man eating sugar' (*siwgr*); and in each case the crafty man, after saying what he is doing, adds, *paid a deud*.

Puns, Tongue Twisters, and Tales Which Never End

That pick-pocket of wit the pun is a common ingredient of juvenile jokelore.

'There was a man in a house and he could not get out. The only furniture was a table. He rubbed his hands until they were sore. Then he sawed the table in half. Two halves make a whole. He shouted through the hole until he was hoarse, jumped on the horse and rode away.'

Almost identical versions of this monstrosity have been received from children in Birmingham, Enfield, and Hindhead. The following is apparently repeated everywhere:

> Long legged Italy
> Kicked poor Sicily
> Right in the middle of the Mediterranean Sea.
> Austria was Hungary
> Took a bit of Turkey
> Dipped it in Greece
> Fried it in Japan
> And ate it off China.

Some children (in Forfar, Kirkcaldy, and Spennymoor) even manage to ball-bounce to these words.

Puns are, of course, the basis of their conundrums (the relationship of a doormat to a doorstep is a 'step-farther'; the way bees get rid of their honey is 'they cell it'). Occasionally a pun is the pivot of a popular saying ('We opened the window and influenza'). The pun plays a prominent part in their every-day repartee ('My ice-cream is dripping' – 'Oh that's funny I thought it was ice-cream'), and in their duplicities ('Pick up that hammer.' 'What 'ammer?' 'You're daft'). And it need hardly be mentioned that pun-ishable jokes such as the following abound:

'There was an elephant called Nuts, and a man was going to take him out to show him to the people. When the man said to Nuts, "Sit Nuts", the elephant would sit. One day a man on the other side of the fence started shouting, "Pea-nuts! Pea-nuts!" and Nuts did.' (*Girl, 13.*)

Tongue twisters. The child's delight in the coincidence of sound is nowhere more apparent than in the pleasure he takes in tongue twisters or, as he sometimes calls them, 'jaw busters'. 'Peter Piper', 'The Leith Police', 'Unique New York', 'A proper copper coffee pot', 'A stewed sow's snout', 'Three grey geese in a green field grazing', and 'She sells sea shells on the sea shore', continue to be favourites as they were fifty years ago. Peter Piper indeed, has been picking pickled peppers since the eighteenth century.[1] The following are also much in vogue:

A tutor who tooted the flute	A woman to her son did utter
Tried to tutor two tooters to toot.	Go, my son, and shut the shutter.
Said the two to the tutor:	The shutter's shut, the son did utter,
Is it harder to toot, or	I cannot shut it any shutter.
To tutor two tooters to toot?	
	How much wood could a woodchuck chuck
There's no need to light a night-light	If a woodchuck could chuck wood?
On a light night like tonight,	As much wood as a woodchuck would chuck
For a night-light's a slight light	
On a light night like tonight.	If a woodchuck could chuck wood.

An attraction of the woodchuck rhyme is the number of changes which can be rung on it, for instance: 'How many cookies could a good cook cook, if a good cook could cook cookies?' and 'How much oil can a gumboil boil, if a gumboil can boil oil?' and, possibly cleverest, 'How many cans can a cannibal nibble, if a cannibal can nibble cans?' Also much repeated are the passages:

'Of all the felt I ever felt, I never felt a piece of felt which felt the same as that felt felt, when I first felt the felt of that felt hat.'

And,

'Your Bob owes our Bob a bob. If your Bob doesn't give our Bob the bob your Bob owes our Bob, our Bob will give your Bob a bob in the eye.'

And,

'Our Dicky wants to know if your Dicky will lend our Dicky your Dicky's Dicky-bow; if your Dicky won't lend our Dicky your Dicky's Dicky-bow, then

1. The rhyme has been found, set to music by Dr Samuel Arnold. in *Juvenile Amusements*, published 1797.

our Dicky won't lend your Dicky our Dicky's Dicky-bow when our Dicky has a Dicky-bow.'

Each of these is a perennial, for it takes children a long time before they cease to be amazed that one word can have more than one meaning.

The tale without an end. This is another stock joke. The tale usually begins: 'It was a dark and stormy night, and the Captain said to the Bo'sun, "Bo'sun, tell us a story," so the Bo'sun began ...' Or it may be: 'It was a dark and stormy night, the rain came down in torrents, there were brigands on the mountains, and thieves, and the chief said unto Antonio: "Antonio, tell us a story." And Antonio, in fear and dread of the mighty chief, began his story: "It was a dark and stormy night, the rain came down in torrents, there were brigands on the mountains, and thieves ..." ' And such is any child's readiness to hear a good story that the tale may be told three times round before the listeners appreciate that they are being diddled.

There are never-ending songs, too, songs like 'There's an 'ole in my bucket, dear Liza, dear Liza', 'There were ten in a bed and the little one said: Turn over!', and the amusing ditty 'He gave her kisses one (and she said: This is fun)', which leads up to 'He gave her kisses ten (and she said: Begin again)'. The best known of this breed is undoubtedly:

> There was a man called Michael Finigan,
> He grew whiskers on his chinigin,
> The wind came out and blew them in ag'in,
> Poor old Michael Finigan, begin ag'in.

And very popular are the verses which tell of an inquisitive bear, sung to the tune 'For he's a jolly good fellow':

> The bear went over the mountain,
> The bear went over the mountain,
> The bear went over the mountain,
> To see what he could see.

When the bear gets to the top of the mountain all he sees is 'the other side of the mountain', or 'another mountain', and so he goes on mountaineering, seeking a change of view, until the singers, not the bear, are exhausted.[1]

1. Each of these pieces is also current in the U.S.A., except that in the first tale American children say: 'It was a dark and stormy night, some Indians were sitting around the camp fire when their chief rose and said ...' French children (at Albi, Tarn) say: 'Un jour, c'était la nuit, j'étais assis tout debout sur mon lit. Je lisais mon journal qui n'était pas écrit à la lueur d'une bougie éteinte, quand soudain j'entrevis dans l'ombre un muet qui disait: "Un jour, c'était la nuit ..." ', etc., which is also akin to 'One fine day in the middle of the night'.

Ghoulism

When children are about ten years old they enter a period in which the outward material facts about death seem extraordinarily funny. They ask each other: 'You going to be burnt or buried?' They have catch phrases: 'It's not the cough that carries you off, it's the coffin they carry you off in.' They have mock laments:

Poor old Peggy's dead,
She died last night in bed.
We put her in a coffin
And she fell right through the bottom,
Poor old Peggy's dead.[1]

Little Willie's dead,
Jam him in the coffin,
For you don't get the chance
Of a funeral of'en.

They inscribe their names on the flyleaf of their schoolbooks:

When I am dead and in my grave, and all my bones are rotten,
This little book will tell my name, when I am quite forgotten.[2]

And certain songs, like Whyte-Melville's 'Wrap me up in my tarpaulin jacket', Montrose's 'Clementine' ('In the corner of the churchyard where the myrtle boughs entwine, grow the rosies in their posies fertilized by Clementine'), and the popular song 'When I die don't bury me at all, just pickle my bones in alcohol', become an obsession, chorused over and over again, and apparently giving endless pleasure. With the greatest good humour they chant 'The Infirmary Blues':

Whenever you see the hearse go by
And think to yourself that you're gonna die,
Be merry, my friends, be merry.

They put you in a big white shirt
And cover you over with tons of dirt,
Be merry, my friends, be merry.

1. Also recited by children in New Zealand: *Western Folklore*, vol. xii, January 1953, p. 18.
2. This is an old verse. In a copy of *An Exposition on the Church Catechism*, in the Municipal Library at Bath, a youthful owner, about 1825, has inscribed:

When I am dead and in my Grave and all My Bonds arotton
the Greedy worms will eat my Flish and I shall be forgotten.

Similarly, in 1736, a girl embroidered on her sampler:

When I am dead, and laid in grave, And all my bones are rotten,
By this may I remembered be When I should be forgotten.

(M. B. Huish, *Samplers and Tapestry Embroideries*, 1913, p. 44). The lineage of a lesson-book scribbling is, of course, easier to trace than that of an oral verse – it leaves more evidence!

They put you in a long-shaped box
And cover you over with tons of rocks,
Be merry, my friends, be merry.

The worms crawl out and the worms crawl in,
The ones that crawl in are lean and thin,
The ones that crawl out are fat and stout,
Be merry, my friends, be merry.

Your eyes fall in and your hair falls out,
And your brains come tumbling down your snout,
Be merry, my friends, be merry.

Version from boy, 13, Croydon.

In a more sombre mood they tell the tragic story of Mother Lee, a tale dating perhaps from the nineteenth century and reminiscent of the old traditional ballad 'The Cruel Mother':

There was an old girl called Old Muvver Lee,
   Old Muvver Lee, Old Muvver Lee,
There was an old girl called Old Muvver Lee,
   Under the walnut tree.

She 'ad 'er baiby on 'er knee, on 'er knee,
   on 'er knee,
She 'ad 'er baiby on 'er knee,
   Under the walnut tree.

A carvin' knife was in 'er 'and, in 'er 'and,
   in 'er 'and,
A carvin' knife was in 'er 'and,
   Under the walnut tree.

She ran it through the baiby's 'art, baiby's 'art,
   baiby's 'art,
She ran it through the baiby's 'art,
   Under the walnut tree.

The rich red blood went runnin' dahn, runnin' dahn,
   runnin' dahn,
The rich red blood went runnin' dahn,
   Under the walnut tree.

The corny cops came runnin' dahn, runnin' dahn,
   runnin' dahn,
The corny cops came runnin' dahn,
   Under the walnut tree.

They strung 'er up and 'ung 'er 'igh, 'ung 'er 'igh,
    'ung 'er 'igh,
They strung 'er up and 'ung 'er 'igh,
    Under the walnut tree.

Version recited in dead-pan manner by boy, aged about 11, Waterloo, London. At the end of each verse one finger was quietly raised pointing up to the walnut tree.

In their skipping ropes, too, children sometimes sing unexpected lines:

Mother, mother, I feel sick,
Send for the doctor, quick, quick, quick.
Doctor, doctor, shall I die?
Yes, my dear, and so shall I.
How many carriages shall I have?
One, two, three, four . . . [1]

And, in similar unaffected manner, Scottish children 'caw' the ropes faster and faster as they chant the dirge:

Ding dong my castle bell,
Farewell to my mother,
Bury me in the old churchyard
Beside my elder brother.
My coffin shall be white
Six white angels by my side,
Two to sing and two to play
And two to carry my soul away.

Death, which when they were younger they may have regarded as a frightening and private subject, has now come out into the open. They have found that it is still a long way off, and these songs are a sign of their emancipation.

1. This verse, collected in London, Halifax, and Swansea, evidently goes back quite a long way for there was an inquiry about it in *Notes and Queries*, 24 December 1864. It is also a well-known rope-rhyme in America; and a French-Canadian version, recorded in the *Journal of American Folklore*, vol. liii, 1940, p. 165, begins:

Maman, Maman, je suis malade, Maman, Maman.
Un médecin, un médecin!
Vite, vite, à l'instant . . .

A. L. Lloyd, *Lilliput*, September 1952, p. 57, gives a new version:

Mother, mother, I am ill,
Send for the doctor from over the hill.
In comes the doctor,
In comes the nurse,
In comes the lady with the alligator purse.
Penicillin, says the doctor,
Penicillin, says the nurse,
Penicillin, says the lady with the alligator purse.

The strange lady with the alligator purse is, as Patricia Evans points out in *Jump Rope Rhymes*, 1955, a recurring figure in American child rhymes, and Mrs Evans gives a verse much like Lloyd's, collected in San Francisco.

Spookies

Yet another entertainment is the 'spooky' rhyme or story recited when the lights are low, as when members of a gang gather together in their hut or den, and the wind whistles through the chinks of the door, fluttering the candle flame. One of them tells a story to the new-comers in a slow blood-curdling voice, saying the traditional words very quietly so that the listeners have to crane their heads forward to catch the words, and then – the *raison d'être* is always the same – the last word is suddenly shouted. 'It is to frighten a child,' explains an 11-year-old Birmingham girl, rather unnecessarily, after supplying the following example:

'Once upon a time there was a small girl who was reading a large book, when to her surprise she read that if she went to a house which was not far from her, she could get, by asking the caretaker, some treasure which was hidden there.

'So she went along to the house, and she knocked on the door, and a small voice said, "Come in." She went in, and she saw a small man seated at a table. Very timidly she said, "Is it right that if I asked you for some treasure in the house I could have it?"

'And the little man said – "YES!" '[1]

Not only are they careful to wait until it is dark before they tell these stories, they hope first to create an atmosphere of mystery and excitement. In the dormitories of girls' boarding schools after lights out, one girl whispers to another 'This is the dead man's eye, pass it on,' and she drops a peeled grape into the other girl's hand. Another says 'This is the dead man's hand, pass it on,' and in the darkness holds out a clammy rubber glove filled with sand.

Sometimes the tension of the stories is increased by repeated duplication of an adjective such as 'old, old', or 'dark, dark':

> In a dark, dark wood, there was a dark, dark house,
> And in that dark, dark house, there was a dark, dark room,
> And in that dark, dark room, there was a dark, dark cupboard,
> And in that dark, dark cupboard, there was a dark, dark shelf,
> And in that dark, dark shelf, there was a dark, dark box,
> And in that dark, dark box, there was a GHOST!

Versions from Alton, Eastbourne, Enfield, and Swansea.

1. Each of the tales in this section, collected from the recitation or writing of children in the 1950s, is paralleled in a collection of 'frightening rhymes' collected in the nineteenth century from schoolchildren in Edinburgh and printed in the *Miscellanea of the Rymour Club*, vol. i, pp. 108–10, 1911. A story of the same genre is given by Robert Chambers, *Popular Rhymes of Scotland*, 1869, p. 64; and two truly horrifying examples, one of them from Surrey in which a dead lady's 'golden arm' is stolen, and the other from Glasgow in which a black man gives away one of his black fingers, are related by, respectively, George Sturt, *A Small Boy in the Sixties*, 1927, pp. 141–2, and Clifford Hanley, *Dancing in the Streets*, 1958, pp. 49–50.

Or again, they make the narrative personal by naming one of the company present:

'I am the ghost of the cave, and I am coming to haunt you tonight, *Margaret*, *Margaret*, I'm on your one step [*said in a mesmeric coming-nearer voice*],

> *Margaret*, I'm on your two step,
> *Margaret*, I'm on your three step,
> *Margaret*, I'm on your four step,
> *Margaret*, I'm at your bedroom door,
> *Margaret*, I'm at your bedside,
> *Margaret*, I'VE GOT YOU!'

Girl, 12, Alton, and correspondent, Tyneside, c. 1895.

The most haunting of these quietly told tales with electrifying endings is probably also the oldest, for it was in print by 1810.[1] Its popularity today amongst children is, nevertheless, almost certainly due to an unbroken chain of retelling through the years, rather than to print. They say 'Let's play "The woman all skin and bone"', or 'Let's do "The woman in a churchyard"' (the tale is currently known in two versions), and the children crouch around in the darkest part of the room while the narrator recites in a sepulchral voice:

> There was a woman all skin and bone
> Who lived in a cottage all on her own,
> Oo-oo-oo!
>
> She thought she'd go to church one day
> To hear the parson preach and pray,
> Oo-oo-oo!
>
> When she got to the wooden stile
> She thought she'd stay and rest a while,
> Oo-oo-oo!
>
> When she reached the old church door
> A ghastly ghost lay on the floor
> Oo-oo-oo!
>
> The grubs crawled in, the grubs crawled out,
> Of its ears, eyes, nose, and mouth.
> Oo-oo-oo!

1. *Gammer Gurton's Garland*, 1810, p. 29; reprinted with a note thereon in *The Oxford Dictionary of Nursery Rhymes*, 1951, pp. 260–61.

Oh you ghastly ghost, she said,
Shall I be like you when I am dead?
   YES!

Version from girl, c. 12, Welshpool.

A woman in a churchyard sat,
   Oo–oo–ah–ah!
Very short and very fat,
   Oo–oo–ah–ah!
She saw three corpses carried in,
   Oo–oo–ah–ah!
Very tall and very thin,
   Oo–oo–ah–ah!

Woman to the corpses said,
   Oo–oo–ah–ah!
Shall I be like you when I am dead?
   Oo–oo–ah–ah!
Corpses to the woman said,
   Oo–oo–ah–ah!
Yes, you'll be like us when you are dead,
   Oo–oo–ah–ah!
Woman to the corpses said –
     [*piercing deathlike scream!*]

Version from girl 10, London.

Such a story could have been the 'sad tale' young Mamillius began to tell on a winter's day long ago. He, too, knew that the story must be told softly, so softly that 'Yond crickets shall not hear it', and he began his tale in the same way: 'There was a man dwelt by a churchyard.'

Scout and Guide Songs

Another kind of song is the Camp-fire or Party song. These are often action songs, like 'Underneath the spreading chestnut tree', and 'We pushed the damper in'; or rounds such as the eighteenth-century song 'Sandy he belongs to the mill', and 'Softly sings the donkey', and 'Why doesn't my goose lay as much as thy goose, when I paid for my goose twice as much as thine?' Their effectiveness much depends on the way they are sung, and the company in which they are sung, and, it may be added, the discomfort in which they are sung, for British children are like their fathers in feeling especially convivial when conditions are wet and dreary.

I went to the animal fair,
All the birds and the beasts were there,
The gay baboon by the light of the
        moon
Was combing his yellow hair.
The monkey fell from his bunk
And dropped on the elephant's trunk.
The elephant sneezed, and went down
        on his knees
And what became of the mon-key,
        mon-key, mon-key, mon-key,
        monk?

*Usually sung as a round. Norman
Douglas gives it as a skipping rhyme in
'London Street Games', 1916, and
Scarborough children still use it as such.*

O Jemima, look at your Uncle Jim,
He's in the duck pond, learning how
        to swim;
First he does the breast stroke,
        then he does the side,
And now he's under the water,
        swimming against the tide.

*Sung to the Soldiers' Chorus in Gounod's
'Faust'.*

Salome was a dancer
She danced the hootchie-cootch,
She shook her shimmy shoulder
And she showed a bit too much.
Stop! said King Herod,
You can't do that there 'ere.
Salome said, Baloney!
And kicked the chandelier.

*Also used for skipping in San Francisco,
according to Patricia Evans, 'Jump
Rope Rhymes', 1954.*

There was a bloomin' spider,
Climbed up a bloomin' spout,
Down came the rain
And washed the spider out.
Out came the sunshine
Dried up all the rain,
Up the bloomin' water spout
The blighter went again.

*Version from East London. It has been
known for half a century, usually as
'Incey Wincey' or 'Ipsey Wipsey
Spider'. The story is enacted with
fingers and thumbs.*

The following favourite accumulates on the principle of 'The House
that Jack built'. It was repopularized by the American folk-singer Burl
Ives in 1953, but had been current in Britain for anyway forty years before
his visit:

> There was an old woman who swallowed a fly;
> I wonder why
> She swallowed a fly.
> Poor old woman, she's sure to die.
>
> There was an old woman who swallowed a spider,
> That went oops-oops right down inside her;
> She swallowed the spider to catch the fly,
> I wonder why
> She swallowed a fly.
> Poor old woman, she's sure to die.
>
> There was an old woman who swallowed a bird;
> How absurd
> To swallow a bird.
> She swallowed the bird to catch the spider . . .
>
> There was an old woman who swallowed a cat;
> Fancy that!
> She swallowed a cat . . .

> There was an old woman who swallowed a dog;
> She went the whole hog
> And swallowed a dog . . .
>
> There was an old woman who swallowed a cow;
> I wonder how
> She swallowed a cow . . .
>
> There was an old woman who swallowed a horse;
> She died, of course!

The following is a good example of an action song, calling for strict co-ordination of voice and movement:

> With my hands on myself, what have I here?
> This is my brain-box, and nothing to fear.
> Brain-box and wiggy-wiggy-waggy-woo,
> That's what they taught me when I went to school.
>
> With my hands on myself, what have I here?
> These are my eye-blinkers, nothing to fear.
> Eye-blinkers, brain-box, and wiggy-wiggy-waggy-woo,
> That's what they taught me when I went to school.

It accumulates, with appropriate pointings and actions, to the ninth and final verse which goes:

> With my hands on myself, what have I here?
> These are my globe-trotters, nothing to fear.
> Globe-trotters, knee-benders,
> Bread-box, chest-protector,
> Chin-chopper, mouth-clicker,
> Nose-wiper, eye-blinker,
> Brain-box and wiggy-wiggy-waggy-woo,
> That's what they taught me when I went to school.

There are, too, the marching songs, of which the following is probably the most popular, sung in the United States as well as in Britain, and by members of the fighting forces (with 'improvements') as well as by members of the Boys' Brigade:

> Left, left, I had a good home and I left,
> Left, left, I had a good home and I left,
> Left my wife and four fat babies, left 'em –
> Right, right, right in the middle of the kitchen floor.

And, of course, there are the songs which good-humouredly describe the joys and woes of life under canvas, such as 'We're all together again', and 'Whate'er befall, I'll still recall those happy camping days', and the following which is sung, very solemnly, to the lugubrious tune of 'There's a long, long road a-winding to the one that I love':

> There's a long, long worm a-crawling
> Across the roof of my tent.
> I can hear the whistle calling,
> And it's time I went.
> There's the cold, cold water waiting
> For me to take my morning dip.
> And when I come back I'll find that worm
> Upon my pillow-slip.

Such songs, it is true, partially owe their circulation to adult troop leaders, but they are often well known to children not attached to any youth group.

3 Wit and Repartee

THE schoolboy has long had an enviable reputation for wit. His impudent sallies in a verbal tussle with the devil are commemorated in the ballad of 'The Fause Knicht upon the Road' which probably dates back to the fifteenth century; his 'innocent and impertinent talk' was a sport to Pepys; and the story will probably often be retold of how his quaint idiom once silenced even Churchill. According to Detective Inspector W. H. Thompson, when Winston Churchill – who could not stand whistling – was at the height of power in 1940, he met a lad in Downing Street whistling loudly and asked him brusquely to stop.

'Why should I?' said the boy, unconcerned.

'Because I don't like it and it's a horrid noise,' growled Churchill.

'Well, you can shut your ears, can't you?' retorted the boy.

And Churchill, the master of oratory, after a moment's astonished anger, is said to have turned and walked on, happily murmuring to himself, 'You can shut your ears, can't you?'[1]

The fact is that schoolchildren, constantly fending for themselves amongst their fellows, acquire an armoury of ready responses, and a lack of inhibition about using them. 'Some people,' remarks a young informant, 'have a bright answer to whatever you say. If you ask them where they have been they reply "Oh! just so far and no further." When you question "Who have you been with?" they answer "Me, myself, and I." Then there is the time you ask how many people were there at the football match, and they answer, "The biggest part of a good few." Then you ask them "Why?" and they answer you "Z." Then a person tells you to do something, and you inquire "What for?" and they answer "Five."'

There is no question of this humour being original. In fact it may be thought one of the curiosities of juvenile lore (though it has come about strictly in accordance with the laws which govern the conduct of all oral matter) that more than 200 years ago such responses were what Dean Swift termed 'genteel and ingenious conversation', examples of which,

1. W. H. Thompson, *I Was Churchill's Shadow*, 1951, p. 40.

according to his own account, he spent eight-and-twenty years collecting, not in playgrounds and backstreets, but in the drawing-rooms of the aristocracy.[1] Each of the following quips which Swift noted down in the times of Queen Anne and George I are perpetuated today by schoolboys and girls.

Colonel Atwit. Pray, Miss, how old are you?
Miss Notable. Why, I'm as old as my Tongue, and a little older than my Teeth.

Mr Neverout. Pray, Miss, why do you sigh?
Miss Notable. To make a Fool ask, and you are the first.

Colonel Atwit. Pray, Miss, where is your old acquaintance, Mrs Wayward?
Miss Notable. Why, where should she be? You must needs know; she's in her skin.

Mr Neverout. Pray, Madam, do you tell me [the time]; for I have let my Watch run down.
Lady Answerall. Why, 'tis half an Hour past Hanging-time. [Children now say 'half past kissing time'.]

Mr Neverout. Hey, Madam, did you call me?
Miss Notable. Hay; why, Hay is for Horses.

None of these specimens are likely to have been new even when Swift first heard them as smart dialogue; and he himself made a point of this. He believed that there was not a phrase in his collection which had not 'received the stamp and approbation of at least one hundred years'. And in confirmation we may cite Miss Notable's cheeky reply to the inquiry where Mrs Wayward was: 'She's in her skin', a joke (common amongst young schoolgirls today) which we have found in George Gascoigne's *Supposes*, 1566, the first English prose comedy:

Dulippo. Ho, Jack Pack, where is Erostrato?
Crapino. Erostrato? Marry, he is in his skin.
Act 1, *sc. iv.*

And also, appropriately, in *Anecdotes of a Boarding School*, vol. i, 1783, p. 130, one of the earliest of school stories:

Martha. Pray can you tell me where Miss Candid is?
Miss Catch. In her skin, when she jumps out, you may jump in.

---

1. *A Complete Collection of Genteel and Ingenious Conversation, According to the Most Polite Mode and Method Now Used at Court, and in the Best Companies of England*, 1738.

Crooked Answers

Urchins seem to take a connoisseur's pleasure in evading questions which are inconvenient to them. If another child asks them their name and they do not want to give it, they say 'Same as me Dad's.' If the questioner persists, 'What's your Dad's then?' they reply, 'Same as mine.' (See Chapter 9, p. 176.) If asked 'Where do you live?' they reply sharply 'In a house.' If asked 'How old are you?' they reply 'As old as my tongue and a little older than my teeth.' Asked 'What are you going to be when you grow up?' a girl replies 'A woman I hope.' It is part of the fun of such retorts that they adhere ostentatiously to the truth. And these prevarications baulk and irritate the questioner, without, perhaps, giving real offence. But should the children think a person is being unnecessarily nosey, or asking questions which are downright foolish, they are likely to give more impertinent answers.

To one who asks inquisitively 'What are you looking for?' they reply tartly 'Looking for my shadow', or, 'Looking for last year's snow.'

'Where are you going?'
'There and back again to see how far it is.'
'Where *are* you going?'
'Daft, are you coming?'
'Where have you been?'
'To see my Aunt Fanny's ghost wrapped up in brown paper.'
'What did you do that for?'
'To make fools spier [ask] and you're the first.' (Kirkcaldy)

To people who see them doing something obvious, such as pumping up a bicycle tyre, and ask 'What are you doing?' they reply 'Frying eggs.'

'What for?'
'Five.'
In Scotland, 'What fur?'
'Cat's fur, ever seen it on dogs?'
(In Illinois: 'What fer?'
'Cat's fur – to make the kitten's breeches.')
'Where's the cat?'
'Up the cook's funnel hanging on a nail.'
'Where's your brother?'
'Up the spout, sparrow catching.'
'Could you say that again?'

'You 'eard. I don't boil my cabbages twice.'

And to people who ask an unanswerably stupid question, they recite:

> Twelve and twelve makes twenty-four
> Shut your mouth and say no more,

or reply, 'Does an elephant hate peanuts?' or 'Can a wren take a crane for a lark?' or other inanity – it being well known that 'Jolly silly questions deserve jolly silly answers'.

The distinction between this repartee and the guile which is featured in the next chapter (Chapter 4) is that while a child practising guile creates a desired opening so that he can make a prepared response: 'I've just remembered...' 'What?' 'You're a fool and I'm not,' or 'I'll tell you one thing and that's not two.' 'What's not?' 'Three' – whereas, that is, the trickster artfully prepares his ground, usually with malicious intent – genuine repartee is a quick follow-on to a question or remark which just happens to crop up. Someone says innocently, 'Do you know what?' and the joker quickly replies 'I know his brother.' An innocent remarks 'I feel like a cup of tea' and the joker retorts, 'You don't look like one.' An inquirer asks 'What's on at the cinema this week?' and is promptly informed, 'The roof.' Indeed the more normal the request for information may be the more likely are there to be a variety of crooked answers for it, so that sometimes it becomes almost impossible to obtain a straightforward answer to that most innocuous of questions concerning the hour of day:

'What's the time?'

'Time you knew better.'

'What's the time?'

'A minute to the next.'

'What's the time?'

'About now.' 'Ten o'clock next Wednesday.' 'Half past kissing time and time to kiss again.' 'Half past, quarter to strike, ten minutes to the lamp post.' 'Half past, quarter to strike, just turned septic.'

'What's the time?'

'The same time as it was this time yesterday.'

What's the time?	What's the time?
Half past nine	Half past nine
Put the napkins on the line.	Hang your breeches on the line.
When they're dry	When the copper
Bring them in	Comes along
And don't forget the safety pin.	Pull them off and put them on.
Alton.	*Alton. Similar from Bath, Hillingdon, and Reading.*

'What's the time?'

'Time-you-bought-a-watch!'[1]

The only way to obtain the correct time may be to prick the pride of the 'Big Ben' owner, challenging: 'What's the time by your old tick-tock what doesn't go?'

'Does go. Five to nine.'

'Ah! time flies.'

'No it don't it goes on wheels.'

Having the Last Word

In any juvenile exchange of pleasantries the esteemed feature seems to be not the quality of the wit, but the ability to have the last word.

First boy: 'If I had a face like yours I'd put it on a wall and throw a brick at it.'

Second boy: 'If I had a face like *yours* I'd put it on a brick and throw a wall at it.'

Every method is employed, however old and feeble, to turn an insult back on him who offered it. If a youngster is accused of having some peculiarity or mental defect, the standard retort is '*You* can't talk.' If named an animal: 'You know what you are, you're nought but a big baboon', the prompt reply is 'Yes, dad.'[2] If someone taunts a boy climbing a tree, 'Monkeys like to be high up', he retaliates 'Where donkeys can't get.' If one boy, watching another do something childish, sneers 'Babies will play', the other replies 'And monkeys will look on.' The remark 'Little things please little minds' is countered with 'And little drawers fit little behinds – like yours.'

'A witty reply' is given by a 14-year-old Bishop Auckland boy named Sowerley. 'If a boy says to me: "They don't call everybody Sowerley."'

'Me. "It'd be better if they did."'

'Boy: "Aye, for fools."'

'Me: "Aye, for fools like you."'

This type of parlance seems to be about the first knowledge a newcomer acquires on attending one of our national dispensaries of learning.

1. Such jokes can also be pedagogic. P. H. Gosse tells of an old schoolmaster he knew, about 1820, whose wife had a habit, when she wanted to know the time, of shouting into the schoolroom, 'What's a clock?' to which the old ruffian would reply, 'A pretty round thing up a-top o' Market-house.' (*Longman's Magazine*, vol. xiii, 1889, p. 524.)

2. Eric Partridge in *The Shaggy Dog Story*, 1953, p. 15, gives an 'ancient Greek' story: 'A pert youth, meeting an old woman driving a herd, called "Good morning, mother of asses!" "Good morning, my son!"'

When they say to him 'You're a soppy date', instead of denying it, he learns to reply: 'And you're another,' or 'I haven't far to go to find a mate,' or 'Same to you with knobs on,' whereupon, in a form long prescribed by tradition, a battle of (simple) wits develops:

'Same to you with knobs on and brass buttons down the back.'

'Same to you with iron fastenings.'

'Steel clamps.'

'Gold screws.'

'Same to you with silver rivets and don't forget to polish them. They'll get rusty if you don't.'

'Same to you with a ton of atom bombs on top of you.'

'Same to you with a sackful of squashed tomatoes down your front.' – a dialogue which may be terminated, as on the occasion when this example was recorded, by the bigger boy saying:

'You shut up or I'll give you a perishin bash on the boko with a poker.'

But to threaten physical action is to confess mental defeat. A better answer is the rhyming one which Lancashire girls customarily give:

> Same to you with knobs on,
> Cabbages with clogs on,
> Elephants with slippers on,
> And you with dirty knickers on.

The tussle may then continue feebly with the well-worn sentiments: 'Same to you and no returns', 'Double ditto, no back chat', 'No more of your lip', 'You slab-sided son of a sea cook', 'You low-down heeled son of a no good beef steak', 'Do me a favour – drop dead'. Or a wordy retort which girls, in particular, learn off by heart, so that they can say it quickly and hold the floor:

'Are you insinuating that I should tolerate such diabolical insolence from an inferior like you? Your intellect is not sufficiently developed to comprehend the verbosity of my remarks. If it were not for taking off my fur gloves and showing my diamond ring to the atmosphere I would slap your saucy face.'

Alton version.

'Are you insinuating that I am tolerating such diabolical insolence from a little piece of animosity such as you? If so, I presume that your presumptions are precisely incorrect and that your diabolical system is insufficient to comprehend my meaning. If it weren't for the discomforture of removing my velvet glove from my lily white hand, I'd slap you across the face with this five pound note. Come, Fido!'

Swansea version.

66

To which the appropriate reply is: "Ark at 'er now. Every time she opens 'er mouth she says something.'

'You cheeky brat, shut your mouth.'

'Shut your own, it's closer.'

Juvenile Correctives

Many traditional witticisms, almost invariably sarcastic, draw attention to ill manners. Of a person who does not shut doors they inquire: 'Where were you born – in a field with the gate open?' To a person who gets in the light they say: '*Your* father wasn't a glazier.' [1] To a person who pushes in front: 'That's right, age before beauty' or 'Muck before a shovel.' To a person who keeps asking for things to be done for him: 'When did your servant die?' (This from small children in Hackney.) To a person who kicks ('when you don't feel like retaliating'): 'You're not in a stable – only donkeys kick.' To a person who speaks well of himself: 'When did your trumpeter die?'

A whole series of stock remarks comment acidly upon a person's costume. If a boy's cap is on skew-whiff: 'Are you wearing that cap or just walking underneath it?' If a boy's shorts are coming down they remark: 'The ship's cat is dead – he's got his trousers at half mast.' If a girl's slip is showing they say 'S.O.S.' (Slip On Show), or 'It's snowing in Paris', or ask 'Is your name Seymour?' A boy with his shirt hanging out is called a 'Dicky Dout' or 'Giddy Gout':

> Dicky, Dicky Dout,
> Your shirt hangs out,
> Four yards in and five yards out. [2]

And, of course, anything hanging out is pulled. If a boy is seen to have a fly-button undone, they remind him, 'There's a star in the East', or 'You've dropped sixpence', and go on repeating it, mystifying him, until he takes the hint. And they call 'Spud' after anyone with a hole in his sock – the hole itself being a 'potato' – or, in Aberdeen, they jeer: 'Your mother's making cheese.'

1. Thus, also, in Swift's *Polite Conversation*, 1738, p. 13: 'Prythee, Tom, sit a little farther I believe your Father was no Glasier.'

2. This cry is far from new, as may be seen, for instance, in *Folk-Speech of South Cheshire*, 1887, p. 171. In the United States children commonly chant:

> I see London, I see France,
> I see someone's underpants.

To those with unpleasant habits they are equally outspoken. To a nose-picker they chant:

> Friday, pie-day,
> Keep your nose tidy.

To a sniveller: 'Yer lip's bleedin, wipe yer nose.' To a sniffer (in Forfar): 'Snif weel and yer nose'll lift mair nor a shovel.'

Someone with a cold is mocked by pinching their own nose and repeating:

> I've got a code id by doze,
> An doebody doze
> I've got a code id by doze.

What adults dare not tell their best friends, children are willing to bellow across the playground. ''Ere, take a whiff of 'im!''

Inky pinky, pen and inky,
I smell a dirty stinky.
11-year-olds, Birmingham.

I think, I think, I smell a stink,
I wonder whose it can be?
Girl, 14, Kirkcaldy.

Parker is kind and *Parker* is strong,
Parker is nice, but he doesn't half
pong.
Boy, 12, Croydon.

Horse, pig, dog, goat,
You stink, I don't.
Boy, 12, Welwyn.

I'm a kid, you're a goat,
You smell, and I don't.
Alton and Portsmouth.

Roses are red, violets are blue,
Onions stink, and so do you.
Girl, 14, London.[1]

The accused one responds, 'The trouble with you is your nose was put too near your mouth.'

Indeed there is a verbal specific for almost every juvenile ailment. To a liar they may say 'You're a filthy fifty-one-a-r' (LIar) and chant 'You liar, you liar, your pants are on fire.' The accused one retorts 'And you're a gentleman – that's another lie.'

Of one who talks too much (i.e. a chatter-box, gas-bag, gramophone, jabbering ape, parrot, walkie-talkie, or windbag) they remark blithely,

---

1. These cries are prevalent in many forms. This last couplet also goes: Roses are red, violets are blue, skunks do stink, and so do you' (Croydon), 'Hitler stinks and so do you' (Aberdeen, 1952), and, more subtly, 'Lavender smells, and so do you' (Worcester). The beginnings of the first rhyme 'Inky pinky' can be seen a century ago in the counting-out lines:

> Ink, pink Pen and ink;
> A study, a stive, A stove, and a sink!

(J. O. Halliwell, *Popular Rhymes*, 1849, p. 134), and it is often employed for 'dipping' today. Nearly all these derisive cries are also well known in the United States.

'Been working overtime at the gasworks, mate, haven't they?' or 'He's got a tongue like a dog's tail, it's always wagging.'

Of a lazy-bones (someone who has a 'dose of lazyitis') Kirkcaldy kids chant:

> Davy Doubts, Laird o' Louts,
> Played wi' chuckie stanes.
> A' the bairns got cheese and bread,
> But Davie ne'er got none.

A very common ode recited for the benefit of the impatient goes:

> Patience is a virtue, virtue is a grace,
> Both put together make a very pretty face.

To which the impatient responds:

> Patience is a virtue, virtue is a grace,
> Grace is a little girl who doesn't wash her face.

When someone without a seat complains 'Where shall I sit?' the fashionable retort is 'Oh – sit on your thumb.' Whereupon the modern Miss Notable responds: 'I would, but there's a nail in it.' When someone asks, rather helplessly, where they shall put something, the chorus begins: 'Oompah, oompah, stick it up your jumper.'

Habitual grumblers in London's East End receive the poetic injunction: 'Oo, shut yer moanin' 'ole.' A child who interferingly tells them how something should be done is snapped at, 'Go and teach your grandmother to suck eggs.'[1]

Should a small child, feeling himself aggrieved, threaten, 'Tell me mum of you', they jeer:

> Tell her, smell her,
> Kick her down the cellar.

Alton, Pendeen, Swansea.[2]

Should a child complain, 'Tell me dad', they are equally undaunted:

> Tell him, smell him,
> Take him out and sell him.

Alton.

1. An ancient retort. It appears not only, inevitably, in Swift's *Polite Conversation* but in various forms in the sixteenth and seventeenth centuries: 'To teache our dame to spynne' (1542); 'Go learne your gooddame to get Bairnes' (*c.* 1598); 'Teach your grandma to grope her duck' (1616); and 'Teach your grandame to sup sour milk' (1670). See M. P. Tilley, *Proverbs*, 1950, p. 273.

2. This is the same cry of defiance that unregenerate youngsters uttered in Victorian days. The couplet is recorded in Bodleian MS. Eng. misc. e. 39 f. 118, and was apparently current in Manchester in the middle of the nineteenth century.

In Scotland, if a like situation arises, they taunt:

> Tell, tell, yer Auntie Bell,
> And get tuppence tae yersel'.
>
> *Kirkcaldy.*

Or,

> Tell, tell, yer Auntie Bell,
> Tae buy a rope and hang hersel'.
>
> *Forfar.*[1]

To those they have offended they offer the mock apology:

> Beg your pardon, grant your grace,
> – I hope the cows will spit in your face.

To 'don't-cares' the traditional saying is:

> Don't care was *made* to care,
> Don't care was hung,
> Don't care was put in a pot
> And boiled till he was done.
>
> *Hackney version.*

And those who find themselves excluded jeer back at the crowd:

> Birds of a feather flock together,
> And so do pigs and swine;
> Rats and mice do have their choice
> And so do I have mine.[2]

Wordsmanship

It is common practice to snub a companion who makes irritating use of words such as 'Well!' 'What?' 'Why?' and 'Eh?'

1. There are also mock threats to 'tell':

> I'm going to tell of you,
> You put me in the dustbin
> And made me black and blue.
>
> *Sale.*

> I'm going to tell of you,
> You went upstairs
> And kissed a kangaroo.
>
> *Sale.*

> A'm going to tell my ma on you,
> You sat on a dyke,
> And smoked a pipe,
> And never gave me a draw.
>
> *Aberdeen.*

> I'm going to tell on you,
> You sat on the piano
> And ate a banana,
> And wudna gie me a bite.
>
> *Forfar.*

Names and jeers for a child who really does commit the sin of the telling appear on pp. 209–11.

2. First noted in print by J. O. Halliwell, *Nursery Rhymes*, 1844, p. 152. It is an extension of the old proverb 'Byrds of a fether, best flye together' (1578).

Arguing with someone who keeps saying 'Well-l . . .' the pert-tongued demand: 'What's the good of a well without water?' (If quick-witted, the first retorts: 'To throw rubbish like you in.')

To one who exclaims 'Well! Well!'

– 'Two wells make a river and you in the middle make it bigger.'

'Well! Well! Well!'

– 'Three big holes in the earth.'

'Do you know what?'

– 'You're a monkey and I'm not.'[1]

'What?'

– 'Watt made a steam-engine.'

'What?'

– 'Watt died long ago. Pardon took his place.'

In some districts they rap out rhyming rebukes:

'What?' – 'Squat! Eat your dinner while it's hot' (Pendeen).

'What?' – 'Pot, poke your head in the teapot. Bring it out red hot, that's all the sense you've got' (Alton).

'What?' – 'Pot, kiss the kettle when it's hot. You're a monkey and I'm not' (Welshpool).

'What?' – 'Pot, cats' tails all hot. You cook 'em, I'll eat 'em' (London).

'What?' – 'Pot, you're a donkey and I'm not. You walk on four legs, I walk on two. The last donkey I saw was very like you' (Dublin). [2]

People who keep pestering 'Why? Why?' are fobbed off with: 'Because Y has a long tail' (Alton).

'Y's a crooked letter and you can't straighten it' (Ruthin and Welshpool).

'Y is a letter you ought to know better' (Lydney).

'Y is a crooked letter, just talk to me straight' (Lincoln).

'Why? – Z!' (Croydon).

'Why! Y's not Z and Z's not Y – that's why!' (Market Rasen).

> Why? – Wheat is better than rye,
> You would know it if you had it to buy.
>
> *Knighton.*

> Why? Why? Why?
> Give him a dig in the eye.
>
> *Dublin.*

1. In Ruthin children say: 'Wyddost ti be? Pwys o dê.' (Do you know what? A pound of tea.)
2. An Aberdeenshire child says 'Fit?' (for 'What?') and they reply 'It's nae a fit, it's a leg.' A Cardiganshire child says 'Whart?' and receives the information 'It's not a wart it's a pimple.'

Why? – Z!
Butter on your bread,
If you don't like it
You'll have to go to bed.

South Elmsall.

Likewise the user of the vulgar interrogative 'Eh?' is proffered the agricultural advice: 'Buy straw, it's cheaper' (Croydon); 'Horses eat it, want a bag?' (Enfield); 'Horses eat it, cows chew it' (Oxford); ''Ay's long stuff, can't eat a truss in a month' (Market Rasen).

Eh? – Straw,
What you can't eat – gnaw!
What you can't gnaw – nibble!
What you can't nibble –
Give to the devil!

Alton.

Eh?
B.
Cat's in the cupboard
And can't see me.

Sale, Manchester.

Eh?
—t a bob eggs.

South Elmsall.

Similarly, in response to the call 'Hey there!' they shout back: 'Hay's in the stable', 'Hay's good for horses and asses like you', or 'There's plenty of 'ay in the fields!'[1]

In fact there seems to be a stock retort for every trite expression. To one who says 'You ought not to do that', they reply 'Aught stands for nothing.' To one who exclaims 'I can't get over that!' they suggest 'Well jump over it!' To one who keeps 'wondering', they moralize: 'You'll wonder and wonder till crows build in your bottom and then you'll wonder where they get the sticks from!'[2] To one who keeps saying 'Maybe', the Forfar child chants:

Mebbe aye, mebbe no,
Mebbe I suppose so.

1. In the 1880s, according to Flora Thompson, Oxfordshire village women used to chant 'Ay-Ay-Ay! Ay for 'osses, straw for cows, milk f'r little pigs, and wash for gert ole sows – like you!' (*Still Glides the Stream*, 1948, p. 53). In Illinois, in a similar situation, children retort: 'Save your 'ay and marry a cow.'
2. Cf. G. F. Northall, *Folk-Phrases of Four Counties*, 1894, p. 35, 'You should not think till the crows build in your bum and then you should wonder how they got the sticks there.'

Similarly to one who ventures 'I dare say':

> Daresay aye, daresay no,
> Daresay I suppose so.

To one who says 'Excuse me' – 'Excuse anything nowadays.' To one who says 'I beg your pardon' – 'Don't beg, you're big enough to steal.' To one who exclaims 'Oh!' the immediate response is 'P.' To one who keeps saying 'she' in an impolite manner the reproof is: 'Who's *she*, the cat's mother?' To one who inadvertently says something in rhyme ('I shan't because I can't') they jeer in sing-song voice, 'Ha! ha! You're a poet and you don't know it', or 'That's a rhyme if you take it in time.'[1] To one colloquially saying good-night 'Nightie, nightie', their good-humoured riposte is 'Pyjama, pyjama'. And should a master be so off his guard as to acquire the habit of exclaiming 'Boys will be boys', sooner or later his class will be responding 'And girls will be mothers.'

Stale Jokes and Stale News

They come down like a ton of bricks on people who tell a stale joke. 'Do you know where Smudger takes his girl?' gags the would-be comic, 'He takes her behind a bush because it's very *privet*.' Whereupon the 'ripe one' is complimented: 'Oh lor, last time I heard that the tears rolled down my bib.' 'I laughed till my teething ring choked me.' 'Aren't you funny, sonny? I tickle myself to make me laugh.'[2] His applause is the hollow laughter of:

> Ha, ha, ha, hee, hee, hee,
> Elephant's eggs in a rhubarb tree.

The bearer of stale news is similarly ridiculed. He who breathlessly acquaints his public with the fact 'Do you know what? Miss Thompson

---

1. Similarly in *Polite Conversation*, 1738, p. 21:

Neverout. Well, Miss; I'll think of this.
Miss. That's Rhime, if you take it in Time.
Neverout. What! I see you are a Poet.
Miss. Yes; if I had but the Wit to show it.

And amongst American youngsters (according to *The Child's Book of Folklore*, New York, 1947, p. 72):

> You're a poet, and don't know it,
> But your feet show it – they're Longfellows!

2. A *Gargantuan* joke, given by Urquhart, Book I, ch. xi, 1653.

has a fiancé', is drily informed: 'Queen Anne's dead.'[1] 'That's like seven-days-old bread, it's stale.' 'Tell us news, not history.' 'Where did you dig that up?' 'Always first with the news, aint he?' 'Oh, gor blimey, you're slow.' 'Cor, you're a bit late, mate.' 'That's as old as the hills, try something new.' 'Old Lightning – you're history.' 'Wake up England!' 'No you don't say! – You're kidding.' 'That's got whiskers on it.' 'That's corny. I knew that before you 'er born.' 'King Tut's dead, so what?' 'Oh, stale buns. I've heard that thousands of times.' 'Shave the whiskers off it.' 'Gosh, news! Now tell us the one about the three bears.'

Should the news purveyor also consider his information to be odd, commenting, 'Isn't it funny', they echo:

> Isn't it funny, a rabbit's a bunny,
> It has two ears, four legs, and a tummy.
>
> *Very general.*

> Isn't it funny, the cat's got money,
> And I've got none.
>
> *Shrewsbury.*

> Isn't it funny to see a bunny
> Take a watch from the pocket in his tummy.
>
> *Cleethorpes.*

> Isn't it funny, a rabbit's a bunny
> It lifts up its tail and loses its money.
>
> *Market Rasen.*

Should the slow one also think her news to be marvellous, saying, for instance, 'Did you ever? Betty's come to school in trousers, did you ever?' they chaff:

> Well I never! Did you ever
> See a monkey dressed in leather?
> Leather eyes, leather nose,
> Leather breeches to his toes.
>
> *Hayes, Middlesex.*

> Well I never! No I never
> See a pig without a feather.
>
> *Manchester.*

---

1. Appropriately, this expression did not come into vogue until long after Queen Anne's death. It is first found in George Colman's *The Heir at Law*, Act 1, sc. i, 1797. Swift in *Polite Conversation*, 1738, p. 5, has 'Queen Elizabeth's dead'. Farquhar in *Sir Harry Wildair*, 1701, Act II, sc. ii, has 'The King of Spain is dead'. John Ray in his *Proverbs*, 1670, p. 163, gives 'My Lord Baldwin's dead'.

Well I never! Did you ever
See your mother in the gutter
Making butter for her supper?

Pendeen.

Hif ye efer seen the like
O yer grannie oan a bike
And yer mither oan the handlebars?

Luncarty.

Street Jeers

There is also a small group of special jeers for anyone unusual seen in
the street. Someone with a beard has 'Beardie!' or 'Fungus face!' shouted
after him. (The cry 'Beaver!' is a thing of the past.) They call 'Bald 'ed!'
after anyone with a mop of hair, 'Look at him robbing the barber.' Someone with a crew-cut is a 'Bean head', 'Bullet head', or 'Convict number
99'. In Newcastle when a barber has been over-enthusiastic, they sing out
'Scottie the scalper uses a knife!'

The over-dressed (i.e. 'a posh or dolled-up person', toff, swell, snob,
nob, big-wig, lord, or la-di-dah) is plagued with the words:

> Smarty, smarty, gave a party,
> – But nobody came.[1]

When a Teddy boy passes by: 'How d'you get your boots on – with
vaseline?'

After a policeman they chant – when he's safely round the corner:

> Policeman, policeman, don't catch me,
> Catch that boy behind that tree.
> He stole sugar and I stole tea.
> Policeman, policeman, don't catch me,

and so many other verses that they have a section to themselves (pp. 395–
7).

After a postman ('Slottie Johnnie' in Aberdeenshire) children in Scotland chant:

> Postie, postie, number nine,
> Tore 'is breeks on a railway line.

[1]. This refrain has possibly been picked up from American servicemen, for the chant is
endemic in the United States. See, e.g., *New York Times*, 6 August 1939, sec. ii, p. 4/8;
A Rocket in My Pocket, Carl Withers, 1948, p. 113; and the *Journal of American Folk-
lore*, vol. lxiii, 1950, p. 425. In Iowa (1958) children have a longer verse:

> Smarty, smarty, smarty, thought she'd have a party,
> Nobody came but a big fat darkie.

In Angus children still chant after the lamplighter the evocative verse of long ago:

> Leerie, leerie, licht the lamps,
> Lang legs and crookit shanks.[1]

When a Highlander passes by they remark, none too quietly, 'Cauld blows the breezes up my kneezes.' After a sailor they yell, 'Yer troosies will fit yer battleship.'

When gipsies, usually known as 'gyppoes' or 'hoboes' (or 'diddies' in the west of England, and 'tinks' in Scotland), are first sighted, Forfar children 'always' shout, 'Tinkie, tinkie, torn breeks' after them, and Radnorshire children say that they taunt:

> Gipsy, gipsy joker,
> Get a red hot poker.

But the passers-by who come in for the most derision, other than policemen, are bicyclists. When boys see an antiquated machine they shout: 'Any old iron!' or 'What do you call that crate?' or 'Sell that crock and buy a bike.'

To a rider wobbling on his bike: 'Get off and milk it.'

To any cyclist passing by: 'Hi mate! Yer wheels are going round', or 'Watch out, your back wheel's tyred.'

Each of these calls is traditional, and appears to be known throughout the country. (According to our correspondents most of them were already being shouted at the beginning of the century.) There are also traditional responses by the one who is riding the bike:

Boy walking: 'Your back wheel's trying to catch up your front one.'
Boy on bike: 'Put your head in and stop it.'

Boy walking [as reported from Kirkcaldy]: 'Yer back wheel's gaen roond.'
Boy on bike: 'So's ma front ane.'
Boy walking: 'Aye, but no backwards.'

Boy walking: 'Where are your lights?'
Boy on bike: 'Next my liver.'

Boy walking: 'Where's your bell?'
Boy on bike: 'Where d'you think – gone egging!'

1. In 1826 Robert Chambers (*Popular Rhymes of Scotland*, p. 153) recorded as a familiar serenade amongst boys in Peebles:

> Leerie, leerie, light the lamps,
> Lang legs and short shanks,
> Tak' a stick and break his back,
> And send him through the Nor'gate!

4 Guile

IT seems that even the petty verbal stratagems they practise on each other are traditional. One boy will say 'I one my mother', and get another lad to say 'I two my mother', and will continue 'I three my mother', and the other say 'I four my mother', and so on, 'I five my mother', 'I six my mother', 'I seven my mother', until the unsuspecting one says 'I 'ate my mother', whereupon he who plays the trick will roar with laughter and give himself the prize for wit, little thinking that he is flogging a joke his father and his grandfather knew, and schoolboys knew and practised in the reign of George III (see hereafter, p. 85). He will say 'Think of a number, double it, add two, add three, add one more, halve it, take away the number you first thought of. Your answer is three', and be practising a hocus-pocus which can be traced back for seven generations.[1] He will say 'King Charles the First walked and talked half an hour after his head was cut off', and be hawking a trifle which was known to children in the eighteenth century.[2] He will say 'Heads I have it, tails you don't', and be catching someone with a deceit which Dean Swift conceived to be perfect.[3] He will press a cold sixpence on a comrade's forehead and feign that it sticks there, challenging him to shake it off, and be perpetuating an illusion which has passed from brow to brow since Shakespeare's time.[4]

These tricks they have for scoring off one another cover almost the whole anatomy of personal humiliation. Some of them evoke responses

1. It is given in *The Art of Teaching in Sport*, 1785, pp. 62–3.
2. It appears amongst jokes, not all original, in *A Choice Collection of Riddles, Charades, Rebusses, &c.* by Peter Puzzlewell, Esq., 1792, p. 20.
3. Jonathan Swift, *Some Remarks on the Barrier Treaty*, 1712 (ed. 1883, vol. iv, p. 371). It was not new then. Thomas Shadwell mentions it in his drama, *Epsom-Wells*, 1673, Act II, sc. i, 'They cheat . . . worse than Cross I win, Pile you lose'; and Butler refers to it in *Hudibras*, 1678, III. iii. 685.
4. The prank is apparently alluded to by the dramatist Edward Sharpham in *Cupid's Whirligig*, 1607, K3, 'Holde vp your head Tobias, and looke and you can see a penny in my browe'; and by Thomas Burton in his *Diary*, 9 March, 1658/9. Roger North is almost certainly referring to it in his *Examen*, 1740, II. v, p. 324. And it is described in *The Girl's Book of Diversions*, 1835, p. 111; and in *Notes and Queries*, 9th ser., viii, 1901, p. 189.

which give (or are assumed to give) permission for physical action. 'What does a ship do first when it comes into harbour?' 'Ties up.' ('You flick the person's tie out' – Boy, 13, Lydney.) 'Spell pin backwards.' ('And when she does, nip her' – Girl, 12, Cleethorpes.) Some bamboozle a child into admitting unsavoury characteristics. ('If frozen water is iced water, what is frozen ink?') Some trap him or her into saying a rude word, or embarrass by the apparent indelicacy of their proposition. Some sneak up on him and make him look daft or babyish or a dunce. 'Do you learn Guzzinta in your form?' 'No, we haven't done that yet.' 'Don't they teach you two guzzinta four?' (Royal Grammar School, Worcester). In some he is sent on sleeveless errands (see under April Fools' Day), or is put in considerable discomfort (see especially under New Boys), or is nearly made mad with baiting ripostes to what seemed serious questions. But with all of them, however momentarily aggressive, however slight the alleviation of wit, there is one compensation which is immediately apparent to the victim: he now knows the trick, *he can now try it on somebody else.* It is this which makes him accept being fooled with general good humour. And it is this fact which endlessly prolongs the life of these jokes, the good and the bad, without discrimination.

'I know what you are going to say next.' 'What?' 'I knew you'd say what.'

'I'll make you say black.' 'You won't!' 'What are the colours of the Union Jack?' 'Red, white and blue.' 'There! I said you'd say blue.' 'No, you said I'd say black.' 'Yes, and now you have said it.'

'I can make you into a Red Indian.' 'How?' 'How!' and the first boy raises his right hand head high.

Tricks Inflicting Pain

A trick will sweep through a school like a disease, one child passing it on to another, until nearly everyone in the school has succumbed to it.

Younger children, particularly young boys, say: 'Do you want a chestnut?' 'Yes.' 'Well, there's your chest' (*poke*) 'and there's your nut' (*smack*).[1] 'Do you know my patent wigwam?' 'No.' 'Well, there's a wig' (*tousling person's hair*), 'and there's a wham' (*in person's stomach*). 'Do you collect stamps?' 'Yes.' 'Here's another for you' (*stamping on his foot*). 'Do you like ice-creams?' 'Yes.' 'Do you like fourpenny ones?' 'Yes.' 'I'll give you one' (*punching him*).

[1]. 'Just contributed,' writes a teacher, 'by my six-year-old son, and I remember it vividly before 1914.'

Small girls say: 'Do you know Tony Chestnut?' (*Toe-knee-chest-nut*).

Girls take a person's hand and lift up each finger in turn, 'The sheep says baa-baa ... The cow says moo-moo ... The dog says bow-wow', and when they come to the little finger they say, 'The cat says me —' and they bend the person's finger back until she cries 'Ow!'

They have, in Ipswich, a finger game called 'Playing Schools'. A girl interlaces her fingers with another girl's fingers, and bends and straightens them saying:

> 'Sit down, stand up,
> Sit down, stand up.'

She then says 'Let's have an arithmetic lesson,' and she counts on the girl's fingers, '1 + 1 = 2. 2 + 2 = 4'. Then she interlaces their fingers again and repeats:

> 'Sit down, stand up,
> Sit down, stand up.'

'Now we'll have a spelling lesson,' and she touches the finger tips:

> 'D-O-G spells dog.
> C-A-T spells cat.'

Then she interlaces their fingers again and repeats:

> 'Sit down, stand up,
> Sit down, stand up.'

'Now,' she says, 'we'll have a singing lesson,' and she squeezes the interlaced fingers until the other child yells. 'You are out of tune,' she says.

Both boys and girls have the rhyme:

> Adam and Eve and Pinch-me
> Went down to the river to bathe.
> Adam and Eve were drowned,
> Who do you think was saved?

If an innocent replies 'Pinch-me', the invitation usually receives prompt and careful attention. ('You say "It's a pleasure",' remarks a Presteigne girl.) The catch is, however, so old and memorable it has almost descended to being nursery property.[1] So they have to disguise 'Pinch-me', calling

---

1. According to a correspondent to *Notes and Queries*, 10th ser., iv, 1905, p. 77, the lines were already 'well known as a schoolboy's catch for the innocent new boy and for our unwary sisters' about 1855.

him 'Nipmetight' or 'Kickmehard' or 'Leathermewell'; or they say the rhyme in other ways:

Adam and Eve and Nipmewell
Went in a boat to sea.
Adam and Eve fell out,
Who was left?

> *Boy, 10, Blackburn.*

Adam and Eve and Pinch-me
Went down to the river to bathe.
Adam and Pinch-me got drowned,
Who do you think was saved?

> *Girls, Swansea. The cleverdick thinks a mistake has been made and replies Eve ('eave), and they tell him to run to a basin.*

Punch and Judy ran a race
Round and round the market place,
Judy stopped to tie her lace,
Who won?

> *Cleethorpes, Forfar ('Judy fell and skinned her face'), Kirkcaldy, Oxford, Swansea, 'When the person says "Punch", you punch them'.*

James and John and Little Nippon
Went down to the river to bathe;
James and John fell in and were drowned,
Which of the three was saved?

> *Girls, Kirkcaldy. The girl is nipped until she utters the magic word "Nipp-off".*

Pinch-me, Pinch-me, and Treadon-mytoes,
Went down to the river to bathe.
Two of the three were drowned,
Who do you think was saved?

> *Girl, 14, Knighton. A three-way catch.*

The cock, the hen, and the pullet,
Went into the barn to lay.
The cock and the hen came out again,
And which do you think did lay?

> *Boys, 11, Knighton. 'When they say "pullet", pull their hair.'*

As well as being popular in Britain, this catch is an international favourite.[1]

It seems to be mostly older and city children who employ the following somewhat fierce artifices.

A boy says 'Hit me.' The new-comer does so, usually tentatively.

'What did I say?'

'Hit me.'

'All right I WILL!' and a hit is delivered which is far from tentative.

A boy says 'Hit me and I won't hit you back,' and after the dupe's half-hearted effort, hits him good and hard in *front*.

1. Thus:

Adam and Eve and Pinch-me-tight
Went over the river to see a cat fight;
Adam and Eve got back all right,
Who didn't?

> *East Texas.*

Knijp-me-eens en Krab-me-eens
Die zaten in een bootje;
Knijp-me-eens die viel er uit,
Wie bleef er toen nog over?

> *Holland.*

Pince-mé et Pince-moi
Sortent dans un bateau;
Pince-mé tombe dans l'eau,
Qu'est-ce qui reste?

> *France.*

Juan y Pínchame se fueron a bañar;
Juan se ahogó
¿Quién quedó?

> *Spain.*

A tough, with an appearance of friendliness, says 'Do you know the best thing I can draw?' 'No, what?' 'My hand across your face', and he demonstrates his proficiency.

A popular trick, of uncertain wit, is performed by a boy saying:

> See my finger, (*holding out finger*)
> See my thumb, (*holding out thumb*)
> See my fist
> And here it come! (*gabbled very quickly and acted upon*)

Or, in Aberdeen:

> That's a triangle, (*joining thumbs and forefingers*)
> That's a space, (*making a circle*)
> That's my hand
> And that's your face! (*smacking face*)

In both cases a specious authority for the actions is given by the key words being in rhyme.[1]

In Enfield a greenhorn is instructed to say 'No' to everything.

'Turkey.'

'No.'

'Goose.'

'No.'

'Duck.'

'No.'

So he is punched, standing where he is. 'Seems senseless,' comments a master, 'but it happens and is thought very funny.'

Alternatively, in different places, boys tell a person to 'look at this finger nail', and when he peers forward slap his nose.

They draw a person's attention to their elbow, and when he glances down, hit him on the head with their fist.

They tell him to pick up a piece of paper on the floor 'and when he bends down,' says a 12-year-old, 'smack him a good one on the bottom.'

And when a person has become properly scared, they raise their fist sharply, as if to hit him again, and then carry their hand on upwards and scratch the back of their head. 'Wot's the matter, chum? I ain't going to 'it yer.'

1. Milder forms of the joke go:

Pull my finger	Pull my finger,	Suck your finger,
Pull my thumb,	Pull my thumb,	Suck your thumb,
(*victim does so*)	Tell your teacher	Don't do either,
I'll tell a p'liceman	What you done.	Chew some gum.
What you've done.	*London, Alton,*	*Long Island,*
Weymouth.	*and Newcastle.*	*U.S.A.*

And, 'Pull my pinkie [little finger], you're a tinkie' (Forfar).

Country children, too, can play a venomous trick. They say 'Nettles don't sting this month', and confirm their statement by grasping a nettle leaf firmly. The 'towney' touches the leaf gingerly and cries out with pain, whereupon the country child jeers, 'Nettles don't sting this month – but they do sting *you*!' Then, perhaps, to make amends, he extends the stranger's rural lore by finding a dock leaf, spitting on it, and rubbing the affected part, chanting, as in Chaucer's time:

> Dockin go in, nettle go out,
> Dockin go in and pull nettle out.[1]

In a similar vein, the village boys of Upton Magna in Shropshire joke, 'Cuckoos don't sing this month.' And when the visitor expresses surprise the boys explain, 'They only sing "Cuckoo".'

'Made You Look'

An extraordinarily popular trick, an all-year-round variety of the Common *Aprilus Primum*, is to say 'Look! What's that on the ground?' and when a person looks, cry 'Monkey looking for monkey nuts' (to which the wise have a crushing retort, 'Aye, apes tell them to'). Another is to keep pointing up in the sky 'He's got one! A mauve one!' and when anyone follows their gaze, to chant:

> Made you look, made you stare,
> Made the barber cut your hair.
> Cut it long, cut it short,
> Cut it with a knife and fork.

Alton, Bath, Enfield, Manchester, Oxted, Shrewsbury.

Or,

> I made you look, I made you stare,
> I made you cut the barber's hair.
> The barber's hair was rough and thick,
> I made you use his walking stick.

Newcastle.

Or,

> I made you look, I made you stare,
> I made you cut the barber's hair.
> The barber's hair was full of fleas,
> I made you eat a bit of cheese.

Aberystwyth.

1. Cf. *Troylus and Cryseyde*, iv. 460, *c.* 1385, 'But kanstow pleyen raket, to and fro, Netle In, dokke out, now this now þat, Pandare?' The particular verse-charm quoted above is from 11-year-olds in Penrith, Cumberland (1957).

Or,

> I made you look
> You dirty duck. (*hitting him*)
> *Newcastle.*[1]

To make someone a further fool, they say, 'Look up!' and when he does so:

> Look up, look down,
> You owe me half a crown.
> Look at the door,
> You owe me more.

Or again, 'Look, there's something on your tongue.' The person puts out his tongue. 'Good dog!'

Spitting Jokes

The following are not, perhaps, worth a £5 fine on a corporation bus, but pass for wit in the backstreets.

One boy says to another, 'Think you're strong d'you?' and, on receiving an affirmatory reply, spits on the ground, and challenges, 'Pick that up.'

A boy goes up to one to whom he wishes to show disrespect, and says, 'D'you want something to do? – You do?' and spits on the ground, crowing, 'Well, pick the bones out of that.'

A trick popular with 10–12-year-olds (Birmingham, Lydney, and Shrewsbury) is called 'The Duck Pond'. A boy takes someone's hand, and professes to trace on it the plan of a farm. 'Here's where the barn is, and here's where the cowshed is, and here in the middle,' he says, spiting into the person's hand, 'is the duck pond.'[2]

---

1. In Maryland, U.S.A.,

> Made you look, made you cry,
> Made you buy a penny pie.
> Look up, look down,
> You're the biggest fool in town.

In Virginia,

> Made you look, you dirty crook,
> Stole your mother's pocket book.
> Turned it in, turned it out,
> Turned it into sauerkraut.

2. Cf. F. M. Böhme. *Deutsches Kinderlied und Kinderspiel*, 1924, nr. 1288,

> Ich sage dir wahr,
> deine Hand is klar,
> ich sage dir was,
> deine Hand ist naß.

The speaker spits into the other's hand as he says this.

Trick Bets

The artful ones use dodges like these: 'I can jump higher than a house.'
  'Bet you can't.'
  'Bet I can, did you ever see a house jump?' (Boy, 9, Alton.)
  'Can you jump over these railings?'
  'No.'
  'I'll take off my shoes and jump over them.'
  'Bet you can't.'
  'Bet I can.' He takes off his shoes and jumps over them. (Boy, 14, Bishop Auckland.)
  'I can jump that stream.'
  'Bet you can't.'
  'Give me a penny and I'll jump over it.' He places the penny on the ground and jumps over it. (Boy, 11, Luncarty, nr. Perth.)

And each year there are some half million new schoolchildren who will be amazed by the diddler who can bite half an inch off a poker (he bites half an inch away from the poker), who can kiss a match-box inside and out without opening it (he kisses it indoors and outside), who can push someone's head through the inkwell in a desk (he puts his finger through the hole and pushes someone's head), or who says 'I can put myself through a key-hole' (he writes 'myself' on a piece of paper and shoves it through).[1]

Self-Incrimination Traps

It is considered high sport to trap the unwary into admitting that he is daft, a dunce, a blockhead, a monkey, and such-like enormities. They recite, in 'Adam and Eve and Pinch-me' fashion:

'Doh, Ray, and Me, went into the nut house. Doh and Ray came out, who was left in?'

or,

'I know three monkeys. One's called Doh, one's called Ray, what's the third called?'

'Person will reply "Me"', says an 11-year-old Blackburn boy. 'Then you say "Oh! I didn't know you were a monkey".'

1. Each of these jokes is more than a hundred years old. See, e.g., *The Girl's Book of Diversions*, 1835, pp. 103–6, and *Fireside Amusements*, 1850, pp. 92–5.

'If you and I had a race to the madhouse who'd get there first?'

'If he says "You" then you reply, "Yes, to open the door for you".' (Boy, 13, Croydon.)

'Can you add this up? 1 ton of sawdust, 1 ton of straw, ½ ton of cotton wool. Have you got all that in your head?' ('The person says "Yes", and you say, "I thought that's what you had in your head".')

'Can you say tea-pot backwards?' ('The person says "pot-tea", and you say you know he is.')

'Do you feel like a cup of tea?' 'Yes.' 'You look like one.'

'Are you soft?' 'No.' 'Are you daft?' 'No.' 'Are you far off it?' 'No.' (You say, 'I thought not'.)

This last is almost one of the triple-question tricks in which the person is led to expect that the answer given to the first two questions will also do for the third:

Do you like apples?	Or,	Do you like white?
Do you like pears?		Do you like pink?
Do you like tumbling down the stairs?		Do you like falling down the sink?

Possibly the rhyming aids the delusion, for these formulas are highly popular, particularly with very young children who have just started school. Our daughter, for example, was five years old when she came home with:

> Do you like coffee?
> Do you like tea?
> Do you like sitting on a blackman's knee?[1]

In the same class are the 'insidious ruses', as P. H. Gosse described them, in which the victim is induced to reply to each question with a prescribed answer.[2] The result, when the victim finally incriminates himself, is – as we well remember ourselves – peculiarly satisfying to the trickster, and is greeted, as one girl puts it 'with screams of laughter from everybody listening'.

1. Cf. the skipping rhyme in *London Street Games*, 1916, p. 53.

> Do you like silver and gold?
> Do you like brass?
> Do you like looking through the looking glass?

2. Philip Henry Gosse was at school at Poole in Dorset from 1818 to 1823. There the children practised the tricks: 'I one my mother', already described, ending 'I eight my mother' ('Here's a wicked footer! He says he hates his mother!'), and 'I'll go to A,' ending 'I'll go to L' ('Lo! what d'ye think? he says he'll go to hell!'). Gosse's account of his boyhood was published, posthumously, as 'A Country Day-School Seventy Years Ago' in *Longman's Magazine*, vol. xiii, 1889, pp. 512–24.

In the following specimens the tenderfoot is instructed to respond 'Just like me' or 'So do I', as the case may be, or to be a key to the other person's lock, or to take the even numbers in a curious count:

'I went up one pair of stairs.'
'Just like me.'
'I went up two pairs of stairs.'
'Just like me.'
'I opened the door.'
'Just like me.'
'I crossed the room.'
'Just like me.'
'I looked out of the window.'
'Just like me.'
'And saw a monkey.'
'Just like me.'

> *Castle Eden, Co. Durham. Very similar versions from Bishop Auckland, Cleethorpes, Lydney, Oxford, Peterborough, Reading, and South Elmsall.*[1]

Let's play 'Eight Steps' they say. They draw the steps with a chalk and warn their victim that she must say 'So did I' to everything that happens on the steps.

'I went up one step.'
'So did I.'
'I went up two steps.'
'So did I.'
'I went up four steps.'
'So did I.'
'I saw a cat.'
'So did I.'
'The cat saw a rat.'
'So did I.'
'The cat ate the rat' (*said quickly*)
'So did I.'
'Get away from me you horrid thing eating rats.'

> *Elizabeth Healy, 'The Irish School Weekly', 9 December 1950.*

'I am a gold lock.'
'I am a gold key.'
'I am a silver lock.'
'I am a silver key.'
'I am a brass lock.'
'I am a brass key.'
'I am a monk lock.'
'I am a monkey.'

> *Alton and Cambridge.*[2]

'As I was walking up a scabb't lane I met a scabb't horse. I one it.'
'I two it.'
'I three it.'
'I four it.'
'I five it.'
'I six it.'
'I seven it.'
'I ate it.'

> *Aberdeen, Edinburgh, Forfar, Glasgow, Kirkcaldy. Similar from Swansea, but used as a counting-out rhyme.*

Further versions start 'I one a dead dog, I two a dead dog' (Radcliffe), 'There was a bad apple in a field, I one it, I two it' (Sale), 'There wiz a horse on top of a stair and we fought for it, I one'd it, I two'd it' (Forfar),

1. Previously recorded by J. O. Halliwell, *The Nursery Rhymes of England*, 1844, p. 105. The trick is also commonly practised by American youngsters, as are most of the others given here.
2. Halliwell collected this, too, in 1844 (p. 103); and it was one of the tricks Dick Bultitude played on visitors when he took charge of his father's office in the City. (*Vice Versâ*, 1882, p. 297.)

'I love say one' leading up to 'I love say ten' (Oxford), and 'I went round a corner to A in a basket' (the unhygienic result coming towards the end of the alphabet).[1]

With an appearance of innocence they ask: 'Tell me, which hand do you stir your tea with?'

'The right.'

'You dirty creature, why don't you use a spoon?'

'Did you get wet this morning?' (On a fine day.)

'No, of course not.'

'You should 'ave if you'd washed.' (Girl, 10, Ipswich.)

'Do you clean your top teeth with a toothbrush?'

'Yes.'

'What do you clean your bottom with?'

'A toothbrush.'

'It must be dirty!'

'Tell me, which would you rather do:

> Run a mile,
> Jump a stile,
> Or eat a pancake in a field?'

And it causes no little merriment if the last of these activities is selected.[2]

To snare a child into using a rude word or uttering an impoliteness they instruct him to repeat quickly: 'I chased a bug around a tree, I'll have his blood, he knows I will!' (this one is top favourite), or 'Shut up

1. Cf.: 'J'ai monté un escalier.'   'Ich bin in den Wald gegangen.'
  'Comme moi.'   'Ich auch.'
  'Je suis entré dans la chambre.'   'Ich bin zu einem Baum gekommen.'
  'Comme moi.'   'Ich auch.'
  'J'ai vu une petite boîte.'   'Ich hab einen umgehauen.'
  'Comme moi.'   'Ich auch.'
  'Je l'ai ouverte.'   'Ich hab einen Sautrog daraus gemacht.'
  'Comme moi.'   'Ich auch.'
  'Il y avait une grosse bête.'   'Die Säue haben draus gefressen.'
  'Comme moi.'   'Ich auch.'

> W. W. Newell, 'Games and Songs of American Children', 1903, p. 141 n.

> F. M. Böhme, 'Deutsches Kinderlied und Kinderspiel', 1924, nr. 1289.

For references to further parallels in French, German, Estonian, Slovenian, and Abyssinian, see Paul G. Brewster, *American Nonsinging Games*, 1953, pp. 122–3.

2. This piece of rustic wit continues to be much practised, particularly among village children (heard in places as distant from each other as Eckington in Derbyshire, and Weston-super-Mare). In a version in *The West-Somerset Word-Book*, 1888, p. 638, 'What'll ee take? A hursty rake, a zin burnd cake, or a blackbird under the hill?' each of the alternatives is a catch. After the choice has been made, the person learns that he has chosen either rancid bacon, or a dried cow-clat, or the devil.

the shutters and sit in the shop' (to be said three times over), or 'Polish it in every corner, polish it behind the door.' ('It is the boys who tell us these,' say the girls.) They ask a chump: 'If a man who catches flies is a flyer, what is a man who catches bugs?' They say 'Spell *olic* and say "stars"', or 'Spell *I cup*' or 'Spell *up* and say "up" after it'. They tell him to say 'off' after each colour they name: 'Pink, red, orange, green, blue.'

'Oh it's awful!' giggle the girls, but at the 12–13 mark most of them seem to know these catches; and during the past fifty years many a young child's introduction to a word, and knowledge that it is naughty, must have been through these tricks, for nearly all are also remembered by correspondents who were young in Edwardian or Victorian days.

Minor Imbecilities

They try to make each other out to be little more than infants. 'What's that black stuff they put on the roads?' 'Tar.' 'Baby, can't say thank you.' 'What are the initials of Girl Guide?' 'G.G.' 'Baby, can't say horse yet.'[1]

They welcome little quips, however feeble. 'Have you got tulips?' 'No.' '*Haven't* you two lips?' 'What's the first letter in the alphabet?' 'A.' 'You shouldn't say "Eh?"' you should say "Pardon".' 'What's the fifteenth letter in the alphabet?' 'O.' 'I ain't touched you yet.' (Collected from boys in East London.)

They make out that they, or their companions, cannot spell. 'England, Scotland, Ireland, Wales, all begins with A.' 'Eggs and bacon, bacon fat. In four letters spell me that.' 'I saw Esau sitting on a see-saw, how many S's in that?' 'Londonderry, Cork, and Kerry, spell that without a K.'

If a fellow met a fellow	Round and round the rugged rock
In a field of fitches,	The ragged rascal ran.
Could a fellow tell a fellow	How many r's are there in that?
Where a fellow itches.	Now tell me if you can.
How many 'f's in that?	*Common in Scotland.*
Birmingham and Manchester.[2]	

1. In the United States: 'I can make you talk baby talk, spell "Sir".' These tricks are largely practised by children who are only just out of the infant stage themselves.

2. This sort of joke was current among children in George III's time. For instance in *Mother Goose's Melody*, 1780, p. 41, appears:

> Pease-porridge hot
> Pease-porridge cold,
> Pease-porridge in the pot
> Nine days old,
> Spell me that in four letters;
> I will, THAT.

Some of these catch-questions may seem like riddles, but the distinction lies in the way the question is asked. Usually when a riddle or conundrum is being posed a person is aware of it. The questioner either introduces his joke with the direct challenge, 'Can you solve this riddle?' or the question is itself so absurd ('What is the difference between a big black cloud and a lion with toothache?') that the person asked is immediately aware that some ingenious answer is expected of him. With a catch the person is unprepared for a trick; guile is employed to make the question look innocent. 'You know your great-great-great-grandfather?' 'Yes.' 'No you don't, because he's dead, ha! ha!' The catch is often given the appearance of being a genuine request for information. 'Where did King John sign Magna Charta?' and the person who tries to remember his history is unprepared for the sally, 'Don't you know? He signed it at the bottom.' The classic problem 'Why does a new-laid egg float but a boiled egg sink?' which Charles II is reputed to have set members of the Royal Society, is almost analogous. When the gathering of Stuart scientists confessed themselves baffled, the king explained, 'The answer is simple. It doesn't.' This is on a par with the modern schoolchild's duplicities: 'Do you say the yolk of an egg *is* white or the yolk of an egg *are* white?' and (on a Thursday), 'Is it *Wed*nesday or Wed*nes*day?' Or, 'A man owned a peacock on one side of a fence and it laid an egg in another man's garden on the other side of the fence. Whose was it?' Or, 'If two fat men were under a little umbrella, why didn't they get wet?' Or, more tortuous, 'Supposing, supposing, three camels were dozing, two got up and went away, how many were left?' Each of these questions is pure fraud, the answers being that peacocks don't lay eggs, or that the egg belonged to neither man, 'it was the peahen's' (Boy, 12, Lydney); [1] that the fat men didn't get wet 'because it wasn't raining' (Boy, 12, Market Rasen); and that no camels were left, 'I only said supposing' (Girl, 13, Kirkcaldy).

Trick Spelling and Arithmetic

Endless fun is had with the delightful word Constantinople. 'Constantinople is a very big word, if you can't spell *it* you're a very big dunce.' And: 'I'll help you spell Constantinople by giving you one syllable at a

---

[1]. Italian children are up to this trick too: 'Un gallo ha fatto un uovo sul confine italo-francese. A chi appartiene l'uovo?' And Mr Neverout in *Polite Conversation*, 1738, is similarly crafty: 'Miss, can you tell which is the Gander, the white Goose or the grey Goose?' (p. 156, but misprinted in original edition).

time. Con.' 'C-O-N.' '*Stan.*' 'S-T-A-N.' '*Ti.*' 'T-I.' '*No.*' 'T-E?' '*No!*'
'T-I-E.' '*No!*' And so on. ('No', of course, is the next syllable to be
spelt.) 'Ha, ha, pull his nose. Carn-stan-'is-nose-pull'd!' [1]

'What's the word that everybody spells wrongly?' 'WRONGLY.' 'Close
your eyes and spell *ice* without the "e".' 'I-C.' 'No you can't, you twerp,
your eyes are shut.' 'Spell *hungry horse* in four letters.' (M.T.G.G.) 'Spell
blind pig in two.' (P-G – that's pig without an eye.) [2] 'Spell tram.' 'T-R-A-M.'
'What's the first letter?' 'T.' 'What comes after T?' 'R.' 'No, supper.'
'How many letters are there in the alphabet?' 'Twenty-six.' 'No,
twenty-three. You and I aren't in it, and the angel said "Noel".'

They guy the arithmetical problems set in school with similar relish.
'If it took five men one day to dig a field, how long would it take ten men
to dig the same field?' 'Half a day.' 'No, it was done already.' 'There
were six birds on a tree. A boy shot one. How many were there left?'
'Five.' 'No, none – they all flew away.' 'Four return trains went out of a
station, one went east, one went west, one went north, one went south.
How many came back?' 'I dunno, four?' 'No, three – one went west.'
'A shepherd and his dog and a hundred sheep in a field, how many feet had
they?' 'Let me see, four hundred and six.' 'No, two – a dog has paws and
sheep have trotters.' 'Twenty copy-cats by a river. One dived in. How
many left?' 'Nineteen?' 'No, none – all the rest copied.'

Either-Way Tricks

However puerile are these jokes, there can be few people so nimble
witted that they can face all of them without loss of dignity. Some of the
quizzes, indeed, are double-edged. They catch a person whichever way
he answers them. Boys ask 'Have you stopped beating your wife?' and,
as the great jurist Sir Travers Humphreys has pointed out, recalling the
jest from his own schooldays, the question cannot be answered by a simple
'Yes' or 'No'. 'Would you rather be a bigger fool than you look or look
a bigger fool than you are?' 'It does not matter which way a person
replies,' remarks a 13-year-old girl, 'once he has answered you say "I'm

1. The trick of getting a person to spell Constantinople syllable by syllable, very popular
with children today, appears to have been common at parties a century ago where it was
set as a penance for one who wished to redeem a forfeit. See, e.g., *The Girl's Book of
Diversions*, 1835, p. 113. In the United States children say, 'Mississippi is a hard word to
spell. Spell *it*.' In Holland, 'Amsterdam die groote stad. Mes hoeveel lettres spel je *da*?'
2. This spelling must have gratified thousands of small scholars. Even *Punch*, when
young, allowed it to appear in its pages: vol. iv, 27 May 1843, p. 215.

afraid that's impossible".' Probably Dick Bultitude made a similar comment, seventy years earlier, when he surprised callers at his father's office in the City with this same query (*Vice Versâ*, 1882, p. 297). 'Are you a P.L.P.?' a constant query today (Alton, Bath, Forfar, Ipswich, Lydney, Manchester) will doubtless continue to be popular for the same reason. If a person elects to reply 'No', they turn their back on him in distaste saying, 'You're quite right. You're not a Proper Looking Person.' If he says 'Yes', they say 'Ah, I thought so,' and resting themselves against him, cry out: 'He says he's a Public Leaning Post!'

They also have fake mathematical problems of the same character – a correct answer being impossible because the questioner can alter the interpretation of the question after the answer has been given. 'There were twenty *sic* sheep in a field. One died. How many were there left?' (Twenty-five sheep or nineteen sick ones.) 'Four *te* cups on a table. One broke. How many left?' (Three tea cups or thirty-nine indeterminate ones.) 'Six *Tay* salmon went under a bridge. Two were caught. How many were left?' (Four Tay salmon, or fifty-eight less superior fish.)

Embarrassers

Embarrassers are of two kinds. In the first kind the person thinks that he is being set a sensible problem to test his ingenuity (like the problem of the fox, the goose, and the sack of corn which a man had to ferry across a river), and the answer turns out to be buffoonery, usually of a personal nature. For instance:

'There was a donkey in a field and on one side of the field there was a ten-foot stone wall, and on the next side there was a wide deep river, and on the third side there was a thick prickly hedge, and on the fourth side there was a steep high cliff. In a field close by there was a heap of carrots. How did the donkey get to the carrots?'

'Jump over the wall?'

'No, it was too high.'

'Swim the river?'

'No, he couldn't swim.'

'Push through the hedge.'

'No, it was too thick and prickly.'

'Climb the cliff.'

'No, it was too steep.'

'Well, I don't know.'

'Nor did the other donkey.'[1]

Likewise:

'If it took a week to walk a fortnight, how long would it take a flea to cross a treacle barrel?'

'I don't get what you mean.'

'Are you stuck?'

'Yes.'

'So was the flea.'

'If you were unarmed and you were walking along and met a bear, what would you do?'

'Turn round and run away.'

'What! with a bare behind?'[2]

In the other kind of embarrasser the point is not so much the cleverness of the answer as the embarrassing nature of the question. The person does not like to answer the question because of the implication he sees in it. Then, when he is told the innocuous answer, he is the more embarrassed for having been embarrassed.

'If you went into a field with your trousers down what would you do?'

'I – er – what would *you* do?'

'Pull them up, of course.'

'If you were walking along the street without any trousers on and you saw a copper what would you do?'

'I'd run.'

'*I'd* pick it up.'

And there is the little verse they recite:

> Margery Daw on the beach
> Went to swim out of reach,
> She lost her stockings and everything,
> What do you think she came home in?

'And what's the answer?' we asked. 'Can't you guess?' they said. We didn't feel inclined to speculate and said we would prefer them to tell us what she came home in. 'Twilight', they said cheerily.

1. Primitive highlanders of Arkansas and Missouri, according to the *Journal of American Folklore*, vol. xlvii, 1934, p. 89, say: 'Thar was a pore ol' starvin' mule on one side o' th' river, an' a fine big haystack on t'other side. Th' river was too deep t' ford an' too swift t'swim, an' thar warn't no bridge. How did th' mule git th' hay?'

'I caint figger it out. I give up.'

'Uh-huh, that's jest what t'other mule done!'

2. News of this old trap, still much employed by the simpler members of the community, reached Parliament 11 March 1949, when quoted by Mr Ralph Morley, the Member for Southampton.

5 Riddles

A CURIOUS feature about riddles is the way many children, when they hear them, like writing them down and making collections of them. No other species of oral lore, not even the proverb, has been collected so often; and in the past adults gathered them as much, or more than children: witness Harriet's 'only literary pursuit' in *Emma*. Printed riddle books, too, such as the one Alice Shortcake borrowed from Master Slender, have been popular for more than four centuries (latterly only with children), and consequently it is easier to find out about the age of a riddle than the age of any other kind of schoolchild lore. It is possible, for instance, to establish that many of the riddles which modern children send to the editor of a comic in the expectation of reward are 150 years old; that a good handful of the riddles have been exercising young wits for a full 300 years; and that just a few date back almost to the Middle Ages. The poser told us by a 12-year-old boy in Oxford:

How deep is the ocean? – A stone's throw;

and the mind-stretching query from a Presteigne lad:

How many balls of string would it take to reach the moon? – One, if it was long enough;

are to be found in a riddle book *Demaundes Joyous* which was 'Enprynted at London in Fletestrete at the sygne of the sonne' by Wynkyn de Worde in 1511:

What space is from y⁰ hyest space of the se to the depest – But a stones cast.

How many calues tayles behoueth to reche frome the erthe to the skye – No more but one and it be longe ynough.

It may be remarked, too, that both these riddles had appeared earlier in continental collections, in, for example, *Demaundes joyeuses en maniere de quodlibetz*, printed before 1500, and *Les Adeuineaux amoureux*, printed about 1478.

Furthermore, catch riddles such as 'What water never freezes?' (Hot water), 'How do you know the difference between a sheep and a goat?' (By looking at them), and 'What is most like a horse but isn't a horse?' (A mare), or – as a delightful Maryland version goes – 'What has a head like a cat, feet like a cat, tail like a cat, but isn't a cat?' (A kitten), either appear in the collection of 1511, or have close counterparts in it.

True Riddles

A 'true' riddle is a composition in which some creature or object is described in an intentionally obscure manner; the solution fitting all the characteristics of the description in the question, and usually resolving a paradox. For instance (all examples from present-day children):

What goes up when the rain comes down? – An umbrella.

What can go up a chimney down but can't come down a chimney up? – An umbrella.

What goes up but never comes down? – Smoke (according to boys in Dublin); Your age (according to boys in Knighton).

What holds water yet is full of holes? – A sponge.

What gets wet when drying? – A towel.

What goes to sleep with its shoes on? – The milkman's horse.

Sometimes these riddles fall into groups in which each riddle is cast in the same mould; and, traditionally, a riddler tries to cap the previous riddle with a query which varies only in a word or two. The following four are from Scotland, the last of them possibly being a recent addition:

What goes into the water red and comes out black? – A red-hot poker.

What goes into the water black and comes out red? – A lobster.

What goes into the water white and comes out black? – A miller's boot.

What goes into the water yellow and comes out of it white? – A baby's nappie.

A somewhat similar group includes: 'What has four legs and can fly?' (Two birds), 'What has yellow feathers and four legs?' (Two canaries), and 'What has six eyes and cannot see?' (Three blind mice). These unnatural monsters belong to the same menagerie as the eight-legged creature with two hands and wings (a man on horseback carrying a hawk) which used to amaze Stuart youngsters. Indeed many true riddles are venerable compositions, as may be seen in the following annotations:

What goes up a tree with its head turned downwards? – A nail in your boot.

> *Boy, 13, Knighton. Cf. 'The Booke of Meery Riddles', 1629, 'What is it that goes to the water on the head?—It is a horse-shoe naile.'*

What grows in winter, dies in summer, and grows with its roots upwards? – An icicle.

> *Boy, 10, Alton. Cf. 'A Booke of merrie Riddles', 1631, 'What doth with his roote upwards grow, and downward with his head doth show? – It is an icesickle.' 'The Puzzle Cap', c. 1840, 'What is that which only grows in winter, and with its root upwards? – An icicle.'*

What goes through the hedge and through the hedge and leaves its tail behind? – A needle and thread.

> *Boy, 13, Evenjobb, Radnorshire. Cf. MS. Harley 1960, c. 1645, 'Wᵗ is that as goes throw the heye [hedge] & leves his gutes after it? – a neele and thride.'*

What goes w'ee train, comes back w'ee train, is nae use t'ee train, and the train cannae go without it? – Noise.

> *Children, Forfar. Cf. 'Riddles, Charades, and Conundrums', 1822, 'What is that which a coach always goes with, cannot go without, and yet is of no use to the coach? – Noise.'*

What gets bigger the more you take from it? – A hole in the ground.

> *Boy, 9, Dublin. Cf. 'Mince Pies for Christmas', 1805, 'What thing is that which is lengthened by being cut at both ends? – A ditch.'*

What does your mother look for and hopes not to find? – A hole in your sock.

> *Girl, 12, Kirkcaldy. Cf. 'The Booke of Meery Riddles', 1629, 'What is that one seeketh for, and would not finde? – That is a hole in his shooe.'*

The following quaint riddle was possibly not appreciated by the 11-year-old girl in Oxford who wrote it down for us:

'What can go under the water, and over the water, without getting wet? – An egg in a duck's back.'

Three hundred years earlier a youngster in the Holme family of Chester, possibly Randle Holme, had written down in his collection:

'Wᵗ is that as goes under water & ouʳ water & touches not the water. – an egge in a ducks belly.' (MS. Harley 1960.)

Such a riddle offers endless scope for investigation since it is also known internationally, being found in French, German, Norwegian, Spanish, Roumanian, and Arabic collections.[1] The study of riddles is, in fact, such a rewarding one (the comparative and historical materials being so abundant), that we have sometimes found ourselves tempted to ask children for riddles to the exclusion of everything else. It is an exciting experience, for

1. For foreign parallels to riddles in this section and the next (Rhyming Riddles) see Professor Archer Taylor's massive work *English Riddles from Oral Tradition*, University of California Press, 1951. Sometimes the foreign versions give evidence that a riddle is substantially older than its earliest appearance in English literature would indicate. For instance, Taylor shows (pp. 673–6 and 863–4) that the riddle 'What gets bigger the more you take from it?' was known on the Continent long before the nineteenth century.

instance, to walk into a schoolroom in one of the poorest quarters of Dublin and hear a 9-year-old urchin give the cryptic description of a maid milking a cow,

> Ink ank under a bank
> Ten drawing four,

being already aware that this was how the riddle was posed in Charles I's time:

> Clinke clanke under a banke,
> Ten above foure and neere the stanke.[1]

and being able to tell oneself that it was highly unlikely that the child, or any of his forebears, had ever seen these words in print, for during the centuries of the riddle's existence it has only been printed two or three times, in obscure places.

Rhyming Riddles

Children who ask each other rhyming riddles may well be reciting in the playground pieces of poetry as worthwhile as any they are made to recite in the schoolroom. The descriptions these riddles give of their solutions (for nearly all rhyming riddles are true riddles) are usually phrased highly imaginatively in terms of something else. Thus a candle is seen as a little girl in a white petticoat, a cabbage is thought of as made of numerous patches set on top of each other, and a ring is described as a bottomless vessel to put flesh and blood in. Such images are, perhaps, the fittest introduction to poetry that a child can have.

Rhyming riddles are also sometimes of considerably antiquity. Among the examples children have given us is a metrical version of one of the oldest riddles in the world – the riddle of the Sphinx; four riddles which were known in Charles I's time; and four which, although apparently traditional, do not seem to have been previously recorded, for they are not included in Archer Taylor's comprehensive collection.

A MAN

Walks on four feet
On two feet, on three,
The more feet it walks on
The weaker it be.

> *Girl, 15, Kirkcaldy. Cf. Taylor, 46–7. The same girl asked us: 'What walks on four feet in the morning, two feet at noon, and three feet in the evening?'*

A BRAMBLE

First I am as white as snow,
Then as green as grass I grow,
Next I am as red as blood
Lastly I'm as black as mud.

> *Girl, 14, Kirkcaldy. Cf. Taylor, 1384–93 and 1561.*

1. *A Book of merrie Riddles*, 1631, no. 59. Cf. also *Les Adeuineaux amoureux, c.* 1478, p. lxxxix, cited Eugêne Rolland, *Devinettes*, 1877, p. 21.

A SQUIRREL

Riddle me, riddle me,
    riddle me ree,
I saw a nut cracker
    up in a tree.

> *Boy, 13, Knighton. Apparently common, since also known in Alton, but not previously recorded.*

AN EGG

A wee, wee hoose
Fou, fou o' meat,
Neither door nor window
To let you in to eat.

> *Girl, 14, Kirkcaldy. Cf. Taylor, 1135. This wording is more metrical than any previously recorded.*

A FINGER

White and thin, red within,
With a nail at the end.

> *Girl, 13, Aberystwyth. Not previously recorded.*

THE WIND

I went to town
And who went with me?
I went up and down
But nobody could see.

> *Child, Harrow. Not previously recorded.*

A SHEEP

Round the rocks
And round the rocks
The ragged rascal ran,
And every bush he came to,
He left his rags and ran.

> *Girl, 15, Kirkcaldy. Cf. 'Meery Riddles', 1629, 'What is that: goeth through the wood, and leaveth on every bush a rag? It is snow.'*

A CABBAGE

Patch upon patch
Without any stitches,
If you tell me this riddle
I'll buy you some breeches.

> *Girl, 12, Welshpool. Cf. Taylor, 1438.*

HAIR

Riddle me, riddle me, what is that,
Over the head and under the hat?

> *Boy, 12, Oxford. Cf. Taylor, 1436.*

A RING

The King of Cumberland
Gave the Queen of Northumberland
A bottomless vessel
To put flesh and blood in.

> *Girl, 9, Birmingham. Cf. Taylor, 1172–3.*

A GRINDSTONE

There's a thing behind the door,
The more you feed it, the more t'will
    roar.

> *Girl, c. 10, Pendeen. Recorded in 1629, 1631, and c. 1645. Not found in England again until now. Cf. Taylor, 387 and 481.*

A THIMBLE

It is a little house,
It has a hundred windows
Yet it won't hold a mouse.

> *Girl, 12, Berriew. 'A Booke of merrie Riddles', 1631, gives an alternative and better solution: a spider's web.*

A GLOVE

As I was walking along the road
I saw a black thing in a furrow,
Neither flesh or neither bone
Yet it had four fingers and a thumb.

> *Girl, 11, Oxford. Cf. Taylor, 24.*

A LIGHTED CANDLE

Little Nancy Netticoat
Wears a white petticoat,
The longer she lives
The shorter she grows,
Little Nancy Netticoat.

> *Girl, 12, Ford, Shropshire. Other versions from Aberystwyth, Birmingham, and Market Rasen. Cf. MS. Harley 1960, c. 1645, and Taylor, 607–30.*

As I was walking along the road I saw a brown house,
Inside that brown house was a white house,
Inside that white house was milk,
What was it?

Girl, 11, Oxford. Not previously recorded, but cf. Taylor, 1161–4.

Rhyming riddles are also, of course, preserved in the nursery ('Humpty Dumpty sat on a wall' is the best known example), and a collection of them appears in *The Oxford Nursery Rhyme Book*, 1955, pp. 147–55.

Punning Riddles

To a child, a punning riddle is as delightful as a 'true' riddle, his mind being just as excited by a word which has two uses, as by a word-picture which can have two interpretations. 'What goes out without putting its coat on?' (A fire), 'What runs but never walks?' (A river), 'What runs through a field but does not move?' (A lane), 'What goes up and down stairs without moving?' (A carpet), 'What turns without moving?' (Milk), 'What stays where it is when it goes off?' (A gun), are examples in point. Each of these, it will be noticed, contains a verbal duplicity implying, as is usual in such riddles, animate movement in an inanimate object.

An old and well-known riddle (told us by a number of children) in which the verb does not imply movement is 'What is put on a table, cut, but never eaten?' (A pack of cards); and another exception is when the verb is used in a legitimate but misleading sense, as in 'What is it that every man overlooks?' (His nose).

If, however, the pun is a substantive one, an inanimate object is generally made out to possess living members, as a head, face, neck, feet, or hands, thus: 'What has got teeth but cannot bite?' (A comb), 'What has a neck but cannot swallow?' (A bottle), 'What has fingers but cannot use them?' (A glove), 'What has an eye but cannot see?' (A needle), 'What has a head and four legs but cannot walk?' (A bed). Such riddles are so simple that children can, and do, make them up for themselves; their favourite enigmatical subject being a clock which is described as the dirtiest thing in the house (because it has hands and does not wash its face), or the shyest thing in the house (because it keeps its hands in front of its face), and so on. Yet even a feeble specimen of this type such as 'What has three feet and cannot walk?' (A yard rule) can lay claim to a pedigree, for it appears, along with the riddle on the pack of cards, in a collection entitled *Riddles, Charades, and Conundrums*, printed in 1822.

Conundrums

'What is the difference,' they commonly ask each other, 'between a riddle and two elephants sitting on a bun?' and the excruciating answer agrees with their highest literary expectations: 'One is a conundrum and the other is a bun-under-'em.' The schoolchild's appetite for conundrums bears out what has already been said about his love of puns and word mutilation. For more than a hundred years children have likened a spectator to a bee-hive because he is a beholder (bee-holder); a schoolboy to a postage stamp because he is licked and put in a corner; a caterpillar to hot bread because 'it's the grub that makes the butterfly'; and an empty room to a room full of married people because there is not a single person in it.[1]

In particular they think any poser remarkable in which the solution contains a double pun:

What is the difference between a warder and a jeweller?
One watches cells and the other sells watches.

What is the difference between a ball and a Prince?
One is thrown in the air and the other is heir to the throne.

What is the difference between a letter ready for posting and a lady going along a road?
One is addressed in an envelope and the other is enveloped in a dress.

If possible they also like a suggestion of rhyme in the solution: the difference between the two objects often being little more than a spoonerism.

What is the difference between a big black cloud and a lion with toothache?
One pours with rain and the other roars with pain.

What is the difference between a lazy schoolboy and a fisherman?
One hates his books and the other baits his hooks.

What is the difference between an angry circus owner and a Roman hairdresser?
One is a raving showman and the other is a shaving Roman.

What is the difference between a cat and a comma?
A cat has its claws at the end of its paws and a comma has its pause at the end of a clause.

1. Each of these similes, repeated by present-day children, has been found in literature of the first half of the nineteenth century. See respectively: *The Boy's Own Book*, 1829, p. 436; *The Quarterly Review*, June 1850 ('One you lick with a stick, the other you stick with a lick' – this riddle seems to have been in circulation for almost as long as there have been adhesive postage stamps); *The Girl's Own Book*, 1832, p. 151; and *The Riddler's Oracle*, 1821, p. 81.

Sometimes, after asking this sort of question, they introduce a catch. 'What is the difference between a horse pulling a cart and a pillar box?' 'I give up.' 'You don't know the difference between a horse pulling a cart and a pillar box – I won't send *you* to post my letters!' Or they ask a conundrum with a sting in its tail: 'What is the difference between a thought, a sigh, a mink coat, and a monkey?' and when the person confesses himself baffled, explain: 'A thought is an idea, a sigh is "Oh dear!", a mink coat is too dear, and a monkey is *you* dear.'

The less ingenious a conundrum may be, however, the more likely is it to be well known, and a really infantile joke such as 'When is a door not a door?' is, of course, remembered even by adults, and becomes nursery lore. Many a small child's introduction to the strange word 'ajar' must have been through being asked this enigma.[1] Other conundrums of this genre include: 'When is a tap not a tap?' – 'When it is dripping.' 'When is a boy not a boy?' – 'When he's abed.' 'When is a sailor not a sailor?' – 'When he's aboard.' 'When is a cow not a cow?' – 'When it is turned into a field.' And, 'When is milk not milk?' – 'When it is turned into a saucepan.'[2]

Similarly the 'Why – Because' conundrums usually involve only a single pun, for instance the vintage joke: 'Why doesn't a railway engine sit down?' – 'Because it has a tender behind.'[3] And many a young riddler has fun postulating that burglars never break into sculleries for fear of a copper being there; that soldiers are tired on the 1st of April because they have just had a March of thirty-one days; that it isn't safe to sleep in trains because trains run over sleepers; and that we sing 'Amen' in church and not 'A-women' because they are hymns not hers.

Similar simplicities currently popular include: 'What key is hardest to turn?' (A donkey), 'What bill never needs paying?' (A duck's bill), 'What kinds of fish do you wear on your shoes?' (Soles and eels), 'What four letters frighten a thief?' (O.I.C.U.),[4] 'What long word has only one

---

1. It appears in *The Boy's Own Book*, 1829, p. 436, and *The Girl's Own Book*, 1832, p. 155. In 1843 *Punch* (vol. iv, p. 74) cited it as an example of a riddle so trite that it could be supplied in quantity.
2. Robert Chambers, *Fireside Amusements*, 1850, p. 138, has 'When is a lady not a lady?' – 'When her bonnet becomes her.' *Punch*, vol. xxvi, 1854, p. 3, offered without apology, 'When is an ox not an ox?' – 'When it is turned into a meadow', having already in vol. i, 1841, p. 101, introduced the political specimen: 'When is Peel not Peel?' – 'When he's candi(e)d.'
3. Probably not new even when it appeared in *March's Penny Riddle Book*, c. 1855.
4. Cf. *The New Help to Discourse*, 1669, p. 17, 'What three vowels are pernicious to debters? An. These three, I O U.'

letter in it?' (Envelope), and, a question constantly asked, 'Who is given the sack as soon as he starts work?' (A postman).

Their favourites, none the less, are those ingenious inquiries, easy to remember, and as amusing to answer as to ask, in which words of similar sound are duplicated both in question and answer:

Why did the owl 'owl? – Because the woodpecker would peck 'er.
Why did the fly fly? – Because the spider spied 'er.
Why did the viper vipe 'er nose? – Because the adder 'ad 'er 'andkerchief.
What did the ear 'ear? – Only the nose knows.

Equally cunning are those in which a noun is made to do the work of a verb:

Why did the window-box? – Because it saw the garden fence.
Why did the hen-run? – Because it saw the tree bark.
Why did the cowslip? – Because it saw the bulrush.
Why did the moonbeam? – Because it saw the skylark.
Why did the cellar stair? – Because it saw the compass point.
Why did the coal scuttle? – Because it saw the kitchen sink.
Why did the jam-roll? – Because it saw the apple-turnover.
Why did the penny stamp? – Because the threepenny bit.

Sometimes, in this type, the joke occurs only in the answer:

Why did the lobster blush? – Because it saw the salad dressing.
Why did the shortcake sing? – Because it saw abundance.[1]

Or the formula is slightly different:

Can the orange box? – No, but the tomato can.

As will be apparent, children are wonderfully word-conscious, more so, indeed, than the majority of their elders; and it is not extravagant to suggest that these little word-plays, hackneyed though they sound to adult ears, give youngsters genuine aesthetic satisfaction.

Wellerisms

Whereas a professional comedian 'throws away' a Wellerism in an aside (' "Meet you at the corner"', as one wall said to the other'), children, with their more laborious sense of humour, produce them as riddles. ('What did one wall say to the other?' – 'Meet you at the corner.') In this

1. A schoolboy contributed this to the *Junior Mirror*, 30 November 1955. In *The Girl's Own Book*, 1832, p. 153, appears: 'Did you ever see a bun dance on a table? – I often see abundance on tables.'

way they are, as it were, able to savour the jokes more fully, particularly the punning ones.

What did the earwig say when it fell off the wall? – 'Ere we go.

What did the chicken say when it came out of the egg? – Marmalade (Ma me laid).

What did the bull say when it swallowed a bomb? – Abominable.

What did the policeman say to the lady who was bathing naked? – Diploma (Dip low, ma).

What did the window say when a tree fell through it? – Tremendous.

What did Noah say when he heard the rain come down? – 'Ark.

What would Neptune say if the sea dried up? – I haven't a notion (an ocean).

A young child may even, on occasion, be in possession of one of these jokes for several weeks before he understands it (as we ourselves remember with 'What did the earwig say'), although when at last he 'underconstumbles' he may perhaps delight in it all the more. But when speaking of the slowness and limitations of juvenile wit it has to be remembered that the point of any jest presupposes knowledge of what is normal, or the humour (of the words or situation) cannot be appreciated. The Wellerisms which children think funniest are therefore those using the phrases with which they are the most familiar:

What did the mouse say when it broke its tooth? – Hard cheese.

What did the ground say when it began to rain? – If this goes on for long my name will be mud.

What did the big tap say to the little tap? – You little squirt.

What did the big rose say to the little rose? – Hiya bud.

What did the big chimney say to the little chimney? – You're too young to smoke.

What did the big goat say to the little goat? – You can't kid me.

What did the monkey say when he was cutting off his tail? – It won't be long now.

What did the man say when he fell off the railway bridge? – Hard lines.

A craze for Wellerisms is apt to develop in a school in the same way that there are still sometimes crazes for limericks, Little Audrey jokes, Knock-knocks, and Shaggy Dog stories. But the Wellerism, which is older than any of these, also gets around more.

Catch Riddles

When a child asks a catch riddle, such as 'Why did the chicken cross the road?' or 'Why does the Duke of Edinburgh wear red, white, and blue braces?' the person is as it were tricked into thinking that he is being asked a conundrum, and that an ingenious or far-fetched answer is expected of him. The answer, however, turns out to be not a complicated play on words, but the simple truth stated in an ignominiously humdrum manner. ('Why did the chicken cross the road?' – 'Because it wanted to get to the other side.' 'Why does the Duke of Edinburgh wear red, white, and blue braces?' – 'To keep his trousers up.') Unlike the answers to the conundrums, the answer to a catch riddle tends to make the person who has failed to answer it feel foolish.[1]

Once, however, any one trick riddle has been asked, a person will probably be able to answer several, for they tend to follow collateral lines of thought. 'Why did the cow look over the wall?' – 'Because it couldn't see through it.' (*The Girl's Book of Diversions*, 1835, contained this, and it has been popular ever since.) 'Why does a pigeon roost on one leg?' – 'Because if he lifted the other he would fall.' (Egyptian children ask: 'Why does a pelican stand on one leg?') Similarly, the answer to 'Why does a miller wear a white hat?' is 'To keep his head warm' (this chestnut appeared as long ago as 1805 in a collection entitled *Mince Pies for Christmas*); and the answer to 'Why does a policeman wear silver buttons?' is the obvious one: 'To do his coat up.' But the answer to 'Why does a bear wear a fur coat?' is unexpected. A bear wears a fur coat 'because it would look ridiculous in a macintosh'.

Sometimes the answers to these catch riddles are so absurdly straightforward that they would not catch anybody whose mind had not first been bemused by a series of conundrums.

What does a diamond become when it is placed in water? – Wet.
If you went over a cliff what would you do? – Fall.
Which boy in the school wears the largest hat? – The boy with the largest head.
What is most like a cat looking out of a window? – A cat looking in at a window.
What makes more noise than a pig under a gate? – Two pigs under a gate.

1. And unlike the conundrums, but like the true riddles, catch riddles are international. The schoolmaster who recently wrote to *The Sunday Times* complaining that every term he was pestered by boys asking him why the chicken crossed the road, would obtain no relief by fleeing overseas. In Holland children ask: 'Waarom steekt een kip de weg over?' In Italy: 'Che cosa fa la gallina quando passa da un marciapiede a un altro?' In Porto Rico: '¿Cuándo la gallina cruza la carretera?' And German children not only revel in the query, but say that Hannibal had the same motive for crossing the Alps: he wanted to get to the other side. Likewise children in Italy ask: 'Perchè Garibaldi alla battaglia di Calatafimi portava le bretelle tricolori?' (Why did Garibaldi go to the battle of Calatafimi wearing tricolour braces?)

Nevertheless these catches seem to serve their purpose, for each of them has been part of schoolchild lore for more than a century.

A little more perspicacity is required, perhaps, to know why black sheep eat less than white sheep (there are fewer of them), and which is the left side of a pudding (the side that is not eaten), and the number of eggs a giant can eat on an empty stomach (one egg), but such problems are not impossible of solution to one who appreciates that the literal meaning of a question may be different from its colloquial meaning. Yet even a pedagogue – although he is asked such questions often enough – might be forgiven for not knowing the correct answers to: 'What smells most in the science lab.?' (The nose), 'How many hairs in a cat's tail?' (None, they are all on the outside), 'What is the best way to make a clean sweep?' (Wash him), 'How would you make a Maltese Cross with one match?' (Strike it and stick it up his jumper), and the wholly unfair deceit, 'There were two Bishops in Bed. Which one wore the nightie?' (Mrs Bishop).

The Fun of Riddling

The skilful riddler is, of course, he who switches quickly from one type of riddle to another, never letting his opponent know the kind of question he is being asked. He may for instance start with a verbal charade (although charades are less popular than they used to be):

> My first is in south but not in north,
> My second is in picture but not in film,
> My third is in fourth and also in worth,
> My fourth is in book and also in cook,
> My fifth is in toe but not in sew,
> My sixth is in life but not in death.

He may follow with a punning riddle, such as the old favourite (recorded in 1856): 'What is black and white and red all over?' and then try an enigma in which the answer is a let-down, being a letter of the alphabet: 'What comes once in a minute, twice in a moment, but not once in a thousand years?' (first recorded 1835). He may ask a hidden-name riddle such as the one about the Westminster scholar named Andrew (the prototype of which was written down more than 300 years ago in MS. Harley, 1960), or the one about Eve, recently written down for us by a schoolgirl in Aberdeen:

> In the middle of the garden was a river,
> In the middle of the river was a boat,
> In the middle of the boat was a lady,

Who wore a red petticoat.
Eve ye dinna ken her name
It's yer ain self to blame,
'Cause I telt ye in the middle of the riddle.

He may ask what is virtually a true riddle, 'The more you take, the more you leave behind. What are they?' (Footsteps), then follow with a catch question, 'What tea-pot can you never get a cup of tea from?' (An empty one), or 'What is Australia bounded by?' (Kangaroos), or 'Which is heavier a pound of feathers or a pound of lead?' (a question recorded in 1849, and also known to French children: 'Qu'est-ce qui pèse le plus, une livre de plumes ou une livre de plomb?'), and then require an explanation of something seemingly impossible:

'There was a man who was married and had two daughters. He quarrelled with his wife so he married his eldest daughter, he then married his youngest daughter. How could this be?' (He was a clergyman.)

Alternatively he may show off his wit with an enigma in which all the fun lies in the answer, for instance a 'chain answer' proving that a carriage is nothing (A carriage is a trap, a trap is a gin, gin is a spirit, a spirit is a ghost, and a ghost is nothing), or ask a three-part or four-part conundrum involving a triple or quadruple pun:

'If a monkey, a small boy, a cockerel, and a blackman lost their knees, what would they do?'

(The monkey would go to the bank and ask for some 'apennies, the little boy would go to the butcher and buy kidneys, the cockerel would go to London because that's where cockneys are, and the blackman would go to Africa because that's where the negroes.)

The subject-matter of a riddle also adds to the fun. In much the way that a number of riddles in *Demaundes Joyous* have a biblical setting, ridiculing the quibbles of medieval theologians, so young scholars today enliven their studies with what, for many of them, is the nearest approach to erudite humour. 'When was hockey mentioned in the Bible?' (When Moses dribbled down his beard), 'When is a walking-stick mentioned in the Bible?' (When Eve presented Adam with a Cain), 'Where did Noah strike the first nail in the ark?' (On the head), and, almost proverbial, 'Where was Moses when the light went out?' (In the dark).[1]

1. Only a little river-rat like Huck Finn could be so ingenuous as to comment: 'If you knowed where he was, what did you ask me for?' (*The Adventures of Huckleberry Finn*, 1884, ch. xvii.) Today, the would-be-clevers enlarge on the answer and say that when the light went out Moses was 'under the bed looking for the matches', or 'under the bed in his night shirt'. The earliest we have found the joke is in *The Riddler's Oracle*, c. 1821, p. 84.

Again, children are fascinated by blackmen and Chinamen, as their rhymes and songs bear witness, and jokes and riddles about Africans and Orientals are numerous. 'If a blackman dies, what do the others do?' – 'Go blackberrying.' 'What is never white and never right?' – 'A negro's left arm.' (Similarly the catch: 'It's not right or fair is it?' 'What isn't?' 'A blackman's left hand.') 'Why is a short negro like a white man?' – 'He's not at all black.' 'Four blackmen had a fish and chip shop. What was their telephone number?' – 'Blackfriars 1234.' And endless fun is had at the expense of Chinamen and how they talk, or are supposed to talk. 'If a Chinamen had a toothache what time would it be?' – 'Tooth hurtee.' And they catch each other by asking: 'How high is a Chinaman?'

'About five foot?'

'No, how high is a Chinaman?'

'Five foot two?'

'No, How Hi is a Chinaman.'

6   Parody and Impropriety

PARODY, that most refined form of jeering, gives an intelligent child a way of showing independence without having to rebel. Children who recite 'Our Father which art in heaven, bought a pair of braces for two and eleven', or who chant, as boys used to do when Matins was attended more regularly,

> Dearly beloved brethren,
> The Scripture moveth us in sundry places,
> For to go and seek the donkey races,
> For to confess our manifold sins,
> And to see which donkey wins,

or who joke, as Welsh children sometimes do,

> Amen, ceffyl pren   (*Amen, a wooden horse*
> Yn treio mynd ir nefoedd wen,   *Trying to go to a white heaven*)

are not necessarily irreverent. It is just a thing they do. It is as if children know instinctively that anything wholly solemn, without a smile behind it, is only half alive.

Hymns and Carols

As is well known, hymns come in for an amount of parodying, especially from children at denominational schools – the children who know them best.

Jesus loves me	*Gentle Jesus*
Jesus loves me, I don't think,	Charlie Chaplin, meek and mild,
He took me to a skating rink.	Stole a sixpence from a child,
He drank whisky, I drank beer,	When the child began to cry
Jesus loves me – I'm a leer.[1]	Charlie Chaplin said goodbye.

1. Scottish. Compare a verse American children say:

> Jesus, lover of my soul,
> Lead me to the sugar bowl,
> If the sugar bowl is empty,
> Lead me to my mother's pantry.

The above two verses are probably new, but most hymn parodies have long whiskers on them. The following pair, which children very commonly sing today, are a legacy from their grandparents.

While shepherds watched their flocks by night

While shepherds washed their socks by night
All seated round the tub,
A bar of Sunlight soap came down
And they began to scrub.

While shepherds watched their turnip tops
All boiling in the pot,
A lump of soot came rolling down
And spoilt the bloomin' lot.

Sometimes the modern version is less audacious than the version known in an age supposedly before juvenile emancipation.

There is a happy land, far, far away,
Where they have bread and jam three times a day.
Oh, how the angels yell,
When they hear the dinner-bell,
There is a happy land, far, far away.

Sixty years ago the words were as follows, and seem to have been extraordinarily popular (known in places as different as Eastbourne and Hay in Breconshire):

There is a happy land, far, far away,
Where little piggies run, three times a day.
Oh! how they squeal and run,
When they hear the butcher come,
Three slices off their bum, three times a day.

Carols, too, receive ludibrious attention; and it is not unusual for small Christmas singers at the door to offer their own words to the familiar tunes, especially if they feel that the people inside are taking an unnecessarily long time about showing their appreciation.

Nowel, Nowel

No ale, no beer, no stout, sold out,
Born is the king with his shirt hanging out.

Manchester.

We Three Kings

We three kings of Orient are,
One in a taxi, one in a car,
One on a scooter blowing his hooter
Following yonder star.

Birmingham, and very general.

O come, all ye faithful

O come, all ye faithful,
Butter from the Maypole,
Cheese from the Star supply,
And milk from the cow.
Bread from the baker,
Lard from the grocer,
O come let us adore Him . . .

(Or, 'O come and pull the cork out' or, in exasperation, 'O come let's kick the door in'.)

Swansea, and similar elsewhere.

Hark! the Herald-Angels sing

Hark! the jelly babies sing,
Beecham's pills are just the thing,
They are gentle, meek and mild,
Two for a man and one for a child.
If you want to go to heaven
You must take a dose of seven;
If you want to go to hell,
Take the blinking box as well.

London, and general.[1]

Most popular of all are parodies of 'Good King Wenceslas':

Good King Wenceslas looked out
　On the Feast of Stephen;
A snowball hit him on the snout
　And made it all uneven.
Brightly shone his conk that night
　Though the pain was cruel,
Till the doctor came in sight
　Riding on a mu-oo-el [mule].

*Bournemouth, Huddersfield, Loughton,
Swansea. A generation old at least.*

Good King Wenceslas drove out
　In his Austin Seven,
He bumped into a trolley bus
　And now he's up in heaven.

*Alton, Dorking, Swansea. Probably
composed c. 1932.*

Good King Wenceslas walked out
　In his mother's garden.
He bumped into a Brussels sprout
　And said 'I beg your pardon'.

Alton, Dorking, Gloucester.

Good King Wenceslas looked out
　In his pink pyjamas.
What d'you think he hollered out?
'Lovely ripe bananas.'

Alton, Bath, Loughton, Swansea.

Good King Wenceslas looked out
　When he was on 'telly',
Chased his page all round the screen
　And punched him in the belly.

Dorking, 1954.

Nursery Rhymes

Once children have settled down at school, the very natural desire
they have to loosen the apron-strings of their home life is well shown
in their changing attitude to nursery rhymes. A short year or two before

---

1. This verse seems to have come into vogue some time about the beginning of the First
World War when the current street joke concerned the difference between Beecham's
pills and Lord Kitchener – 'One sends you out the back and the other out the front.'
The parody has even come to the ears of Parliament. On 11 June 1952 Sir Beverley
Baxter in a debate on the B.B.C. charter informed the House: 'It is said that Beecham's
told a certain church that they would supply their hymn books, provided that they could
do some concealed advertising. One day at Christmas the congregation sang:

Hark the herald-angels sing
Beecham's pills are just the thing,
Peace on earth and mercy mild,
Two for man and one for child.'

'Hansard', 5th ser., vol. dii, col. 275.

they probably loved the familiar jingles. The words of the verses seemed to them inviolable; and a way of teasing them, when four or five years old, was to make deliberate mistakes: 'There came a big spider who drank all the cider and so the poor doggie had none.' A misrecitation like this used to infuriate them. But now, seven or eight years old, they establish their independence by parodying the rhymes their parents taught them. Mary's lamb, deservedly, comes in for particular ridicule.

Mary had a little lamb,
  Its feet were black as soot,
And into Mary's bread and jam
  Its sooty foot it put.
Now Mary was a careful child,
  Avoided every sham,
She said – one little word that
    meant
  The mother of that lamb.

Mary had a little lamb,
  It was a greedy glutton.
She fed it on ice-cream all day
  And now it's frozen mutton.

Mary had a little lamb,
  She fed it castor oil,
And everywhere the lamb would go
  It fertilized the soil.

Mary had a little cow,
  It fed on safety pins;
And every time she milked the cow
  The milk came out in tins.

Mary had a little lamb,
  She also had a bear;
I've often seen her little lamb,
  But I've never seen her *bear*.

Mary had a little lamb
  With which she used to tussle;
She pulled the wool from off its back
  And stuffed it in her bustle.

Mary had a little lamb
  Its stomach was lined with zinc,
And everywhere that Mary went
  It drank up all the ink.

Mary had a little lamb,
  Her father shot it dead,
And now it goes to school with her
  Between two chunks of bread.

Mary had a little lamb,
  You've heard this tale before,
But did you know she passed her plate
  And had a little more?

Mary had a little watch,
  She dropped it on the fender:
When she bent to pick it up,
  Pop! went her suspender.

Mary had a wristlet watch,
  She swallowed it one day,
And now she's taking Beecham's pills
  To pass the time away.[1]

Little do the children realize that in trying to escape from one tradition they are plunging headlong into another. Some of these parodies have been on one set of young lips after another for half a century or more. The first parody quoted, for instance, goes back at least to 1886.[2] The nursery rhyme itself only goes back a further half century.

1. This used to be sung to the tune 'It ain't gonna rain no more'. It is now sung to 'The Happy Wanderer'.
2. It appeared in *Truth*, 30 September 1886: 'Mary had a little lamb, With coat as black as soot, And into Mary's cup of milk It put its dirty foot. Now Mary, a straightforward girl, Who hated any sham, Rapped out a naughty little word That rhymed with Mary's lamb.'

Popular Songs

Parodies of popular songs are endless, and sometimes keep going endlessly. The following version (supplied by 11-year-olds) of C. K. Harris's song has survived two world wars and is perhaps better known to the rising generation than the original words:

> After the ball was over
> She lay on the sofa and sighed.
> She put her false teeth in salt water
> And took out her lovely glass eye.
> She kicked her cork leg in the corner
> And hung up her wig on the wall,
> The rest of her went to bye-byes,
> After the ball.

These parodies, almost songs in their own right, seem to belong to the big cities. They are sometimes adult or student songs which come to the children from a friendly elder brother, or from surreptitious listening at the half-open door of a public house. In the Gorbals district of Glasgow precocious little keelies joyfully chorus to the tune their forebears took to the trenches long ago:

> Goodbye Gartnavel, farewell Barlinnie Square,
> It's a long way to Milton, but by Duke Street you'll get there.
> There's a wee convict waitin'
> Wi' a big ball and chain,
> He's been in Gartnavel fifteen years,
> But now he's out again.

Gartnavel is a mental hospital and Barlinnie and Duke Street are prisons. In Aberdeen 12-year-old girls croon what they call a 'nonsense' song:

> When it's spring time in the Model,
> The Model of East, North Street,
> The flechs [fleas] begin to yodel,
> The lughers [lodgers] canna sleep.
> They rise and light a candle,
> And wash their sweaty feet.
> When it is spring time in the Model,
> The Model of East, North Street.

The Model is a lodging-house in one of the poorest quarters of Aberdeen. In the cities of South Wales, they sing to the same tune:

> It was spring time in the Rockies,
> The rain was falling fast,
> A bare-footed tramp with boots on
> Came slowly whizzing past.

> He went round a straight crooked corner
> To see a dead donkey die,
> He took out a pistol to stab him,
> And shot himself right in the eye.

In the west of Scotland they chant, count-out, or play two-balls, and, in Swansea, skip to, their own version of another military heirloom, a song which the army itself has improved upon from time to time:

> Mademoiselle from Armentières, parlez-vous,
> She hasn't been kissed for forty years, parlez-vous.
> The Prince of Wales was put in jail
> For riding a horse without a tail,
> Inky-pinky parlez-vous.

'The ball is thrown against the wall until the last line when it is stotted [bounced] quickly on the ground,' says a Fife 14-year-old. But why the Prince of Wales should be put in jail for riding a horse without a tail not even the wise teenagers know.

More heart-warming, because nearer real life, is a parody of 'I love a lassie' which would have pleased Sir Harry himself, a verse roared by small children at the Dean Orphanage in Edinburgh (1955):

> I love an aipple,
> A Cawperay 'tive aipple,
> A hale big aipple tae mesel'.
> We'll cut it up in quarters
> And gie it tae the squatters,
> Mary, my Scots Bluebell.

Another version, one of persisting popularity, is today used for 'dipping':

> I had a sausage, a bonny, bonny sausage,
> I put it in the oven for my tea.
> I went down the cellar
> To get the salt and pepper,
> And the sausage ran after me.

A correspondent remembers that this was current in her childhood about 1915, not very long after the original song was written.

Recitations

Through parody children get their own back on the great ones. Tennyson, Longfellow, Watts, and other climbers on Parnassus are brought down to street level. 'Half an inch, half an inch, half an inch onward, into the Detention Room rode the six hundred.' 'How doth the busy little bee delight to bark and bite, and gather honey all the day and eat it all the night.' Most of all they have their revenge on Mrs Hemans, and the heroic lines at one time regularly set for recitation.

The boy stood on the burning deck,
His legs were covered with blisters;
His father was in the public house,
With beer all down his whiskers.

The boy stood on the burning deck,
His legs all covered in blisters;
And when his pants began to burn
He had to borrow his sister's.

The boy stood on the burning deck
Picking his nose like mad;
He rolled them into little balls
And flicked them at his Dad.

The boy stood on the burning deck
Melting with the heat;
His big blue eyes were full of tears
And his shoes were full of feet.

The boy stood on the burning deck,
Selling peas a penny a peck.
Did he ever wash his neck?
No, by heck!

The boy stood on the burning deck
Playing a game of cricket;
The ball rolled up his trouser leg
And hit the middle wicket.

These crisp but emotionless little verses may be termed 'slick rhymes'; their inspiration, if not their source, is the adult epigram. They do not have the circulation of the play rhymes, but seem to appeal, curiously strongly, to the grammar-school type of child.

The Improper

It is a commonplace that some of the rhymes and jokes which run around with children are mildly indelicate. London suburban youngsters have taken to chorusing:

> I got a girl in Waterloo
> She don't wear no – yes she do!
> I got a girl in Leicester Square,
> She don't wear no underwear.

In Hackney small girls encourage the skipper in the long rope with the lively words and tune:

> Oh the black cat piddled in the white cat's eye,
> The white cat said, Gord blimey,
> I'm sorry, sir, I piddled in your eye
> I didn't know you was behind me.

Bangor children find that an innocent hand-clapping game goes neatly to the words:

> As I sat under the apple tree,
> A birdie sent his love to me,
> And as I wiped it from my eye,
> I said, Thank goodness, cows can't fly.

The appeal of such verses is obvious. They have rhythm, a nice meeting of sounds, and a pinch of wit. They would gain circulation (this tends to be overlooked) even without the attraction of being improper.

It may be dangerous, as Sir David Maxwell Fyfe once warned, to confuse children with angels. Yet it is also true that a child may be never more innocent than when repeating a rude rhyme. Dorothy Baker in her tale of a waif's upbringing in the back streets of a Midlands town, tells of a classmate who, her first day at a new school, when the teacher asked for a volunteer to say a piece of poetry, stood up and recited:

> Ham, ham, pig's bum,
> When I have a party
> You shan't come.
> Bread without butter,
> Tea without sugar,
> Ham, ham, pig's bum.

Whereupon 'a tiny smile curved the teacher's lips as she gravely thanked Hetty and asked for any other volunteers'. And the afternoon passed off peacefully, if extra quietly.[1]

In the same way Leila Berg, in *Junior Bookshelf*, November 1953, tells how her 7-year-old announced at tea that his teacher had asked who could say a poem, and he had been the only one to put up his hand. When Mrs Berg proudly asked what poem he had recited, he told her:

> Up in the mountains,
> Lying on the grass,
> I saw a Chinaman
> Sliding on his
> Ask no questions,
> Tell no lies
> I saw a Chinaman
> Doing up his
> Flies are a nuisance
> Flies are a pest,
> I saw a Chinaman
> Putting on his vest.

1. Dorothy Baker, *The Street*, 1951, pp. 29–30.

It had, it seemed, become one of his favourite poems, one which he put on a level with W. H. Davies's 'School's Out', and the various 'Hums' of Pooh. When asked what the teacher had said about his recitation, he grumbled: 'She said she could not hear a word.'

These two stories are not isolated cases. Just as one child can be unaware of what he is saying, so can innocence bless a crowd.

> I'm a man that came from Scotland
> Shooting peas up a Nannie goat's bottom,
> I'm the man that came from Scotland
> Shooting peas away.

'These remarkable words' (writes a valued Swansea contributor) 'are sung to the tune "Men of Harlech". I have known of their existence for at least forty years. During our school Coronation Tea, 1937, we were entertained by a local concert party. Their orchestra played current popular numbers which the children sang. One item was a medley of national tunes beginning with "Men of Harlech". Immediately the whole audience of 450 – dear little girls aged five years to eleven years – broke into these words. I was sitting on the hall floor among them: there was not a smirk on any child's face. They were blissfully unconscious of what they were singing and merely making a joyful noise. The pianist nearly fell off his stool in astonishment. He knew that this tune also concluded the medley, and sure enough when he played it the chorus broke out again.

'I have heard [she continues] that the late Sir Walford Davies had a similar experience, when using "Men of Harlech" for community singing with a crowd of Cardiff children. He, too, must have been a very surprised gentleman.'

It would be ridiculous, of course, to suggest that all ribald verses are recited in similar good faith. Much depends on a child's age. The dawn of awareness shows itself in the current craze for the 'Shocking, shocking shocking' and 'Temptation, temptation, temptation' verses which seem to fascinate adolescent girls of about twelve years old:

> Shocking, shocking, shocking,
> A mouse ran up my stocking,
> When it got to my knee
> Wow! what did it see?
> Shocking, shocking, shocking.

Genuinely erotic verse, however, is unusual. That there are villains among children, as among adults, the *News of the World* offers frequent testimony; and from somewhere the ogre child acquires his strange salacious prescriptions, taking criminal pleasure in pressing them on juniors, and

115

inscribing them on the walls of the school lavatory. But we are not here discussing delinquents. The usual group of youngsters whispering together, passing some verse to each other and giggling, though they refuse to tell what it is, are probably interested in nothing more sordid than the deeds of nature, an intimate garment, or a crude word. As likely as not the rhyme will be:

> Red, white, and blue,
> Dirty kangaroo,
> Sitting on the dustbin
> Doing his 'Number Two'.

Or it may be:

> Eeny, meeny, miney, mo,
> Put the baby on the po,
> When he's done
> Wipe his bum
> Shove the paper up the lum;

which is remembered now by three generations. It may be a rhyme in which somebody comes to harm through exercising excessive control (a favourite topic) or who drowns in bed through lack of it. It may be a verse in which the private parts are mentioned, as in the baby-washing songs of Tiny Tim, the adventures of Buffalo Billie at the barber's shop, or of Captain Cook making soup, or one of the innumerable variations on the Popeye theme, with their Freudian symbols, bushes, watering-cans, sceptres, and Union Jacks. But a pointless ditty about a pimple on the belly may be felt to be just as 'shocking':

> Old Mister Kelly
> Had a pimple on his belly.
> His wife cut it off
> And it tasted like jelly.

Acquisition of such a verse seems to be as natural to children as having second teeth. In fact the American anthropologist Mr Carl Withers informs us that this is 'perhaps the most popular jump-rope rhyme of little girls' in the United States. Likewise songs about underclothing, or lack of it, are frequent, for instance a chant such as the following in which the first and third lines are said aloud, while the second and fourth are rendered *sotto voce* to tantalize those just outside the group:

> As I was going down the lane
> *I thought I smelt some kippers.*
> I asked a lady what it was
> *She said it was her knickers.*

In another the humour is so feeble that it seems impossible it could ever have gained wide circulation, yet it is known not only in Britain but in America, where it is apparently a favourite, and recited across the continent from coast to coast:

> Ladies and gentlemen
> Take my advice,
> Pull down your pants
> And slide on the ice.

And there are a whole clan of mock-proper verses, such as young Master Berg declaimed, rhymes which in fact only serve to emphasize the forbidden words they never quite say:

> The higher up the mountain
> The greener grows the grass,
> The higher up the monkey climbs
> The more he shows his
> Ask no questions
> Hear no lies,
> Shut your mouth
> And you'll catch no flies.

Or, old, and so innocent it might almost be recited with propriety at Sunday school:

> Mary ate jam,
> Mary ate jelly,
> Mary went home
> With a pain in her—
> Now don't get excited
> Don't be misled
> Mary went home
> With a pain in her head.

TEN years after the First World War, when we ourselves were at school, there was a verse in vogue amongst us:

> Kaiser Bill went up the hill
> To conquer all the nations;
> Kaiser Bill came down the hill
> And split his combinations.

To the student of oral lore the value of a rhyme such as this is that the era to which it belongs is immediately apparent. Yet the same reservations have to be made when dating topical rhymes as when dating other types of oral verse. One can say only that the rhyme has the trappings of a particular period; or that the date applies only to the particular version which has been collected. It sometimes happens that a rhyme or song which seems to be recent has, in fact, been marching with history for centuries, changing during the years little more than its uniform before appearing on each new battlefield.

In 1952 a group of girls playing with a skipping-rope in a Wiltshire village were heard to sing:

> Kaiser Bill went up the hill
> To see if the war was over;
> General French got out of his trench
> And kicked him into Dover.
> He say if the Bone Man come
> Stick your bayonet up his bum.

Although this verse is a souvenir of the First World War, it cannot be said to have originated in the First World War. During or after the Boer War, Scottish children had a song which went in part:

> B for Booer, K for Krudger,
> J for General French;
> The Bri'ish were up at the top o' the hill
> And the Booers went down in the trench.[1]

1. *Nicht at Eenie* (Samson Press), 1932. A collection of rhymes gathered from oral tradition by Dr A. A. Ramsay and others.

And the last two lines of the Wiltshire song with their reference to the 'Bone Man' seem to echo an even earlier campaign. When Napoleon's shadow fell upon Britain the days were brightened with such verses as:

> When, O when does little Boney come?
> Pr'aps he'll come in August, pr'aps he'll stay at home.

Today in Sutherland, Golspie children still sing (as E. W. B. Nicholson found them singing in Victoria's day):

> Napoleon was a general,
>   He had ten thousand men,
> He marched them up to the top of the hill,
>   And he marched them down again.

And it seems that more than 300 years have passed since the English first sang about hostile armies marching up hill and down. The song,

> The King of France went up the hill
>   With forty thousand men;
> The King of France came down the hill,
>   And ne'er went up again,

was noted three times in Charles I's reign; and, whether or not the statement is correct, James Howell, who became historiographer royal to Charles II, set it on record that 'The King of France with fourty thousand men' originally portrayed the ambitious King Henry IV who 'levied a huge army of 40,000 men' shortly before he was assassinated in 1610.[1]

Topical rhymes, it seems, can have as deep roots as any other kind of oral verse.

1930–1939

Four events which were mirrored in children's songs between the wars were Amy Johnson's flight to Australia, the invasion of Abyssinia, the Abdication, and A.R.P.

In 1930 the woman of the year was the ex-typist Amy Johnson, back from her heroic 19½ days' solo flight to Australia. In every crowded Woolworth's store the gramophones were playing a thin sixpenny record:

> Amy, wonderful Amy,
> How can you blame me
>   for loving you?

1. James Howell, *Epistolae Ho-Elianae*, 1645, p. 32.

To the children she was almost a mythological figure, to be set beside the still popular Daisy who would not – or did she? – ride on a bicycle-made-for-two. The urchins sang

> Amy, Amy, give me your answer do,
> I'm half crazy all for the love of you.
> It won't be a stylish wedding
> We can't afford any bedding
> But you'll look sweet, washing your feet,
> In the Manchester Ship Canal.

In 1935 when Mussolini marched into Abyssinia one of the songs the dance bands were playing was 'Roll along, covered waggon'. Juvenile sentiment was heavily on the side of the ill-armed tribesmen, and almost until the end their faith was strong that in some way or another right would prevail against bombers, and mechanized infantry, and dum-dum bullets:

> Roll along Mussolini, roll along,
> You won't be in Abyssinia long,
> You'll be sitting on the plain
> With a bullet in your brain,
> Roll along, Mussolini, roll along.

Amongst the humorists the fashionable farewell became 'A-be-seein-ya!'

During the first three days of December 1936, the news became generally known that the new king wished to marry Mrs Ernest Simpson. Newspapers such as the *Daily Mirror* were probably correct in their estimation of flapper sentiment when they unhesitatingly came out on the king's side with the argument: Why shouldn't the king marry whom he chooses like anybody else? In the face of this supposed popular sympathy the venom of the rhymes which circulated all over the country in juvenile circles was remarkable.[1]

Contemporary murder cases, too, evoked topical verse. Just as the grisly activities of Burke and Hare, and the axemanship of Lizzie Borden, became subjects of juvenile song in the nineteenth century, so did children sing about the Crowborough 'chicken run' murder:

> Underneath the bright moonlight,
> By the dark Crowb'rough thorn,
> Oh–oh there lies the body of Elsie Cam'ron
> Underneath the chicken run.
> Tuck her up, tuck her up, tuck her up –
> Oh where is Norman Thorne?
> Oh–oh he is sitting in the prison
> Waiting his turn.

1. For a note on the rapidity with which the rhymes circulated see p. 26.

And about Dr Buck Ruxton, to the tune of 'Red sails in the sunset':

> Red stains on the carpet, red stains on your knife,
> Oh Dr Buck Ruxton, you murdered your wife.
> The nursemaid she saw you, and threatened to tell,
> Oh Dr Buck Ruxton, you killed her as well.

The crisis of September 1938, which led to the Munich Agreement, revealed the inadequacy of Britain's air-raid precautions, and made the nation A.R.P.-conscious as no exhortations could have done. Before the end of the year young cockneys were singing, to the well-known tune:

> Underneath the spreading chestnut tree
> Mr Chamberlain said to me,
> If you want to get your gas-mask free,
> Join the blinking A.R.P.

Fourteen years later this verse was re-collected in Aberdeen from girls who said they repeated the rhyme to count the bounces when 'playing balls'. They had not been born when the Munich pact was signed.

The Second World War

In the same way that 'Kaiser Bill' remained a part of the oral lore of schoolchildren after the First World War, Hitler and Mussolini continued to be commemorated in innumerable playgrounds after the Second World War. All the verses given here have been collected from children since the end of the war. The first four are to the tune 'Whistle while you work' featured in Walt Disney's *Snow White*, shown in Britain in 1938.

> Whistle while you work,
> Mussolini bought a shirt,
> Hitler wore it,
> Chamberlain tore it,
> Whistle while you work.
>
> *Girls, 14, Swansea, 1952.*[1]

> Whistle while you work,
> Miss —— made a shirt,
> Hitler wore it,
> Goering tore it,
> Wasn't he a twerp?
>
> *Girls, 16, Loughton, 1951.*[2]
> *Current Portsmouth, 1939.*

1. The teacher who collected this rhyme commented on the fact that Chamberlain was celebrated, instead of Churchill as might have been expected. Our information is that this rhyme was current within a month or two of the outbreak of hostilities, and the Swansea girls were therefore preserving the original wording, although they were only aged about three when Chamberlain ceased to be Prime Minister, and some of them did not know who he was.

2. Their teacher reported: 'I suspected this came from the factories in wartime. The girls strongly denied it and said the rhyme was theirs. They said it in sewing class (*sotto voce*) inserting the name of the needlework mistress.'

The rhyme was still current at the end of 1956 when a small boy was heard singing: 'Whistle while you work, Nasser is a twerp . . .'

Whistle while you work,
Snow White made a shirt,
Hitler wore it,
Mussolini tore it,
Whistle while you work.

Girl, 13, Kirkcaldy, 1952.

Music while you work,
Hitler made a shirt,
Stalin wore it
Moradec [Mussadiq?] tore it.
Music while you work.

Boy, 13, Golspie, 1952.

The following are to various tunes, or no tune:

Calling all cars, calling all stations,
Hitler's lost his combinations.
If you can't find them never mind
them,
Calling all cars, calling all stations.

Girl, 13, Kirkcaldy, 1952.

Calling all cars, calling all cars,
Hitler's lost his Sunday drawers.
Calling all forces, calling all forces,
Hitler's lost his Sunday corsets.

Children, Forfar, c. 1952.

Underneath the churchyard six feet
deep,
There lies Hitler fast asleep.
All the little micey come
tickle his feet,
'Neath the churchyard six feet deep.

*Girl, c. 17, Stockton-on-Tees, 1954. To
the tune 'Underneath the spreading
chestnut tree'.*

Underneath the water six feet deep,
There lies Hitler fast asleep,
All the little tadpoles tickle his feet
'Neath the water, six feet deep.

*Girl, 14, Tunstall (Staffs.), 1954, for
skipping. Also from Aberdeen, 1952.*

In 1944 Hitler went to war
He lost his pants
In the middle of France
In 1944.

*Girl, 11, Market Rasen, 1952, and
Swansea, 1951.*

Down in the dungeons seven feet
deep,
Where old Hitler lies asleep,
German boys they tickle his feet
Down in the dungeons seven feet
deep.

Girl, 12, Forfar, 1954, for skipping.

Heil Hitler, yah, yah, yah!
What a funny little man you are.
With your black moustache and your
hair all – [blah?]
Heil Hitler, yah, yah, yah!

Girl, c. 12, Enfield, 1951, for skipping.

V for Victory, dot, dot, dash,
Hitler lost his wee moustache.
If you find it, let him know,
And he'll give you a bag of dough.

Girl, 12, Kirkcaldy, 1952.

R.A.F. o'er Berlin
Dropping bombs in play;
Hitler in his shelter
Shouting 'Honey Pears'.

Young girls, Dundee, 1952, for skipping.

In 1944 the soldiers went to war
They lost their pants
In the middle of France
In 1944.

*Boy, 9, Alton, 1953. Girl, 7, Gidea
Park, 1955.*

The date rhymes are subject to extension and fluctuation, any relation they bear to historical accuracy being purely fortuitous.

In 1941 old Hitler ate a bun
He got an ache
Which made him quake
In 1941.

In 1942 old Hitler felt quite blue
He left his pants
In the middle of France
In 1942.

In 1943 old Hitler climbed a tree
Down he fell
And went to hell
In 1943.

In 1944 old Hitler went to war
He had no guns
So he said 'Crumbs!'
In 1944.

Boy, Bath, c. 1950.

In 1944 Hitler lost the war
He lost his pants
In the middle of a dance
In 1944.

In 1945 Hitler was still alive
He showed his face
But was in disgrace
In 1945.

In 1947 Hitler thought he'd go to
    heaven
But he missed the train
And went to Spain
In 1947.

In 1949 Hitler went to dine
He lost his pants
In the middle of France
In 1949.

Girls, Swansea, 1953.

This epic was subsequently set in the sixth decade of the century. At the end of 1956 we heard a 7-year-old (Alton) who did not know who Hitler was, recite a verse she had 'just made up':

In 1954 Hitler went to war
He lost his socks
In the middle of the docks
In 1954.

Three Hitler rhymes have been sent by correspondents who heard children chant them during the war:

Hitler, you're barmy,
You want to join the army.
Get knocked out
By a big Boy Scout,
Hitler – you're barmy!

Lancaster. Cf. 'Ginger, you're barmy'.

Who's that knocking at the window?
Who's that knocking at the door?
If it's Hitler let him in
And we'll sit him on a pin,
And we won't see old Hitler any more.

Denbighshire, c. 1940. Cf. 'Vote, vote, vote, for . . .'.

Run, Hitler, run, Hitler, run, run, run,
Don't give the Allies their fun, fun, fun;
    They'll get by
    Without their Hitler pie,
So run Hitler, run Hitler, run, run, run.

London, c. 1940. A debased version of Flanagan and Allen's Palladium parody of their song 'Run Rabbit'.

It wasn't the Yorks that won the war,
  Parlez-vous.
It wasn't the Poles that won the war,
  Same to you.
The Fifty-First were there before
So it was them that won the war,
  Inky-pinky parlez-vous.

  Girl, 12, Aberdeen, 1952.

Now the war is over,
Mussolini's dead,
He wants to go to heaven
With a crown upon his head.
But the Lord said, No!
You must go down below,
All dressed up and nowhere to go.

  Girl, 12, Aberdeen, 1952.

When collected in 1952 both these songs accompanied girls' ball-bouncing games. The girl who sang the new rendering of 'Mademoiselle from Armenteers' said: 'The Fifty-First is a Highland Light Infantry Division. In the middle and end of the lines you put the ball under your leg. It can be played with two balls against the wall.' The other song – although a 12-year-old would not know it – was also being sung, with slightly different emphasis, before victory had been achieved. It was then a cry of longing for the war to be over, and was heard sung by youngsters in Stockton-on-Tees:

> When the war is over Hitler will be dead,
> He hopes to go to heaven with a crown upon his head.
> But the Lord said No! You'll have to go below,
> There's only room for Churchill so cheery-cheery-oh.

And it was also a song of joyous expectation during the First World War. According to a contributor to the *Glasgow Herald*, 13 August 1955, infant keelies in 1918 used to chant:

> When the war is over and the Kaiser's deid
> He's no' gaun tae Heaven wi' the eagle on 'is heid,
> For the Lord says No! He'll have tae go below,
> For he's all dressed up and nowhere tae go.

It would be interesting to know what happened to the verse during the twenty-one years between the wars. Can the crude lines have been quietly passed from child to child through the twenties and the thirties to be re-established in the Second World War, in the way that they are continuing to be handed on now?

1945–1958

The immediate post-war scene was notable, or notorious, for pre-fabs, spivs, the Festival of Britain, flying saucers, the ascent of Everest, the

Coronation, Teddy Boys, and a wave of particularly unsavoury murders. Each of these phenomena left some impression on the child lore of Britain. Not that we must fall into the error of supposing that the young had suddenly become creative. Children merely, as the old proverb has it, 'pick up words as pigeons peas, and utter them again as God shall please'. There was a shortage of cigarette cards for 'flirting' so they took to playing with milk-bottle tops and these round objects got called 'Flying Saucers'. That mirthless flop the Festival of Britain had one entertainment in it, the Skylon, and the term became a nickname for the long-limbed. The chant-verse of throbbing rhythm,

> Down in the jungle
> Living in a tent,
> Better than a pre-fab –
> No rent!

which we had from an 8-year-old girl in Manchester, January 1953, from 14-year-old girls in Aberdeen, repeated while they bounced their balls, March 1952, and from a 10-year-old boy in Caistor, Lincolnshire, who used it for counting-out, March 1952, was not attributable to the emotional vigour of childhood, but to a weekly feature in a Charlie Chester show. Similar sources were probably responsible for other verses of the period. How much of the following parody, from an 11-year-old girl, Hackney, February 1952, is original and how much it is an adaptation of something heard, we have been unable to ascertain.

> We are three spivs of Trafalgar Square
> Flogging nylons tuppence a pair,
> All fully fashioned, all off the ration,
> Sold in Trafalgar Square.

The teacher wrote: 'Victoria tells me her brother, aged ten, made it up. I think they must be a literary family as Victoria is at present engaged on writing a novel. Victoria and her friends skip to the rhyme very fast with a "bump"[1] on the last word.'

The two events which really fired juvenile imagination were the ascent of Everest and the Coronation. This was more apparent in their imitative games ('I wanna be Tensing.' 'All right, but I bags 'Illary.' 'Well let me be Colonel 'Unt') than in the production of any new rhymes.[2] But during

1. A bump is when the rope is passed twice under the feet in one jump.
2. 'Coronations' was a game played not only by British children but, according to the *Daily Telegraph*, 10 July 1953, by children in Western Germany.

the Coronation summer the following suddenly enjoyed widespread popularity:

> Red, white, and blue,
> The Queen's got the flu,
> The King's got the tummy ache
> And don't know what to do.

No disrespect for the new sovereign seems to have been intended. It appears, simply, that in the excitement of the occasion this was the only royal rhyme the children had available. And, according to our correspondents, the same piece of exuberance greeted Her Majesty's grandfather when he came to the throne.

Later in the same year, when Christie the multiple murderer was hung (July 1953) boys had a riddle 'If Christie had two sons what would he call them? – Ropem and Chokem', and we ourselves remember this jest being applied to some similarly unsociable character when we were young.

It is perhaps unnecessary to look for a forerunner to the Teddy Boy joke, 'Do you know a Teddy Boy has just been drowned – in his drainpipe trousers', but the reader of these pages will not have to look far for the precursor of the following playground doggerel, current in Swansea, August 1955:

> There's a boy over there in a gaberdine mack,
> Drainpipe trousers and a D.A. back,
> Slip-on shoes and a rainbow tie,
> Kissing his Teddy girl goodbye!

In 1958 the juvenile commentary on current affairs continued with the verse, sung to the tune 'Catch a Falling Star':

> Catch a falling sputnik,
> Put it in a matchbox,
> Send it to the U.S.A.
> They'll be glad to get it,
> Very glad to get it,
> Send it to the U.S.A.

Legendary Heroes

True immortality, that immortality which does not depend upon the dunning of history teachers, is probably only assured for a hero if he enters the folklore of his country: if he becomes a ballad hero, or the subject of a nursery rhyme, or the centre of a traditional tale such as that of Alfred and the burnt cakes. It is true that in the course of centuries scholars may question the veracity of the tale, and may even doubt whether the hero existed, but this has never deterred a ballad singer, any more than it does his modern counterpart the film director. There may not have been a real Robin Hood or a real Little Miss Muffet, but it cannot be doubted that they live in the national imagination.

Yet, as will be observed in the following sections, perpetuity is not automatically guaranteed for a name when it first enters the main stream of oral tradition. The tale or verse which enshrines the name may continue but a new and more euphonious or exciting name may supplant the old. And this is no uncommon occurrence. Little Miss Muffet, for instance, was known as 'Little Mary Ester' in 1812, and as 'Little Miss Mopsey' in 1842, before the verse became crystallized in its present form; and one of the problems in the study of traditional lore is to determine how it is that an oral verse, or other item which is normally subject to change, eventually gets fixed in a particular shape, of no obvious merit, and is thereafter unalterable.

Lottie Collins

The nineteenth-century music hall, as we have seen, was the original backcloth to a number of verses now thought of merely as children's rhymes. In 1891 clever little Lottie Collins sang 'Ta-Ra-Ra-Boom-De-Ay' in *Dick Whittington* at the Grand Theatre, Islington, putting the song on the lips of 'every 'bus-conductor, errand-boy, and groom-de-ay' in the town, and earning a personal notoriety with the 'verve' (as the posters described it) of her dancing. In no great space of time the schoolchild ditty,

> When I was young and had no sense
> I bought a fiddle for eighteen pence . . .,

which had been popular since the middle of the century,[1] was re-tuned in her honour:

> Lottie Collins, she had no sense,
> She bought a piano for eighteenpence,
> And all she played on it all day
> Was, 'Ta-ra-ra-boom-de-ay'.

1. It had been known to schoolboys since about 1855 according to a correspondent in *Notes and Queries*, 11th ser., vol. xi, 1915, p. 35.

'Ta-ra-ra-boom-de-ay' itself was not closed to 'improvements'. 'One version,' wrote Flora Thompson, 'sung by lounging youths beneath the chestnut tree on the green' went:

> Lottie Collins has no drawers.
> Will you kindly lend her yours?
> She is going far away
> To sing Ta-ra-ra-boom-de-ay!

It was sung, says Flora Thompson, 'with the intention of annoying any girl who might happen to be passing. And she would be annoyed. Shocked, too, to hear such an intimate undergarment mentioned in public.'

For twenty years Lottie Collins glittered in juvenile song. But today though the street boys continue to sing the songs which were dedicated to her, they have forgotten her name. They insert the name of their teacher, or of a particular girl they know; or think (doubtless sometimes along with their teacher) that they have invented something new, something belonging to the mid-twentieth century:

> Diana Dors has no drawers,
> Will you kindly lend her yours?

Charlie Chaplin

The sad and jaunty waif, with his black moustache, baggy trousers, and expressive boots, has become one of the chief figures of juvenile mythology in the twentieth century.

> Charlie Chaplin washing up
> Broke a saucer and a cup,
> How much did they cost?
>
> *Alton, Hackney, and Woolwich, for skipping.*

> Charlie Chaplin sat on a pin,
> How many inches did it go in?
> One, two, three, four . . .
>
> *Cleethorpes, Hackney, Taunton, and Wootton Bassett, for skipping. Also common in U.S.A.*

> Charlie Chaplin meek and mild
> Took a sausage off a child,
> When the child began to cry
> Charlie sloshed him in the eye.
> Yes, Charlie did it,
> Yes, Charlie did it,
> Yes, Charlie did it,
> The kids will tell you so.
>
> *Birmingham, to the tune 'Gentle Jesus'.*

> Charlie Chaplin has big feet,
> *Wilbur Macey* has them beat.
>
> *Maryland, U.S.A.*

Two points seem worth noting about Charlie Chaplin: the speed with which his name entered the vernacular, and the sureness with which it has remained. A variation of a well-known ball-bouncing game goes:

> One, two, three a-lairy,
> My ball's down the airie,
> Don't forget to give it to Mary,
> Not to Charlie Chaplin.

This has been heard in Chelsea, Camberwell and Hackney, it has been reported as current in Montreal, and it is doubtless known in many other places. With words all but identical it is vouched for as having been used for ball-bouncing in Reading at the time when *The Gold Rush* and *The Kid* were first showing. Another verse in the clan, collected from Bishop Auckland children in 1952, can be dated internally:

> The moon shines bright on Charlie Chaplin
> His boots are crackin',
> For want of blackin',
> And his little baggy trousers they want mendin'
> Before we send 'im
> To the Dardanelles.[1]

The Chaplin lore persisted throughout the inter-war period, and it has very rightly been pointed out that before Mr Chaplin's comeback in 1952, a generation was growing up to whom he was little more than a name. Yet he is celebrated, with apparently increasing frequency, in more than one branch of oral lore, and he has in some instances almost completely displaced earlier traditional figures. Even among Scottish children the name Charlie now conjures up the picture of a doleful clown, rather than a bonnie prince. The game 'Farmer, may we cross the river?' known in Scotland as 'Charlie, may we cross the water?' – presumably under the influence of Jacobite songs about 'Charlie over the water' – has, in Fife, become 'Charlie Chaplin, may we cross the water?' Similarly, the nineteenth-century song about Mrs Bence, or Leslie Spence, or 'When I was young and had no sense', sung to the tune of the 'Sultan Polka', and in the 1890s, as we have seen, applied to Lottie Collins, has in Birmingham become:

> Charlie Chaplin had no sense,
> He bought a fiddle for eighteen pence;
> And all the tunes that he could play
> Was 'Ta-ra-ra-boom-de-ay'.

1. That this was current in the First World War is attested by John Brophy and Eric Partridge, *Songs and Slang of the British Soldier: 1914–1918*, 1931, p. 38, who give the air as 'Pretty Red Wing'; by Robert Payne, *The Great Charlie*, 1952, p. 149; and by Atticus, *The Sunday Times*, 5 October 1952, who recalls: 'Thus sang the errand boys and kerbside buskers of my youth, suiting the familiar actions to the theme. I sang it myself, in boyish enthusiasm for the early Chaplin "shorts".'

And one of the most popular of skipping and ball-bounce rhymes in the present day, 'Charlie Chaplin went to France', has almost certainly been overlaid on some earlier song, now lost. Versions which have been collected include:

Charlie Chaplin went to France
To teach the ladies how to dance.
First he did the rhumba,
Then he did the kicks,
Then he did the samba,
Then he did the splits.

> *Spennymoor. Similar at Blaenavon (Mon.), Bressay (Shetland Isles), Dovenby, Hackney, Keighley, Pontefract, Radcliffe, and Wimblington (Cambs.). For skipping. Also Melbourne, Australia.*

Charlie Chaplin went to France
To teach the ladies how to dance.
This is how he taught them:
Heel, toe, whupsy-o,
Heel, toe, whupsy-o,
And don't forget the 'bump'.

> *Enfield. Similar at Birmingham, Cleethorpes, Market Rasen, and Scunthorpe. For skipping.*

Charlie Chaplin went to France
To show the ladies how to dance.
This is what he taught them:
Heel, toe, stampy, birly,
That is what he taught them.

> *Luncarty. Similar at Aberdeen, 'Heel, toe, stamp Gib-err-altar'; Laverstock, Pendeen, Swansea, 'Heel, toe, and over you go'; Welwyn, Woolwich, 'Heel, toe, a-lairey-o!' All for ball bounce.*

Charlie Chaplin went to France
To show the ladies how to dance.
First your heel, then your toe,
Lift up your skirt and round you go.

> *Kirkcaldy, for ball-bouncing. Similar at San Francisco, c. 1950, 'Left foot forward, out you go'. P. Evans, 'Jump-Rope Rhymes', 1954.*

Charlie Chaplin went to France
To teach the girls how to dance.
How many girls did he teach?
One, two, three, four . . .

> *Carlisle 'Evening Sentinel', Pennsylvania, 1929, reprinted 'American Folklore', vol. xlvii, p. 386. For skipping.*

One, two, three, four,
Charlie Chaplin went to war.
He taught the ladies how to dance
And this is what he taught them.
Heel, toe, over you go,
Heel, toe, over you go;
Salute to the king,
And bow to the queen,
And turn your back
On the Kaiserine (or 'submarine').

> *New York City, 1938 (Howard thesis). Similar at San Francisco, c. 1950 (P. Evans, op. cit.). Also 'Yorkshire Post', 29 July 1954, recollection of a Tadcaster reader. Stated to have been current in the First World War by R. Payne, 'The Great Charlie', 1952, p. 150.*

Further, as might be expected, Charlie Chaplin has entered the juvenile lore of other languages. In Yauco, for instance (according to the *Journal of American Folklore*, 1951, p. 74), Porto Rican schoolchildren say:

Si tiens un gatito
No lo saques al balcón
Que viene Chali Chaplin
Y le da con el bastón.

If you have a kitten
Don't take it out on the porch
For Charlie Chaplin will come
And hit it with his walking cane.

Mickey Mouse

The second best-loved figure seems to be Mickey Mouse, created by Walt Disney in 1928.

Mickey Mouse came to my house,
I asked him what he wanted.
He stamped his foot
And broke a cup
And that is what he wanted.

> *Kirkcaldy, Manchester, Market Rasen.*
> *Usually for ball-bouncing.*

Mickey Mouse came to my house,
I asked him what he wanted.
He clapped his hands
And stamped his foot
And that was all he wanted.

> *Bridgwater, Titchmarsh (Northants.),*
> *Swansea, Woking.*

All around the house
To look for Mickey Mouse,
If you catch him by the tail
Hang him on a rusty nail,
Give him to the cook.

> *Dublin. Similar in Scotland and N.*
> *England.*

Mickey Mouse is dead,
He died last night in bed.
He cut his throat
With a ten bob note,
Mickey Mouse is dead.

> *Enfield, Caistor, Aberdeen, Forfar,*
> *Kirkcaldy.[1]*

Mickey Mouse came into my house,
I asked him what he wanted.
A piece an' jam
A slice of ham (or 'A hurlie in the
    pram')
And that was all he wanted.

> *Forfar, Glasgow, Golspie, Kirkcaldy.*
> *For ball-bouncing.*

Mickey Mouse built a house
Under an apple tree,
Mickey Mouse called his house
Number twenty-three.

> *Dublin, for counting-out. London, S.E.7,*
> *for skipping.*

Mickey Mouse bought a house,
What colour did he paint it?
> *Blue.*
B-L-U-E spells blue, and you
    must have it on you.

> *Lydney, Newcastle, Portsmouth. For*
> *counting-out.*

Mickey Mouse in a public house
Drinking pots of beer.
Where's your money?
In my pocket.
Where's your pocket?
I forgot it.
Please walk out.

> *Alton, for counting-out. For precursors*
> *see pp. 30–1.*

1. Tragedies of a similar nature have previously befallen Jack the Ripper (active 1888–9) and President Kruger (died 1904).

Jack the Ripper's dead,
And lying in his bed,
He cut his throat
With Sunlight soap,
Jack the Ripper's dead.

> *Collected in Argyllshire, 'Folk-Lore',*
> *vol. lvi, 1905, p. 460.*

Poor old Kruger's dead,
He died last night in bed,
He cut his throat
With a bit of soap
Poor old Kruger's dead.

> *Eastbourne, c. 1914.*
> *Recollection of correspondent, 1951.*

Jack the Ripper was still commemorated by boys in Worcester *c.* 1935, in a little rhyme:

Jack the Ripper stole a kipper,
Hid it in his father's slipper.

Mickey Mouse, in his house,
Taking off his trousers.
Quick Mum, smack his bum,
And chase him round the houses.

Enfield.

Mickey Mouse was in a house
Wondering what to do.
So he scratched his bun-tiddly-um
Out goes you.

Farnham (Surrey), for counting-out.

Mickey Mouse, like Charlie Chaplin, doubtless benefits from alliteration's artful aid. In some of the verses 'Mouse' is a rhyme word, and therefore not likely to change with time. But this does not of itself ensure Mickey's immortality. Some children, when repeating these rhymes, already name 'Minnie Mouse', 'Matilda Mouse', and 'Mister Mouse', rather than 'Mickey'.

Popeye

The little runt Popeye, the strong-arm, spinach-swallowing sailorman, another cartoon character originating in America, has in his film appearances a simple signature song, or war cry, which is subject to infinite variation, for instance:

I'm Popeye the sailor man,
I'm Popeye the sailor man,
I eat onions and scallions
To fight the Italians,
I'm Popeye the sailor man.

Co. Durham, c. 1943.

Popeye the sailor man,
He lived in a caravan,
He opened the door
And fell to the floor,
Popeye the sailor man.

*Girl, 11, Perth, 1954, for playing
'Doublers', i.e. Two-balls.*

I opeye the sailor man,
He lived in a caravan,
He bought a pianner
For six and a tanner,
Popeye the sailor man.

*Girls, c. 10, Shrewsbury, 1952, for
ball-bouncing.*

I'm Popeye the garbage man,
I live in the garbage can,
I like to go swimmin
With bow-legged women,
I'm Popeye the garbage man.

*Long Island, U.S.A. (Howard thesis,
1938).*

Popeye is still very much alive in oral tradition, but for some reason he chiefly features in verses which are obscene.

Shirley Temple and Deanna Durbin

It is noticeable that the names of child film stars appear in the rhymes more often than the number of their appearances in films would seem to warrant. Shirley Temple and Deanna Durbin are two of the stars most often mentioned in game rhymes, although both are now grown-up, and their heyday was before the time when the children who now celebrate them became cinema-goers. Shirley Temple, in particular, seems on the way to becoming a fixture:

Shirley Temple walks like this,
Shirley Temple throws a kiss,
Shirley Temple says her prayers,
Shirley Temple falls down stairs.

Swansea, 1952, for skipping.

Shirley Oneple,
Shirley Twople,
Shirley Threeple,
Shirley Fourple,
Shirley Fiveple,
Shirley Sixple,
Shirley Sevenple,
Shirley Eightple,
Shirley Nineple,
Shirley Tenple.

Edinburgh, c. 1940, Swansea, 1952.

Who's that coming down the street?
Shirley Temple, ain't she sweet?
She's been on the stage before,
Now she's on the radio.

Swansea, 1939. Not known in 1950s.

Little Shirley Temple
She bought a penny doll,
She washed it, she dried it,
Then she let it fall.
She called for the doctor,
The doctor couldn't come,
Along came the ambulance
Rum, tum, tum.

Aberdeen, Beadnell (Northumberland), Edinburgh, Glasgow, Helensburgh, Newcastle. Collected 1952–4. For ball-bouncing.

Alternative ending:

She phoned for the doctor,
The doctor couldn't come,
Because he had a pimple
On his bum, bum, bum.

Aberdeen and Forfar. Note that all recordings are Scottish or North Country. In the south the hero of this rhyme is 'Ching Ching Chinaman'.

Shirley Temple is a star,
S-T-A-R

Newcastle, North Shields, Swansea, Welwyn, and Woking, 1951–2. Skipping or ball-bouncing.

The following were collected 1952–3 when we were concentrating on this type of rhyme:

Deanna Durbin wears a turban
Red, white, and blue.

Aberdeen, Forfar, Hackney, all for ball-bouncing.

Deanna Durbin, she wore a turban
Until she was 2, 4, 6, 8 . . .

Alton, London, and N. Staffordshire, all for skipping.

Deanna Durbin wore her turban
In-side-out!

Swansea, for 'dipping'.

Deanna Durbin lost her turban
In a pool of water.

Scarborough, for skipping and peppering.

Miss Durbin did, in fact, wear a turban in *Nice Girl?*, shown in Britain in 1941 when turban hats were fashionable.

Dog Film Stars

As would be expected, dog film stars are popular.

> Rin Tin Tin he swallowed a pin,
> He went to the doctor and the doctor wasn't in.
> He knocked at the door, and fell through the floor,
> And that was the end of Rin Tin Tin.

This rhyme has been collected from Pontypool for skipping (1954), from Caistor for skipping (1953), and from Newcastle upon Tyne for ball-bouncing (1952). In the United States Dr Howard collected versions in Maryland (1947), New York (1936), and New Jersey (1934), so the verse has already had a useful life span. In Monmouthshire, and elsewhere, 'Rin Tin Tin' has become a name for 'Tin Can Tommy'.

The dog star 'Lassie' is met in the rhymes:

> Lassie come home,
> Lassie come home,
> Lassie come H-O-M-E.
>
> *Stoke-on-Trent, for skipping, 1953.*

> Johnny is a skipper
> Sealy has a flipper
> Lassie is a collie
> You can have a lollie
> When you jump out.
>
> *Independence, Kansas, 1952.*

Betty Grable

In the period under review Miss Betty Grable (born 1916) was the school-child's personification of what can best be termed 'glamour'. America's highest paid woman in 1946 and 1947 (succeeding Miss Durbin who was the highest paid in 1945), Miss Grable seems in the forties and early fifties to have been the most envied princess in the Hollywood book of fairy tales. The reasons for her sustained popularity with adolescents are difficult to determine, but perhaps have something to do with her being a blonde without ever becoming a siren, and being gay and talented yet as homely as the girl next door. In this context a full-length study of her career would undoubtedly be very worth while. In oral rhymes of a mildly erotic nature she was named many more times than her younger and sometimes more exotic rivals.

> Betty Grable
> Sitting on a table
> Showing off her legs
> To Clark Gable.
>
> *Girls, 12, Aberdeen, 1952.*[1]

> I say, what a smasher,
> Betty Grable's getting fatter,
> Pick a brick and throw it at her.
> If you wish, steal a kiss,
> I say, what a smasher.
>
> *Girls, 13, Swansea, 1952.*

1. Repeated while bouncing two balls against a wall, doing a 'leary' (a kick in which the ball is bounced under the leg) at the end of each line. Miss Grable is reputed to have said that there were two main reasons for her success and she stood on them.

I say, what a smasher,
Betty Grable smoking Pasha.[1]

Girls, 13, Kirkcaldy, 1952.
Boys and girls, 6–7, Ballingry, 1954.

Dictation, dictation, dictation,
Bing Crosby went down to the station.
Betty Grable was there
So pretty and fair,
Dictation, dictation, dictation.

Various versions current, 1952.

Each, peach, pear, plum,
I spy Tom Thumb;
Tom Thumb in the wood,
I spy Robin Hood;
Robin Hood in the cellar,
I spy Cinderella;
Cinderella at the ball,
I spy Henry Hall;
Henry Hall at his house,
I spy Mickey Mouse;
Mickey Mouse in his cradle,
I spy Betty Grable.
Betty Grable is a star
S–T–A–R.

*Boys and girls, c. 10, Matching Green,
an isolated village in Essex, 1954. Also,
identical, Oxted, 1958.[2]*

My name is Harry James,
I'm the leader of the band,
My wife is Betty Grable,
She's the fairest in the land.
She can dance and she can sing
And she can show a leg,
The only thing she cannot do
Is make a bairn's bed.

Girl, 13, Kirkcaldy, 1952.

My name is Macnamara,
I'm the leader of the band.
My wife is Betty Grable,
She's the fairest in the land.
Oh she can dance and she can sing,
And she can show a leg,
The only thing she canna do,
She canna boil an egg.

*Dundee, 1954, for skipping. Glasgow,
1956.*

Beefcake and Cheesecake

If the popularity of a star can be gauged by the number of times he or she
appears in children's rhymes, it may be of interest that, after Charlie
Chaplin, the most popular men seem to be Bing Crosby, Roy Rogers,
James Mason, Danny Kaye, and Bob Hope; and that, amongst the ladies,

1. When a class was asked what was 'Pasha' they replied with one accord: 'Turkish
cigarettes, of course.'
2. Numerous variations exist, for example with the endings:

Henry Hall in the stable	Billy Gate in the stables,	Jeanne Crain in a stable,
Making eyes at Betty Grable;	Out steps Betty Grable;	Out pops Betty Grable;
Betty Grable in the bin	Betty Grable sewing socks,	Betty Grable in the hay,
Making eyes at Errol Flynn.	Out steps Patricia Roc.	Out pops Doris Day.
Swansea, 1954.	*Shrewsbury, 1952.*	*Perth, 1957.*

Jane Russell, Betty Hutton, and Judy Garland are sometimes named in alternative versions of the rhymes given here.

One, two, three a-leary,
I saw Wallace Beery,
Sitting on his bumbaleerie,
Kissing Shirley Temple.

> *Edinburgh, c. 1940. Girl, 14, Kirkcaldy, 1952, for ball-bouncing.*

Down in the jungle
Swinging on a rope
There stands Bob Hope
Washing himself with soap.

> *Girls, 12, Aberdeen, 1952. Similar from girl, 10, Penrith, 1957, with addition: 'Bob Hope is a dope,* D-O-P-E.'

Danny Kaye ran away
On his mother's washing-day.
He never came back till half past eight.
Half past eight is much too late
For a boy like Danny Kaye.

> *Forfar, c. 1952.*

Sonja Henie
Wore a peenie [pinafore]
Red, white, and blue.

> *Girls, 13, Aberdeen, 1952. For playing balls.*

Marilyn Monroe
Fell in the snow
Her skirt blew up
And the boy said 'Oh!'

> *Children, c. 7, Ballingry, Fife, 1954.*

Eexie, peeksie, pearie, plum,
Out steps Tom Thumb;
Tom Thumb in a basin,
Out pops James Mason;
James Mason in a cellar,
Out pops Cinderella;
Cinderella in a fix,
Out pops Tom Mix;
Tom Mix is a star,
S-T-A-R.

> *Luncarty, nr. Perth, 1954. For counting-out.*

Hi, Roy Rogers!
How about a date?
Meet me at the corner
At half past eight.
I can do the rumba,
I can do the splits,
I can do the turn-arounds,
I can do the kicks.

> *Girls, 11, Swansea, 1957, for skipping.*

In 1952 when the catchy tune 'Put Another Nickel In' was being whistled by every lout on the street corner, schoolchildren were ringing changes to the words:

If you like to go for a swim,
Let Bing Crosby push you in;
Swim the rest with Errol Flynn,
It's smashin', smashin', smashin'.

How'd you like to climb a tree,
Sit on Boris Karloff's knee?
You would certainly have to be
His next victim, victim, victim.

On October 1956 as children travelled to Alton in the school buses instead of singing about Robin Hood, they roared:

Liberace, Liberace, riding through the glen,
Liberace, Liberace, with his band of men.

And in May 1958 when the song of the month was 'Catch a falling star', the children were singing of two men whose names, to them, were of equal lustre:

Catch a Perry Como,
Wash him in some Omo,
Hang him on the line to dry.

Catch a Winston Churchill,
Wash him in some Persil,
Hang him on a line to dry.

⁎ American children's film-star rhymes include some of those known in Britain, but on the whole seem to be slicker, more of the autograph-album variety, and closer to adult influence, for example:

Sally Rand has a fan,
If she drops it – oh man!

Sally Rand has lost her fan,
Give it back you nasty man.

If you can't go to Hollywood
You don't have to cry;
Clark Gable is good looking
But so am I.

Clark Gable is a favourite in American rhymes.

British Stars

Amongst the stars with reputations made in Britain Margaret Lockwood seems to have been the favourite. 'Margaret Lockwood is a star, S-T-A-R', was chanted in Swansea, Birmingham, and Stoke-on-Trent, while skipping or ball-bouncing. Others celebrated in street song were Diana Dors (see p. 128), and the radio comedians Charlie Chester (in a version of 'Put Another Nickel In'), and Dick Bentley. In the *Radio Times*, 7 July 1950, a Surbiton reader reported hearing 9-year-old children counting-out:

In 1942, in 1942,
Bentley sailed a canoe,
He struck a rock, the clumsy clot.
That was a good one, was it not?

Whereupon a north London reader, 21 July 1950, brought forward the version:

In 1492
Dick Bentley sailed the ocean blue,
It wasn't a steamer, it wasn't a yacht,
That was a good one, was it not?[1]

In *The Times*, 7 March 1953, a correspondent reported the new skipping rhyme:

I like coffee,
I like tea,
I like radio
and TV.

1. These rhymes stem from the old mnemonic 'In fourteen hundred and ninety-two, Columbus sailed the ocean blue', which is itself sometimes used as a ball-bounce rhyme.

Much might be made of the fact that one of the most popular of street games is called 'Film Stars', and that the names of film stars are replacing flower-names in children's fortune-telling. But, popular as 'film star' rhymes undoubtedly are, it is worth remembering that they do not comprise more than 3 per cent of the oral rhymes which have been collected.

When one contemplates the amount of money, and talent, and publicity which is expended on the cinema, radio, and TV, and the amount of time some children give to these entertainments, it is perhaps remarkable how little the new arts have affected child lore. Indeed, one cannot help gaining the impression that by and large the cinema and TV only have a superficial effect on schoolchildren. It is not, it seems, until the leather jacket and eye-shadow age is reached, at about the time the children are leaving school, that the arc-lamp dream-world really begins to have an effect on their thought and way of living.

However, one instance of film publicity having a transitory influence on children can be recorded.

Davy Crockett

At the beginning of 1956 Walt Disney Productions launched a publicity campaign to make Britain's youth 'Crockett conscious' in preparation for a film *Davy Crockett, King of the Wild Frontier* (released 2 April 1956). The campaign became the most ambitious adult-organized assault on the juvenile imagination since before the war. Toy manufacturers were encouraged to produce 'character' merchandise, and stimulate a Crockett cult. There were Davy Crockett suits (for £2. 9s. 11d. each), Davy Crockett bows and arrows, Davy Crockett hunting spears, Davy Crockett fishing rods, Davy Crockett 'Whistling Pipes of Peace', and even Davy Crockett wall-paper, hair brushes, braces, T-shirts, belts, charm bracelets, transfers, and nougat bars. Most distinctive of all were the Davy Crockett imitation coon-skin hats (at 12s. 6d.), although for every hat sold over the counter half a dozen appeared in the streets made at home from a cast-off fur necktie, with tail large or small hanging down the back of the neck in the approved fashion. In April and May 1956 the campaign reached its climax, and there was a definite spasm of Crockett play. The *British Medical Journal* reported a significant increase in the number of children admitted to hospital with eye injuries. And the children began singing. There was an official Davy Crockett ballad, seventeen stanzas long, with a catchy tune by George Bruns, but the verses the children sang in the playground were not the official ones. Crockett in song became more interesting than a mere American frontiersman.[1] He became Crockett the Spaceman, Crockett the Parricide, Davy Crewcut 'King of the Teddy Boys', and, very popular, a sap Crockett, a crockery-washer. Examples:

> Born in a satellite near the moon,
> His mother was a Martian, his father was a coon;
> He caught his braces on a passing rocket
> And that was the end of Davy Crockett.
>   Davy, Davy Crockett,
>   King of the Universe.
>
> *Perth, c. June, 1956. Enfield, February 1958.*

> Davy Crockett was born on Mars,
> One of the far-off evening stars,
> He came down to earth in a big balloon
> And landed on the common in Abbey Road, Scone.
>   Davy, Davy Crockett,
>   Captain of the M.C.C.
>
> *Scone, May 1956.*

> Born on a mountain top in Tennessee,
> Killed his Ma when he was only three,
> Killed his Pa when he was only four,
> And now he's looking for his brother-in-law!
>   Davy, Davy Crockett,
>   King of the wild frontier.
>
> *Swansea, September 1956. Ilford, April 1957.*

> Born on a table top in Joe's Café,
> The dirtiest place in the U.S.A.
> Fell in love with Doris Day,
> Thought he could sing like Johnnie Ray.
>   Davy, Davy Crewcut,
>   King of the Teddy boys.
>
> *Enfield, October 1956.*[2]

> Born on a roof top in Battersea,
> Joined the Teds when he was only three,
> Coshed a cop when he was only four
> And now he's in Dartmoor for evermore.
>   Davy, Davy Crockett,
>   King of the Teddy Boys.
>
> *Great Bookham, July 1956. Swansea, September 1956. Romford, April 1957.*

1. The original David Crockett (1786–1836), whose history was aggrandized by his own gift for story telling, was a self-educated Tennessee-born backwoodsman, hunter, and militia colonel, who was twice elected to Congress, and was shot after the heroic defence of the Alamo at San Antonio in the war for Texan independence.
2. For two variants and a note on this verse see p. 27.

Glasgow version:

> Born in a tenement at Gorbals Cross,
> Of all the Teddy boys he was the boss,
> Got him a slasher [razor] five feet wide,
> Chopped up his mother and dumped her in the Clyde.
>> Davy Crewcut, Davy Crewcut,
>> King of the Teddy boy gang.

> *Very similar versions, Glasgow and Edinburgh, May 1956;*
> *Perth, January 1957; Brentwood, July 1957.*

> Standing on the corner, swinging his chain,[1]
> Along came a policeman and took his name;
> He pulled out the razor and he slit the copper's throat,
> Now he's wiping up the blood with his Teddy boy's coat.
>> Davy, Davy Crockett,
>> King of the Teddy boys.

> *Swansea, September 1956.*

To the tune 'The Yellow Rose of Texas':

> The Yellow Rose of Texas and the man from Laramie
> Went down to Davy Crockett's to have a cup of tea;
> The tea was so delicious, they had another cup,
> And poor old Davy Crockett had to do the washing up.

This last verse, or slight variants of it, seemed to have reached everywhere by the summer holidays of 1956. There were Crockett jokes, too, of the daft riddle genre: 'What does Davy Crockett call his father?' Answer: 'Dad.' 'How many ears has Davy Crockett?' 'Two, hasn't he?' 'No, three. He's got a left ear, and a right ear, and a wild frontier.'

At the end of the summer Crockett play and costume disappeared as suddenly as it had arrived; only the Crockett songs continued, and still continued (1959) in full throat.

1. Chain, i.e. bicycle chain, used as a weapon in street gang warfare.

THE schoolchild, in his primitive community, conducts his business with his fellows by ritual declaration. His affidavits, promisory notes, claims, deeds of conveyance, receipts, and notices of resignation, are verbal, and are sealed by the utterance of ancient words which are recognized and considered binding by the whole community.

This juvenile language of significant terms and formulas appears to be a legacy of the days when the nation itself was younger and more primitive (a medieval knight offered his opponent 'barlay', and children today in the north-west seek respite with the same cry); and much of this language, like the country dialects, varies from one region of Britain to another. Of barbarian simplicity, the schoolchild code enjoins that prior assertion of ownership in the prescribed form shall take the place of litigation; and that not even the deliberately swindled has redress if the bargain has been concluded by a bond word. Further it will be noticed that the gestures with which the significance of the language is stressed, for example, spitting, crossing fingers, and touching cold iron, are gestures which have been an accepted part of ritual since times long before our own.

Affirmation

Children reinforce the truth by swearing upon their honour, their heart, their Bible, their own life, or, preferably, their mother's. Spitting, linking fingers, holding their hand up to God, and making crosses upon their body, accompany their declarations.

If this catalogue seems impious it should be emphasized that the asseverations in the following pages (mostly collected from 10- and 11-year-olds) are not treated lightly by those who use them. An imprecation such as 'May I drop down dead if I tell a lie' is liable to be accorded the respect of its literal meaning, and distinct uneasiness may follow its utterance, even when the child concerned is fairly certain that he has not departed from the truth. He has very probably heard the tales his fellows tell of violent death instantly overtaking those who have dared to defy an oath; and it may well be that he believes these tales, however strange they sound to adult ears, for childhood is on nodding terms with the supernatural. A Somerset writer for instance has recalled that, in his day, schoolboys had a story in which a sinner was not only immediately struck dead when he perjured himself but became rooted to the spot where he stood 'so that no power on earth – not even a team of horses attached by ropes and chains – could move the body, which stood (like Lot's wife) as a terrible warning to other men and women'.[1]

God and honour. Pledges such as the following are commonplace: 'On my honour', 'Honour bright', 'God's honour', 'Scout's honour', 'Crusader's honour' (or the honour of whoever is the hero of the moment), 'Honest truth', 'Honest to God', 'Honest pirate', 'Honest Injun' (formerly, about 1850, a favourite with New England boys, and perhaps brought to Britain by Tom Sawyer and Huckleberry Finn), 'It's as true as I stand here', 'I tip my heel before you' (Dublin), 'I swear by the open sky' (kissing the earth), 'Truth!', 'Straight!' and, in the Forest of Dean, the dialect equivalent, 'Jonnock!'

The most common oath is 'God's honour', and the child licks the tip of his index finger and makes the sign of the cross on his throat, or, in Radnorshire, crosses his two forefingers saying 'Cross God's honour'. If he says 'I swear honest to God' or 'I swear honest truth' he may raise his hand to an upright position, and, alternatively, say: 'God's word', 'Hand up to God', 'I put my right hand up to Jesus', 'Hate God if I tell a lie'. In Penrith some children say 'Sell't me God!' which means, according to a 12-year-old, ' "May I sell my God (Christ) if I am not telling the truth." In other words, "If I am not telling the truth I am a Judas." ' Or they say 'Cush man', which means 'May man be cursed if it is not true'.

---

1. A. S. Macmillan, *Word-Lore*, vol. i, p. 59, 1926. A number of instances of supernatural retribution following upon the telling of a lie have been formally documented. The fate of Ruth Pierce on 25 January 1753 was inscribed on the Market Cross of Devizes, Wiltshire, 'as a salutary warning against the danger of impiously invoking the Divine vengeance'. According to the inscription she protested that she had paid her full share for a sack of wheat she was buying with three other women, and said she might drop down dead if she had not. 'She rashly repeated this awful wish, when, to the consternation of the surrounding multitude, she instantly fell and expired, having the money concealed in her hand.' In a report of the Coroner's inquest in *The Western Flying Post*, 29 January 1753, the further detail is added that the amount Ruth Pierce was concealing in her hand was three pence.

Similar stories, some of them grisly, may be found in *The Taunton Courier*, 22 April 1857; *The Western Flying Post*, 1 March 1813; *Aris's Birmingham Gazette*, 12 September 1796; and *The Sherborne Mercury*, 21 April 1741. For details see first reference.

'Straight' when given formally with a handshake is usually considered a manly way of expressing honesty, and is taken at its face value. 'Honour bright' has long been a juvenile pledge: witness the apprentice in *Barnaby Rudge*, ch. viii, 'I do ... Honour bright. No chaff, you know.' Scout's, Cub's, Guide's, and Brownie's honour are the only pledges deliberately sown by adults to have taken root, and are sometimes accompanied by a left handshake, or by a salute with the appropriate number of fingers. A Birmingham girl who demanded 'On your Girl Guide's promise, and cut your throat if you lie' seems, however, to have had doubts about the potency of the new pledge.

Bible oath. When a child asks 'Will you take your Bible oath on it?' he does not necessarily require that a Bible be held while the oath is administered. It is sufficient for the other merely to repeat, 'Yes, I'll take my Bible oath on it.' Thus it is in the nature of these ceremonies that the formula is repeated twice, first by the challenger, and then by the one giving the oath. 'Hand on the Bible, it's true?' 'Yes, hand on the Bible I'm not kidding.' 'Kiss the Bible?' 'Sure, I'll kiss the Bible on it.' Alternatively: 'Cross the Holy Bible', 'Criss cross the Holy Bible' (while crossing arms over chest),

> Criss cross the Bible, never tell a lie,
> If I do my mother will die.
>
> *Aberystwyth.*

> Criss cross the Holy Bible, never tell a lie,
> If I do I'll cut my throat, and then I'm sure to die.
>
> *Aberystwyth.*

'Here's my heart and there's the Bible' (Ruthin), 'If I lie I'll spit on the Bible' (Lydney), 'Holy Bible truly Gospel' (Welshpool), 'I swear on the Gospel and on my mother's death bed' (Scarborough). In Dublin a child swears by the Mass Book. In Scotland he may intone:

> Here's my Bible, (*raising his hands with palms towards him*)
> Here's my cross, (*making a cross with his arms*)
> Here's my right hand up to God. (*putting up his right hand*)
>
> *Glasgow, E. 2, and Kirkcaldy, Fife.*

In north Lincolnshire, Yorkshire, County Durham, Westmorland, and Cumberland, he (or, more often, she) elaborates:

There's the Bible open,	Here's the Bible open,
There's the Bible shut,	Here's the Bible shut.
There's a cross for Jesus,	I If do not tell the truth
My throat's cut.	I hope me throat is cut.
Scarborough.	*Durham.*

'First you put both your hands flat in front of you with little fingers together,' explains a Cleethorpes girl, 'then you put both hands as though you were saying a prayer. Then you put two fingers over each other like a cross, then slide one over your throat as if it was a knife.' 'It means you have to cut your throat if you break the promise,' adds a Penrith child.

Crossing the heart and fingers. 'Cross my heart', 'Criss cross my heart', 'Christ cross my heart', and similar vows are usually repeated by girls, and usually with their arms crossed. 'When one crosses one's heart one should do it with arms across the whole of one's chest, touching one's shoulders. Not everyone does it properly,' states a 10-year-old Oxford girl.

Little Yorkshire lasses at South Elmsall write: 'When we make a promise to anyone, they say to us "Cross your heart and spit" or "Cross your heart and hope to die". So we wet our finger and make the sign of a cross on our hearts. Sometimes we put our finger on our forehead then on each shoulder, then on our chest. Sometimes they say to us, "Put three crosses on your heart".'

At Newtonmore, beside the Spey in Inverness-shire, the pledge demanded is 'Cross your heart and bend your knees', and a girl not only has to draw a cross diagonally from each shoulder with her right hand, but get down on her knees – 'and jolly sore they get too,' says one of them.

The term 'Criss cross', cried on its own or in conjunction with 'my heart' or 'my throat', prevails, it seems, in an area extending from Knighton westwards to the sea, and northwards to Liverpool. In country districts around Aberystwyth children cry out, *Cris croes, tân poeth, byddaf farw ar y groes* (Criss cross, hot fire, I will die on the cross). And in Anglesey, where the cry *Cris croes* is also heard, children moisten a forefinger and make the mark of the cross significantly on their forehead, or on their neck.

Further declarations in which a defaulter risks retribution include:

Cross my heart,
If I ever tell a lie
Put a rope round my neck
Then let me die.

Aberystwyth.

Clasp my hands,
Look at the sky,
Cross my heart
And hope to die.

Penrith.

Criss cross tell a lie
God will punish (or punch) me
when I die.

Liverpool.

If I lie I promise to die
So you can punch me in the eye,
Then if I'm dead
You can hit me on the head
with a poker.

Bishop Auckland.

I lie and do you wrong,
May the devil slit my tongue.[1]

Bishop Auckland.

May the floor open
If I have an untrue word spoken.

Sale, Manchester.

Sometimes the child who is making the oath crosses his fingers, and the other child puts his fingers through them, snapping them apart. This rite, called 'Breaking the cross' or 'Break my cross if I tell a lie', is practised in places as different as the new town of Welwyn Garden City in Hertfordshire, and the ancient town of Forfar in Strathmore. It is a rite which has no small significance in juvenile ethics, for amongst children it is well known that crossed fingers not only give protection to their bodies, but unbridled licence to their tongues. The innocent-eyed feel themselves at liberty to manufacture any mis-statements calculated to be to their advantage provided that they keep (perhaps concealed behind their back) two fingers crossed. But if they allow this cross to be broken they are no longer free; they must, even to a teacher, choose words which are capable of covering the truth.

Drop down dead. 'May I drop dead here, if I tell a lie', 'God let me drop dead this minute', 'God strike me stiff and blind', and suchlike imprecations are apparently hazarded almost everywhere. Sometimes, as in Ruthin, two oaths are metrically combined:

> Cross my heart and hope to die,
> Drop down dead if I tell a lie.

In Penrith a girl chants 'to show I am telling the truth':

> God send the lightning to strike my tree,
> And God send the lightning if I tell a lee.

The following has been reported only from Swansea. Two girls link their little fingers and cry 'Pull the dying oath.' From the same school this has also been reported as 'Pull oath', 'Die on oath', 'Dianothe', and 'Diamond oath', an interesting trail of corruption.

The children's practice of staking their parent's well-being on their truthfulness is very general, and almost anywhere they are liable to exclaim: 'On my mother's life!' 'On my mother's death bed!' 'Across my mother's dead body!' or, 'If I tell a lie my mother will die' (Cornwall), 'Mother's death, father's death, I'm not telling a lie' (Glamorgan),

---

1. The best test of veracity Boswell could think of when involved in a difficult situation with two small urchins squabbling in Whitehall, was to ask one of them: 'Will you say, Devil take you?' This imprecation, Boswell records, 'the little gipsy roared out twice most fervently'. – *Journal*, 21 December 1762.

'Mother, Father, will die, if I tell a lie' (Fife). 'You have to tell the truth,' warns a 10-year-old, 'otherwise it's your mother's death.'[1]

In the north-west, that is in Cumberland, Westmorland, the West

Riding, Lancashire, Cheshire, north Derbyshire, and in the north of Wales, spitting plays a prominent part in their attestations. A child, when questioning the veracity of a statement, will demand 'Spit your death' or 'Spit your mother's death', whereupon the challenged one will repeat the words demanded of him and, according to local custom, will spit and cross his throat, or spit over his wrist or little finger, and perhaps cross his throat as well, or, in Liverpool, link little fingers and spit, or, in the West Riding, spit on the ground and declare, 'If I tell a lie may I die on the spot where I spit.'[2]

Cut my throat. Of the oaths current today this is the one which was the most documented

2   Spitting Death

in the nineteenth century, perhaps because it is the most dramatic;[3] and it is general throughout the English-speaking world. It is another instance in which the special properties of spittle are recognized. A child moistens his finger and shows it, and says:

'My finger's wet.'

1. How seriously such oaths are regarded by adults also, in some levels of society, may be seen in the police court report on a 16-year-old Dorset boy accused of murder. It was his mother who asked: 'Will you swear over my dead body you did not do it?' The boy replied: 'I tell you I didn't. I swear over your dead body.' – *News of the World*, 14 February 1954, p. 2.
2. The juvenile practice of making an oath more terrible by spitting was noticed in the eighteenth century by the antiquary John Brand of Newcastle in his *Popular Antiquities*, 1777, p. 101 n.: 'Boys have a Custom (*inter se*) of spitting their Faith, or as they also call it here, their Saul (Soul), when required to make Asseverations in a Matter of Consequence.'
3. See, e.g. G. F. Northall, *English Folk Rhymes*, 1892, p. 336, and S. O. Addy, *Household Tales*, 1895, p. 127.

He wipes it – usually in his armpit – and shows it, and says:

> 'My finger's dry.'

He tilts his head back, draws his finger across his throat, and says:

> 'Cut my throat if I tell a lie.'

Only the most depraved will tell an untruth after repeating such a formula, which is made not a whit the less startling by the miniature stature of some of its practitioners. The wording varies only slightly from one place to another:

Wet my thumb,	I wet my finger,
Wipe it dry,	I wipe it dry,
Cut my throat	I cut my throat
If I tell a lie.	If I tell a lie.
Farnham, Surrey.	*Lydney.*
My finger's wet,	That's wet,
My finger's dry,	That's dry,
God strike me dead	I hate God
If I tell a lie.	If I tell a lie.
Hull.	*Kirkcaldy.*

Sometimes the oath is taken on the blade of a boy's penknife, which is first spat upon: 'See it's wet, see it's dry, cut my throat if I tell a lie' (Bishop Auckland). Sometimes, less elaborately, they say, 'Cut my throat and may I die, if I ever tell a lie' (Scarborough), or 'If I tell a lie, cut my throat and let me die' (Welwyn). In north Devon, more cautiously, 'Cut my mother's throat'. Also 'Slit my throat if I lie' (Croydon), and 'Split my neck' (Lydney). And sometimes there are no words, just a significant gesture across the wind pipe.[1]

Testing Truthfulness

If there can still be doubt about a person's veracity (he may, for instance, have been saying 'Not' under his breath) he is liable to be tested. He may be asked 'What will you eat?' and have to reply 'Fire and brimstone'.[2]

1. During the proceedings of the Lynskey Tribunal held in London in 1948 to inquire into abuses at the Board of Trade, Mrs John Belcher, wife of the ex-Railway Clerk, Parliamentary Secretary to the Board of Trade, won the sympathy of everyone present with her frank evidence as she twice licked her fingers and crossed her throat in this schoolgirlish affirmation of honesty.
2. This traditional torment for the mendacious, inspired by such a passage as *Revelation*, xx. 10, is also recommended in an old juvenile jibe for liars, recorded in *Tommy Thumb's Pretty Song Book*, vol. ii, 1744, p. 35: 'Lyer Lyer Lickspit, Turn about the Candlestick, Whats good for Lyers Brimstone and Fire.'

Or, 'What will you do if it is not true?' 'Tread on hot needles' (Welwyn).

He (or more likely she) may be asked to 'Look up to heaven without laughing', and then be tickled under the chin, a kind of trial by ordeal (Swansea); or may be given the challenge 'Cheese', which means that he has to repeat the word 'cheese' ten times, and 'if he laughs he has not been telling the truth' (Penrith).

A further way of detecting lies is to draw two fingers along the ground and if the fingers remain clean it proves the statement was untrue, but if one of the fingers is dirty it was true (Peterborough).

And it is a well-known sign that a person has told a falsehood if a blister appears on his tongue.[1]

*_** Another curious method of testing truthfulness (perhaps no longer practised, although a similar procedure is still used to decide who shall be 'he' in a game) is described by a correspondent to *Notes and Queries*, 8th ser., vol. ix, 1896, pp. 495–6, as occurring among London boys. 'Sometimes, when a boy has doubt about a matter, he attempts to get to the bottom of it by some such method as the following. After allowing some spittle to rest upon the back of his hand, he will raise the forefinger of the other hand, posing it above the spot whereon the spittle, or "fat", as it is in boyish vernacular termed, rests, at the same time giving vent to the following doggerel:

> Little pig, little pig, tell me a lie,
> And I'll knock the fat clean out of your eye.

And then, at the termination of the recital, he brings the over-poised finger smartly down upon the "fat".' If, as a result, the 'fat' vanished, what had been doubted was true; if the blow caused the spittle to splash over the back of the hand and become more conspicuous than it was before, it was not true.

Bets

A cynical writer in 1902[2] declared that the following scale of affirmations was not unknown among schoolboys: 'Is it true?' 'Yes.' – 'Will you take your oath on it?' 'Yes.' – 'Will you take your Bible oath on it?' 'Yes.' –

1. This is a very old belief referred to by Lyly (1584), Bacon (1597), Shakespeare (1608), Fletcher and Rowley (1623), 'Poor Robin' (1678), Aubrey (1687), Fuller (1732), and Swift (1738). It can in fact be traced back to classical times (Theocritus, *Idylls* xii. 23–24).
2. *Notes and Queries*, 9th ser., vol. ix, p. 375.

'Will you cut your throat if it isn't true?' 'Yes.' – 'Will you bet a penny on it?' 'No, I'll not go *that* length.'

Certainly betting is closely allied to promising. When one Scottish class (Kirkcaldy) was asked how they vouched for a thing being true they variously replied:

'I bet you it's true.'

'Bet you anything. Honest Injun. Cut my throat if I tell a lie.'

'You wet your thumb and hold it up. Then you shout "I bet you".'

'"Bets." Lick your thumb and press it against the thumb of the disbeliever who has also licked his thumb.'

When asked for elucidation they wrote:

'*Bets*. Used when someone is positive something will happen, indicated by licking the thumb, or in the case of boys putting the thumbs under the braces and pulling them out. It shows that a person must think himself right or he wouldn't do it.'

'*Bets*. It is said when two people disagree over a subject, e.g.
Tom: "I say Parkinson will win the 500 c.c. at the races."
Jack: "Dinna be daft, Jimmy Dick'll beat him by a lap."
Tom: "Bets."
Jack: "On."
If both boys lick their thumbs and put them together the bet is on.'

'*Bets*. When two or more people are arguing it is probable that they will be quite angry. It is used mostly in friendly conversation as to perhaps the make of a car. It is done to make a person believe sometimes, but most usually it is done to make sure that the other cannot say that he said something else. It is really the sealing of a wager. The two people lick their thumbs, say "Bets", and press their thumbs together. When the bet is not accepted the other person does not lick his thumb or touch the other's.'

So it is that an ancient manner of securing a wager or bargain – for countless generations an accepted token in Scottish life – lives on and retains its significance in the seclusion of children's playgrounds.

⁎ According to the itinerant pedlar Dougal Graham, born near Stirling in 1724, thumb-licking was already a juvenile practice in the eighteenth century, and he states (*Writings*, vol. ii, p. 10) that in confirmation of the act boys would recite:

> Though kith and kin and a' should revile thee,
> There's my thumb I'll ne'er beguile thee.

This juvenile attestation appears to be alluded to by Allan Ramsay in *A Tale of Three Bonnets*, 1722, when he writes:

> My honest Bawsy, there's my thumb
> That, while I breathe, I'se ne'er beguile ye.

There is no doubt about thumb-licking formerly being a practice which was seriously regarded by Scottish manhood. John Erskine in his *Institute of the Law of Scotland*, Book III, 1773, iii, § 5, p. 447, notes: 'Decrees are yet extant in our records . . . sustaining sales upon summonses of thumb licking, upon this medium, That the parties had licked thumbs at finishing the bargain.' Edmund Burt, writing *c.* 1723 in his *Letters from the North of Scotland*, vol. ii, p. 222, observes: 'Two Highlanders, to make a binding bargain, wet each of them the ball of his thumb with his mouth, and then press their wet thumb balls together.' And Robert Chambers in his *Book of Days*, vol. i, p. 359, recounts an incident in 1642 when a Scottish lieutenant licked his thumb, thereby pledging himself to a duel in which he was killed.

Bargain Making

Making a bargain is similar to making a bet. In parts of Scotland, as already noted, including Edinburgh and Glasgow, the thumbs are wetted and pressed together. In other parts both sides to the bargain spit on the ground. In yet other areas, and in particular in England, children shake hands, or slap hands, or join hands and have the grasp broken by a blow from a third party (South Molton), or stamp on each other's toes (Knighton), or, fairly commonly, link the little fingers or 'pinkies' of their right hands and shake them up and down, occasionally repeating some dirge as a warning to each other:

> Ring a ring a pinkie,
> Ring a ring a bell,
> If ye brak the bargain
> Ye'll go to hell.
>
> *Forfar.*

> Cope a cope that bargain,
> Never cope again;
> Two cross sticks
> Make a broken bone.
>
> *Plymouth.*

More prosaically, they call out: 'It's a deal', 'Done', 'On', 'Fair enough', 'Quits', 'Double quits', 'Square', 'Eeks' (or, in Scotland, 'Eeksie-peeksie', or, in Enfield, 'Touch wood and whistle'), and no going back on an offer is possible once it has been accepted by someone using whichever phrase is recognized as binding in his school.

_{*} The term 'pinkie', a juvenile and nursery word for something small was first noted as being applied to the little finger in Jamieson's *Scottish Dictionary*, 1808. The name is still widely used for the little finger in Lowland Scotland, northern England, and in Holland. Bartlett in his *Dictionary of Americanisms* (1860) states that 'pinkie' was 'a common term in New York, especially among small children, who, when making a bargain with each other, are accustomed to confirm it by interlocking the little finger of each other's right hands, and repeating the following doggerel:

> Pinky, pinky, bow-bell,
> Whoever tells a lie
> Will sink down to the bad place,
> And never rise up again.'

The action of linking the little fingers of the right hand, and shaking the hands with an up-and-down motion, was noted several times in the nineteenth century as an essential rite among children when wishing to bind each other to an engagement. A writer in *Notes and Queries*, 4th ser., vol. xi, 1873, p. 22, recalls the practice as being common among boys in the Midlands, when he was young, while saying:

> Ring finger, blue bell,
> Tell a lie, go t'hell.

Gregor (1881) notes a similar ceremony amongst boys in Banffshire, where the words were,

> Ring, ring the pottle bell,
> Gehn ye brak the bargain,
> Ye'll gang to hell,

and in Fraserburgh, where the pledge was,

> Ring a bottle, ring a bell,
> The first brae it ye cum till,
> Ye'll fa' doon an brack yer neck,
> An that 'ill the bargain brack.

It is also said to be the custom of girls in Smyrna, Asia Minor, when making pledges (*Notes and Queries*, 4th ser., vol. xi, p. 163). The significance accorded to the little fingers when confirming the truth or an engagement may throw light on Lady Percy's threat in *Henry IV, Part I* (II. iii):

'Indeede Ile breake thy little finger Harry, if thou wilt not tel me true.'

Swopping

The chief bargains made at school concern swopping. ('Commonest swops are comics.') And the anxiety of those who swop is centred on the knowledge that after a while one party or the other is apt to regret his bargain and want back, indeed demand back, what has been exchanged. Most of the traditional sayings are aimed at impressing upon the participants the permanence of the deal. They exclaim:

'No backs' (Kirkcaldy).

'No back backers' (Rothesay).

'No gives backs' (Oxford).

'No changey back' (Bishop Auckland).

'No swops back for a million biscuits' (Sale, Manchester).

'Chip chop, can't have it back' (Yeovil).

'Tin tacks, no backs' (Peterborough).

In Dublin the formula amounts to a threat, 'Tick tack, never give back, or God will send you down below.'

In Birmingham one child says 'What colour is coal?' The other replies 'Black.' And the first chants 'No swops back.'

Similarly in Lincoln and Market Rasen one child asks 'What colour is grass?' The other says 'Green.' And the first seals the bargain with: 'No swops back till your mother's a queen.'

And at Enfield, to conclude the transaction, each party gives the strange promise: 'Round the world and back again.'

As a kind of insurance they often emphasize their words with small rites: 'Touch black, no back' (Leeds), 'Touch blacks, no backs' (Liverpool), 'Touch black, never have back' (Aberystwyth). Similar precepts appear to be known throughout Britain, sometimes several versions being current in one place; and while repeating the words 'You touch your shoe or something black.' In Croydon they hook little fingers and shake, chanting:

> Touch teeth, touch leather,
> No backsies for ever and ever.

In Swansea,

> Touch teeth, touch leather,
> Can't have back for ever and ever.

In Laverstock, near Salisbury,

> Touch teeth, touch wood,
> Can't have it back for good.

And in Bishop Auckland, where swopping is also known as 'cooping' (the would-be swopper says 'I'll coop yer my migs [marbles] for yer small dag [knife]'), they bind themselves with: 'No Jackie backs, touch wood', or 'No Jackie backs, touch cold iron'.

Should it happen, however, that one of the parties is not sure that he is getting a good bargain, the mechanism of the swop can, at a number of schools (as far apart as South Molton and Sale, Manchester), be regulated by the deed and declaration: 'Touch white, swop back if I like'.

₌ Formulas recorded in the nineteenth century for making exchange agreements inviolable include:

> Chiff-chaff, never change agen
> As long as the world stands, Amen!
> > 'Leicestershire Words', 1881.
>
> Chick, chock, chino, the world turns round.
> > 'Notes and Queries', 7th ser., vol. ix, 1890, p. 312.
>
> Tick tack, never change back, touch cold iron.
> > 'Glossary of S.-E. Worcestershire', 1894.

Touching cold iron – the blade of a penknife, or the iron heel of a boot –'appears to have been common in the last century. It is curious that none of the present-day sayings seem to have been previously recorded, and that only one amongst them (from Bishop Auckland) specifies iron.

Giving

As with swopping, so with giving. It is a cardinal rule amongst the young that a thing which has been given must not be asked for again; and in some places in England and Ireland the reproach for a meanie who attempts this offence is still the metrical one which was current amongst children who lived in the time of Shakespeare:

> Give a thing, take a thing,
> Dirty man's plaything.[1]
> > Somerset.
>
> Give a thing, take a thing,
> Never go to God again.
> > Cheshire.

1. Thus Thomas Adams in 1624: 'It is . . . a Prouerbe among our children, To giue a thing, and take a thing, is fit for the Deuils darling.' Cotgrave, before him, under *Retirer* in his French–English Dictionary, notes 'To weare a thing and take a thing: to weare the diuells gold-ring.' And Plato (*Philibus* sec. 19E) states that this sentiment was a proverb amongst children in his time.

Give a thing, take it back,
God will ask you, Where is that?
You say you don't know,
Then God will send you down below.

Laurencetown, Co. Galway.

More common now, though not a whit the less effective, is,

Giving's keeping,
Taking back's stealing.

Or the succinct,

Giveses, keepses.

These reproaches are, of course, usually made by the one who is in danger of losing his gift. But the disinterested, too, have no doubts about the rightness of the rule's operation, and will hotly support the permanence of a present once it has changed hands. Even when the original owner may have convinced himself that he intended his benevolence as no more than a loan, the onlookers address the would-be recoverer (as we have overheard) in no equivocal language: 'Lay off it you mangy stinker, let him 'ave it for keeps.'

In the United States such a child, who succumbs to the temptation of wanting back, is termed an 'Injun-giver'.

Gaining Possession

There is, too, a set procedure and vocabulary for gaining possession of an object, and it is noteworthy that in schoolchild society, in which the art of looking after number one is necessarily developed to a high degree, possession frequently goes not to the strongest or the most active, but to the quickest tongued.

There are three recognized ways in which articles may be acquired by verbal dexterity, these are by 'egoing', by 'bagging', and by 'finding-keeping'.

In private schools a child who wishes to dispose of something he no longer wants will give himself the pleasure of holding it up and calling out 'Quis?' and the boy or girl who first replies 'Ego' receives the object and may say (to the horror of the classicist) 'I egoed it'. Whereupon the first child sometimes says 'Baggy no backs' indicating that, however valueless the object may prove to be, it cannot be returned.

In other schools, even in grammar schools, although 'Quis?' is not entirely unknown, the more usual cry is 'Who wants?' to which the loud reply is 'I do'; or, as in Alton, the common procedure, wholly satisfying to the donor, is to throw the object into the air and shout 'Scrambles'. If, incidentally, a sweet or other titbit is being straightforwardly offered to a friend, the usual metropolitan phrase is ''Ere ya' or ''Ere ya, yours for tuppence' to which the response is 'Ya', or 'No fear!' If a boy sees something somebody else has which he wants and is prepared to pay for, his almost invariable inquiry is: 'Wanna flog it?'

When possession of an object, such as a comic, is available to only one person in a group; or when it is a case of everybody having to find a chair or help themselves to cake, the rabble do not wait to be asked or handed what they want but make an immediate claim to it, indicating the seat or slice of their choice, and exclaiming 'Bags', 'Bagsy', 'Baggy mine', 'Bags I this one', 'Bags it me', or 'Bags it for keeps', whereupon, as a writer pointed out as long ago as 1870, 'it is a gross breach of etiquette for anyone to take a thing that has been thus verbally bagged'.[1]

This term 'Bags', or variations thereof, appears to be in general use throughout Britain. There are, however, some dialect alternatives:

Ballow. 'Ballow that' or 'I ballows that'. Current in the West Riding. It is an old-established term and appears in nineteenth century word-books, occasionally pronounced 'balla'.

Barley, usually 'Barley me that'. Sometimes used for asserting a claim in the barley truce-term country (see pp. 168–70). The word has long had this distinctive usage in the north-west. For instance, a Lancastrian correspondent to *Notes and Queries*, 3rd ser., vol. vii, 1865, p. 84, states: 'When a boy I used to ramble on the moors with my companions, and always shouted "Barley" when I found a well-stocked blackberry, or whinberry, bush.'

Bollars. 'I bollars' or 'Boller me'. Sometimes used in Cheshire and Lancashire, e.g. at Northwich and Atherton.

Chaps. 'Chaps me that.' The usual term in Aberdeenshire, Angus, Perthshire, Dumfriesshire, and doubtless many other parts of Scotland for it has long been in common use there.

Chucks. 'Chucks me that.' The common expression today in Kirkcaldy (although fifty years ago the word in vogue was 'chaps'), and also known farther south in Roxburgh.

Chops. Reported as having been used in Glasgow, as a variant of 'chaps' (*Scottish National Dictionary*).

Cogs or *Sags*. These two terms have equal currency in Ruthin, North Wales. 'Cogs' or 'Coggy' is also reported from Bury St Edmunds.

Ferry. Occasionally used for claiming in the West Riding, e.g. in the phrase 'Ferry for picking' (i.e. 'Bags I count out'). Literally it means first (see p. 159).

Fogs or *Fog it*. In use at Shavington near Crewe, Padiham, Shrewsbury, and occasionally in Manchester.

1. *Notes and Queries*, 4th ser., vol. vi, 1870, p. 517.

Jigs it. Common in Manchester and district, and in the area south to Wolverhampton.

Nab it. Derby and Wolverhampton. Probably the same word as 'nab', to steal or seize.

Nag it. Kirkham and Newcastle-under-Lyme. Probably a variant of 'nab'.

Pike I or *Prior Pike.* Given as a Staffordshire term in *Notes and Queries* in 1870, and again in 1924 (4th ser., vol. vi, p. 517; vol. cxlvii, p. 377).

Sags see *Cogs.*

Shigs. Bishop Auckland. Used when somebody has more than one of a thing, for instance more than one ball, and should share them.

Whack it. Levenshulme, Manchester.

When acquiring a thing the third way, by finding, a child may say simply 'Baggy me'. But if the occasion warrants, that is to say when he who has lost the article is near, he will establish his claim to it by invoking the rule that something lost becomes the property of him who finds it.[1] 'When we find anything,' declares one of the South Elmsall 11-year-olds, 'we say:

> Finding's keeping,
> Giving back's stealing.

Everytime we find anything we never give it back. Nearly every week we find something.' It is recognized that the utterance of this formula gives the finder an absolute right to the article. Nevertheless a classmate, another girl of eleven, puts the other point of view: 'If we lose something and somebody else find it we don't get it back, but sometimes we say "Gi'me it, else I'll bash you".'

There are also some sub-clauses in the code. At Sale when something is lost the owner can stake his right to its recovery with the cry 'Claims back' or, if several threaten to take it, 'Claims on all of you'. Again, if something is found when others are present it is necessary for the finder to shout out 'No shares' (very general), or 'Bags it, no halfers' (north country and south-east Scotland), or 'No halfers, no quarters, no cuddy bits' (Lanarkshire), otherwise another child may, on its discovery, cry 'Halves', 'Halfers', or 'Shares', before he can get hold of it, and thus have a right to a part of it or to half its value.

A certain amount of regional variation is noticeable in the 'Finding keeping' formulas, although often two or more formulas are current in the same place. Thus in Lydney 48 children gave 'Finders keepers', 11 gave

1. Hence the story current in William IV's time: ' "What are you beating that boy for?" said a gentleman to a young denizen of the rookery in St. Giles': "You are too big for him. What has he done?" "Vy, he dropped his knife: I picked it up; and now he wants me to give it him back again, and 'cos I von't, he's sarcy." ' – *Napoleon's Book of Fate,* c. 1835, p. 24.

'Findings keepings', 4 gave 'Findings keepings, no man's sneakings', and one gave 'Findings keepings after Good Friday'. Other prominent forms include:

Findings keepings Taking back's stealings. <div align="right">*Widespread.*</div>	Findems keepums, Losems weepums. <div align="right">*Oxford.*</div>
Findings keepings Giving back's cheatings. <div align="right">*Warwick.*</div>	Findsies keepsies, Losers weepsies. <div align="right">*West Country.*</div>
Findings keepings, Losings weepings. <div align="right">*Croydon and Dulwich.*</div>	Finders keeps, Losers greets. <div align="right">*Scotland.*</div>
Finders keepers, Losers weepers. <div align="right">*Widespread; and the usual saying in U.S.A.*</div>	Findie, findie, keeps it, Losie, losie, seeks it. <div align="right">*Bishop Auckland.*</div>

*** These 'Finding keeping' formulas do not seem to have altered much during the past hundred years or so. J. T. Brockett in *North Country Words*, 1829, p. 145, gives:

> No halfers,
> Findee, keepee,
> Lossee, seekee,

which may be compared with the present-day cry in Bishop Auckland. Charles Reade in *It is Never Too Late to Mend*, 1856, ch. lxv, gives, 'Losers seekers, finders keepers'; and Northall in his *Folk-Rhymes*, 1892, p. 335, gives 'Findings, keepings; losings, seekings', as a saying amongst boys in Warwickshire and Staffordshire.

The known history of the cry 'Halves' or 'Halfers' is longer. It is apparently referred to in *J. Cleaveland Revived*, 1659: 'The devided Damme Runs to the Summons of her hungry Lamb, But when the twin cries Halves, she quits the first.' Richard Savage a century later in *Horace to Scaeva*, 1730, exactly describes it:

> And he, who sees you stoop to th' ground
> Cries, halves! to everything you've found.

And Scott in *The Antiquary*, 1816, ch. xxiii, records the northern 'halfers': 'The beggar exclaimed, like a Scotch school-boy when he finds anything, "Nae halvers and quarters – hale o' mine ain, and nane of my neighbour's".'

Claiming Precedence

The term 'bags' for gaining possession of an object is also commonly used for securing a privilege or first place. Thus, at the outset of an informal game of cricket, such as French cricket or Stump cricket, Croydon lads cry: 'Bags first knock', 'Bags I first', 'First bat', or 'Fursie', and whoever speaks first is automatically – or almost automatically – allowed to have first innings. 'Bags' or 'Baggy' is used like this throughout southern England, and is by no means uncommon in the north. But the dialect terms for gaining possession (see previous section) extend to claiming precedence in the same way. Thus a child in Kirkcaldy says 'Chucks me first', and a child in Ruthin 'Cogs I first go', and so on. In Headington, on occasion, a child stresses his bid for priority with the phrase and deed: 'Touch wood bags I first.'

In some places, other terms prevail in certain situations. In Poplar in the East End of London children use the term 'squits' rather than 'bags' when claiming a privilege. If two of them both want to do the same thing, the first to cry 'Me squits' gets his way. In Enfield, to be first in a game of marbles, or last in a game of fag-cards, the vital cry is 'Lardie'. Again, the term 'firsie' (a juvenile elongation of first, see p. 175) is much used in games. In Bishop Auckland, to have first blow in a game of conkers, a boy has to cry 'Firsie jabs'. In some places the claim must be more formal. In Presteigne, for instance, a boy who wishes to have first turn at conkers must complete the rigmarole:

> Iddy, iddy onker,
> My first conker;
> Iddy, iddy ack,
> My first smack.

It is in the north country that the most distinctive terms of precedence prevail. In an area extending from Stoke-on-Trent to Lincoln, and from Lincoln northwards on the east side of the Pennines (see map) the operative word is 'foggy' and to say 'I'm foggy' means 'I have the right to be first'. It is a word which in Newcastle, South Shields, and on Tyneside generally, sounds like 'fuggy'. In West Hartlepool it becomes 'feggy', and in Doncaster is sometimes corrupted to 'folly'.

In this foggy northern territory the children shout 'laggy' if they want last place, a term which they have preserved amongst themselves for no less than three and a half centuries.[1] They determine the order in which

1. In Robert Armin's play *The History of the two Maids of More-clacke* (1609) a boy playing counter-hole says 'Now Iohn, i'le cry first', and John replies 'And i'le cry lagge'. Miege, in his English and French *Dictionary* (1687), confirms this schoolchild use, '*Lag*,

they shall do something by shouting for first, second, and last places: 'Foggy', 'Seggy', 'Laggy'; or, if there are more than three places, they shout: 'Foggy', 'Seggy', 'Thirdy', 'Fourthy', 'Fifty', and so on.

3   Claiming precedence in the north country

In the West Riding, however, in towns such as Bradford, Halifax, and Huddersfield, the term for first is 'ferry', and they cry 'ferry go' for first turn. The dividing line between the area where they say 'foggy' and the area where they say 'ferry' seems to run through Sheffield, Barnsley, Wakefield, and Leeds, for in or around these places both 'foggy' and 'ferry' are reported.

Farther west, in Lancashire, the predominant term is 'firsy', while in Furness, Westmorland, and Cumberland, they again say 'ferry', or more often 'furry'; and 'furry' is reported as far north as Langholm in Dumfriesshire. In this firsy-ferry-furry area the term for second is 'seccy' not 'seggy', and they sometimes say 'leggy' not 'laggy'.

a School-Word that signifies the last, *le dernier*. As the Lag of a Form, *le dernier d'une Classe*.' In this last sense the word is still in common use at Eton.

When an unpopular task is offered, 'Which of you is going to do the washing up?' it is the last person who speaks who must perform the despised duty. However much the laggy-voiced may complain 'S'no fair, I did it yesterday. I don't won-a-do-it', he or she recognizes that it is little good arguing. In the majority of schools if the others are first saying, 'Bags not', 'Baggy no me', or 'Baggy not do', they have exempted themselves. In some places the phrase is simply 'Bar me', 'No-ie me', 'No fears', 'No dice', or (since the most frequent avoiding action is when a tigger, he, or it, is required for a game) 'No it me', 'No on it', 'No mannie', or no whatever is the local name for the chaser. In Oxford the custom is to cry 'Touch ground, turn around, bags I don't do it', and the last to bend down and spin around receives the unwelcome chore.

In the areas where a dialect equivalent to 'bags' is current (pp. 155–6) similar negative operates: thus in Angus they cry 'Chaps no me'.

The word, however, which can be considered the proper cry (since it does not have to be associated with a negative) for exempting oneself from an action is 'fains' (often pronounced *veins*), a word only in occasional use in county schools (more in the south and west than elsewhere), but general in private schools where any job will be fained as soon as noticed. At the end of a cricket match the wide-awake amongst the fielders will say 'Fains take in the stumps', and the others will chorus 'Fains' after him, or – in some schools – immediately bend down, touch the ground with all ten fingers, and then say 'Fains'; and the last to do so automatically carries in the stumps. The only local term which has been reported, directly equivalent to fains, is 'Moans' which is used in the Avon Valley in Wiltshire. This mournful cry seems, however, to be confined to the east bank of the river, to Durnford, Netton, and Saltern. On the west bank, at Lake, Wilsford, and Upper, Middle, and Lower Woodford, the children are content to be like the majority and shout 'Bags not'.

⁎ 'Fains', as used here, is the direct opposite to 'Bags' (and to 'Ego' in response to 'Quis?'), and was recorded in this sense by a correspondent to *Notes and Queries*, 5th ser., vol. vii, 1877, p. 58, who recollected that in his Essex schooldays: 'If a monitor called his fags, and ordered one to get him something, they would say "fain going" or "fain I", and the one who was last had to go.' This is a quite different usage from the truce term 'fains', 'fannies', or 'faynights', which gives temporary immunity or respite in a game; and from the ancient term of prohibition 'fen', prevalent in games of marbles ('fen dobs', etc.), and used by Jo, the crossing-

sweeper in *Bleak House*, 1853, ch. xvi, when he thinks he is being imposed upon: 'I'm fly. But fen larks, you know. Stow hooking it!' (For a note on the derivation of these words see p. 171.)

Secret Keeping

When wishing a person to keep a thing quiet children ordinarily enjoin 'Keep it dark', 'Don't spread it', 'Mum's the word', 'Don't split'; but if they require a vow of silence there are, in some places, special formulas. In Penrith a child swears: 'I vow never to tell as long as the sun and the moon shall endure.' In Swansea: 'Take my oath and take my little finger' (linking little fingers). In Welshpool:

> Cut my throat and wipe it dry,
> If I tell I'll surely die.

In Lydney, according to an 11-year-old girl:

> Prick of the finger, prick of the thumb,
> I won't tell what you've done.

'We prick our fingers with a pin and write it on paper in blood like "*Me and J. B. swears to keep mum*".' Often, of course, the formulas are ordinary imprecations: 'God strike me dead if I split', 'God cut my throat if I tell of you', 'If I let the secret out I'll drop down dead on this spot'.

In and around Market Rasen, in Lincolnshire, children use an old and charming poetic formula (of which they sent ten versions) for testing a friend's ability to keep a secret. They take the person's hand and run their finger round the palm, repeating:

> Can you keep a secret?
> I don't suppose you can,
> You mustn't laugh or giggle
> When I tickle your hand.[1]
>
> *Girl, 11, Market Rasen.*

> Can you keep a secret?
> If you can you must not laugh,
> You must not smile,
> And you must not cry.
>
> *Girl, 12, Normandy-by-Spital, Lincs.*

> Can you keep a secret?
> Tell me if you can
> If you laugh or show your teeth
> You can't keep one.
>
> *Girl, 12, Binbrook, Lincs.*

> Can you keep a secret?
> If you can, tell me your name.
>   *Jean Holland.*
> No, you can't then!
>
> *Girl, 11, Market Rasen.*

1. S. O. Addy in his *Household Tales*, 1895, p. 81, gives a similar verse from the same part of Britain. Cf. a nursery game with American, German and Chinese parallels, in *The Oxford Dictionary of Nursery Rhymes*, 1951, pp. 184–5.

In Ohio children bind themselves to silence by saying: 'Cross my heart and hope to die, lock my lips and throw away the key', and they make the gesture of turning a key in their lips and throwing it away.

Obtaining Respite

Perhaps the most important word in the schoolchild's vocabulary is his truce term. Certainly to the adult observer it is his most interesting word, for when a child seeks respite he uses a term to which there is now no exact equivalent in adult speech. If, when engaged in some boisterous activity with his fellows, a child is exhausted or out of breath, or cuts himself, or has a shoelace undone, or fears his clothes are getting torn, or wants to know if it is time to go home, he makes a sign with his hands, and calls out a word which brings him immediate but temporary relief from the strife. Thus a 12-year-old Cleethorpes girl writes:

'If one gets a stitch while playing chase, one crosses one's fingers and says "Kings" and the person who is "he" does not chase one until one is ready.'

Similarly an 11-year-old Headington girl:

'If you don't want to be tug when you play tig you keep your fingers crossed and call out "cruses".'

A 10-year-old Bishop Auckland boy:

'Scinch – you cross your fingers and walk to the other gang to tell them something.'

A 9-year-old Ipswich girl describing 'Kiss Chase':

'Boys chase girls and if they catch them kiss them. If you don't want to be kissed say "exsie".'

'Sometimes', remarks a boy at Shoreham-by-Sea (where the truce term is 'fains' or 'vains'), 'when people have been saying "vains" too much we say "No vains in the game" before we play a game which contains running about.'

It will be appreciated that uttering a truce term does not of itself imply that a child has given in or surrendered, although it may sometimes be used preparatory to surrendering. A London urchin when fighting may cry 'faynights', whereupon his opponent, on ceasing to belabour him, may inquire 'Wanna give in?' and the boy will perhaps do so ('Okay, you win, leave me alone'). But more often, if a boy says 'faynights' or 'faynights –

hang on a sec' in the middle of a struggle, he does so because he wants to take off his jacket or his glasses before continuing the combat. And before we ourselves appreciated that children were sensitive to the difference between making a truce and surrendering, we were puzzled by the number of boys who declared stoutly (and correctly) that they had no term for giving in.[1]

In England and Wales the usual way a child shows that he wants to drop out of a game is by crossing fingers. Usually it is considered enough if he crosses the first and second fingers of one hand; but sometimes he must cross the fingers of both hands, and hold them up, and he may have to keep his fingers crossed all the time he wants to be immune – even when tying a shoelace. Occasionally feet are crossed as well, or instead; and at Headington, in an extreme situation, the child sits on the ground cross-legged.[2] At Lydney, although the majority cross their fingers and say 'cruce', some say 'cree' and raise their right hand, palm forwards. At Bradford-on-Avon children hold their hand up and extend three fingers. In Ipswich when saying 'exsie', 'exes', or 'scrucies' children hold up only their right hand with crossed fingers: to hold up the left hand or both hands is reputed to be unlucky.

In Scotland, instead of crossing fingers, it is customary to put thumbs up, sometimes licking them first. In Lancashire, although the usual practice is to cross fingers, in a few places, for instance Radcliffe and Nelson, some children raise their thumbs as in Scotland, and in South Elmsall, in Yorkshire, some children declare their immunity by crying 'I've got my thumbs up'.

As will have been noticed, the word a child uses varies according to the part of Britain where he lives. In some places more than one term is current, and occasionally the pupils at a school will between them know four or five terms so that, at the outset, the words appear to be of purely arbitrary adoption. Children at Kirkcaldy High School, for instance, when first questioned, produced the terms: barleys, barrels, bees, tibs, tubs, dubs or dubbies, thumbs, checks, peas, pearls, and parleys.

1. Thus a teacher in the East End of London writes: 'The boys like fighting – often with the intention of inflicting as much damage as possible. When I, consulting your notes, asked them what they said when they'd had enough of the fight and wanted to give in they said: "We don't give in, Miss".' And by way of illustration she adds: 'One boy came to me last week rubbing his head and looking rather white, so I asked him what was wrong. He said, "A boy hit my head against the wall so hard that my memory left it for a minute".'
2. Out-of-the-way actions like this usually belong to individual relief or sanctuary games such as 'Touch Wood', 'Tiggy Touch Colour', 'Stoop for your Life', or 'One two three Block'.

A class at the Southern Grammar School for Girls, Portsmouth, knew: creams, creamos, creamy-olivers, ollyoxalls, olly-olly-ee, double queenie, cross kings, fingers, pax, and also said that they shouted 'breather'.

Further investigation, however, showed more uniformity. At Kirkcaldy, when each child wrote down the terms he or she used, 'barleys' or the similar-sounding 'barrels' was named 42 times, 'thumbs' or 'thumbs up' – which is the truce sign – 20 times, and no other term was mentioned more than five times.

At Portsmouth it was soon clear that the common term is 'creams' – two of the other terms being puns on creams; while 'olly-olly-ee' is properly a call to end a game, and other terms were the recollections of children who had been to primary schools in other areas.

When a sample class of 30 children were questioned at Welwyn, 29 of the 30 gave either 'fains' or 'fainites':

24 gave 'fains' (sometimes spelt 'veins') as first or only truce term

5 gave 'fainites' (sometimes spelt 'vainites')

1 only gave 'pax'.

Investigations at other schools confirm that one term is usually predominant; and it is only these predominant terms which are discussed hereafter and are plotted on the distribution maps.

At Knighton Secondary Modern School, however, it was found that while some children declared that the usual term was 'cree', others were strong for 'barley', and it was realized that the territories where these two truce terms are honoured probably met in the school's contributory area – a region of some 100 square miles – for 'cree' is prevalent to the south around the Bristol Channel, and 'barley' is the usual term in north and mid-Wales.

The map prepared by Mr Frank Noble (Fig. 4) showing the truce terms according to the primary schools which the children had previously attended, does not reveal a clear division, for there is bound to be overlapping on a border. But when a map covers a greater area, as that of Lincolnshire (Fig. 5) prepared by Mr Roy Dunstan from information supplied by students attending Lincoln Technical College, a more definite demarcation line becomes apparent.

A point of interest in the Lincolnshire map is that it suggests that Market Rasen is on the boundary between the 'crosses' country and the territory ruled by 'kings'; and Mr S. V. Vickers, headmaster of the Modern School at Market Rasen, followed this up by interrogating 294 of his pupils whose homes, like those of the Knighton pupils, are spread over a considerable area around the town. His map (Fig. 6) confirms Mr

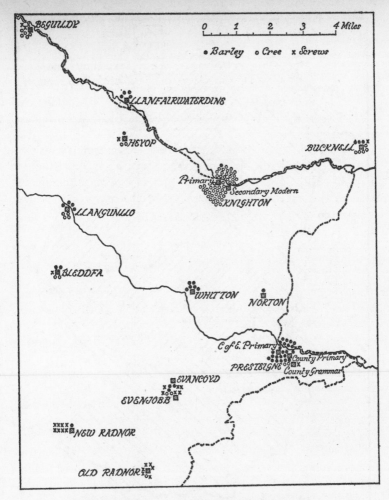

4   Truce terms in the vicinity of Knighton, Radnorshire

Dunstan's findings. Mr Vickers found that although most of his children
were aware of both terms, those coming from the east definitely favoured
'crosses', while those from the north-west preferred 'kings'. It will be
noticed, nevertheless, that while the children living in Market Rasen itself
are fairly evenly divided between 'crosses' (42 children) and 'kings' (30
children), comparatively few children support 'kings' in the immediate
countryside. The situation of urban children being at odds with the

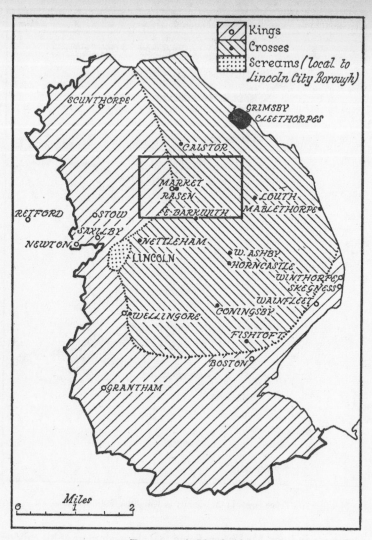

Kings
Crosses
Screams *(local to Lincoln City Borough)*

SCUNTHORPE

GRIMSBY
CLEETHORPES

CAISTOR

MARKET
RASEN
E. BARKWITH

RETFORD

STOW

LOUTH
MABLETHORPE

SAXILBY

NEWTON

NETTLEHAM

LINCOLN

W. ASHBY
HORNCASTLE

WINTHORPE
SKEGNESS

WAINFLEET

WELLINGORE

CONINGSBY

FISHTOFT

BOSTON

GRANTHAM

Miles
0   1   2

5   Truce terms in Lincolnshire

surrounding countryside can also be noted in the other two maps: Lincoln City being unlike the rest of the county with its 'screams', and Knighton being predominantly 'cree' in an area cultivating 'barley'.

In general, however, as we have said, a single truce term, or at most a pair of terms, predominates over a wide area, and Britain appears to be

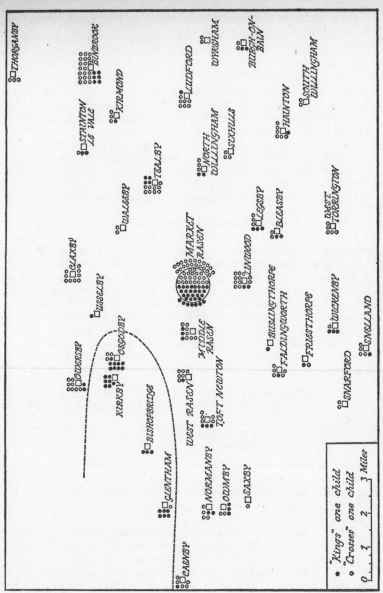

6 Truce terms in the vicinity of Market Rasen, Lincolnshire

divided into nine main truce-term territories. Fig. 7 will, we believe, be found to be correct for about 90 per cent of the juvenile population, especially if the following notes on individual terms are consulted while using the map.

Arley. An occasional shortening of 'barley' in, for instance, Birmingham. Cf. *Arlies* in *The English Dialect Dictionary*, vol. i, 1896, south Cheshire: 'If one boy was chasing another, and the latter cried "arlies", he would expect to be allowed a little breathing space before the chase was resumed.'

Ballow. A form of 'barlow', in north-west England, apparently dying out as a truce term while remaining current for claiming (p. 155). *The English Dialect Dictionary* gives an 1870 Lancashire reference to 'balla my hand' for the temporary cessation of a game; and a contributor to *The Listener*, 18 November 1954, gives 'I'm balluz' (with a short 'a') from her Salford childhood.

Bar. See *bars*.

Barbee. An alternative to 'barlow' in and around Penrith.

Barley. Prevailing term in east Scotland and the Borders, Lake District, north-west England, west midlands, and in Wales except for the south-east where 'cree' prevails. A Birmingham boy, aged 10, writes: 'I don't mean the barley what grows, but when you feel like a rest in a game you cross your fingers and shout "Barley upp!"' In Lanarkshire they sometimes shout: 'Gie's a bawley.' 'Barley' seems formerly to have extended over more of Scotland than it does today. Twenty or thirty years ago in, for instance, Kilmarnock the prevailing term was 'barley' or 'baurley', and not 'keys' as it is today.

** Barley has a wonderfully long history in north-west England. In the fourteenth-century alliterative poem *Sir Gawayne and the Grene Knight*, lines 294–8 read:

> 'And I shal stonde hym a strok, · stif on this flet;
> Elles thou wil dight me the dom · to dele him an other,
>   barlay,
>   And yet gif him respite,
>   A twelmonith and a day.'

When it is remembered that this poem was probably written in Lancashire, and that it is in North-West Midland dialect, there seems little doubt that the word 'barlay', which has troubled many a learned commentator, is one which is still, 600 years later, being glossed by the street-boys of Liverpool and Rochdale.

The term has also long been current in Scotland. Smollett, who went to Dumbarton school, has Maclaymore in *The Reprisal*, 1757, act II, sc. iii, exclaim: 'Never fash your noddle about me; conscience! I'se no be the first to cry Barley.' Scott in *Waverley*, 1814, ch. xlii, describes Edward as 'clean-made and deliver, and like a proper lad o' his quarters, that will not cry barley in a brulzie'. And Jamieson in his *Scottish Dictionary*, vol. i, 1808, is explicit about the word: 'Barley, s. A term used in the games of children, when a truce is demanded.'

Compare 'barley-fummel', the old Scottish call for a truce by one who has fallen in wrestling or fighting. In 'Chrysts-Kirk of the Grene', a poem some-

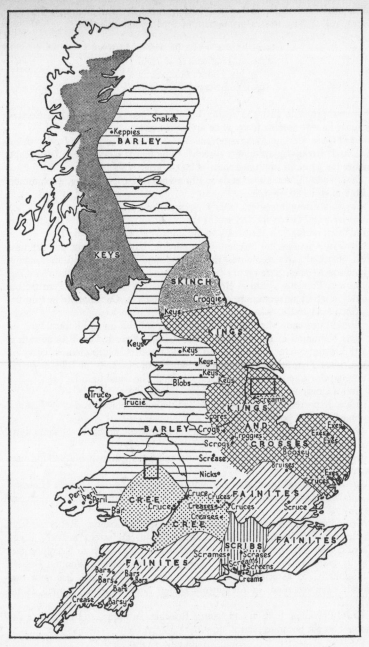

7 Truce terms in Great Britain

times attributed to James I of Scotland (printed in Allan Ramsay's *The Ever Green*, vol. i, 1724, from a manuscript of 1568), verse 15 ends:

> Thocht he was wicht, he was nocht wyss,
> With sic Jangleurs to jummill;
> For frae his Thoume they dang a Sklyss,
> Quhyle he cry'd *Barlafummill*.

It seems probable that the reason his thumb was sliced was that, Scottish fashion, he was holding it up while crying the truce.

Barley-bay. Heslop, *Northumberland Words*, 1892, gives 'barley-bay', 'barley-faa', and 'barley-faa-an'-king's speech'. 'The words always mean the speaker wishes the game to stop until some point of order is settled.'

Barley-bees. The common term in Shrewsbury, 'barleys' being less common. Also known in Edinburgh.

Barley-o. Broughton Beck (near Ulverston) and Preston.

Barley-play. Given for Orkney in the *Scottish National Dictionary*, together with 'barley-brok', 'barlo-brok', 'barrels-broken', and 'bollo-brok'.

Barleys. Aberdeen (or 'barleys on'), Airdrie, Kirkcaldy (most popular term with 'barrels'), Newtonmore. In England and Wales: Lichfield, Ludlow, Manchester (Sale), Shrewsbury (see *barley-bees*), Welshpool.

Barlow. Prevailing term in Bradford and district, Halifax, and Penrith (but not so much in surrounding countryside, see *skinch*). Occasionally in Furness. In Congleton and Ruthin they say 'barlows'. Cf. *ballow*.

Barrels. Common alternative to 'barleys' in Edinburgh and Kirkcaldy.

Bars. Common in Devon (along with 'fains'). Reported from Bondleigh in north Devon; Exeter and vicinity in south Devon. Also reported as 'barsy' or 'barsies' at Plympton St Mary, and 'barsies' or 'bargees' at Billacombe. In Swansea, the other side of the Bristol Channel, the usual term is 'bar'.

Bees. Occasional alternative to 'barley'. Kirkcaldy and Perth.

Blobs. Reported at Great Lever, Bolton. 'Shout "blobs" and cross first and second fingers of both hands.'

Boosey. Isle of Ely. In Cambridge they cry 'bruises', probably the same word, and perhaps a corruption of 'cruces'.

Creams. Prevailing term in Portsmouth, and has apparently been so for more than fifty years. Cf. *screams*.

Creases. Wantage, Berkshire, and north to just across the Thames. 'Creases' is thus the transition term between the 'cree' of north Wiltshire and the 'cruces' of Oxford.

Cree. Prevailing term both sides of the Bristol Channel. Reported from Bridgwater, Burnham, Weston-super-Mare, Bristol (cf. 'screes' in Bath), Barry, Cardiff, Newport, and Monmouth. The area extends north to Knighton (see Fig. 4), taking in Pontypridd and Abergavenny, and east to Wootton Bassett. Occasionally, by association, 'cree' is rendered 'free'. 'Cree' has once previously been recorded: in *The English Dialect Dictionary*, vol. i, 1898, North Wiltshire.

Cribs. Prevailing term in and around Reading, and south to Basingstoke and Hook where it becomes 'scribs' (q.v.).

Croggies. Leicester and district. But 'crogs' at Shepshed, 'scrogs' at Countesthorpe, 'squoggies' at Aylestone. 'Croggie' is also general in West Hartlepool although the usual term in County Durham is 'skinch'. Possibly a form of 'cross-keys'.

Crosses. The usual term in Cleethorpes and north-east Lincolnshire (see Fig. 5). Also found, generally as an alternative, in a number of unrelated places, e.g. at Beaulieu Road Station in the New Forest (as alternative to 'squibs'), Little Habton, near Malton ('I crosses'), Nottingham, and Peterborough ('I've got crosses').

Cross keys. Andover, South Elmsall, Stamford, as alternative to 'crosses'.

Cruce. Predominant term in Lydney and Gloucester, while farther to the east 'cruces' is predominant in Burford, Witney, Oxford, and Headington. Cf. *creases, crosses*.

Den or *denny*. Occasionally used as truce term, from the 'den' or sanctuary of certain catching games.

Exes. The usual term in and around Ispwich and Norwich. Probably a form of 'crosses'.

Eggshell, I'm in my. Common phrase amongst boys in Peterborough. 'No tiggin' in eggshell.' 'I'm still in my eggshell, dopey. My feet are crossed.' Probably from a local sanctuary game.

Fains or *fainites*. The usual term in London, and throughout southern England from Margate to Penzance – except for the 'scribs' and 'screams' of east Hampshire, and the 'bars' of Devon. Also prevails north of London as far as Olney, and Maids Moreton where 'fains' and 'fainites' share currency with 'kings'. Children are often uncertain whether the word begins with an f or a v – expostulating that they have never before been asked to spell it. Variations include: 'fennits' (particularly in Kent), 'fannies' (Laverstock), 'fainies' (Maryon Park), 'fainsies' (Taunton), 'fans' (Gillingham), 'fails' (Poole), 'faylines' (Torquay), 'vainlights' (Peckham), 'vainyards' (Lancing).

*** 'Fains' appears to be the earliest form. 'Fains or fain it – A term demanding a "truce" during the progress of any game, which is always granted by the opposing party' – is recorded in *Notes and Queries*, 4th ser., vol. vi, 1870, p. 415, and said to be in common use by London schoolboys. 'Faints' is not recorded until Barrère and Leland's *Dictionary of Slang*, 1889; 'fainits' not until Farmer and Henley's *Slang*, 1891. 'Faynights' is said by a correspondent to *The Sunday Times*, 25 November 1951, to have been in use about 1900. Professor J. R. R. Tolkien told us that both the term 'fains I', I decline (p. 160), and the truce term 'fains' or 'fainites', are survivals of medieval English, the basic expression being 'fain I'. 'This descends from fourteenth century *feine, faine* "feign", in a sense, derived from Old French *se feindre*, "make excuses, hang back, back out (esp. of battle)".' He noted that the word *fen*, 'ban, bar' (p. 160) is probably derived from *fend*, shortened form of *defend*, since *defend* was used in the French sense 'forbid' from about A.D. 1300 to the time of Milton. 'The formula *fain I*', he added, 'seems to throw light on a line in Chaucer which no editor so far has thought worthy of a note, though its transitive use of *feyne* has no exact parallel. In the *Clerk's Tale*, 529, a servant says "that lordes heestes mowe nat been yfeyned", and seems to mean that "lords' orders cannot be treated with a 'fain I' (I decline), but must be obeyed".'

Finns. Guernsey.

Free. Occasional rationalization of 'cree', for instance at Penmark, near Barry, and Abbots Leigh, near Bristol.

Keppies. 'I'm keppies', holding up both thumbs. Alternative to 'barleys' at Newtonmore, Inverness-shire.

Keys. Prevailing term in western Scotland from Port Patrick in Wigtownshire and Dalbeattie in Kirkcudbrightshire, north to Golspie and Lairg – farther north (Kinlochbervie, Durness, and Wick) no truce term or sign seems to be operative. 'Keys' is the usual term in Kilmarnock and Ayr (in Burns's day it was probably 'barley'), in Rothesay on the Isle of Bute, in Glasgow, and eastwards to Cumbernauld and Stirling. In England it is found in a strip running from Holmfirth and South Elmsall, by Halifax, and up to Stainton in Cumberland. Also reported in the Barrow area.

Kings. Common in eastern England, in an area extending from Leighton Buzzard to the Tees. *The English Dialect Dictionary* suggests much the same area in the nineteenth century. Earliest recording of the term is in Sternberg's *Dialect of Northamptonshire*, 1851, and it is still the usual term at, for instance, Northampton Grammar School.

Locks. Given by several children at Ruthin. At South Elmsall, and at Alfreton in Derbyshire, several give 'lick-lock' or 'lick-lock I'm in my den'.

Nicks or *nix*. Prevailing term in Warwick. According to the *Warwickshire Word-Book*, 1896, it used to be 'nicklas'.

Parley or *parleys*. Reported as an alternative term in Kirkcaldy, Findhorn in Morayshire, and from the Windermere district. Apparently always chiefly a Scottish term. *O.E.D.* quotes the Aberdeenshire poet William Meston, 1723:

> On it [his skull] you might thresh wheat or barley,
> Or tread the grape ere he cry'd parley.

Pax. The usual term in private schools and school stories, 'pax' is group dialect not regional dialect. Thus a 14-year-old prep. school girl in 1954: 'When life becomes too bad you shriek "*Pax*". Once you have uttered this magic word you are safe. To break a *pax* is an unforgivable crime.' And Charlotte M. Yonge, *The Daisy Chain*, 1856, ch. i: ' "*Pax! Pax!*" cried Norman, over all, with the voice of an authority, as he leapt up lightly and set Tom on his legs again.'

Peas. Occasional term in Kirkcaldy, Stirling, and Penrith.

Peril. The established term in the Haverfordwest–Narberth–Foxhall area of south Pembrokeshire.

Queens. Occasionally used in the 'kings' area, but if it was originally a pun it is an old one. Heslop, *Northumberland Words*, 1894, gives 'Queen's Play' as a truce term. Blakeborough, *North Riding of Yorkshire*, 1898, gives 'queenie': 'Whilst anyone had hold of wood, and cried "Queenie", or wet his finger calling out "I'm wet", such for the time being was secure from receiving the last tig (bat or touch) on parting for the night.' In some places, as at Doncaster, a child calls 'Queens' when ready to begin playing again.

Quits. Probably not an 'authentic' truce term, but given by a number of children in different parts of Britain, e.g. Bolton, Croydon, and Sherwood, usually as an alternative to a regional term, and repeated in usual manner holding up crossed fingers. Similar descriptive terms are 'halts' (Frome, Somerset), 'rest' (Hook Norton), and 'stay' (Stoke-on-Trent).

Scores. Prevailing term in Derby. Other terms in use in the town are 'crosses' and 'pax'.

Scrases. The usual term in Alton, and has been so for fifty years, although 'scribs' (q.v.), the predominant Hampshire term, is common in the junior schools. Other Hampshire variants are 'scrims' (Herriard), 'screens' (Denmead), 'scrames' (Winchester, since anyway 1900), 'screams' (Fareham), and 'creams' (Portsmouth).

Screase. Coventry. Cf. *screes.*

Screams. The common term in Lincoln City (see Fig. 6). In 1866 Brogden in his *Provincial Words and Expressions current in Lincolnshire* gave 'screen'. See also under *scrases.*

Screes. Bath. Cf. *cree.*

Screws, screwsies, or *scruces.* The usual term in Ipswich and elsewhere in Suffolk, occasionally in Essex. Cf. *cruces.*

Scribs or *squibs.* Covers an area from Basingstoke and Chertsey (both 'scribs') to Southampton and Horsham (both 'squibs'). At Guildford it is 'scribs'. In some places children use both 'scribs' and 'squibs' – 'It doesn't matter which you say'. See *cribs.*

Scrogs or *squoggies.* Leicestershire. See *crogs.*

Skinch or *skinge.* Almost invariable cry in Northumberland and Durham, and *The English Dialect Dictionary* records the same term in these two countries in the nineteenth century. At Morpeth the cry has been rationalized to 'Flinch'.

Snakes or *snecks.* Inverurie, Aberdeenshire.

Squits. Alternative to 'bruises' (see *boosey*) at Cambridge. At Charlbury, Oxon, they say 'squitsies'. Cf. *quits.*

Truce or *trucie.* Llandudno in north Wales and Llangefni in Anglesey.

Twigs. Two Penrith boys aged 9 and 10 gave this term, and their formmaster, a Cumbrian, aged 42, recollected that in his schooldays they had a custom of crossing two twigs as a sign of 'barley'. He thought it had something to do with the Holy Cross.

Vains, vainites. See *fains.*

THE language used by children attending publicly provided schools is not merely the least recorded of all the varieties of speech spoken in Britain, it is also, some will say, the least recordable. Tongue-tied though a child may be when made to use adult words, his vocabulary can be extensive when speaking his own language. For instance a pair of Hertfordshire 14-year-olds, of not notably high I.Q., when asked about their classmates and invited to set down their epithets for them, promptly came to life and wrote:

'Phumph, lumber bontts [bonce], lush, Gables, square head, pugh, Jimpy, Hepsiba, lofty, big head, Rudolth, hog, scoffer, flippin kid, titty, rocker box, chubby cheaks, chink, coaca, Cowson, screawy, nuts, bolts, Tweedle, woolly wog, Kedah Wong, gilly, ruby nose, Bullet Head, nutty and cominist.'

Nor is the rare child who speaks the argot of the refined adult necessarily unilingual. In a debate in the House of Commons (11 March 1949) the ex-schoolmaster member for Southampton, Ralph Morley, told how, near the school where he was once teaching, there was a girls' school with a teacher who was a very highly trained and enthusiastic elocutionist. 'One day she brought one of her girls into our assembly. The girl recited some poetry and although she was a working-class girl she pronounced "how" as if she had spent some considerable time at Eton and Harrow. When the assembly was over I said to my boys: "I wish you would talk as nicely as that girl whom you have just heard talk." The boys replied at once, and almost in chorus: "You ought to hear her talk in the street."'

Characteristics of Schoolchild Language

Two apparently conflicting emotions are active in schoolchild language: respect for tradition and desire for fun. Respect for tradition shows itself in their words of honour, as we have seen, and in the retention of many dialect words, for instance names for birds and animals: blackie (blackbird), barker or growler (dog), moggy (cat), drummer (snipe), horse-stinger (dragonfly), Joey (owl), Scribbly Jack (yellowhammer), spuggy (sparrow), and stiggy (starling). Their love of fun, on the other hand, is shown in the constant welcome given to slang and innovation. Money, for instance, is variously referred to as: brass, lolly, tin, dough, mazuma, moolah, dosh (common), sploosh, bees and honey, and champagne coupons. A pound is a 'quid', a 'smacker', or a 'nicker'; ten shillings is 'half a nicker' or 'half a bar'; five shillings is a 'dollar'; one shilling is a 'bob', 'dienner', or 'thumber'; sixpence is a 'kick', 'sprat', or 'tanner'; a threepenny piece is a 'bit' or 'tiddler'; and twopence is 'deuce'. Coppers are referred to as 'mouldies'.[1] A penny is a 'clod' or a 'dee' (usually spoken of as 'one dee'), a halfpenny is a 'meg' or 'rusty meg', a farthing is a 'mite', and to have nothing is to be 'skint' or 'boko'.

Occasionally children's names for things are expressive, almost amounting to poetic speech: a postman, in Aberdeen, is 'Slottie Johnnie', a tramp, very generally, is a 'milestone inspector', the floor is the 'dog's shelf', a boy's mouth is his 'cake hole', his stomach is his 'breadbasket' or 'porridge bag', and large feet are 'beetle crushers'.

Chiefly, however, children go in for short sharp words, as in their more usual names for parts of the body: 'nob', 'nut', 'loaf', 'bonce', 'block', and 'dome' for head: 'mug', 'dial', and 'phiz' for face; 'conk', 'beak', 'snitch', 'snout', 'snot-box', 'snorer', 'snozzle', and 'boko' for nose; 'gob' for mouth; 'flaps' or 'lugs' for ears; 'mitts', 'dukes', or 'paws' for hands. Sometimes they have the most breath-saving past tenses: 'tug' for tigged (i.e. touched), 'scum' for skimmed, 'thunk' for thought, and 'knat' for knitted.

But perhaps the most distinctive feature of juvenile parlance is the use of the standard endings, -ass, -bug, -cat, -dick, -gog, -guts, -pot, -puss, -sides, and, most of all, -ies or -sy, endings which are regularly affixed to certain words. These syllables are used either to replace the second half of a word, as: newbug, rasbug, strawbug, goosegog, and wellygogs (Wellington boots); or to turn a verb or adjective into a descriptive noun, as: creep-ass, squall-ass, copycat, stare-cat, tease-cat, funny-dick, cleverdick, greedy-guts, grizzle-guts, lazy-guts, scabby-guts, fuss-pot, stink-pot, swank-pot, blubber-puss, sleepy-puss, sour-puss, sobersides, solemnsides, and – in games terminology – onesies, twosies, commonies, shotties, farsy, nearsy, plainsy, and dumbsy. In fact the addition of 'ies' is so common it

1. On Derby Day boys at Chessington call out to motorists returning from the races, 'Throw out your mouldies', and scramble for anything thrown.

is sometimes added where not absolutely necessary, for instance in the school chant: 'Easties are beasties, Northies are horsies, Westies are besties.' Sometimes, indeed, the addition is a matter of conscious preference; thus a Dulwich girl, giving the rhyme,

> Good night, sweet repose,
> Mind the mosquitoes don't bite your toes,

added, 'That's how I was told it, but I always say "reposes" and "toeses" because I like it better.'

Their Own Name

Children attach an almost primitive significance to people's names, always wanting to find out a stranger's name, yet being correspondingly reluctant to reveal their own. They have ways of avoiding telling their name. They answer, 'Haven't got a name, only got a number.' They say, 'Same name as me Dad.'

'What's your Dad's then?'

'Same as mine.'[1]

And there is the recurrent set-piece: 'What's your name?' 'Sarah Jane.' 'Where do you live?' 'Down the lane.' 'What's your number?' 'Cucumber.' 'What's your shop?' 'Lollipop.' 'What's your town?' 'Dressing-gown.' It can be a blessing to a new child to know a formula like this. Girls circle round a new girl, crying 'What's your name? What's your name?' and the circle will disperse only if the untrue ritual answer is forthcoming. Sometimes a game can be joined only if the correct response is made to 'What's your number?' 'Cucumber.' Real Sarah Janes, Mary Janes, and Elizabeth Janes are teased with the pointless questions. And sometimes children recite the curious catechism, or catechize each other,

---

1. Cf. the French child:

> – Comment t'appelles-tu?
> – Je m'appelle comme mon père.
> – Et ton père?
> – Mon père s'appelle comme moi.
> – Comment vous appelez-vous tous les deux?
> – Nous nous appelons l'un comme l'autre.

(E. Rolland, *Rimes et Jeux de l'Enfance*, 1883, p. 301.)

for no reason except that children have been doing so since time long ago.

What's your name?
Mary Jane.
Where do you live?
Down the grid.
What number?
Cucumber.
What street?
Pig street.
Lancaster.

What's your name?
Lady Jane.
Where do you live?
Cabbage Lane.
What's your number?
Bread and cucumber.
What's your address?
Bread and watercress.
Market Rasen.

What's your name?
Baldy Bain.
What's your ither?
Ask ma mither.
Glasgow.

What's your name?
Mary Jane.
Where do you live?
Down the lane.
What do you keep?
A little shop.
What do you sell?
Ginger pop.
How many bottles do you sell
  in a day?
Twenty-four, now go away.
Swansea, for skipping.

What's your name?
Elecampane (or 'elegant pain').
What's your number?
Cucumber.
What's your road?
Big black toad.
Nottingham.

In Alton, Hampshire, the very clever have lately learned to say:

My name is:
Addi, addi, chickeri, chickeri,
Ooney, pooney, om pom alari,
Alla balla whisky,
Chinese salt!

In the United States:

What's your name?
Puddin Tame.
Ask me again
And I'll tell you the same.
Maryland.

What's your name?
John Brown.
Ask me again
And I'll knock you down.
New Jersey.

*** The Maryland verse has previously been recorded in *The Sussex Archaeological Collections*, 1861, 'What's yer naüm? Pudden and taüm; Ax me agin, and I'll tell ye da saüm', given as current 'thirty or forty years ago' (i.e. *c.* 1825). 'Pudding and Tame' seems to preserve the name of the fiend or devil, 'Pudding-of-Tame', listed in Samuel Harsnet's

Popish Impostures, 1603. A number of similar formulas were collected in the nineteenth century, e.g.:

> What do they call you? Patchy Dolly.
> Where were you born? In the cow's horn.
> Where were you bred? In the cow's head.
> Where will you die? In the cow's eye.
>
> *J. O. Halliwell, 'Nursery Rhymes', 1844, p. 162.*

What's your name? Mary Jane.
Where do you live? Womber Lane.
What do you do? Keep a school.
How many scholars? Twenty-two.

How many more? Twenty-four.
What's your number? Cucumber!

Birmingham, G. F. Northall, 'English Folk-Rhymes', 1892, p. 317, q.v. for further references.

Other People's Names

Needless to say children are not respecters of names once they have learnt them, and have a fondness, in particular, for giving a familiar sound to those names which are unfamiliar to them. Thus Edwin Schiff becomes 'Bedouin Chief', Clara Dace becomes 'Clear-a-space', and Fred Maddox becomes 'Fresh Haddocks'. (Baden-Powell, at Charterhouse, was known as 'Bathing Towel'.) Puns or abridgements are introduced whenever possible. A boy with the surname Wood will be called 'Splinter', a boy surnamed Bell will be 'Dinger'. Sedgewick will be reduced to 'Sedge', and Nixon to 'Nick'; Poulton will be turned to 'Polly', and June become 'Spoon'.

Children like names which fall into patterns, and for more than a hundred years they have been fitting people's names into peculiar spell-like mocking chants.

Maggy, my maggy,
My rick stick staggy,
Hum bug,
Belly bug,
Bandy-legged Maggy.

Aberdeen.

Jenny, my benny,
My rick stick stenny,
Hum bug,
Belly bug,
Bandy-legged Jenny.

Same formula, applied to Jenny.

Similar is:

Joan the roan,
The rix stix stoan,
The iron-nosed,
The copper-nosed,
The bandy-legged Joan.

London.

Joan Hassall, when a girl, was called:

Joan to oan,
Pepp-in-tus scoan,
Frastockadilla moan,
Fring frang-froan.

Surrey.

178

Sometimes this play on names is known as 'new spelling' and goes:

Shirley-wirley,	John-won,
Nick and nirley,	Nick and non,
Pam birley,	Pam bon,
Bobby rirley,	Bobby ron,
That's the way to spell Shirley.	That's the way to spell John.
Cambridge.	*London.*

*** Amongst American children the formula usually seems to be on the lines of: 'Annie bom bannie, tilly Annie, go sannie, tea legged, tie legged, bow legged Annie.' This follows fairly closely the formulas current in Britain at the end of the nineteenth century. Northall, 1892, p. 304, says that the following was employed by children in the Midlands before 1850: 'George, Porge, the rix-tix Torge, The rhibo, the rhambo, The cocktail'd George.'

Traditional Nicknames

Certain nicknames belong by tradition to the bearers of particular names, and children seem to be as familiar with them as are servicemen and factory workers. Charlie is known as 'Chuck', Derrick is 'Dekker', Maurice is 'Mogga', and Michael is 'Spike'. There are inevitable pre-fixes to certain surnames: 'Nobby' Clark, 'Pincher' Martin, 'Dusty' Miller, 'Spud' Murphy, 'Tug' Wilson, and 'Shiner' Wright. One-syllable names tend to be elongated: Brown becomes 'Brownie', Jones becomes 'Jonesey', and Smith is rarely left alone, becoming 'Smitty', 'Smithy', 'Smutty', or 'Smudger'. Unlike the adult world, children attach stock jokes to certain names. Any Dennis is, on the slightest pre-text, named 'Dennis the Menace', Eustace is 'Useless', Claud is 'Clumsy', and Mary is greeted with the silly query 'Where's your lamb?' Certain scraps of doggerel are associated with particular names, and many a Tom, Dick, and Charlie has complained that these verses have followed him throughout his school life.

Bobby	Bobby, Bobby, number nine, Sewed his breeks with binder twine.
Charlie	Charlie, Charlie, chuck, chuck, chuck, Went to bed with three young ducks.
Dan	Dan, Dan, the dirty old man, Washed his face in a frying pan.

David	Davie, Davie, fie for shame,
	Kissed the girls in a railway train.
	Davy, Davy,
	Stick him in the gravy.
George	Georgie Porgie, pudding and pie,
	Kissed the girls and made them cry.
Mary	Mary, Mary,
	Quite contrary.[1]
Peter	Peter's pop kept a lollipop shop,
	And the lollipop shop kept Peter.
Richard	Dicky, Dicky Doubt,
	Your shirt hangs out.
Stephen	Stephen, Stephen,
	Cut the loaf even.
Tom	Tam, Tam Parker,
	Went up the lum farten.

Kirkcaldy.

In Wales, says an Aberystwyth girl, when someone unpopular is called Jones she is followed with the cry:

> *Elizabeth* Jones broke her bones
> Tumbling down cherry stones.

A Knighton girl adds:

> Bach Jones, a bag of bones,
> A belly full of fat;
> When he dies he shuts his eyes,
> And what do you think of that?

And everywhere the common rebuttal by the child who is called a name is the philosophical recitation:

> Sticks and stones may break my bones
> But names will never hurt me.
> When I'm dead and in my grave
> You'll be sorry for what you've called me.

'That's the worst of calling people names, they reply "Sticks and stones",' remarked a 9-year-old, bitterly. 'I mostly don't call people names.'

1. One Mary who was teased by this rhyme was the Mary in Mrs Hodgson Burnett's *The Secret Garden*, 1911.

Approval and Disapproval

Few terms change in fashion more decisively than those expressing approval. From about 1947 the word of the decade was 'smashing'. Lord Russell of Liverpool (*Daily Telegraph*, 2 July 1953) justly remarked: 'In my school days it was "topping" and "ripping". These were followed by "super" and "wizard" and now, I regret to say, everything is "smashing".' With some children the word broke into every sentence. Roller-skaters outside on the pavement were heard saying, 'It's smashin 'ere. You come over this side – smashin an' smooth. Get along smashin.' A good 'book' (i.e. a magazine) was said to be 'smashin', a film was 'smashin', a film star – of the opposite sex – was a 'smasher' (thirty years earlier he or she would have been a 'stunner'; a hundred years earlier a 'spanker'), and a show-off was derided: 'I say what a smasher, two fried eggs and a gammon rasher!'

Other superlatives in favour were: bang on, beezer,[1] bonza, flashy, lush (by far the favourite adjective with Oxford children in 1953), luscious, smack on, snazzy, and spazzy (used particularly of costume), spiffing, spivving or spivvy (a girl might be 'spivvy stuff'), smacking, smasho, super (still very common), super-duper, super-slobby-dobs (used of 'anything that tastes nice like ice lollies'), supersonic (a most popular superlative since 1952), swell, whizzing, whiz-bang, whizzo, whizzol, and wizard (still common).

Cries of jubilation include: Wow! Whacko! Goody gumdrops! Lovely grub! and By gog jolly custard!

Terms of disapproval, on the other hand, scarcely alter from generation to generation. Except for the new lamentations 'grue' or 'grooh' (from gruesome) and 'chiz' or 'chiz-chiz' (cross between chisel and swiz?), juvenile repugnance continues to be expressed by the old standbys: blinking awful, bloomin orrible, boring, cheesy, chronic, corny, daft, disgraceful, flipping awful, foul, fusty, frowsy, ghastly, hateful, idiotic, lousy (very frequent), mardy, mildewed, mingy, misery-making, mouldy, mucky, nasty, no fair, no good, orrid (usual spelling), outrageous, pesky, putrid, poor effort, revolting 'just like turnip and swede', rotten, rotten shame, rotten swiz, scabby, shocking, soppy, spiteful, stale, stingy, stinking, super-ghastly – Ugh! O lor! Gosh! Golliwogs! What a chiz!

1. On 21 January 1956, D. C. Thomson & Co., Dundee, launched a threepenny comic called *Beezer* Some terms of approbation might well be dated by the names given to children's comics, as *Champion* (published in 1922), *Wizard* (1922), *Triumph* (1924), and *Dandy* (1937).

Such words, needless to say, are looked upon as unexceptionable. Every few years the could-be-true story reappears in the press of an old lady saying to her granddaughter: 'My dear, there are two words I wish you would promise me never to use. One is "swell" and the other is "lousy".'

'Sure, gran,' says the good-natured schoolgirl, 'I'll promise. What are the two words?'

School Dinners[1]

The possessors of young and healthy appetites are lyrical about their food. School dinners are 'muck', 'pig swill', 'poison', 'slops', 'S.O.S.' (Same Old Slush), and 'Y.M.C.A.' (Yesterday's Muck Cooked Again). A current joke is 'School Dinners by Major Sick'. And the meals may be queued for, devoured, or left on the plate to the music of:

Come to the cook-house door,
Come to the cook-house door,
Fill your belly full of jelly,
Come to the cook-house door.

Newcastle. Sung to the bugle call.

What's for dinner? What's for dinner?
Irish spew, Irish spew,
Sloppy semolina, sloppy semolina,
No thank you, no thank you.

Lydney. Sung to 'Frère Jacques'.

Say what you will,
School dinners make you ill,
And shepherd's pie
Makes Davy Crockett cry;
All school din-dins
Come from pigs' bins
  – That's no lie.

Alton, Great Bookham, and Tooting. Became current October 1956. Sung to 'Out of Town'.

If you stay to school dinners
Better throw them aside,
A lot of kids didn't,
A lot of kids died.
The meat is of iron,
The spuds are of steel,
If that don't get you
Then the afters will.

Brentwood and Enfield. Current April 1957. Sung to 'Sixteen Tons'.

'Today's Menu'

Splishy splashy custard,
  dead dogs' eyes,
All mixed up with giblet pies,
Spread it on the butty[2] nice and thick,
Swallow it down with a bucket of sick.

Manchester.

Slab a pab of custard, green dog eye,
All mixed together with a dead cat's
  eye,
Slap it on thick,
Then swill it down with a cup of cold
sick.

Blackburn.

1. The School Meals service was started in Britain during the Second World War. According to a count made in the autumn of 1955, 3,018,000 children in England and Wales (or 48·3 per cent of those present on the day of the count) were taking a meal at school; the cost for 1956 being estimated at £31,000,000, on top of the 9*d.* contributed by parents in respect of 90 per cent of the meals. Despite the children's (traditional) views on the subject, the School Meals service has undoubtedly contributed to the physical well-being of the rising generation.

2. *Butty*, Mancunian dialect for a sandwich snack.

Scab and matter custard,
Green snot pies,
Dead dog's giblets
Dead cat's eyes
And a cup of sick to wash it down.

Lydney.

Hotch scotch, bogie pie,
Mix it up with a dead man's eye,
Hard boiled snails, spread it thick,
Wash it down with a cup of sick.

Ipswich.

Food in general is referred to as 'bait' ('from fish bait'), 'chuck', 'grub', or 'grubber', 'munchie', 'tuck', or 'tucker'; and as 'scranner' in Ossett, Yorkshire (where 1*d.* buns are 'penny scranners').

Stew, a not infrequent component of school dinners, is 'spew', 'dog's dinner', or, in Croydon, 'nutty slack'.[1] A meat pie is 'cat's meat' or 'growler' (Manchester), mince being 'hound pudding', and cottage pie 'resurrection pie'. 'Armoured cow' proclaims that tinned corned beef is on the menu. 'And when pork or ham arrives for school lunch (which is not often),' says the headmistress of a rural junior school, 'we get in *fairly* sotto voce tones, "Yum, yum, pig's b—".'

Sausages are 'bangers', 'snorters', ''ossies', or 'dogs', and the gravy which goes with them, avers a Croydon boy, is 'bilge, tar, pitch, crude petroleum'.

Potatoes are 'murphies', 'pots', 'spuds', or 'taties'. Roast potatoes are 'Rocks of Gibraltar'. Beans are 'peens' (Kirkcaldy), and baked beans, 'cowboy's breakfast' (very general). Peas are 'bullets' or 'cannon balls'; and pea soup is 'London fog' (Portsmouth), an inversion of the usual saying.

School cabbage is 'garbage' or 'seaweed' apparently all over Britain. Turnips are 'neeps', or 'tumshies' in Scotland, or 'snaggers' (in Bishop Auckland). Tomatoes are generally 'squashers', and 'rabbit's food' is any green salad.

A thick slice of bread is almost always described as a 'door step'; fried bread is 'frizzled monkey'. Margarine or 'marge' is 'Maggy Anne'. Spaghetti, naturally, is 'string' or 'worms', and macaroni is 'drainpipes' or, occasionally, 'filleted worms'. Cheese pie (in Manchester) is 'splidge'.

Children are, if possible, even less complimentary about the sweet course than about the first course. Any kind of milk pudding is 'slosh' or 'baby pudding'. Rice pudding, says a Manchester boy, is 'Three-six-five pudding' ('because it is served every day'). Should the cook-house, which is fortunately sometimes several miles away, be so rash as to send chocolate rice it is, of course, 'mud'.

---

1. After an inapt term coined by the Ministry of Fuel (1952) for a poor quality coal, obtainable off the ration. The nuts were few and far between.

Tapioca or sago is 'fishes' eyes', 'frogs' eyes', 'fishes' eyes in glue', or, very commonly, 'frog spawn'. It is a little more attractive when called 'snowball pud', and less so under the title 'snottie gog pie'. 'Cat's fish' is, perhaps, an apt term for semolina ('sister Ina') when it has become a bit dry in its travels, so is 'tadpoles in a pond' for sultanas in sago, and 'steamed stodge' describes itself.

'Spotted Dick', in Cornwall known as 'tiggy pudding', may, when it is the true roly-poly shape, be called 'Bugs in the bolster' (Portsmouth). 'Green sling' (custard), 'old man's dung' or 'squeezed cow giblets' (warm treacle), or 'Brylcreem' (white sauce), may be poured over it. Garibaldi biscuits are 'squashed flies' or 'fly pies', and Eccles or currant cake is 'flies' cemetery'. A plain suet pud and treacle, or red-jam roly-poly, passes as 'dead baby'. 'Apple nellie' (in Bishop Auckland) is apple pie, 'fuggen' (in Cornwall) is pastry with currants in it, 'atom bomb' (1952) is a tart with cream on the top, and graphically, pink blancmange is popularly known as 'baby-in-the-bath'.

'Shows who has had the most,' says the boy who has finished first, looking around at the others still eating. 'Shows who has got the biggest mouth,' replies his neighbour.

Dinner Grace:

> For what we have put back on the dish
> May the school chickens be truly grateful.

Or, when there is to be a second sitting:

> For what we have put back in the dish
> May second dinner be truly thankful.

Drinks

> Through the lips and round the gums,
> Look out, stomach, here it comes!

In Yorkshire, if children want a drink, they say 'let's have a draw'; or if it is to be a quick draught – from a bottle or under a tap – they call it a 'swag', which in Wales and southern England is a 'swig', and in Lincolnshire a 'swig-swag'.

Water is deliberately pronounced 'waiter' in Knighton, and 'watter' in Cleethorpes. More widely it is referred to as 'juice', or 'Corporation pop'.[1]

1. And 'Corporation hair-oil' is the commodity with which they (sometimes) flatten their hair of a morning.

Tea is 'char', 'grog', or 'jungle juice'. Weak tea may be 'gnat's piss', and milk is commonly 'cow juice'.[1]

And almost throughout England, from Pendeen to Bishop Auckland their favourite beverage is 'pop', which covers all acid drinks and minerals. 'Fizz' or 'fizzstuff', or 'Gassy George', are merely occasional comic alternatives. But in Lydney lemonade (or cider) is 'squonk', and in Kirkcaldy it is commonly 'skoosh' (literally, a squirt), which can also be ginger ale, and it is sometimes 'scud' or 'squirty', and far in the North, in Golspie, they call it 'snoddy' or 'lemon snoddy'.

The one drink exclusive to children is the Scottish and North Country 'sugarolly water' which they make out of a fragmented liquorice stick, sugar, and warm water, shaken up in a bottle, and left as long as possible in a cupboard until the concoction becomes nice and black. This they offer (just a sip) with the words:

> Sugarolly watter, black as the lum,
> Gaither up sticks (or 'peens') and ye'll a' get some.

Before the war juvenile salesmen were to be seen all over the cities of Edinburgh and Glasgow, but today, although still manufactured by enthusiasts, the refreshment is said to be going out of fashion.

*** 'Sugarolly water', also known as 'Spanish juice', or 'Spanish liquorice water' ('fit for a lady's daughter'), or, in the West Riding as 'spaw water' (i.e. spa water), or 'popololly', used to be a favourite beverage at Easter ('Spanish Day'), and is still made at this holiday by the Pace Eggers around Halifax. See *Leeds Mercury Supplement*, 11 April 1896 (E.D.D.). *Rymour Club Miscellanea*, vol. ii, 1913, p. 77, giving rhyme similar to today's from Kingarth School, Bute. *Word-Lore*, vol. ii, 1927, p. 191. *Sunday Mail* (Glasgow), 30 December 1951, p. 7. *John o' London's Weekly*, 'Passing Remarks' by Jackdaw, 30 May and 27 June 1952.

Ice-Creams

Cornet, Brick, and Lollipop
Taste very nice when bought from the shop.
'Saying' quoted by girl, 13, Welwyn.

The sale or ice-creams of 'I screams' ('I scream, you scream, we all scream for ice-cream') increased considerably after the war, partially due

1. The juvenile users of this phrase would be surprised to learn that it belongs to the eighteenth century, being included in Francis Grose's *Dictionary of the Vulgar Tongue*, 3rd ed., 1796. Similar schoolboy witticisms are 'cow grease' (butter), 'cackle fruit' (eggs), and 'sky juice' (rain).

to better all-the-year-round distribution; partially, perhaps, due to a determined publicity campaign by the manufacturers (not least in the children's comics);[1] and partially due to their relative cheapness. A good ice-cream could (in 1959) be bought for 3*d*. and most children who wanted to were able to afford one out of their pocket money.

In the big cities such as London and Birmingham, ice-cream is still sometimes referred to as 'hokey-pokey', or, more usually, 'okey-pokey', and youngsters may be heard chanting on appropriate occasions:

> Okey-pokey penny a lump,
> The more you eat the more you jump.[2]

The greatest innovation after the war was the 'ice-lolly', a manufacturer's clever idea (about 1945) of putting a fruit-flavoured water-ice on a stick. Ice-lollies sold for as little as 1½*d*. each (against 6*d*. for a drink), and ousted from favour the boiled-sweet lollipop, although lollipops could (in 1956) be bought which looked like fried eggs, or strawberries in cream, or were an image of Davy Crockett. Each of the 33,000 schoolchildren who, in 1953, watched Coronation procession on the Victoria Embankment was treated to an 'ice-lolly' during the seven-hour wait.

Sweets

Sweets are referred to as 'comforters', 'goodies' (a common term), 'sucks' or 'suckers' ('sookies' in Scotland), and 'quenchers'. They are also 'candies' in Cleethorpes (American influence?), 'chews' in Aberystwyth, 'trash' in Knighton, and always 'spice' in the West Riding ('Gi' us a spice'). 'Lollies' is also becoming a general term, and so is 'gobstoppers' for 'any sweet difficult to chew', as humbugs, large aniseed balls, and fruit drops. (The true, colour-changing gob-stopper was for long unobtainable during and after the war.) Most boys call toffee 'stickjaw', and consider that a better name for 'liquorice sticks' is 'stickerish licks'. Bubble gum, the new fad, with its tempting picture card in each

1. For instance, in 1953 Messrs T. Wall & Sons Ltd, the ice-cream manufacturers, a company in the Unilever group, cleverly instituted the 'Lucky W' finger-sign (made by joining together the point of each thumb and extending the forefingers), and this sign definitely caught on, for a while, in the juvenile world.
2. 'When the Indians came to England to sell Ice cream they said Okey Pokey Penny a lump' (Girl, 9, Birmingham). Except that she means 'Italians', she may be right, for *perhaps* they cried *O che poco!* (O how little!)

packet, is known as 'beetle fat'. Other sweet-shop favourites appear to be the same as in the nineteen-twenties, in fact bull's eyes, jelly babies, and dolly mixture, have entered schoolchild language as descriptive nouns.

For the record, a one-man High-Street confectioner, much patronized by schoolchildren, was found to be offering (south of England, summer 1954):

Barrat's Sherbet Fountains 12 drams net. Price 2*d*. each with liquorice 'straw'. 'Contents – Sugar, Cornflour, Citric and Tartaric Acid, Sodium Bi-Carb, Flavouring.'

Delvin's Sports Sweet Cigarettes 2*d*. a packet (of ten) with 'Famous Footballer' picture cards.

Dollar Film Star Bubble Gum 1*d*. for a single thin pink slab. 'Free in each packet glamorous Film Star Photograph.' (The one opened contained a picture of Miss Marilyn Monroe.)

Mackintosh's Rolo 6*d*. a tube (Chocolate-coated toffees).

Flying Saucers 'Something New!! (Mint Flavoured)' 2 for 1*d*. (Having the appearance of small gob-stoppers.)

Razzle-Dazzle 'Chewing Gum Balls for blowing big bubbles' 2 for 1*d*. 'Watch the colours change and then blow bubbles with the gum.'

Blue Star Pure Sherbet Sucker 1*d*. (In three-cornered paper bag with liquorice tube inserted.)

Tommy's Aniseed Balls 12 a penny. (Smaller, if memory is correct, than pre-war.)

Mars 'are marvellous' *Bars* 6*d*.

Bassett's Liquorice Allsorts 7*d*. per quarter.

Big Chief Dream Pipe 1*d*. each. (The pipe was made of a liquorice tube and had a sugar cigarette sticking in the pipe bowl.)

Beatall Lollies 1½*d*. each. (These were in fact lollipops on sticks.)

The name 'lolly' has apparently become general even in the trade. There were also round '*Football Lollies*', the size of small ping-pong balls, not on sticks. The proprietor said that he had recently had '*Traffic Light*' lollipops which when sucked turned from red to yellow to green. Also giant gob-stoppers at 1½*d*. each which had 'sold like hot cakes'. One small boy spent a regular 2*s*. 6*d*. a week pocket money on them.

Greedy-Guts

They ask a greedy-guts ('gutsy' for short) 'Do you eat to live or live to eat?' hoping he will give the self-incriminating answer. They call him: dustbin, hollow legs, hog, face-packer, gluttons, gobble-guts, Gobble Gobble Gertie, gorgey, greedy glutton, greedy-devil, greedy-grabs, greedy-hog, greedy-muffin, greedy-pig (and jeer 'The greedy pig who needs a dig'), guts, guts-ache, gutsy sod, gutter, guzzler, guzzle-guts, hungry guts, Hungry Horace, piggy, pig-hog, piganog (pig-an'-'og), pig-bin, and rumble tummy.

*** The term 'greedy-guts' is more than 400 years old; and the stock question they ask him may be almost as venerable, for Elizabethans (amongst them Northbrooke, Florio, Stubbes, and Greene) were fond of quoting the adage 'Wee must not liue to eat, but wee must eat to liue', a sentiment they had found in Plutarch and Cicero. The name Gobble Gobble Gertie, on the other hand, dates only from 1954 when a perpetually ravenous Eskimo woman was featured in a *Beano* picture story.

Fatties

> Roger Edward Ford ('*chap in our form*')
> He weighs sixteen stone,
> That's not skin and bone,
> Roger Edward Ford . . .
> > '*Song*' – Boy, *13, Croydon.*

The unfortunate fat boy, the 'ton of flesh', 'barely on two legs', who can 'pack a double-decker in his belly', and whose 'bacon bonce' (face) is flanked with 'slobber chops', is known as: back end of a bus, balloon, barrage balloon, barrel, barrel-belly, barrow-guts, big-belly-bump, Billy Bunter the Second, blood tub, bouncer, Buster, chubby, chunky, Crystal Jellybottom, diddle diddle dumpling, Falstaff, fat belly, fat duck, Fatty Harbuckle,[1] flab, football, glutton, grub-tub, guts, hammy-bones, jelly-belly, jelly-wobble, Jumbo, lumpy, lump of lardy, piggy, pillar-box, podge, porker, Porky, porridge, pud, plum-pudding, pudding-pie, rubber-guts, sausage, slob, slug, steam-roller, swell-hide, tank, human tank, ten-ton, tubs, tubby (Tubus and Magnus Tubus in grammar schools), and Two-Ton Tessy.

The names Bessy Bunter, Fatima, and Tubbelina, are usually reserved for girls.

1. This has been collected as 'Fatty Harbuckle' (London, Portsmouth, Oundle, and Worcester), 'Fatty Harbottle' (Birmingham), 'Fatty Arbicle' (Welshpool), and 'Fatty Artabuckles' (Frostburg, Maryland). None of the children who used the term, nor their teachers, realized that they were perpetuating the name of the talented corpulent comedian Roscoe Arbuckle (1887–1933) of the early Mack Sennett single-reelers. A similar name-term 'Fatty Goering' was in use amongst girls at Cleethorpes in 1952.

Skinnies

Skinny-malinky long legs
Big banana feet,
Went to the pictures
And fell through the seat.
Boy, 12, Helensburgh.[1]

Thin people inspire almost as many names and jokes as fat people, but the laughter is less mortifying; the names cannot insinuate self-indulgence, they are merely descriptive, as: bag o' bones, bean pole, Bony Moroney (Glasgow), broomstick, daddy-longlegs, drain pipe ('Thin enough to go up a drain pipe'), fuse-wire, hair-bones, hairpin, lamp-post, walking lamp-post, Lanky Liz, Lanky Panky, 'Long and lanky, skinny and cranky', Swanky Lanky Liz (a character in *Beano*), L.S.D. (Long Skinny Davy), matchstick (sometimes abbreviated to 'matchy'), needles, needle-legs, pencil slim, pipe cleaner, rake (very common – and medieval[2]) or raky, razor blade, rib skin, scarecrow, scraggy, skin and bones,[3] skinny, skinny-flint or skinflint (curiously common in this sense), skinny guts, Skinny Liz, skinny-malink, spaggy or sparrow (one with long thin legs), Spindle Dick, spindle legs, spindleshanks, spindle sticks, taper, Thinima (opposite to Fatima), tin ribs, and, of course, such names as Tubby. 'Look at him sideways, teacher'll think he's absent.' 'He's as fat as a matchstick with the wood shaved off.'

Lankies

Inevitably there is a fusion of terms between those for the thin and lanky lad and those for the overgrown. In the following the chief emphasis is on height, 'Lofty' being the most popular nickname, followed by 'Longshanks' ('Lean old lanks got long shanks', 'Lean old lank looks like a plank'), and Long John Silver ('Six feet two and a tealeaf', 'Six feet of misery'). Other epithets include: Everest (not heard before the ascent of Everest), flagpole ('Cold up there mate?'), freak, Gulliver, giddy lamp-post (the idea being that he is so tall it makes one giddy), maypole,

1. A Scottish rhyme only heard north of the Border; but the term 'skinny-malink' travelled south long ago, and is well established in England.
2. Thus *c.* 1387, Chaucer, *Prologue*, 287, 'And leene was his hors as is a rake'.
3. In U.S.A., 'skinbone'. Alternatively 'string bean'. Thus Marilyn Monroe, the girl with the greatest 'physical impact' on the 1950s: 'At twelve I was pretty thin. The boys used to call me "string bean".' – *Picture Post*, 15 August 1953.

Spike (common in London), Skylon,[1] skyscraper, snowy ('Brush the snow off your head'), spider, stilty ('Get down off your stilts'), streak or streaker, Tower of London, walking barge pole, walking lamp-post, walking telegraph pole, Wagstaffe. Also, of course, giants are named facetiously, Tich, Shorty, and Tiny Tim, in the good old manner that Will Stutely jested about the height of the seven-foot John Little, calling him 'Little John'.

Little 'Uns

A chap who has got duck's disease is most often labelled 'Tich' in a friendly manner, or 'squirt' or 'little squirt' in a less friendly manner. Alternatively: ankle biter, dolly mixture (after a species of very small sweet), dumpy, flea, half-pint, imp, Jenny (in Scotland), junior, kipper, microbe, midge, nipper, penguin, pint-size, Pip, poached egg, shorty ('Get off your knees, Shorty'), shrimp, small fry, snitch or snitchy, squib, squit (thus also Anstey in 1889, 'He's not half a bad little squit'), stubby, stumps, stumpy, squiddy, twinkle toes ('Put some manure in your boots'), tiddler, tiger, Tiny Tim, Tom Thumb, tot, and, very common, weed. Also, inevitably: lofty, longshanks, Goliath, etc.

Red Heads

Red heads attract a barrage of nicknames: beetroot, blood nut, carrots, carrot-top, carroty-pow (Forfar), copper crust, coppernob, fire bucket, fire head, flame, flarey, foxy, fury, ginge, ginger, ginger conk, ginger mop, gingernob, gingernut, Ginger Tom, gingy, glow-worm, mad head, reddy, red kipper, red mop, red thatch, red paint brush, Rufus, and Rusty (accompanied by hints that he was left out in the rain when a baby). He is uncoverably open to insult:

Ginger, you're barmy,
You'll never join the army.
You'll never make a scout
With your shirt hanging out,
Ginger, you're barmy.
Versions throughout England.

Rusty nut fell in the Cut (canal)
And frightened all the fishes.
A fish jumped up and bit his nut
And made him wash the dishes.
Liverpool, and similar in Birmingham.

1. The term Skylon, after the perpendicular show-piece in the Festival of Britain, 1951, was found two years later to be a name for the lanky not only in London but as far away as Ruthin.

Red hair, carrot nose,
Pull the string and up he goes.
Versions throughout Scotland.[1]

Red head, gingerbread,
Five cents a loaf.
*Missouri, 1950. 'American Folklore',
vol. lxiii, p. 435.*

'Ginger, you're barmy, getcher 'air cut' has been a greeting to copper-
nobs ever since it was a catch phrase in the Harry Champion song, written
by Fred Murray. Other salutations are, 'Wat'cher, fire cracker', and the
simple 'Red hair, your head's on fire'. It is generally taken for granted
that the owner of a flaming top-knot is also the possessor of a fiery disposition. He is referred to as 'a strong-tempered buz', 'red-hot ginger',
and 'spitfire'. For all this, it is generally conceded that 'Ginger for pluck'
is a true saying.

The Funny Faced

Nothing is easier than to deride someone's face:

Oh *Sheila* dear,
Your face is queer,
It looks just like
A chipped pear.
Girls, c. 12, Aberdeen.

Roses are red,
Cabbages are green,
My face may be funny
But yours is a scream.
Girl, 13, London.

Sly nose, ugly face,
Ought to be put in a glass case;
If you want to know his name,
His name is *Georgie Smithers.*
Boy, 15, Headington.

Oh, *Judy*, you're a funny'un,
With a face like a pickled onion,
A nose like a squashed tomato,
And teeth like green peas.
Very general.

'Oh, *Judy*, you're a funny'un' is sung to the tune of 'The Ash Grove',
and to judge by the number of versions received, occasions for its utterance
are to be found all over Britain, the subjects not always being juvenile, and
not necessarily outside the teaching profession.

A funny-faced person may also be called 'Goofy', or 'Enoch' (after a
character in the radio-show 'Happidrome' of the 1940s?), or 'Ugly Mug'
or 'Fish Face' ('a name for someone who has a long face and dopey eyes'),
or, of course, 'Monkey Face':

Ha! ha! ha! He! he! he!
You've got a face like a chimpanzee.

In Scotland a common jibe of mock solicitude is 'Wha ca'd ye parten face,
an' ye sae like a crab?' Someone with a large mouth is called 'Froggy',

1. In 1913 (Rymour Club, *Miscellanea*, vol. ii, p. 80) it was recorded as:

Red hair, carrot nose,
Gie't a lick, and off it goes.

and it is presumed that he was fed with a shovel when young. Someone with out-size side-flaps is referred to as 'Big Lugs'.

There are also, according to juvenile observers, people with 'ferret' noses, 'pig' noses, 'jelly' noses, long 'cucumber' noses, 'Peggy parrot' noses ('What a beaut'), 'cheese cutters', and 'Rudolphs', that is to say red noses ('Buy a poppy!' 'Put that light out').[1]

Other unfortunates are 'Spotty Dicks', the unwilling possessors of freckles or 'Dalmation' faces, people whose one idea while earnestly applying T.C.P. or May-dew in the privacy of their bedrooms is to make inappropriate the names their friends call them: Bumps, Dimples, Crater-face, Freckles, Freckle-faced faggot, Leopard, Mealyface (hence 'School dinners'), Measle nob ('Look she's got the measles'), Pepper pot, Pimple bonce, Poxie, and Scabby guts. 'If that's your face it's a dashed disgrace, I thought it was your bottom in the wrong place.'

Spectacles

A girl or boy with spectacles is known as 'Four-eyes', 'Specky four-eyes', '*Annie* four-eyes', and at Headington, Oxford, is faced with the jeer:

> Four eyes, double chin,
> Enough to make the monkey grin.

Occasionally he is 'Eye balls', 'Glass eyes', 'Googlie eyes', 'Goggles', and 'Specky Jock' (Scotland), but none of these names is thought as funny as 'Four-eyes'.

The term 'giglamps' for spectacles (used by Cuthbert Bede in 1853) is on the wane, and few people now are nicknamed 'Giglamps' for wearing them (as Kipling was at Westward Ho), although derivatives persist in the picture strips. The supposedly brainy young 'tec in the *Eagle* strip 'P.C. 49' was known as 'Gigs' (1956), and the bespectacled freckle-faced heroine of a school serial in *Mickey Mouse Weekly* (1952) was called 'Gig-frecks'. Needless to say, the myth that spectacles denote superior intellect not merely persists but is taken for granted.

** In New Zealand boys chant: 'Four eyes, four eyes, Glass eyes, bye byes!' (Brian Sutton-Smith, *Our Street*, 1950, p. 64). The term to be four-eyed is older than might be supposed. It appears in *The Vocabulary of East Anglia*, vol. i, 1830, p. 120.

1. The name Rudolph comes from the popular song 'Rudolph, the Red-Nosed Reindeer', 1949.

School Subjects

> If your school should be in a flood
>   Do not scream or cry,
> Stand upon a Latin book
>   For that is always dry.

In the bus taking them to school, someone says: 'What's the first lesson today?' Someone replies: 'Dictation.' And then all the young ones burst out:

> Dictation,
> Pollygation,
> Three pigs on a railway station,

or 'Dictation, botheration, put teacher in the p'lice station', which one teacher heard repeated so often she had to put an absolute ban on it. There is, however, a scarcity of rhymes about school subjects and, other than the old lament 'Multiplication is vexation',[1] the only lesson which evokes any verses seems to be Latin:

> Detention, detention, detention,
> I've forgotten my Latin declension.
> The Second or First?
> The Third is the worst.
> Detention, detention, detention.
>
> *Northgate Grammar School.*

> Latin is a subject
> That no one enjoys;
> It killed the ancient Romans
> And now it is killing boys.
>
> *Kirkcaldy High School.*

> Latin is a dead tongue,
> Dead as dead can be,
> First it killed the Romans,
> Now it's killing me.
> All are dead who wrote it,
> All are dead who spoke it,
> All are dead who learnt it,
> Lucky dead, they've earnt it.
>
> *Selhurst Grammar School. Versions of this are also repeated by American children.*

The fact that most of the nicknames for school subjects are presumably wholly juvenile in conception, being without benefit of adult prototypes, makes them of particular interest. Some of the popular terms, which apparently give children great satisfaction, are little more than straightforward abbreviations, thus: Compo (Composition), Domaski or Dommeca (Domestic Science), Gogers, Geogo, or Jig-jog (Geography), and

---

[1]. Multiplication is vexation,
   Division is as bad,
   The Rule of Three
   Does puzzle me
   And practice drives me mad.

   Girl, 11, Birmingham.

Multiplication is mie vexation
And division quite as bad,
The Golden Rule is mie stumbling stule,
And Practice makes me mad.

Manuscript, c. 1570 (cited in Davies's 'Key to Hutton's Mathematics', 1840, p. 17).

Fizzy or Phiz-jig (Physics). Others are merely rhymes, half-rhymes, per-
versions, or puns: 'Fart' for art – or 'Treacle tart' or 'Apple tart' which
can, perhaps, be dignified by being called rhyming slang – 'Draftwork' for
craftwork, 'Laffs' for maths, and 'Mystery' for history, like the Mock
Turtle in *Alice in Wonderland*; and possibly it was from the Liddell
children themselves that Dodgson had the idea of the Mock Turtle's
syllabus: 'Reeling and Writhing, Mystery, ancient and modern, with
Seaography', and the subjects taught by the old conger eel, 'Drawling,
Stretching, and Fainting in Coils', for children, today, sometimes speak
of painting as 'Fainting', and sketching as 'Stretching' (e.g. at Spennymoor). One feels Lewis Carroll would have liked the current terms Physical Torture (for P.T.) and Religious Destruction or Ridiculous Kapers
(for R.K.), and might, if he had thought of it, have awarded the Gryphon
a 'stiff cat' for passing an 'eggs, ham, and bacon' in 'Bilge and Stinks'
(Biology and Chemistry), all common terms with the twentieth-century
schoolchild. He might, too, have seen sense in the wisecracks which,
according to Mr Geoffrey Potter (to whose minutiae we owe much),
scientifically minded boys indulge in when, at about twelve years old, they
begin to take up their subject in earnest:

'What is the matter?' 'That which occupies space.'

'What is Boyle's Law?' 'A boil on your bottom makes recumbency
painful.'

'What happens when an irresistible force meets an immovable body?'
'Infinite heat.' (Said with great solemnity and knowingness.)

And the rhyme:

> Poor Old Stinker's dead and gone,
> His face you'll see no more:
> For what he thought was H_2O
> Was H_2SO_4!

This last is of folkloristic interest for it is a direct transmogrification of
traditional lines spoken of old by the yuletide mummers.[1]

1. See 'Old Abram Brown is dead and gone', in *The Oxford Dictionary of Nursery Rhymes*, 1951, p. 52.

> Nobody loves me, everybody hates me,
>   Going in the garden to eat worms;
> Big fat juicy ones, little squiggly niggly ones,
>   Going in the garden to eat worms.
>
>   *Song for the unhappy.*

SOMEBODY they dislike, 'a person with whom you are not pally', may be called (general terms): beast, clot, dreg, dumb cluck, erk, gawp, kid, monkey ('little monkey' in particular), pig, rat (usually 'dirty rat'), rogue, rotter, rotten dog, and stinker. In Kirkcaldy a bossy person is 'pawpy'. In Bishop Auckland 'Dog Harry' is a general term of reproach.

The girls gang up on 'an unfriendly person' and chant:

> I know a little girl sly and deceitful,
> Every little tittle-tat she goes and tells the people.
> Long nose, ugly face, ought to be put in a glass case,
> If you want to know her name, her name is *Heather Lee*.
> Please *Heather Lee*, keep away from me;
> I don't want to speak to you, nor you to speak to me.
> Once we were friends, now we disagree,
> Oh, *Heather Lee*, keep away from me.
> It's not because you're dirty,
> It's not because you're clean,
> It's because you've got the whooping-cough,
> Pooh! You awful thing!
>
>   *Versions from fifteen schools throughout Britain (much*
>   *employed also for skipping).*

Compared with the piercing exactitude of the jeers for specific offences (e.g. crying and tale-bearing, hereafter), the rhymes expressing general dislike have an impersonal air. One has the feeling, often correct, that the children are being rude just for the fun of being rude. The recipient can take little harm from taunts such as the following:

Brian Johnson is no good,
Chop him up for fi-er wood;
When he's dead, boil his head,
Make it into ginger bread.

*Versions from fifteen schools in Britain,
also common in the United States.*

God made the French,
God made the Dutch,
Whoever made you
Never made much.

Caistor, Lincs.

Tiddly Winks old man,
Suck a lemon if you can;
If you can't suck a lemon
Suck an old tin can.

Versions from eleven schools in Britain.

Hubbah hubbah ding ding,
Look at the legs on that thing.
What thing? That thing.
Hubbah hubbah ding ding.

Helensburgh and Kirkcaldy.

A particular pleasure, as has already been remarked, is to liken a companion to one of the lower orders of creation:

Donkey walks on four legs,
And I walk on two,
The last one I saw
Was just like you.

That's the way to the zoo,
That's the way to the zoo,
The monkey house is nearly full
But there's room enough for you.

To one singing:

Sweetly sings the donkey
As he goes to grass,
He who sings so sweetly
Is sure to be an ass.

Toorally oorally oorally oo,
They're wanting monkeys at the zoo.
I'd apply if I were you
And get a situation.

⁎⁎* Each of these jeers is widespread, and has a pedigree going back to the nineteenth century. 'Donkey walks on four legs' was recorded by J. O. Halliwell in 1842 (*Nursery Rhymes of England*, p. 134); 'Sweetly sings the donkey' is to be found in nineteenth-century autograph albums; and 'That's the way to the zoo' was the chorus of a music hall song, popular *c.* 1880 (see *East Anglian Magazine*, September 1951, p. 13).

Spoil-Sports, Sourpusses, Spitfires

The children frequently mention spoil-sports as being the people they most dislike. 'When playing games,' says a 9-year-old in Dovenby, Cumberland, 'if one of the girls falls out we shout sulky puss or spoil sport or Baby baby bunting Daddy's gone a hunting for a rabbit skin to lap the baby in or Water works.' The young in Newcastle shout:

Trouble maker, trouble maker,
Fetch a pan and a cake we'll make of her.

To a moaner who keeps whining 'Oh dear me!' Forfar children put the question, 'Fat's dear aboot you and dirt sae chaip?' A peevish person is referred to as a Cross-patch, Old Grousey or Grumpy, Misery, Mardy-

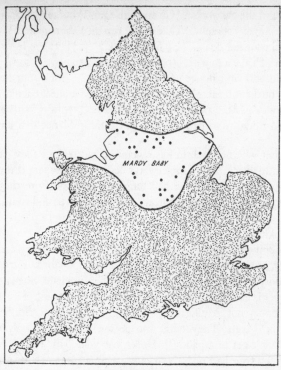

8　Mardy area

To people in Derbyshire, Leicestershire, Nottinghamshire, and areas adjoining, the term *mardy* has a meaning of its own. It is used, in the first instance, of a spoilt child (i.e. a marred child), hence generally, as above, of a peevish or moody child (considered the natural consequence of being spoilt), and, thirdly, of a soft child or cry-baby (see p. 207), the result of too much cosseting. A Derby 8-year-old says: 'In class, when something has gone wrong, a child leans over to you and whispers "Mardy-baby" or "Mardy mardy mustard, can't eat custard".' The word was much used by D. H. Lawrence, a native of Nottinghamshire, see, for example, *The White Peacock* (1911), and *Sons and Lovers* (1913).

baby, Peevy, Sourpuss, or Sulky Sue. In Glasgow, when having fun with somebody who does not take it as fun, they chant:

> Roses are red, Violets are blue,
> Lemons are sour and so are you.

A name for one 'with a grim glum face' is 'Smiler'. When someone thoroughly unwelcome turns up they comment, 'Look what the cat's brought in' or 'Look who it ain't.' When accosted by an irritating person who 'gets their goat' or 'gets their needle', they complain 'Why don't you drop dead?' (very common), or suggest: 'Go and get lost', 'Go chase yourself round the gasworks', 'Go and run round yourself', 'Go and take a running jump at yourself', 'Take a long run off a short pier', 'Walk into the sea until your hat floats', 'Go fish a brick', 'For Pete's sake wrap up', 'Pipe down', 'Take a powder' (particularly to a grumpy person), 'Suck a lemon', 'Go boil your bonce', 'Go fry your face', 'Stick your head in a gas oven' ('bucket of water', 'coal hole', etc.), 'Go and eat coke', 'Dry up and blow away'. If the person takes the hint and withdraws, they comment 'Good riddance to bad rubbish' or 'Good riddance to a dirty dish clout'.

To find out whether a child has a good or bad temper they run their finger down his back. If the finger stays cool, good temper; if the finger becomes hot, the person has a bad temper. In Radnorshire they test a child by plucking a hair from his head, and pulling their moistened finger and thumb along it; if the hair remains straight it shows a placid temper, but if it kinkles it reveals an ill temper.

A short-tempered person is spoken of as being: catty (very common), crusty, fiery, grizzly, niggled or niggly (Headington, Oxford), ratty, shirty, snappy, snooty (meaning easily irritated), and sharp-edged. Such a person, whose temper is easily provoked, may be named: Our bomb, Fire-blower, Hot pot, Pepper pot, Mulligrubs,[1] Radish, Temper puss, Spitfire (very common), or Vixen. They taunt the person: 'Now don't fly off the handle', 'Don't get in a paddy', 'Don't lose your bait' ('rag', 'rise' or 'wool'), 'Keep your hair on', 'Now, now, temper! temper!' In Aberdeen they taunt:

> *Lorna*'s in a ragie
> Pit her in a cagie.[2]

Clever-Dicks

Their terms for the bright boy or girl show both admiration and contempt. They are willing to acclaim anyone who habitually comes top of the class without apparent effort, naming him Genius, The Brains, Miracle Man, Professor, and Topper; but they look down upon the one who has to work

---

1. 'Said while the teaser rubs the head of the offended person' (Pendeen, Cornwall).
2. In the United States, where 'mad' means 'cross' or 'in a rage', the common gibe is:

> *Mary*'s mad, and I am glad,
> And I know what will please her,
> A bottle of ink to make her stink
> And a nigger boy to squeeze her.

hard to keep first place. Such a person is a 'swotter', 'swotpot', or 'stew-pot'. They snort 'You swot!' if they find him preparing work before a lesson. 'Swotting' or 'mugging up' is only considered good form if a person is on the point of taking an exam. A couplet common in schools around Peterborough is:

> He that works and does his best
> Gets the sack like all the rest.

People who keep at their work are Ants, Bookworms, Slaves, Plodderoners, and Old Grindstones. A clever boy is most often styled a 'clever-dick', or, less frequently: brainy pup, brilliant bonce, cleverguts, cleverpot, clever-sides, cleversticks, jingler, know-all, squelch, and (in Oxford) Brain Basil – all terms which may also, on occasions, be ironical, meaning that he is: artful, over-witty, too clever by half, a show-off, a snob, or a 'poshy guy'.

Dafties, Fools, and Dunces

The most common, and pertinent (and most resented), of all child-to-child abuse is saying that a person is daft in the head.

> You're daft, you're potty, you're barmy,
> You ought to join the army.
> You got knocked out
> With a brussel sprout,
> You're daft, you're potty, you're barmy.
>
> *Market Rasen version.*

A person who is 'wanting in the upper storey' is: bats, batty, barmy, crackers or a crackpot, daffy, dippy, dithering ('You're daft and dithering, wipe your chin and stop dribbling' – Cleethorpes), dizzy, a dope, a dopey dick, dotty, goofy or goopy, a gowk (in Scotland), a ninny, a nit-wit, nutty, potty, a pot-head ('You're daft, you're potty, you're made of treacle toffee' – Newcastle). He is cracked, he's cuckoo, he's loco, he's nuts, he's not all there ('Yer out of your waggon' – Bishop Auckland), he's not plumb, he's off his rocket ('Off your rocket' is a development of 'off your rocker'). He is – scatty, screwy, scearie (in Perth), off his chump (head, nut, block), has a screw loose, a tile loose, is a bit touched, a bit wrong in the head, soft in the head, half baked, a stupe, and in Bishop Auckland, for some reason, a rajah.

'Don't be so nutty, you dull ass.'

Answer: 'If you're right in the head, I'll stay as I am.'

All these words imply, or are intended to imply, that the subject is not in full possession of his mental faculties; but this is not necessarily the case if he is called a fool.

Willie Carey is a fool
Like a monkey on a stool,
When he's dead
Lay him on a bed
And bake his head with gingerbread.

Headington.

Lydia Smith is a fool,
Like a donkey on a stool.
When the stool began to crack,
All the fleas ran down her back.

Alton, Enfield, Norfolk, Lydney, and similar versions from elsewhere.

Joe Egg is a fool,
He tied his stocking to a stool.
When the stool begins to crack
All the beetles run up his back.

Market Rasen.

Oor Leebie is a fule,
And a donkey at the skule.
If she had a langer tail,
I would hang her up for sale.

Forfar. Known to date back to 1910.

Jean Mactaggart is a fule (or 'feel'),
She's made up wi' brose an' meal,
Brose an' meal makes her fat,
That's the way she's a cheeky cat.

Aberdeen.

Tammie Ross is an ass,
For a donkey he would pass,
If he only had a tail
We would hang him up for sale.

Dundee.

Being a silly fool, or behaving like a fool, may mean only that the person is acting the goat, doing idiotic things, behaving foolishly. He is – a clown, a clot, a fathead, a mutt, a muggins, an oaf, a bit of a twerp, a silly goop, a proper Charlie. He has behaved like a chump, like a donkey, or a goose, or a juggins. They say 'You fool, you must be potty to do such a thing.' They do not say that he *is* potty, but that he is behaving as if he were.

A dunce is slightly different again. He may be sane, good at games, and seldom act the fool, but he lacks scholastic abilities, he is dense, slow on the uptake, he has got a thick head.

Dunce, dunce, double D,
Doesn't know his A.B.C.

Market Rasen, Oxford, Ruthin, Shrewsbury. Also given as a popular rhyme in 1898 ('The English Dialect Dictionary').

Dunce, dunce, double D,
Cannot learn his A.B.C.
Put a cap on then you'll see
What a silly boy is he.

Headington and Portsmouth.

Silly-Dick he has no brains,
Soon he didn't have no veins.

Oundle.

In this rhyme the fool is the dunce type:

Jimmy Snaps is a fool,
Send him to the baby school,
Give him one, give him two,
Tell the teacher what to do.

Kirkcaldy.

The difference can be seen in the three terms: soft in the head, fathead, and blockhead. The significance, of course, of all terms varies according to how they are used, but someone who is 'soft in the head' is generally understood to be dippy; a 'fathead' is a fool, or someone who has done something stupid; and a 'blockhead' is someone who is dense.[1] He is a 'big-'ead' (very common), a 'thick-head', with a 'head full of lead', or 'bone from the knees up' (a Suffolk saying). He is – a clodpoll, a dim-wit, a dull-dick, a dullard, a dunderpate, a know-nothing, a numbskull, a corner-boy (or corner-girl). He is – a brainless chump, a brainless gorm, a pea-brain, or a putty-brain.

He may also be called a 'booby'; to boob something is to make a mess of it, to get it wrong, and the booby prize is awarded to the one who is bottom of the class. But booby is not the usual term for a dunce; it is more often applied to a simpleton, and the children seem to associate it with crying. A booby is a foolish cry-baby, possibly arrived at from the term 'boo-baby' and the word 'booing' for crying (very common: see under Cry-Babies). To warm one's hands by slapping oneself is to 'beat the booby'.

Again, it may be noted that to be a clot, a dumb clot, or a 'dumbless thing', is not necessarily to be a dunce. These epithets may be used to describe someone who has merely behaved idiotically, or who is a 'no-good', or a duffer; that is to say a person not proficient in an activity which is esteemed: no good at games, or no good at carpentry, physically awkward, a 'clumsy clot'.[2] Similarly a 'yob' (backslang for boy) has come to mean a lout. The terms 'scatterbrain', 'featherhead', 'empty vessel', are applied, in particular, to people who are vague or forgetful. A 'dilly-day-dream' (or just 'dream'), or a 'Joseph' (after Joseph's dream) is a person who has his mind on other things. And the word 'sap', which at Eton is primarily used to castigate someone who is over-keen on his work (equivalent to 'swot'), the children define as meaning a sissy or a softy ('soft in that he does not do anything wrong'), and suggest other moist alternatives, as 'milksop', 'soppy date', a 'wet', or a 'drip'. 'What's on the bread today?' 'You with I-N-G at the end.' 'Is your hair wet? There's a big drip under it!'

1. An inscription written in the margin of a schoolbook by an 11-year-old in 1710 has a familiar ring about it. 'Alexander Meason can write better nor Robert Barclay, but he is a blockhead at countins.' – *Notes and Queries*, 9th ser., vol. xi, 1903, p. 145.
2. *Clot* is now common in the juvenile world, aided by the frequency with which it appeared in the balloons in the *Eagle* picture strip 'P.C. 49'.

Copy-Cats, Cribbers, Cheats

Imitation is not considered the sincerest form of flattery.

Copy-cat
Stole a rat
Put it in his Sunday hat.

Girl, 12, Ipswich.

Copy-cat,
Dirty rat,
Sitting on a policeman's hat.

Boy, 7, Alton.

In Aberdeen, the girl accused of being a copy-cat replies: 'A didna ken the co-opie [the Co-operative] selt cats.'

A copy-cat is not, however, one who copies off, or over-looks, another person's work. Such a person is almost always a 'cribber' (although in Welshpool a 'cribber' is a cry-baby), or in Cheshire a 'cog'. A book which gives answers, whether or not used legitimately, is a 'crib'. Someone who cribs, when nobody else is cribbing, is a 'cheat' or a 'swindler'. Amongst London boys a cheat is generally referred to as a 'wog', sometimes a 'clot'. The girls cry out 'Cheats never prosper' or just 'cheater'.

Swankpots

Swankpots come in for stern disapproval. All over Scotland, in Edinburgh, Glasgow, Perth, Kirkcaldy, and Helensburgh, children make sport of a swankpot by chanting the lines:

There she goes, there she goes,
Peerie heels and pointed toes.
Look at her feet,
She thinks she's neat,
Long black stockings and dirty feet.

In Kirkcaldy the verse sometimes begins, 'There she goes, there she goes, like an elephant on her toes'; and in Edinburgh they say, 'Nae stockings and claurty [filthy] feet', but the intensity of their dislike is without variation.

In England a swankpot is known as a Swanky Liz, Swanky Lanky Liz, or Swanky Pants. Girls try to prick her pride with verses such as:

Charmian Smith, tall and slender,
She's got legs like a crooked fender.

Headington.

Long legs, crooked thighs,
Little head, and two eyes.

Cleethorpes.[1]

1. An adaptation of an old riddle describing a pair of tongs. See *The Oxford Dictionary of Nursery Rhymes*, 1951, p. 267.

Oh *Susan Johnson*
Thinks herself a treat,
Long skinny banana legs,
And umbrella feet.

Newcastle upon Tyne.

Hands together,
Eyes closed,
Mary Popham
Has big toes.

Pendeen.

The show-off or conceited person is also known as an 'ego' ('someone full of own importance'), a 'porky prig', a 'snobby', a 'stuck-up peacock', Miss Prim and Proper, Miss Hoity-toity, and, most of all, is said to be 'toffee nosed' (very general). A boaster is a 'jet-brain', a 'puff-bag', a 'big brass drum', and is asked 'When did your trumpeter die?' Someone bumptious or conceited is 'big nob', and references are made to the way his 'bonce' is swelling ('You'd better watch that head of yours ... It's getting so big it will blow off your shoulders one day.'[1]) But the application of these terms is wide. They may, for instance, be thrown in the teeth of someone whose only sin is to have done too well in class.

Nosey Parkers

Nosey people are known as: Flap-ears, Keyhole Kates, Nosey-Parkers, or Peep-eyes. They earn such remarks as: 'Keep your nose out of other people's pies', 'Nosey Parker, squashed tomato', 'Quizzy flies never grow wise', and 'Quizzy monkeys burn their noses'.

People with quizzy tongues who ask about things which are none of their business, get for answer: 'Ask no questions and receive no lies',[2] or,

Ask no questions
And you'll be told no lies;
Shut your mouth
And you will catch no flies,

or, 'Shim shams for meddlers' (Oxford), or 'Curiosity killed the cat' (to which the rather lame reply is 'Satisfaction brought it back'), or 'M.Y.O.B.', 'Mind your own beeswax', 'Mind your own biz'.

Mind your own business,
Fry your own fish;
Don't poke your nose
Into my clean dish.

Bathampton and Birmingham.

Mind your own business,
Eat your own fat;
Don't poke your nose
Into my best hat.

London N.E.

1. A jibe given by Michael Croft, *Spare the Rod*, 1954, p. 66.
2. Echoing the words of Tony Lumpkin: 'Ask me no questions and I'll tell you no fibs.' – *She Stoops to Conquer*, Act III, sc. i, 1773.

Mind your own business And don't mind mine Kiss your own sweetheart And don't kiss mine.	Mind your own business And I'll mind mine Stitch your own breeches And I'll stitch mine.
Alton and Stockton-on-Tees.	*Manchester.*[1]

If I'm soft, you're hard,
If I'm butter, you're lard,
If I'm treacle, you're cheese,
Mind Your Own Business, Please.

Yorkshire.

'Ask me another,' a Croydon boy told his inquisitor, 'and I'll buy you a book of answers.' And in Ruthin, Welsh-speaking children say:

Paid a holi, cynffon doli, Ar ddydd Sul mae eisiau holi.	(*Don't ask questions, tail of a dolly,* *You ask questions on a Sunday.*)

Stare-Cats

They resent being stared at and voice their resentment. 'Stare, stare, like a bear, then you'll know me anywhere' (very general). 'Stare, stare, you big fat bear, when you get married you'll have no hair' (Co. Durham and Lincolnshire). 'Stare, stare, pull your mum's hair, pull your dad's whiskers, I don't care' (Huntingdonshire). And, from 8-year-olds in Broken Hill, Northern Rhodesia:

Stare, stare, like a bear,
Call your mother 'Ginger hair',
Chase your father round a chair,
Like a sausage in the air.

'You cheeky thing.' 'Like another pennyworth?' 'Have you got your eyeful? If not I'll come and fill it with ink.' 'Who are you looking at?' And the accused one retorts:

I'm looking at you with your face so blue
And your nose turned up like a kangaroo,

1. These verses probably have many years' employment behind them. According to Flora Thompson, *Still Glides the Stream*, 1948, p. 53, Oxfordshire village women in the nineteenth century used to say:

You mind your own business and I'll mind mine.
You drink the pigs' wash and I'll drink wine!

Harriette Wilson in her *Memoirs*, 1825, ch. viii, records that her schoolboy nephew George Woodcock sent her footman the 'eloquent words':

Five and four makes nine.
Mind your business, and I'll mind mine.

Or, as in days gone by:

> A cat can look at a king,
> Can't I look at an ugly thing?

₊ Thus James Kelly in his *Collection of Scottish Proverbs*, 1721, p. 11: 'A halfpenny Cat may look at a King. An Answer to them that ask you, why you look at them, or what you look at.' Similarly, four centuries ago, John Heywood in his *Dialogue . . . of All the Prouerbes*, 1546, II. v: 'What, a cat maie looke on a kyng, ye know.'

Cowards

The boy who will not jump from a wall which everyone else has jumped from, or who will not take part in a prank or accept a challenge, is 'yellow', a 'yellow-belly', hence (amongst children in Oxford) 'eggy' or 'yolky', or (in West Yorkshire) 'custard lugs'.[1] He is a 'scaredy', a 'scare-baby', and may have 'Windy' shouted after him as he slinks away. In private schools he is a 'funk', or a 'funk-pot', or has 'got the collywobbles'. In Pontefract, reports a 13-year-old: 'If a boy is a coward he has to fight the cock of the school. He has got to go into a field with a ring of boys round him. The coward has to stop and fight with the cock for a minute, then he is let off.' In Scotland he is called a 'feardy gowk', or a 'scaredy gowk'. ('They shout at you, "Ya scaredy, yer feart, ye darna dae it",' says a Langholm boy.) In Peterborough, where the lads are notoriously severe, they threaten him: 'Spit and run you skunk of a coward.' But everywhere and most of all, he who lacks the necessary resolution is styled a 'cowardy custard', and desperate-faced, shuffle-footed, he beats his ignoble retreat to the tune of:

> Cowardy, cowardy custard,
> Can't eat bread and mustard.
>
> *London.*

> Cowardy, cowardy custard,
> Your bones will turn to mustard.
>
> *Preston.*

> Cowardy, cowardy custard,
> Dip your head in granny's mustard.
>
> *Pendeen.*

> Cowardy, cowardy custard,
> Three bags of mustard,
> One for you,
> And one for me,
> And one for cowardy custard.
>
> *Glasgow.*

> Cowardy, cowardy custard,
> Fell in his mother's mustard;
> The mustard was hot,
> He swallowed the lot,
> Cowardy, cowardy custard.
>
> *Lydney.*

1. It seems to be only in the twentieth century that yellow has become the token of faint-heartedness. In the seventeenth, eighteenth, and nineteenth centuries yellow denoted jealousy. Possibly the change has come about through the phrase 'cowardy custard', now that *costard*, the old contemptuous name for a head, is forgotten, and the word 'custard' brings to mind a vision of bright yellow sauce.

Or, 'Eat a pound of mustard' (Swansea), or 'Sit you in the mustard' (Oxford), or, 'Rub your nose in mustard' (Ruthin), or 'Wash your face in mustard' (Forfar).

*** 'Cowardy custard' jeers seem to have been repeated at least since the days of William IV. In 1836 the Christmas entertainment at the Adelphi Theatre, London, a production in which Thomas 'Daddy' Rice took part, was entitled *Cowardy, Cowardy, Custard, or Harlequin Jim Crow and the Magic Mustard Pot.*

Cry-Babies

Amongst boys to use the word 'crying' is sometimes held to be almost as sissy as the act itself. A lad must say 'blubbing',[1] or 'bawling', or 'squalling', according to the custom of his school, or the district in which he lives. In southern England the usual term is 'booing', while in Scotland and the north-east of England it is often 'bubblin', hence a cry-baby is a 'bubbly baby', 'bubbly Jock', or 'mum's big bubbly bairn', just as in London the wet-faced child is a 'boo-baby' or 'booby'.

Other local terms for crying are: babbling (Whitehaven), blabbing (Lydney), blabbling (Derby), blabbering (Isle of Ely), blahing or blarting (Birmingham, Hanley, Wolverhampton), blaring (Norwich), bleating (Birmingham), moaning (the general term in Liverpool), and slobbering (Rochdale). In Welshpool the common term is 'cribbing' and a cry-baby is a 'cribber'; in Croydon they sometimes speak of 'mizzogging' and 'mizzog'; in the area of Blackburn, Bolton, Manchester, Stockport, and Halifax the term 'skriking' is common, the noun being 'skriker'; and in Dublin the usual word is 'whinging', hence 'whinger', a term also still used in Cumberland, and occasionally heard in Liverpool. In Scotland, as well as 'bubblin', they speak of 'girnin' and, of course, 'greetin', hence epithets like 'girnie bubbler', 'girnie gowk', and 'greetin-faced teenie'. 'Girning' is also fairly general in Cumberland, and in the North Riding where it is pronounced 'gennin', while 'bubblin' is heard south to the Tees.

Some of the terms have different shades of meaning. In the West Riding the degrees of intensity are said to be firstly 'bluthering', which is quietly whimpering, then 'rooaring', and then 'skriking', which is yelling

---

1. The term favoured in most private schools, including *The Fifth Form at St Dominic's* (1887) where a character is described as 'a horrid young blub-baby'. 'Blubber-face' has been heard in Manchester, 'blubber-bib' in Bolsover, and 'blubber-puss' in Kirkcaldy.

blue murder. In Fife 'grump' and 'peenger' apply more to people who are snivelling and fretful than openly sobbing. Similarly, especially in the south-west, a person is said to be 'grizzling' when he is merely whining and complaining, the brat himself being styled 'grizzle-guts' or, in Wiltshire, 'grizzle-grunt', while in the North Midlands a like condition is expressed by the word 'mardy' (see under Spoil-Sports).

Croydon boys have twenty names for a cry-baby: baby bunting, blubber, boo-baby, boo-hoo, diddums, grizzle-guts, howler, leaky, Lumleyite (after a local boy), moaner, mother's little darling sissy, slobber-baby, sniveller, softy, tap, Tearful Tilly, water-can, water-hog, waterworks, and weeping willow.

Gloucestershire children comment: you babby, big baby, cuddled baby, mummy's baby, diddums do it to you, cry-a-lot, big gob, booby, poor babba, mother's blubber, mother's pet, mamma's little sugar, grizzly guts, milk sop, misery, pautey pipe, sniveller, sissy, squall-ass, spouter, and wet-eyes.

Elsewhere the weak one may carry the label: babbity (in Glasgow), baby-cake, bubbles, crybaby Joe, drip, drainpipe, fountain-spouter, jelly baby, lassie boy (Scottish border); mardy-baby, mardy bum, mard 'un, or mardy-mardy-mustard (North Midlands); Moan-a-lot or Mona Liza (Liverpool), mummy's darling boo-hoo, pansy face, softie, slaver-chops (Lancaster), squealer, suckie thumb, sugar baby, smiler, taps, titty-titty-baby (Birmingham), and District Waterworks, or Waterworks Willie.

He or she may receive the advice: 'Go back to your bottle', 'Don't make it wet on a dry day', 'Mammy have to rock you to sleep'. The dry-faced smirk to each other: 'He's got water on the brain', 'He's turned on the tap', 'Don't worry, he's just left his napkins', 'He's just fallen out of his cot'.

They shout at the sorrowing figure:

'Baby, baby, brown bread and gravy' (*Bishop Auckland*).

'Baby, baby, fish and taty' (*Scarborough*).

'Baby, baby, bunting, cried for apple dumpling' (*Lydney*).

'Cry-baby, cry-baby, half a pound of onions' (*Lydney*).

'Cry-baby, cry-baby, one, two, three' (*Dovenby*).

'Sugar babby, sugar babby, one, two, three' (*Dublin*).

'Ha, ha, ha, hee, hee, hee, *Barbara Jones* is a big baby' (*Knighton*).

The tearful child tends to feel that the calls are entirely personal; newly made up to apply only to him. He wonders if he will escape from the shame of the hateful verses:

Cry, baby, cry,
Put your finger in your eye,
And tell your mother
It wasn't I.

Very general.

Cry baby bunting,
Daddy's gone a hunting,
To get a little rabbit skin
To wrap the baby bunting in.

London S.E. 7.

Cry, baby, cry,
Put your finger in your eye,
Tell your mother what you've done
And she'll give you a sugar plum.

Caistor.

Cry baby bunting,
Your daddy's gone a hunting,
Mummy's fetching rabbit skins
To wrap poor baby bunting in.

Holmfirth.

Cry, baby, cry,
Punch him in the eye,
Hang him on the lamp post
And leave him there to dry.

Lincoln.

Big head bucket baseball,
Kick it like a caseball,
When your mother gives you one
You cry for another one.

Birmingham.

Baby bunting, laugh and cry,
Push your finger in your eye,
Call your mother from upstairs,
And tell her it wasn't I.

Swansea.

Georgie Porge, pudding and pie,
Kissed the girl and made her cry.
When the boys came out to play
Georgie Porge ran away.

Liverpool.

Baby, baby, laugh and cry,
Stick your finger in your eye,
Go home and tell your mother
The crow pecked your eye.

Laurencetown, Co. Galway.

Hay is for horses,
Straw is for cows,
Milk is for babies
That cry out loud.

East Orange, New Jersey.

Yet, newly made-up as the children often believe these verses to be, most of them have been helping tears to flow faster for generations.

*** 'Cry, baby, cry', the verse most often repeated both in Britain and the United States, may once have followed Charles Lamb, for he quotes it, 'What, the magnanimous Alexander in tears? – cry, baby, put its finger in its eye, it shall have another globe, round as an orange, pretty moppet!' in 'All Fools' Day' published in *The London Magazine* for April 1821. It seems to have been well known a century ago, appearing in nursery rhyme books such as J. O. Halliwell's (1842) and Charles Bennett's (1858). Appropriately enough, most of the other verses, too, have nursery backgrounds, and date back to the eighteenth or early nineteenth centuries (see *The Oxford Dictionary of Nursery Rhymes*, 1951, nos. 25, 180, and 181).

Sneaks

One who blabs to a teacher or to a senior is a 'blabber-mouth', 'rotten sneak', 'dirty tell tale tit'. Young children, in particular, will hound him (as we have witnessed) until he is almost pulp, a quivering sobbing heap having to bear the double agony of blows and reiterated refrain:

> Tell tale tit,
> Your tongue shall be slit,
> And all the dogs in the town
> Shall have a little bit,

a threat which has been stinging in the ears of blabbers for more than 200 years.[1] The tell tale is christened Beaky, the sneaky ('Sneak baby, sneak, your pants do leak!'); he is – a sly, a snitch or snitcher (common, especially in the Midlands), a splitter, a squealer, a snake in the grass, a stool-pigeon or 'stoolie'; he is – a tout, traitor, quisling, or widemouth.

There are dialect names for him. In the Potteries, mid-Wales, and north to Birkenhead they speak of him as being a 'cant', hence 'canty, canty, custard', and say he has been 'canting'; in South Wales he is a 'cleckie' (from the Welsh *clecian*, to gossip), and he is sometimes termed a 'penny cleck' (Ruthin). In Shropshire and Lancashire he is sometimes a 'clat' ('Clit, clat, clit, your tongue shall be slit'), and in Cumberland a 'cripe'. In Scotland a tale-bearer is a 'clype' or 'clypie' (hence 'Clype the clout'), and also, in Fife, a 'clashbags' (a word which fifty years ago was 'clash-pans'). In South Elmsall they sneer at a 'gobbie', in Swansea at a 'gabbie' or 'mouthie', in Welwyn at a 'peaky' or 'pinky', in Derby at a 'split-splat', in Birmingham at a 'twit' (A Lydney boy calls him a 'tell-twit'), and in Liverpool and Newcastle-under-Lyme they name him a 'tit-bag'. Less specifically he is a 'blasted rotter', 'creep-ass', 'sook' (in Scotland), 'dirty dog', 'teacher's pet', and 'spoil sport'. He is likened to as unpleasant objects as come to the speaker's mind, notably: skunk, slimy snake, sly cat, rat, toad, or turd, and, if the blab is a boy, he is given a girl's name, like 'Janet', for his supposedly feminine failing.

1. It appears in *Tommy Thumb's Pretty Song Book*, vol. ii, 1744, p. 37: 'Spit Cat, Spit, Your tongue shall be slit, And all the Dogs in our Town Shall have a bit.' It is recorded again, exactly as known today, in *Mother Goose's Melody*, 1780, p. 45, and also in *Juvenile Amusements*, 1797, no. 2.

In the same way that his name varies from locality to locality, so does the recital to which he is the unwilling audience:

Tell pie tit,
Your tongue shall be slit,
And all the little dickey birds
Will have a little bit.

Newcastle. (In Market Rasen, 'Blab tale tit'.)

Tell tale tit,
Your tongue will split,
And every dog in Huddersfield
Shall have a little bit.

Huddersfield.

Tell tale tit,
Your tongue shall be split in half,
Then won't we laugh!
Tell tale tit.

Lydney.

Tell tale titch,
Your tongue shall be slitch,
And all the little puppy dogs
Shall have a little bitch.

5-year-old boy, Hampstead.

Canty canty custard,
Ate a pound of mustard,
Burned his tongue and home did run,
Canty canty custard.

Welshpool. Cf. rhymes for cowards.

Tell tale tit,
Your mother can't knit,
Your father can't walk
Without a walking stick.

Fairly common in both England and Scotland.

Tell tale tit,
Yer mummie canna knit,
Yer daddie canna go to bed
Without a dummy tit.

Rothesay, Isle of Bute.

Tell tale tit,
Yer mother canna knit,
The only thing that she can do
Is sook a bairn's tit.

Aberdeen.

Telly-pie-tit
Sat upon a wall,
Eating raw cabbages
And letting bits fall.

West Hall, Cumberland.

Hide-and-go-seek,
Yer mother's a leek,
Yer father's a cabbage,
And yor a wee sneak.

Glasgow. Adaptation of a hide-and-seek call.

The following recitation is prevalent in Dublin:

Tell tale tattle
Buy a penny rattle
And tie it to a cow's tail.

This verse may be compared with verses current in the United States, where a sneak is often called a 'tattle tale':

Tattle tale, tattle tale,
Hang your britches on a nail.

Long Island, N.Y.

Tattle tale, tattle tale,
Hanging on the bull's tail.

Long Island, N.Y.

₊ The last of these rhymes (collected by Dr Howard) is of interest in that similar lines appear in Courtney and Couch's *Cornwall Glossary*, 1880:

Tell tale, pick a nail,
Hang to the bull's tail.

Most other tell-tale verses which have been recorded in the past have been from Scotland and the North Country:

Clash-pyot, clash-pyot,
Sits in the tree.
Ding doon aipples
Ane, twa, three;
Ane for the lady,
An ane for the laird,
An ane for the clash-pyot
It sits in the tree.

W. Gregor, N.E. of Scotland, 1881.

Tell! Tell! Tell!
Tell yer Auntie Bell
Tae buy a bottle o' stinkin' ale
And tak' a dram til hersel'!
Tell, Tell! Tell!

Forfar c. 1900. J. Rodger, 'Lang Strang', 1948.

Tell Pie Tit
Laid an egg and couldn't sit.

Doncaster. S. O. Addy, 'Sheffield Glossary', 1888–90.

Claik-pie, claik-pie,
Sits in the midden;
Licks up my dirt
And daes my biddin'.

Dunfermline. 'Rymour Club', 1911.

Claik-pie, claik-pie,
Sits in a tree,
Blabs awa to hissel
Like O Dear Me.

'Nicht at Eenie', Samson Press, 1932.

Johnny Brown is a telly-pie-tit,
Sits on the church wall,
Eating an apple and kepping a ball:
His tongue shall be slit
And all the little dogs shall have a bit.

M. and R. King, 'Street Games of North Shields Children', 1930. Version current 1895.

Crawlers

One who makes up to a teacher is recognized as being in a slightly different category from an outright sneak, although almost as nauseous. The usual epithets are 'toad', or 'toady', 'worms', 'crawler', or, in Camberwell, 'grease boy' or 'grease rat'.[1] He is a 'goody-goody', a 'namby-pamby'. He hands in his work on time, and does chores without being asked. 'Creeping are you?' they say, 'You creeper', 'You bummer', and more explicit names, according to their knowledge. Should he become, or be thought to have become, a teacher's pet, he quickly falls under the designation 'Pet' or 'Petty', 'Teacher's good boy' (and 'good' is given a suggestive significance), 'Holy angel, little innocent'. Their attitude, however, may be not unmixed with envy at the legends. 'Who's teacher's pet boy and was given a racing bicycle? Tain't fair. Teacher takes him home to tea. Why can't I be somebody's favourite?' And the pet, of course, can

1. 'Grease rat, shan't play with us.' 'Grease is a very popular word in school just now, and seems to be short for "greaser" – i.e. sycophant, soft-soaper, teacher's pet, and, by extension, anyone disapproved of.' – Mr Linden Huddlestone, Camberwell.

stand up for himself. 'Jealous! You go and hang yourself, I'll give you the rope.'

Bullies

'In Birmingham,' states an 11-year-old, 'we say to a bully or to a boy who shows off: "Big head, bucket, base-ball, your head is like a case-ball".'

In Ecclesfield an abusive term for a bully is 'Ichabod'. In Enfield a big boy, particularly a pugnacious one, has 'whopper' prefixed to his name, thus 'Whopper Williams'. Another term prefixed is 'stinker' as in the following account of how to deal with a bully, written by a 12-year-old.

'In S——[a village in Oxfordshire] there is a well-known bully usually named Stinker *Maynard*. He is always fighting younger boys so we tried our usual "bully bounce" on him. This is how it is done: the victim is captured and tied to an object consisting of two ashen poles. The bully is then dragged up a very bumpy hill to shake him about. He is then untied and hung upside down from a tree by his feet for a few minutes until he begs for mercy. The captors then hoist him down and fight him until he says he will leave us alone. This is done to every bully in our village.'

'The way we get even with a bully,' writes a Liverpool boy, aged 14, 'is a group of about ten boys lift him on their shoulders and run him into a group of boys who are just standing around and talking. They are then annoyed and set on him too. There is no special name for this.'

'For getting even with a bully,' writes an Edinburgh boy, aged 12, 'chalk or write on a piece of paper "KICK ME HARD" and pin or stick on to his back.'

It is noticeable that bullies, whose crime is a physical one, arouse the desire for physical retribution more strongly than any other offender of the juvenile code.

Sending Away

Children are not squeamish about telling an unpopular kid that he or she is not wanted, and juvenile language is well stocked (and apparently always has been) with expressions inviting a person's departure, for instance: 'Away with you – no salt in our sugar!', bamboosh, bat off, beat it, beetle off, bugger off, bunk (or 'Do a bunk!'), buzz off (and facetiously 'What does the bee say? – Buzz!'), cleaff off (Lincoln), clear off (often used patronizingly 'Clear off, son', 'Clear out, you kids'), crab (Manchester), dig the dirt, disappear, do a mickey, dog off, drift, fizz, flit, float away, f— off, get scarce, get weaving, gerraway (often with a threat '– or else!'), git (short for 'get going'), go and bale out, go and have a roll, go and jump in the cut (= canal, Liverpool), go and run up a tree (or 'Run up a tree and branch off'), 'Go home your ma's got cake', go on – blow, hit grit, hit the trail, hop it (often spelt as one word 'oppit'), hook it, make yourself scarce, mooch (Liverpool), move along, move off, nash away (Kirkcaldy), on your way lad, pack your bags and go, push off, quit, remove your carcass, scarper, scat, scoosh (Kirkcaldy), scoot, scram, scramoosh, scrub off (Lydney), scudabunk (Scotland), shag off, shave off (Birmingham), shift off, shit off, shove off, skedaddle, skidoosh, skip it, sling your hook, split the breeze, take off, travel, turf or turf out of it, vamoose, vanish, waft away, catch a passing sputnik, and (one child) 'Would you mind going please'.

₃ These terms supplied by twentieth-century children may be compared with those in Shakespeare's day given by Carew in his *Epistle on the Excellency of the English Tongue, c.* 1595: 'When wee would be rid of one, wee vse to saye *Bee going, trudge, pack, be faring, hence, awaye, shifte,* and, by circumlocution, *rather your roome then your companye, Letts see your backe, com againe when I bid you, when you are called, sent for, intreated, willed, desiered, inuited, spare vs your place, another in your steede, a shipp of salte for you, saue your credite, you are next the doore, the doore is open for you, theres noe bodye holdes you, no bodie teares your sleeue,* &c.'

The present-day directions are, of course, not infrequently accompanied by a personal description or family history of him whose absence is required. The following excommunication is commonly pronounced in Aberdeen:

> Awa ye ham,
> Yer mither's a bam,
> Yer auld man's a darkie.

Bam is a local term in Aberdeen for a silly ass.

Inducing Quiet

If a child has no authority for obtaining quiet he can seek it by brute force, by verbal force, or by guile. Verbal force can be very persuasive. 'Be quiet or I'll make yer', 'I'll hit you if you don't shut your gob', 'Button yer lip',[1] 'Button thy flaps' (Devon), 'Cut the cackle', 'Dry up', 'Glove it', 'Go chew a bar', 'Hold yer tongue', 'Hold your clack' (Oxford), 'Hud yer wheest' (Kirkcaldy), 'Hush up', 'Let's 'ave a bit of shush', 'Let's hear this pin drop', 'Mind your gob' (South Elmsall), 'Pipe down', 'Put a sock in it', 'Put a cork in it', 'Put wool in your hole', 'Put your head in a bucket of water three times and bring it out twice' (said 'particularly to persons one dislikes'), 'QUIET!' 'Quit the racket', 'Shsss!', 'Sharrap!', 'Shut your cake-hole', 'Shut your chops', 'Shut yer face' – 'fizzog' – 'flycatcher' – or, 'gate' ('gate' is surprisingly common), 'Shut your Gazette' (Bishop Auckland),[2] 'Shut your gob, you got one ain't you?', 'Shut the hatch' or 'Shut the hatch the wind's getting in', 'Shut your 'ole', 'Give it a drink', 'Shut your larrup' (Lydney),[3] 'Shut your neck', 'Shut that big trap o' yours',[4] 'Shut your ugly dial', 'Stop gasbagging', 'Shut up, big gob', 'Stew it', 'Stow it', 'Wrap up and wind your neck in'.

Guile is practised chiefly by girls. The quickest way of getting silence is to say 'Cave! Someone's coming'. This will make everyone so quiet one can hear their hair growing. But it is not a wise stratagem, 'Cave' being a special warning word (see under Keeping Lookout, p. 399–40) and life becomes unpleasant for the child who uses it improperly. It is more constitutional, and almost as effective, to say: 'The first person to speak after me is a monkey' ('ape', 'ass', 'donkey', etc.), 'Next person to speak has to wash Hitler's dishes' (still current 1952). 'Silence in the pig market, the fat pig wants to speak', 'Silence in the pig market or the pigs won't sell' (Market Rasen), 'Silence in the frying pan the sausage is going to speak', or, very common today, 'Silence in the court, the donkey wants to talk', or 'Silence in the court, the monkey wants to talk, Speak up, monkey, speak.'

It may be that in the ensuing lull a bold wag will say:

> Silence reigns
> And we all got wet.[5]

1. 'Button your lip' was already schoolboy slang in the first half of the nineteenth century (*Notes and Queries*, 4th ser., vol. i, 1868, p. 603), and was possibly current in Stuart times. John Trapp in his *Annotations* (on Matthew xxii. 46), 1662, remarks: 'How easily can God button up the mouths of our busiest adversaries.'
2. The *Gazette* is a local newspaper, and the boys selling it in the evening are renowned for their raucous voices.
3. Larrup or lerrup, West Country dialect for a rent or tear, to which an offensive mouth may be likened. Cf. 'Shut yer rip' (Kirkcaldy).
4. Boys in Birmingham about 1930 used to chant 'Shut your silly trap, trap, trap, trap, trap, trap, trap', to the tune of Boccherini's Minuet.
5. In Swansea they say 'Silence reigns. Hark! It's pickering.' ('It's pickering to rain' is a local expression when a few drops begin to fall.)

And thereafter, the spell being broken, another wag may mock the original with:

> Silence in the court
> While the judge blows his nose
> Stands on his head
> And tickles his toes.

But on the whole these formulas work with satisfying ease, bringing about that fragile thing which, as the riddle says, 'is broken every time it is named'.

** 'Silence in the pig market' dates back as long as living memory. Writers in *Notes and Queries*, vol. clxxiv, 1938, pp. 155, 196, 233, recall, from the nineteenth century, 'Silence in the pig market and let the old sow speak first', and the enigmatical 'Silence in the pig market of Anjou'. Northall in his *Folk-Phrases*, 1894, records, 'Silence in the pig market, and let the old sow have a grunt'.

A sort of mock reproof, which was popular a generation ago, went:

> Silence in the gallery,
> Order in the pit,
> The people in the boxes
> Can't hear a bit.

Intimidation

Despite the schoolchild code concerning private possessions there are, needless to say, occasions when the ownership of an object is disputed in no regular manner. A rising tide of exasperation can be glimpsed in the demands used in one metropolitan classroom when, having exhausted the should-be-respected words 'Bagsy', 'Baggy mine', and 'I bags it', the inmates continued: 'S'mine', 'Dat's mine', 'I found it so it's mine', 'It's mine my mother bought it for me', 'Cor, gi's it', 'Hand over', 'Hi those is mine, you f—ker' (accompanied by the conventional upward thrust of two raised fingers), 'Beat you up if you don't let me have it!'

The demand to hand over has elsewhere been heard expressed in the words: 'Cough it up', 'Dish it out', 'Dub up' (North Country), 'Fork over', 'Gie it over' (Scotland), 'Gimme' (very English), 'Show it up', 'Turf it up', 'Unwrap', followed by the normal threats, 'Wait till I get hold of you',

> Stand and deliver
> Your money or your liver,

'Hand it over – or else', – 'I'll bash you up' (the most usual suggestion), 'I'll bluter you' (Kirkcaldy), 'I'll clop you one', 'I'll clout you', 'I'll do you', or 'I'll do you up' (a threat of sinister implication in London S.E.), 'I'll fell you', 'I'll floor you', 'I'll maulicate you', 'I'll slosh you', 'I'll snickersneeze you' (Market Rasen), 'I'll spiflicate you', 'I'll swat thee' (Yorkshire), 'I'll pick you up and drop you', and similar offers of injury or extermination. Or, more anatomically specific: 'I'll knock your block off', 'I'll chin you', 'I'll give you a thick ear', 'A'l ge you a jelly nose, a black eye, and a custard lug' (thus spelt by a Langholm lad), 'Ar'll knock thy teeth down thy throat' (thus spelt by a Bishop Auckland lad), 'I'll nut you', 'I'll punch yer 'ead in', 'I'll knock your head off and put a cabbage on', 'I'll knock yer belly where your back should be', 'Mind your back, your belly's in danger', and, 'I'll knock you for six', which has also been heard as 'I'll knock you through the sound barrier'. The girls' great threat: 'I won't like you any more.'

In Warwickshire a rhythmic threat is current:

> See my finger,
> See my thumb,
> See my fist,
> – You'd better run.

a warning which is fairly widespread, too, amongst boys in the United States.

Fighting

'If a fight is on,' writes an 11-year-old Londoner, 'people gather round and shout "fight, fight, fight", witch is shortened to "oih, oih, oih, oih". If a prefect or master comes on the scene everybody shouts out "Boo-ooo-ooo-ooo" till puffed or blowen out.' Spectators offer the favoured protagonist such encouragement as: 'Bash him one', 'Bash the daylights out of him', 'Bat him on the nob', 'Biff him on the boko', 'Bruise him', 'Clock him' (i.e. hit him on the face), 'Dong him on the dome' (head), 'Get him in the guts', 'Give 'im a crafty clip in the ear 'ole', 'Go on, lam into him', 'Mash him', 'Slosh him on the dial', 'Sock him on the kisser', 'Get in and kill him'.

The spectators' interest in the result of the fight may indeed be more than that of mere onlookers. In every group of boys there is, as in the animal world, an established order of physical superiority, and it is when this order is challenged that most fights seem to occur. A half sheet of paper picked up off a classroom floor, and handed to us by a teacher, is headed: *If I can beat you up put your name*. Beneath follows a neat column of signatures. Seven small boys have attested to the cock's prowess. He can, as they express it, 'scrap the class'. He may even be 'cock of the school'. Their prudent pen-and-ink admission of his superiority should in their case obviate the necessity for any violence. Only the bold wit amongst them will ask 'Wanna fight do you?' and when the cock says he does, will reply: 'Let me hold your coat.'[1]

Challenges. The commonest challenge is 'Put up your mitts' or, in East London, 'Stick up yer mitties'. Alternatively, 'Put your spars up', 'Raise your dibs, son', 'Put up your maulers', 'Show me your rockers', 'Roll up your sleeves', or 'Wanna make something of it, eh?' The Liverpudlian says 'Come on I'll 'ave you a go', 'Want a barney, do you?' or 'I'll have you a scrap'. The Yorkshire lad says 'A'll 'ave you a feit'. The Camberwell tough mutters 'I don't take the mic-mac. Put your dukes up. Hold that.' To call anyone a 'yellow belly' is of course, tantamount to issuing a challenge to fight. 'You're scared.' 'I'm not.' 'Well come on then'. And many a combat has been agreed upon with the polite but ominous words 'Meet you after school in the playground.'

In Aberdeen, a girl reports she has heard the boys saying:

> Off with the jackets,
> Up with the sleeves,
>   Biff, Bang,
> Down on your knees.

'It is usually the boy who is sure he is going to win who says it.'

From the folklorist's point of view the most interesting challenges are those which are still customary in the north. In Stoke-on-Trent one boy seizes another securely and hammers him on the right shoulder or biceps with his clenched fist, repeating:

> One, two, three,
> If thee 'its me
> I'll be boss of thee,
> So one, two, three.

---

1. The expression 'cock of the school' is now more in use amongst boys in the north of England than in the south. In the eighteenth and nineteenth centuries it was general. Thus Swift, *Grand Question*, 1729: 'At cuffs I was always cock of the school.' Likewise young Osborne in a letter from Dr Swishtail's academy, *Vanity Fair*, 1848, ch. v: 'Dear Mama . . . There has been a fight here between Cuff & Dobbin. Cuff, you know, was the Cock of the School. They fought thirteen rounds, and Dobbin Licked. So Cuff is now Only Second Cock.'

This is called 'having one's dups'. The other lad must fight or accept the challenger's suzerainty. In south Yorkshire, where the practice also obtains, they say as they strike 'There's thi dabs' ('Gi him his dabs', cry the onlookers when the fight is on), and, again, the challenged one must fight or submit. In the country around Sheffield a boy will say, 'A'll put cock on thee if tha doesn't feit me'. By this he means that he will put cock's spit (the victor's spittle) over the other's hand or finger if he refuses to take him on, and, likewise, will thereafter be the other's superior.[1]

Retribution

In some schools children have a standard way, sanctioned by custom, of 'getting their own back' on a miscreant.

'The way in which we punish a boy who has been disagreeable is by setting upon him and carrying him to the tap and putting his head under it and switching it on. This is called ducking' (Boy, 14, Liverpool). 'If one boy is not fair his head is put down the lavatory and the chain pulled' (Boy, 11, Oxford). 'They are ducked under a pump with their hands tied behind them' (Girl, 12, Ecclesfield). 'If a person does something which doesn't please us we cry "scrag him" or "pan him", or "floor him". If any of these are said everybody bashes him' (Boy, 13, Langholm).

The term 'scragging' is recurrent everywhere, and seems in fact to be different from giving someone a 'beating up' or 'bashing'. One boy makes the distinction: 'To scrag is a more gentle way of having a kind of hurtful revenge. You pull his hair and take his tie off and that sort of thing.'

Other discomforts for the insufferable: 'Everybody ignores him or makes up rude verses about him.' 'Call names at, shun.' 'Sit the person on a lighted stove (only done to very unpopular persons).' 'Stick a pin through the middle of person's nale.' 'Get a grip on person's knee and pinch hard. When you get the right spot it is very painful.' 'Dig your knuckle in his back between his shoulders and move it slightly.' 'Punish a person by holding her still and unplatting her hair.' 'Sew sleeves of coat up.' 'Bother or tease.'

Recommendations by boys in East and South-East London: 'Bash him

1. These north country challenges are undoubtedly old. For nineteenth-century accounts see William Henderson, *Folk Lore of the Northern Counties*, 1866, p. 19; S. O. Addy, *Household Tales*, 1895, pp. 131–2; *Notes and Queries*, 8th ser., vol. ix, 1896, p. 90; *English Dialect Dictionary*, vol. i, 1898, p. 682 (South Lancashire); and cf. John Jamieson, *Scottish Dictionary, Supplement*, vol. ii, 1825, p. 459; W. Gregor, *Folk-Lore of N.-E. Scotland*, 1881, p. 21.

up.' 'Beat him up.' 'Bounce him.' 'Bump him.' 'Bundle him.' 'Scalp him.'
'Scrag him.' 'Scrap him' (here defined as debagging him). 'Shin him'
(i.e. kick him). 'Slash him.' 'Splatter him.' 'Stretch him.' 'Expel him
from the gang.' 'Make him do something daring.' 'Pinch, punch, or under
the arch.' 'Put him under the mill.' 'Put a firework in his letter box and
wallop him.' (Definitions of some of these terms appear in the next section.)

Country children suggest: 'Nettle walking', also given as 'Nettling'
and 'Slinging in nettles', 'Hedging', which is similar, 'Throwing burrs at
person',[1] and 'Rubbing', which is rubbing the flower of the dandelion on
the person's face (Chapeltown, near Sheffield). 'Make him eat dirt.'
'Baptize with dirt.' 'Throw stones at his feet to make him dance.' 'Take
off his shoes, and put water, grass, and earth down his neck.' 'Spit in his
face.' 'Make him cut his finger.' 'Put itching powder down his neck' – the
'itching powder' being made of the soft centres of rose hips before the
seeds are ripe – in Leicestershire known as 'itchy-backs'.

Further suggestions, some possibly wishful rather than factual, though
obtained in a very tough district: 'Tie him to a lamp post and throw mud
in his face.' 'Tie him on a tree and swing him across a very wide dyke
blindfolded.' 'Tie him up and fling tuffets or any fruit at him and then
torture him.' Usual saying whilst inflicting torture: 'Mummy's little
cissy.' Saying by the one being tortured: ''Ere, nark it.'

Ordeals

The following ordeals, or ones similar, appear to be common to many
schools in Britain.

Sending to Coventry. 'When someone does something most of the class
disagrees with, we send that person to Coventry which means we never
speak to them. Sometimes one or two people hold their noses with their
fingers and say that the place smell where they have been. Another name
for this is "giving them a cold shoulder".' – Girl, 10, Birmingham.

Sending to Coventry is often preceded by a class committee, which
deliberates the length of time the person should stay in Coventry, and
enforces the sentence. Nobody may speak to the child, 'not even the person's best friend', except during class, and if anybody does he is liable to

1. Edward Moor, born 1771, recounts in his *Suffolk Words* how throwing burrs 'on girls'
clothing, or rubbing a handful of them well into the long haired (and the odds in my days
were also *lousy*) scalp of a boy were common pieces of wickedness'. And Shakespeare,
who let nothing in nature pass, has Celia saying, 'They are but burs, Cosen, throwne
vpon thee in holiday foolerie' (*As You Like It*, I. iii).

be put in Coventry himself; and care is taken to ensure that two people in Coventry do not get talking to each other. In Aberdeen the punishment is also known as 'Solitary'.

*** The phrase 'to send to Coventry' became proverbial in the second half of the eighteenth century. Its origin is unknown, but it may come from a one-time Parliamentarian practice, mentioned by Clarendon in his *History of the Rebellion* (vi, § 83), of sending Royalist prisoners to Coventry for safe keeping. The punishment is referred to in many school tales, e.g. in Maria Edgeworth's story 'Eton Montem' in *The Parent's Assistant* (1795), in *Tom Brown's School Days* (1857), *Jack Harkaway's Schooldays* (1871), and in *Vice Versâ* (1882).

Bumps. The 10-year-old Birmingham girl quoted above, says of 'Bumps': 'This is also for someone who is unpopular. Two pretty hefty people get hold of the person's legs and arms and bump them on the ground. The boys mostly do this, and the girls are "sent to Coventry".' The operation, in Camberwell carried out with the cry 'Bounce him, boys', in Alton called 'bumpers', and in Scotland generally known as 'dumps' or 'dumping' (a term which also embraces thumping a person on his backside with the bent knee), is also ritually inflicted on children's birthdays (q.v.). In Newcastle 9 to 11-year-olds have a rhyme, when either bumping or ducking:

> Bump, bump, salty water,
> Give the dog a drink of water,
> One, two, three, *drop*!

*** Compare Edward Moor, who was at school in the 1770s: 'The punishment of a schoolboy for telling tales or for any act of treachery, coming immediately under the summary jurisdiction of his peers, is *bumping*: and this is performed by prostrating the coatless culprit on his back, in the immediate vicinity of a large block of wood, or of a wall. A strong boy seizes the right ankle and wrist, another the left, and lift him off the ground; and after a preparatory vibration or two to give a due momentum, he comes in violent contact with the block, *a posteriori*. This is repeated six or eight more times, according to the enormity of the offence, or the just resentment of the executioners.' – *Suffolk Words*, 1823, p. 53. Around Halifax, *c.* 1900, this practice was termed 'free-bumming' (correspondent).

Running the Gauntlet. Although well known by this name, the ordeal is also termed the 'House of Whacks' (Camberwell), 'Under the Arches'

(Enfield and London), and, very generally, 'Under the Mill' or 'Through the Mill'. A Knottingley lad, aged about 13, writes:

'When boys are not agreeable and are bullies they are put through the mill. This is a kind of torture, and about twenty boys or less, as the case may be, put their hands flat on the wall, with arms outstretched to form a tunnel. The bully has to go through the mill four times. The first time he has *rain*, this is a good slap from each boy. The second time he gets *lightning*, this is a rabbit-punch. The third time he gets *thunder*, this is a prod with the knee. Fourth time he gets *hailstones*, this is a very hard punch in the back. I can assure you the bully will behave after this.'

The mill may also be made by two lines of boys facing each other, making an arch with one hand, and inflicting punishment with the other. Or the offender may be given a 'frog march' along the line of boys, that is to say be forcibly conducted along the line with his arms twisted behind his back.

In less severe form Running the Gauntlet is inflicted on the loser in such games as Bad Eggs and Donkey, as part of the game.

*** Pieter Brueghel the Elder (1525?–1569) depicts children making one of their playfellows run the gauntlet in his famous picture *Kinderspiele*. Running the gauntlet was at one time a regular military punishment, and was made a legal punishment in America in 1676.

Frog Marching. This can be and, indeed, usually is inflicted independently of Running the Gauntlet. 'The person is marched backwards with his arms locked by two boys. He is marched through mud, puddles, bushes, etc.'

Stretching Board. 'Four boys get the bully, two grab his arms and two grab his legs, and they pull.' Alternatively, in a classroom, and more painfully, 'Stretch the body on desk with boys pulling each end of the boy.' – Brentwood, Camberwell, Peterborough, and Pontefract.

Wylums Torture. This punishment, said to be 'popular in Langholm', is in a sense the opposite of the Stretching Board. Thus a 12-year-old: 'You lay them on the ground stomach downwards. Then put one hand under their chin and with the other hand lift their legs so that their legs touch their head. It usually takes more than one to do it.'

Piling On. This is done either 'to hurt a person if he has done wrong', after he has been forcibly thrown to the ground, or, as opportunity occurs, during rough play, when somebody accidentally falls, and one of the company jumps on top of him, yelling 'Pile on', a summons readily obeyed by everybody else rushing up and adding their weight on top of the fallen one. The summons 'Pile on' seems to be understood everywhere from Guildford to Golspie, but in Liverpool the usual cry is 'Piley on', and in Lydney 'Pile on sacks'.

*** In New Zealand the common call is 'Sacks to the mill', a formula which was known in Oxfordshire until the end of the nineteenth century (*English Dialect Dictionary*), and which goes back more than 300 years. In Mabbe's translation, 1622, of Alemán's novel *Guzman de Alfarache* appears the passage: 'When there was nothing to be done at home, your Lackies ... would ... fright me with Snakes, hang on my backe, & weigh me downe, crying, More sackes to the Mill.' Biron, in *Love's Labour's Lost* (IV. iii), may also be referring to the sport when he exclaims, 'More Sacks to the myll. O heavens I have my wish.'

The Chamber. 'One boy is put between the door and the wall, then damp leaves are thrown over him.' – Boy, 13, Laindon, Essex.

Tortures

The most common torture is to 'do a barley-sugar', also expressed verbally in the threat 'I'll barley-sugar you', which is to twist a person's arm round until it hurts, usually behind his back, so that the sufferer has – according to which way his arm is being twisted – to lean backwards or bend forwards excessively to alleviate the pain, and is thus utterly at his tormentor's mercy. The hold is also known as 'Red hot poker', 'Fireman's torture', and 'Nelson's grip' or 'Nelson's twist' (after the wrestling hold).[1]

Less dangerous, but equally painful, is a 'Chinese burn', also known as 'Chinese torture' and 'Chinese twist' (in the United States 'Indian burn' or 'Indian torture'), in which the perpetrator clenches the victim's wrist with both hands and 'twists both ways at the same time, like wringing the dish cloth'. This torture is particularly unpleasant if the victim's arm is already twisted behind his back. If the operation is conducted merely by squeezing a piece of flesh between the thumb nails and rubbing in opposite directions it is termed 'Snake's bite'.

'Boring', 'Worming', or 'Fixing the points' is done by fixing the points of the thumb and forefinger as hard as possible on either side of the upper

[1]. Arm twisting was of course another unpleasantness suffered by the unhappy Mr Bultitude. ' "Very well, then," said Coggs firmly, "we must try the torture. Coker, will you screw the back of his hand, while I show him how they make barley-sugar?" And he gave Paul an interesting illustration of the latter branch of industry by twisting his right arm round and round till he nearly wrenched it out of the socket.' (*Vice Versâ*, 1882, p. 73.)

arm bone, near the muscle, and working them back and forth rapidly over the bone, an action which is quite horribly painful.

The same limb suffers in a ritual practised at a village school near Alton, in which the person's arm is held out straight and taut, with the words,

> Skin a rabbit, skin a hare,
> Chop it off just *there*!

and the side of the hand is brought down sharply on the victim's forearm.

A 'Rabbit's Punch' is delivered by pulling a child's head forward, usually by his hair, and slicing the back of his neck with the side of the hand.

'Cresting' or 'Giving one's crest' is done in the changing rooms. If a boy's bare back is slapped hard enough with the flat of the hand it leaves a red clear imprint, for all to see, on the recipient's flesh. The aggressor then announces he has branded the boy with his crest.

Hand or finger crushing does not seem to have a special name, unless it is the undescribed torture 'Ginot handshake' in Aberystwyth. The art of hand crushing lies in taking hold not of the palm of the hand but the line of knuckles at the root of the fingers, squeezing them tightly, and grinding them back and forth. It is the friction of these bones being rubbed against each other which causes the shooting pain up the wrist.

A 'Barber's rub' or 'Dry scrub' is administered by firmly massaging the customer's scalp at his temples and the nape of his neck with the knuckles: an operation which is more painful than the uninitiated might suppose.

A 'Bee sting' consists of sharply twisting a pinch of short hair on the temple, a growth which is particularly sensitive to interference, as is also revealed by 'Side-hair tweak'.

'Cumberland creep' is the name of a little torment practised in Chelmsford, and possibly elsewhere, which involves twisting the longer hair on the top of a person's head around a pencil or ball-point (preferably one with a clip), and then pulling.

A 'Chinese hair cut' is traditional in many places. The tool employed is the inner sticky stem of a stalk of grass such as cocksfoot, which can be easily pulled from the outer casing if the stalk is opened at a knot. This inner stem is drawn through the person's hair, and is considered to be successfully 'giving a hair cut' if, as usually happens (especially when performed on a girl with long silky hair) it draws some of the hair out with it.

Hair Pulling

If a girl has made herself obnoxious, or is so rash as to announce that it is her birthday (see under Birthdays, pp. 324–5), her hair is pulled ceremonially, once for each year of her age, plus very often 'one for luck', or 'one to be a good girl in future'. In Manchester they then ask: 'A bull or a goose?' If she replies 'goose' she is let loose, but if she replies 'bull' she receives a further pull. Alternatively they ask: 'A hen or a goose?' If she replies 'goose' she is let loose, but if she replies 'hen' her hair is given another ten pulls.

In Blackburn, Lancashire, the child is asked: 'Cock, hen, goose, or gander?' If she replies 'cock' they say 'Give a good knock'; if 'hen' – 'Pull again'; if 'goose' – 'Let loose'; if 'gander' – 'Whither do I wander'. (Information from boy aged 10, and girl aged 11.)

In Swansea they hope for even further sport. The tormentors ask 'Hen or goose?' If the child replies 'goose' she is let loose, but if she says 'hen' they sing out 'Do it again', and pull her hair again, a tug for each year, and keep on holding. She is then asked: 'Brick or a stone?' If she says 'stone' they say 'Leave her alone', and her hair is released, but if she replies 'brick' they 'Give her a kick' and still hold her hair. They then ask 'Duck or a feather?' If she chooses 'duck' that is 'Bad luck', but if she chooses 'a feather' she can be consoled with the thought that it is now 'Good luck for ever'. (Information from teacher of 12-year-old girls.)

In Newcastle a girl is told to 'say soap', and when she does so the others chorus 'Pull the rope', suiting their actions to their words by pulling her hair. (Information from 9 and 10-year-olds.)

*** These formulas, which appear to be widespread in Britain, are not new. The trick 'Say soap, pull the rope' was known in Edwardian days; and about 1930 a native of Ulverston taught his daughters what had become a nursery jingle:

> Wrangel a wrangel a
> Pig-a-machine,
> All his mighty men:
> Fly, cock, goose, or hen.

He would hold on to a lock of hair, and the daughter had to choose one of four alternatives. If she chose 'fly' the father would say 'Let it go by – wrangel a wrangel all over again'; if she chose 'cock' he would say 'Pull an' a knock – wrangel a wrangel all over again', and pull her hair and knock her head; if she chose 'goose' he would say 'Never let loose –

wrangel a wrangel all over again'; if she chose 'hen' he would simply say 'Wrangel a wrangel all over again'.

Similar formulas are current in the United States, but employed for ear-pulling. In East Texas Dr Howard collected the ritual verse:

> Goosie goosie gander,
> Say goose –
> Turn 'im loose.
> Say gander –
> Pull 'im way out yonder,

and the ears were pulled or released according to the child's answer. In his *Negro Folk Rhymes*, 1922, pp. 75 and 262, the negro folklorist Professor T. W. Talley recalls from his youth a ritual game in which a leader chanted:

'Goosie, goosie, goosie-gander! What d'you say?'

If the child addressed replied 'gander' the leader cried:

'Ve'y well. Come in de ring, Honey! I'll pull yō' years way yander!'

Both would then grasp hold of each other's ears and tug.

It seems certain that somewhere, sometime, this game played in the nineteenth century by coloured folk in the United States, and the ordeal which little girls undergo in Britain today, must have had a common ancestor. In Scotland in Georgian times, according to Jamieson,[1] children had a kind of sport in which one lad took hold of another by the forelock, saying to him:

'Tappie, Tappie tousie, will ye be my man?'

If the answer was the affirmative, the first continued, 'Come to me then, come to me then', giving the other a smart pull towards him by the lock he was holding. If the reply was in the negative, he gave the interrogated one a push backward, saying, 'Gae fra me then, gae fra me then'. Jamieson believed that tappie tousie retained 'a singular vestige of very ancient manners' and he associated the play with the old-time custom in which, when a free man wished to become a great person's bondman (so that he could be assured of his maintenance) he rendered himself 'in his court, *be the haire of his forehead*; and gif he thereafter withdrawes himselfe, and flees away fra his maister, or denyes to him his nativitie: his maister may proue him to be his bond-man, be ane assise, before the Justice'.

1. John Jamieson, *An Etymological Dictionary of the Scottish Language*, vol. ii, 1808, *tappie-tousie*.

A GENTLEMAN residing in Plymouth in 1852 stated that in his boyhood it was a common practice with children when they saw a white horse, to 'spit three times', and to 'go where the spit goes' (as the initiating phrase expressed it), in order to be lucky. The *modus operandi*, he said, was to eject the spittle as far as possible, to proceed to the spot where it fell and eject again, and then standing upon the spot where that fell make a third ejection. And he added the comment: 'The practice, notwithstanding the progress of education, has not entirely died out, as I find my own children have been taught the charm, or whatever it may be called.'[1]

This statement, that the juvenile custom of paying superstitious regard to the white horse 'has not entirely died out' could have been made a hundred years later, as shown by the following:

'If you see a white horse spit three times.'

Girl, 11, Perth, 1954.

'If you see a white horse you must spit over your left shoulder.'

Girl, 20, Bath, 1952.

'When you see a white horse you should cross your fingers and spit over them.'

Girl, c. 20, Bath, 1955.

'If I see a white horse I usually spit and wish a wish. This wish is supposed to come to pass.'

Girl, 14, Aberdeen, 1952.

'If you spit when you see a white horse it is lucky. If you see it twice it is unlucky.'

Boy, 12, Ongar, 1957.

'If you see a white horse spit on your heel and you will have luck.'

Girl, 12, Aberystwyth, 1953.

'If you see a white horse you wet your finger and touch the sole of your shoe and say a poet's name and say this verse:

> White horse, white horse,
> Bring me luck today or tomorrow.'

Girl, c. 12, Aberystwyth, 1953.

1. *Notes and Queries*, 1st ser., vol. vi, 1852, p. 193.

'It is considered lucky to see a white horse if you spit on your shoe and say

> White horse, white horse, give me good luck,
> Today or tomorrow may I pick something up.'

Report from a teacher, Clun, Shropshire, 1953.

'If you see a white horse, to bring luck you must spit on the sole of your shoe and then rub it in the ground.'

Report from an aunt of two small girls, Gloucester, 1956.

'In the West Country, if children see a white horse, they mark the sole of their shoe with the sign of a cross.'

Report from a parent, Plymouth, 1953.

Occasionally, white horses are regarded as straightforward signs of good luck, and no protective action is taken.

'If you see a white horse it will bring you good luck.'

Girl, 14, Stoke-on-Trent, 1954.

'If you are walking down a street before school starts, and you see a white horse the horse brings you luck.'

Girl, 13, Forfar, 1954.

'If you see a white horse in the street, wish a wish and it is sure to come true.'

Girl, 13, Golspie, 1952.

'Upon seeing a white horse:

> White horse, white horse,
> Bring me good luck.
> Good luck to you,
> Good luck to me,
> Good luck to everyone I see.'

Report from a parent, Sheffield, 1949.

Usually, however, there is some rite or prohibition if ill luck is to be averted, and a wish granted.

'If you see a white horse you must not look at its tail.'

Girl, 20, Bath, 1952.

'Seeing a white horse in the street is considered lucky. If one wishes, and does not turn or look back until the horse has gone out of sight that is believed to make the wish successful.'

Girl, 14, Aberdeen, 1952.

'If you see a white horse, look round, and if you see a girl with red hair your wish will come true.'

Girl, 14, Knighton, 1952.[1]

1. Confirmed by several Radnorshire children. The converse can also be true. 'If you see a red-haired person you should look for a white horse, if you wish to be lucky.' – *Girl, 15, Forfar, 1954.*

'When you see a white horse, wish a wish, cross your fingers, and keep them crossed until you see a dog.'

Report from teacher of infant class, Luncarty, nr. Perth, 1954.

'If you see a white horse, cross your fingers till you see a black dog.'

Boy, 12, Market Rasen, 1953.

It is not necessary here to inquire into what may be the origin of these duties performed before the white horse. Whether or not they are, as has been suggested, a memory of Crusader knights setting out for the Holy Land, or a relic of Christianizing paganism and the Saxon worship of the horse, or whether they have been with us even longer, like the excavation which still shines on a Berkshire hillside, is for scholars to argue about elsewhere. The point we wish to make is the one which is apparently demonstrated, and is strange enough in itself: that a ritual respect for the white horse has long been the rule rather than the exception with that part of our population which is most newly arrived. And we may observe that this deference to the white horse is no lone survival from the past.

Outwardly the children in the back streets and around the housing estate appear to belong to the twentieth century, but ancient apprehensions, even if only half believed in, continue to infiltrate their minds; warning them that moonlight shining on a person's face when he is asleep will make him go mad, that vinegar stops a person growing no matter how young he is, that a bleeding wart never stops bleeding and the person will bleed to death. They confide to each other that a stone-chip picked up off a grave brings a curse upon him who takes it; that a nose which is too long may be shortened by rubbing it with wet grass on the night of a new moon; and that if a photograph in a frame is dropped and the glass breaks, a painful accident will befall the subject of the photograph. 'I shudder if I break a mirror, fearing seven years' bad luck,' says a 14-year-old Yorkshire girl; and a Radnorshire lad affirms, 'If you break a mirror they say seven years' bad luck to you. This is true in my family.' With simple faith they accept beliefs which have not changed since Shakespeare's day: that if a dog howls outside a house or scratches at the floor someone is going to die in that house; that if owls screech at night it is a sign of death; that if a person hears of two deaths he will assuredly hear of a third; and in evening places where children meet the telling of each dark precept is supported with gruesome instances. They begin to share the awe felt by Mole in *The Wind in the Willows* when Ratty warned him of the hundred things an animal had first to understand before entering the Wild Wood: 'passwords, and signs, and sayings which have power and effect, and plants you carry in your pocket, and verses you repeat, and dodges and tricks you practise; all simple enough when you know them, but they've got to be known if you're small, or you'll find yourself in trouble.' It is such dark thoughts which cause children at Brierley Hill in south Staffordshire to hide their little fingers when an ambulance goes by for fear that their finger-nails will drop out; which induce children in the Gower Peninsula to spit when they see a dead animal and cry:

> Fever, fever, stay away,
> Don't come in my bed today;

and which lead children in Scotland when they see a large black slug or snail to spit on it, declaring 'It's no ma Dye, an' it's no ma Grannie' (reported from Ballingry, Cowdenbeath, and Gartcosh, near Glasgow). And one wonders how many bishops are aware of the jockeying for places which goes on beforehand among the candidates for confirmation when word gets about that to be confirmed with the bishop's right hand is lucky, but to be confirmed with his left hand means bad luck.

Juvenile Attitude to Folklore

The beliefs with which we are concerned here are those which children absorb through going about with each other, and consequently mostly involve happenings out-of-doors: people met in the street, objects found in the road, and mascots carried with them to school. We find, what is understandable, that the younger schoolchildren treat the beliefs and rites of their companions more seriously than those practised by their parents and grandparents; although it is also noticeable that later (14-years-old onwards) the child-to-child superstitions tend to be discarded, along with the rest of the lore, and even forgotten, while the more domestic traditions, which are passed down in the family, are mentioned with increasing frequency.

When asked how much they believe in their superstitions most children will say (as they feel they are expected to say?) that all superstitions are silly. But it may, in passing, be observed that few people, adult or juvenile, are above doing what is silly. As a 10-year-old Nottinghamshire girl candidly confessed, 'If I want to have good luck I do very funny things,' and she went on to say:

'First of all I close my eyes and wave my arms about ten times.
'Secondly I always wear my vest inside out and my jumper back to front. I did that in the selection examination and that brought good luck. When I

heard the results that I had passed, as soon as I got home I changed everything round if I had not done it would have brought bad luck.

'If I am going in for a competition I do not do that, I put a glove on my left hand and suck my other hand at night. I did that once in a Competition and I won first prize – a bike.'

Further it may be remarked that when a practice or omen is termed a 'superstition' it is generally one which is not believed in by the person so referring to it. When collecting this lore from children we have not asked for 'superstitions' as such, but have inquired after the 'magic practices' they knew, or asked for their 'ways of obtaining luck or averting ill-luck'.

Many charms and rites are of course practised by children 'just for fun', because everybody else practises them, and it is the fashion. Other charms, although recognized as being 'probably silly', are repeated because they also feel that there 'may be something in it'. Others, again, are practised because it is in the nature of children to be attracted by the mysterious: they appear to have an innate awareness that there is more to the ordering of fate than appears on the surface. And yet other practices and beliefs are undoubtedly so taken for granted that it is not appreciated that the custom or belief is in fact superstitious. It must, after all, be borne in mind that the children here under observation are only at the stage of mental development sometimes ascribed to a savage tribe, whom anthropologists are not at all surprised to find dominated by superstition. And what might be surprising, and even alarming, would be to find a new generation with so little imagination that it was unable to be a Tom Sawyer and be stirred by curious fancies.

The children's beliefs do not, as may first appear, consist of a miscellany of unrelated scraps. Looked at all together they are seen to fall into a definite pattern, and the dominant motives which emerge in the things that they feel bring good luck or evil, e.g. dislike of seeing the backs of objects (ambulances, mail vans, hay wains; also blind men, men with wooden legs, and nuns); reluctance to anticipate events, for instance not putting water in a jar before the first tiddler has been caught; and love of safeguards as shown in their addiction to lucky charms, scapegoats, and finger-crossing, probably satisfy psychological impulses as well as following the path of tradition.

Ambulances

An understandable instance of a custom attaching itself to an inanimate object is the hospital ambulance fetish. Amongst children throughout

England the sight of an ambulance passing in the street instantly evokes a self-protective charm. 'I was bringing a bunch of orphans to a party in my car yesterday,' reported a Manchester teacher (1953), 'when one of them saw an ambulance. "Touch your collar and look for a four-footed animal", she commanded the rest'; and this practice appears to be commonplace, the rite very often being decreed in rhyme:

Touch collar
Never swallow
Never get the fever,
Touch your nose
Touch your toes
Never go in one of those.

Newcastle.

Touch collar
Never swallow
Never catch the fever,
Not for you
Not for me
Not for all the family.

Stoke-on-Trent.

Touch your collar
Touch your toes
Never go in one of those,
Touch your knee
Touch your chin
Never let the burglar in.

Oxford.

Touch your collar,
Be a scholar
Never catch diseases.

Cumberland.

Cross my fingers
Cross my toes,
Hope I don't go
In one of those.

Birmingham.

Hold your collar
Never swallow
Never die of fever.

Woking.[1]

In the many accounts which have been received no significant differences have been noted between the rhymes from one part of the country and another, and sometimes more than one version is known in a locality. Thus, despite present-day prevalence, the custom appears to be of recent date. No adult seems to have noticed this juvenile obeisance previously, and the earliest we have heard of the rhyme being used is in Bayswater about 1930 (Stoke-on-Trent version). But the practice of looking for a four-footed scapegoat (a dog often being specified) is of course older than the introduction of ambulances, and a similar search is called for when a funeral goes by (q.v.). The children are precise in their injunctions:

'Every time you see an ambulance hold your collar until you see a four-legged animal.'

Girl, 12, South Molton, Devon.

'If you see an ambulance hold your collar and don't swallow till you see a dog. If you don't do this the person in the ambulance will die.'

Girl, 15, Loughborough.

'To see an ambulance means that you will go to hospital. To break the curse you must see a four-legged animal.'

Boy, 12, Chapeltown, Yorkshire.

1. In Halifax a variant in 1954 went, 'Hold your collar, never swallow, D.D.T.'

'You will have bad luck if you see an ambulance and not a black dog within five minutes.'

Girl, *13, Pontypool*.[1]

'If you see an ambulance you must touch wood or you will have bad luck. When the ambulance is out of sight you must keep your fingers crossed until you see a four-legged animal and if there is more than one of you, you must have it the one who saw it first can uncross their fingers, and the others not until they see other animals.'

Girl, *10, Birmingham*.

'If we see an ambulance we say "Touch wood, no returns" and put our hands on someone's head.'

Boy, *10, North Shields*.

'When an ambulance passes in the street one is supposed to spit on the ground. If one fails to carry out this, one is supposed to be taken to hospital and pins and needles will be stuck in one.'

Girl, *14, Aberdeen*.

It is noticeable that unlike some of the older, adult-maintained superstitions, no child dismissed taking protection against an ambulance as silly.

Omens on the Way to School

The children's statements about white horses and ambulances have been set down in some detail to show how widespread a belief can be, and how there may be minor variations in its observance.[2] The beliefs which follow are less fully treated. This does not necessarily mean that they are less common or that fewer records have been obtained about them. Superstitious regard for some objects, such as beetles, bridges, cats, hay carts, ladders, falling leaves, lumps of coal, and cracks in the pavement, seem to extend to every corner of Britain; and these beliefs, and the customs which accompany them, are far from being the 'fast perishing relics' they are sometimes assumed to be.

1. In Wales it appears to be the back of the ambulance which is most feared. In Aberystwyth, 'When we see the back of an ambulance we cross our fingers and say "I hope I don't go in one of those"' (Girl, 12). In Swansea a teacher says that to ward off the ill luck girls look for three black dogs.
2. With regard to white horses it should be mentioned that records in the nineteenth century indicate that children had as many ways of greeting their appearance then as they have now. It was not an invariable rule to spit three times as it was at Plymouth, and as latterly in Perth. In 1882 children in Yorkshire used to spit just once to avert ill luck when they met a white horse; children in Oxfordshire spat just once but on meeting a *pair* of white horses; and children in Birmingham spat not to avert ill luck but to bring good luck (see *Notes and Queries*, 6th ser., vi, 1882, pp. 9 and 178).

It must always be remembered that although to an adult a particular belief may seem like a coelacanthine survival from the past, to the school-child who learns it from his mate the belief is a novelty; it is something just learnt, and often excitingly full of possibility for his immediate welfare.

When a child steps out of his home to go to school, whether he lives in a remote hamlet or in one of the backstreets of a great city, he is on his own, and looking after himself. The day ahead looms large and endless in front of him, and his eyes are wide open for the prognostics which will tell him his fortune.

Beetles. Nearly all children seem to be wary of beetles. 'A black beetle crawling on your shoe means that one of your friends is going to die,' says a 12-year-old Barnsley boy. And most of all they are careful not to kill one, for it is well known to them: 'If you kill a beetle a rainy day will follow.' In Swansea they say:

> Step on a beetle, it will rain;
> Pick it up and bury it, the sun will shine again.

The superstition is so rigorously observed that, as one teacher (Norwich) remarks: 'Every insect akin to a wood-louse is hailed as a "rain-beetle" and one is warned not to kill it.'[1]

Birds. 'If a bird dirts on you' it is lucky (very general). 'If you see a flock of birds you must cross your legs and wish' (Langham, Rutland). 'To see a white bird is unlucky' (Beccles).

See also *Crows*, *Cuckoos*, and *Magpies*.

Blind men. It is lucky to see a blind man in the street (Lydney), and especially lucky to help him (Alton).

Bridges. It is unlucky to walk under a bridge when a train is going over, or to go over a bridge when a train is passing under. If a train does come the usual custom is to cross fingers (very general). It is also considered inadvisable to talk when under a bridge. A Sussex boy says: 'If you do you must touch a green object or you will get bad luck.' The ban on speaking also extends to railway passengers when the train is going through a tunnel. An Angus boy complains: 'One day I was in a train going to Edinburgh and I tried talking and as sure as fate I lost a half-crown on the train.'

Cats. It is considered good luck if one meets a black cat and says 'black cat bring me luck', or if one strokes it three times from head to tail, and then makes a wish. But a black cat does not necessarily bring luck: much

---

1. For a touching account of how even a simple superstition like this can affect a sensitive child, see James Kirkup, *The Only Child*, 1957, p. 20.

depends on the creature's behaviour. The consensus of opinion seems to be that if the cat sits in front of one, or walks ahead in one's path, all is well. But if it runs away, turns back, or walks round one, or if it crosses one's path, and in particular if it crosses one's path from left to right, it is very bad luck. A Golspie boy says, 'You must spit to avoid a terrible accident which is bound to happen.' A Welsh girl says one must make the sign of the cross and turn completely round. A Shropshire girl says one must turn round three times. And a boy in Manchester says that if a black cat crosses in front of a car from left to right, it means a puncture. To see a white cat on the way to school is taken to be a sign of trouble ahead.

Chimney sweeps. The sight of a chimney sweep, in particular the back of a chimney sweep, is considered unlucky in Stoke-on-Trent. One girl there says that to avert ill luck at the sight of a sweep 'you touch your collar till you see a horse, a dog, and a cat'.

Cross-eyed women. 'It is unlucky for a cross-eyed woman to look at you' (Girl, 13, Stoke-on-Trent). 'When somebody who is boss-eyed goes by you spit on the ground' (Girl, 15, Headington).[1]

Crows. If a child sees one crow only, and especially if no one else sees it, bad luck will follow, possibly death or accident. Two crows, however, are a good omen. This fact is known to children even when they do not know the rhyme: 'One crow for sorrow, two for joy, three for a letter, four for a boy.' In Ruthin children say: 'Dwy fran ddu, lwc dda i mi' (Two black crows, good luck to me).

Cuckoos. 'If, when you hear a cuckoo for the first time, you turn over the money in your pocket, you will have money all the year round.' This belief is shared with French children. It is also held, particularly in Wales, that where a person is when he first hears a cuckoo, there will he be in twelve months' time; and a Knighton boy adds he will be doing the same work.

Dogs. The sight of a spotted dog is lucky (fairly general), and is supposed to bring luck in, for instance, exams if one crosses one's fingers (Boy, 15, Oxford). Three white dogs together are also a sign of good luck (Girls, Swansea). The coincidence of an ambulance, a tricycle, and a dog with spots is, however, a sign of ill luck (Boy, 11, Ongar). So is a black dog crossing one's path (Boy, 13, Brentwood); and 'it is bad luck if a dog passes a horse on the same side of the street' (Boy, 12, Forest Hill).

---

1. In *Secret Memoirs of the late Mr. Duncan Campbell*, 1732, p. 61, it is observed that some people will defer going abroad, though called by business of greatest consequence; thus 'if, happening to look out of the Window, they see a single Crow; or going out, are met by a Person who had the Misfortune to squint; either of these turns 'em immediately back'.

Dung. 'To step on horse dung means good luck' (apparently everywhere), and it is similarly propitious if a child accidentally walks in a dog's mess (Brierley Hill).

Funerals. To see a funeral is nearly always considered an ill omen. It is particularly unlucky to count the number of cars in the procession (Aberdeen), to see the coffin through glass (Aberdeen), to pass a coffin and a wedding at the same time (Newcastle), or for a hearse to be followed by a horse, dog, or bird (Eltham, S.E. London). In Loughton girls cross their fingers until the funeral has passed. In Ipswich, Swansea, and York, the protective action is the same as for an ambulance:

> Touch your head, touch your toes,
> Hope I never go in one of those.

In Essex they hold their collar until they have seen a dog or a bird; in Yorkshire until they have seen a dog and a horse; and in Aberdeen children spit. One Aberdeen girl says that spitting when one sees a hearse is more than a protection, it brings luck.[1]

Hares. 'If you see a white hare you are unlucky, but if you see a black hare you will have luck' (Girl, 15, Knighton).

Hats. It appears to be important to be the first in a group to spot a straw boater. In King's Lynn, Norfolk, the child who sees one first says:

> I pinch you, you can't pinch back,
> For I see a man in a white straw hat.

In Portsmouth and Lincoln the child says quickly 'First luck, strawboater' or 'Foggy straw benjer' and licks his finger or thumb and claps the back of one hand with the palm of the other. In Luton he says 'Pit, pat, my straw hat', and hopes to touch it. In Nottingham children cross their fingers until they have seen three dogs. In Forfar they spit. In Sale, Cheshire, they also spit, and the boys there add that they spit on seeing anything white, whether it be a white horse, white cat, white flannels, or white straw hat.

Hay Carts. It is usually considered lucky to meet a load of hay, but it is apparently always considered unlucky to see the back of a hay wain. This has been reported in almost identical terms by children in different parts of Britain, for example a 14-year-old Loughton girl:

> 'If you see a hay cart and wish, your wish will come true, provided you don't see the back of it.'

1. Francis Grose in his *Provincial Glossary*, 1787, p. 62, records: 'If you meet a funeral procession, or one passes by you, always take off your hat: this keeps all evil spirits attending the body in good humour.'

A 12-year-old boy, Southwark, S.E. 17:

'You must not look at the back of a van or lorry load of hay. If you don't look at the back, good luck.'

A girl student, about 18, Kidderminster:

'When you see a truck load of hay along the road make a wish but never look back.'

In Pasadena, California, children express the belief in rhyme:

Load of hay, load of hay,
Make a wish and turn away.

A girl from Dunvant, near Swansea, however, states that it is only unlucky if one sees the moving haystack disappear round a bend or over the crest of a hill, and it is at this point that one must look away.

Horses. White horses receive the most attention; but piebalds are also remarked upon and generally considered lucky (Aberdeen, Barnsley, Swansea). However, an Aberdeen girl says that one should shut one's eyes until it has passed. A Knighton boy says, 'Lucky to see a piebald horse, but must spit over the right shoulder, close eyes and wish. Must not see tail.' And a young girl who has travelled much in Scotland and the north country, particularizes: 'If you see a piebald horse you are lucky, but if you see a skewbald horse you are unlucky.'[1]

Ladders. Walking under ladders is usually recognized to be injudicious, and a 13-year-old Forfar lad writes: 'I once heard a boy say that if you walked under a ladder on the way to school you were supposed to get the strap that day.' But certain precautions can be taken to avert the misfortune. In South Molton, Devon, children do not speak until they have seen a 'four-legged animal'; in Bath they cross their fingers and keep them crossed until they have seen five dogs; in Aberystwyth it is suggested that the fingers should be kept crossed until three dogs and three horses have been counted and then the person may have a wish; in Knighton four dogs are deemed sufficient as long as seen quickly; in Swansea, Preston, and

1. A cartoon by C. Raven Hill depicting country children, in *Punch* 25 April 1906, bears the caption: *The Piebald Superstition*, 'Come on, Billy! Come on an' wish! Wish for something! 'Ere's a lucky horse!' An informant, recalling the same period, states that at Chester boys used to cross their fingers and wish, spit over left shoulder, and say 'Shakespeare come true'.

Alton one dog is enough. In Southwark (London, S.E. 17) after boys have walked under a ladder they spit to avert ill luck, and this action is held to be efficacious in a number of places (a Stoke-on-Trent girl says that one should spit over one's shoulder). In Aberdeen, however, where superstitious spitting is prevalent, it is suggested that walking under a ladder can be turned to advantage, for if a person does so and then spits he not only negatives the ill luck, but changes his luck for the better. Similarly in Penrith a boy says that if one spits first and then hops under the ladder it will bring good fortune.[1]

Lady drivers. A lady driver portends bad luck, and in Wales and Monmouthshire it appears to be common practice among children when they notice a lady driver to cross their fingers until they have seen a dog. A Stoke-on-Trent boy says that he keeps his fingers crossed until he has seen not only a dog, but a bird and a cat as well.

Ladybirds. To find a ladybird on the way to school is regarded as a good omen. 'We hold it on our hand,' say 11-year-olds at Market Rasen, 'and chant:

> Ladybird, ladybird, fly away home,
> Your house is on fire, your children are gone,
> Except the little one under a stone,
> Ladybird, ladybird, fly away home.'

The following variant is known in Alton:

> Ladybird, ladybird, fly away home,
> Your house is on fire, your children at home;
> One is upstairs making the beds,
> The others downstairs are crying for bread.

In Earlham, near Norwich, 'even the youngest children', says a teacher, 'call the ladybird by its East Anglian name "Bishy bishy barnabee".'[2]

Leaves. 'To catch a leaf as it falls from a tree gives a wish or a day's luck.' Knowledge of this is ubiquitous, and leads to some extra exercise being taken in September and October.

1. The custom of spitting when walking under a ladder is recorded in Hone's *Year Book*, February 1831, col. 253: 'To prevent ill luck . . . when you pass under a ladder, you must spit through it, or three times afterwards.' Walking under a ladder is also considered unlucky by children in France, and around Vichy they say that if a child does so he will not grow any more.
2. For a note on ladybird rhymes, both British and Continental, see *The Oxford Dictionary of Nursery Rhymes*, 1951, pp. 263–4.

Magpies. The future is foretold according to the number of magpies seen and the particular version of the old rhyme which is locally indigenous, for its message can be contradictory:

One for sorrow,
Two for mirth,
Three for a wedding,
Four for a birth.
Bedford (and England generally).[1]

One for sorrow,
Two for joy,
Three for a present,
Four for a letter,
Five for something better.
Llanfair Waterdine.

Ane's joy
Twa's grief
Three's a wedding,
Four's death.
Forfar, Angus.

Mail vans. To see a mail van is lucky (Liverpool), unlucky (Loughton), lucky if one touches wood (Aberdeen), unlucky if one sees the back of it (Swansea). In Aberdeen, say a group of 14-year-old girls, if a mail van passes, the first to see it cries out 'First for the Royal Mail Van', the second who sees it cries 'Second for the Royal Mail Van', and so on; or, if the van is stationary, the first who runs to it and touches the crown painted on the side, and then the second, and then the third, fourth, fifth, and sixth, can have a wish or other expectation, according to the formula:

One's a wish,
Two's a kiss,
Three's a disappointment,
Four's a letter,
Five is better,
Six is the best of all.

Monkey-puzzle trees. 'Never speak while passing a monkey-puzzle tree' (Boy, 13, Forfar).

Nuns. In Swansea when girls see a nun they open their coat until they see a four-legged animal, then button the coat up again. One child explained: 'It has something to do with letting in the Holy Ghost.' In Edinburgh to see three nuns walking together is considered a lucky omen. But in Ireland it has been noticed that children do not like seeing the back of a nun when she is walking away from them, and Catholic and Protestant children alike spit to ward off evil.

Oil patches. Oil or petrol marks on a wet road are sometimes held to be spots where a rainbow has stood. 'It is said that if one walks over an oily patch in the road one will get one's sums wrong' (Girl, 15, Ipswich).

Rabbits. 'If a rabbit crosses your path in front it is lucky but if it passes by the back it is unlucky' (Boy, 12, Romford).

1. This version is also the one quoted in the *Supplement* to Johnson and Steevens's Shakespeare, vol. ii, 1780, p. 706, except that the last line goes 'four for death'.

Rain. The old chant,

> Rain, rain, go away,
> Come again another day,

or variations thereof, is still commonly repeated.[1] But amongst small children in infants schools a more humorous verse is now very frequently recited:

> It's raining, it's pouring,
> The old man's snoring;
> He got into bed
> And bumped his head
> And couldn't get up in the morning.

This rhyme, apparently unknown a quarter of a century ago, now circles the English-speaking world.[2] In the north, however, the traditional poetic greetings to Jupiter Pluvius are still not forgotten.

It's raining, it's raining,	Rainy, rainy, rattlestones,
It's raining on the rocks,	Dinna rain on me,
And all the little fisher girls	Rain on John o' Groat's house
Are lifting up their frocks.	Far across the sea.
North Shields children.	*Golspie children.*

Rainbows. It is very generally believed that to point at a rainbow is unlucky, and, in particular, that it will bring back the rain. Sometimes it is said that one may wish upon a rainbow; and a master at Ballingry, Fife, found his class believed that the first to see a rainbow was lucky, provided the person called out to his friends 'First to see a rainbow'. He recollected that this had also been the practice when he was a boy (at Cowdenbeath, *c.* 1944), 'and we also applied it when the electric street lights went on at night'.

Sailors. It is held, apparently everywhere in this island, that to touch the edge of a sailor's collar brings good fortune. (In France children try to touch the red pom-pom on the sailor's cap.)

Snow. In the north country, when 'the old woman is a-picking her geese', children encourage the downfall with the words:

Snow, snow, faster,	Alley, alley, aster,
Alley, alley, baster.	Come down faster.
Leeds.	*Newcastle upon Tyne.*
	(Also said to rain.)

1. James Howell in 1659 recorded, 'Raine, raine, goe to Spain: faire weather come againe' in his *Proverbs*, p. 20.
2. A correspondent who left school in 1928 remarks that she never knew it, but that her brother, twelve years younger, knew it; and her daughter said (1951), 'Oh! everybody knows that.' The rhyme is also well-known in Australia, and the earliest we know of it being current was in New York in 1938.

Spiders. It is a sign of good luck to find a small spider on one's clothes, and in Swansea it is thought that one will have new, whatever garment it is found on. More generally, it is supposed that the spider will bring luck of a financial nature, small spiders (especially red ones) being known as 'money spiders'. Thus a Newbridge girl notes: 'If a money spider comes on you they say it will bring you money before the day is out.' A boy in Annesley says that the spider should be picked up and thrown over the shoulder: 'People say it brings you luck, and you will find threepence on your shoulder.' But care should be taken not to kill the spider. A Pontefract boy states: 'If someone sees what is called a money spider, he is supposed to become rich in a short time, however, if he kills one of these spiders something terrible is supposed to happen to him.' It is a common dictum:

> If you want to live and thrive
> Let a spider run alive.

And it is often held (Liverpool, Newcastle, Presteigne, South Molton) that if a spider is killed it will start raining.

Trains. An 11-year-old girl at Annesley, Nottinghamshire, says, 'When I see a backing train I wish for something.' A 14-year-old girl, Newbridge, Monmouthshire, writes: 'If you see a smoke ring coming from an engine you can wish once, and if you see two smoke rings you can wish twice.' A student from Luton reports: 'If one saw a train (goods or passenger) being driven by two engines then one said, "That's double engine, my good luck". If you saw the last carriage or truck then the good luck changed to bad.' A girl from Slough, aged about 12, states: 'If you throw a halfpenny from a bridge at a railway engine and it stays on, it is a good luck omen.'

See also under *Bridges.* It is possible that a number of other railway superstitions exist which have not yet been collected.

Wooden legs. A 14-year-old Stoke-on-Trent girl says, 'If you see a man with a wooden leg spit over your little finger', and another girl, a form mate, reports that a number of people believe it is bad luck to see the back of a man with a wooden leg before one sees his front.

Lines on Pavements

One of the inexplicables is the amount of lore which has become associated with flagstones, and apparently all children, when the fever is on them, are punctilious about the way they walk along an ordinary pavement. To step on a crack in a stone, or on the lines between the stones, is invariably taken to be unlucky, and the precise catastrophe which will follow is very often known to them, for instance: 'You will get your sums wrong' (Ipswich); 'Your hair will fall out' (Loughton); 'You will fall downstairs next day' (Manchester); 'You will break your spine' (Newcastle upon Tyne). Stepping on lines is also very generally held to restrict a girl's matrimonial prospects. 'Stand on a line and you'll marry a darkie' or 'Tread on a line and you'll marry a negro and have a black baby' are sayings repeated in many parts of Britain (e.g. Aberdeen, Aberystwyth, Barnsley, Edinburgh, Ipswich, Langholm, Liverpool, Loughton, Market Rasen, and Peterborough).[1] Sometimes children deliberately run the risk of stepping on a line to discover what will happen to them. A 14-year-old Aberdeen girl says:

'A way of telling whom one is going to marry is by hopping in and out of the squares on the pavement and if one stands on a black line then one is going to marry a negro, but if one should stand on a crack in the middle of the square then one is going to marry a person of one's own country. If one stands with one foot on each, then one is going to marry a foreign person.'

In Lancashire and adjacent parts of Cheshire and the West Riding, children have the quaint saying:

> If you tread on a nick
> You'll marry a brick (or a 'stick')
> And a beetle will come to your wedding.

Around Sheffield, they chant:

> If you stand on a line
> You'll marry a swine;
> If you stand on a square
> You'll marry a bear.

The fable that sillies who step on lines will be chased by bears when they reach the corner of the road, unforgettable in A. A. Milne's *When We Were Very Young* (1924), is recounted throughout southern England where it is

1. An informant tells us that the saying, 'Tread on a line and you'll marry a negro and have a black baby', was current in Cardiff, *c.* 1910. Another informant recalls that around Kennington, as long ago as 1890–93, ill fortune was thought to follow treading on cracks, and some said that the person's mother would turn black.

Whether or not it is a result of superstition, there appear to be some people who have a lifelong aversion to placing their foot on two stones at once. Dr Fisher, Master of the Charterhouse, told Croker that in the quadrangle of University College Johnson would not step on the juncture of the stones, but carefully on the centre; and according to Lord Elton, General Gordon when walking along a pavement would zigzag in order to avoid the cracks.

variously asserted: 'bears will bite you', 'they will squeeze you', 'they will eat you'. It is also exotically reported that snakes will chase you home (Norfolk), or that you will marry a snake (Manchester); that you'll drown in the sea (Loughton); that each time you tread on a line you kill a fairy (one boy, Peterborough), or that 'you walk on the old man's toes' (Oxford). Old Nick's, perhaps?

Further sayings, apparently not peculiar to any locality, associate the lines with broken crockery. In Ballingry, Fife, if a person treads on the lines he is said to be 'breaking God's plates'. In Aberdeen if he walks on cracks (as distinct from lines) he is 'breaking the devil's dishes', or his 'mother's best china dishes', and the more cracks he walks on the more he breaks. (Aberdonians give this as an alternative to marrying a blackman.) In parts of East Anglia, if a child steps on lines or cracks, or slips off the kerb, it is said he will break his mother's best teapot.

In Peterborough and Swansea the mother's attitude is reflected in the jingle:

> Tread on lines your mother's kind;
> Tread on squares your mother swears.

And in Portsmouth it is reported that children also take notice of the water-courses across the pavement:

> If you tread on a crack, or tread on a spout,
> It's a sure thing your mother will turn you out.

* In America pavement lore appears to be more uniform than in Britain. Recordings made in recent years in Illinois, Iowa, New Jersey, Louisiana, New York State, Ohio, and Texas, have all been similar. The child says 'Step on a crack', and continues 'You'll break your mother's back' or 'You'll break your grandmother's back', or 'Break the devil's back'.

Finding Things

It is not usually considered enough merely to find a lucky object. If the finder is to benefit by his encounter he must go through prescribed actions with his find, step on it, threaten it, spit on it, implore of it, or, very often, throw it away. The only exception seems to be the four-leaf clover, the discovery of which appears to be felt singular enough to be lucky in itself.

Buttons. 'When you pick up a button say,

> Button, button, bring me luck,
> Or else I'll break you up.'
>
> *(Girl, 14, Oxford.)*

'If a button with four holes is found, it is a sign that you may soon hear good tidings' (Girl, 15, Forfar).

Cigarette packets. 'When one is walking down the street and espies an empty cigarette packet with the picture of a black cat on it, the following verse is repeated, provided that one foot is covering the packet:

> Black cat, black cat, bring me luck,
> If you don't I'll tear you up.'

This is reported by a young cockney – 'Black Cat' being a brand of cigarettes manufactured by the North London firm, Carreras Ltd. In other parts of Britain other brands are considered auspicious. In Lydney, Monmouth, Manchester, and Oxford, the charm is repeated when a 'Willy Willy Woodbine' packet is found. In Aberystwyth and Swansea they look for 'Player's Navy Cut':

> Sailor, sailor, bring me luck,
> Find a shilling in the muck.

(Identical chant in both places.) 'If we don't find any money, we come back and tear it up if it is still there.' In Ipswich and environs the invoked brand is 'Churchman's Tenner', of local manufacture, the cry being:

> Red Tenner, red Tenner, bring me luck,
> If you don't I'll tear you up.

*** This regard for the occult properties of certain discarded cigarette packets (although not previously recorded) does not appear to be new. One informant, from Llanelly, recalls 'stepping on Woodbine packets and wishing' about 1910; and an East Suffolk girl affirms that she learnt the Red Tenner charm from 'the older people in our village'.

Clover, four-leaf. To find a four-leaf clover is everywhere regarded as one of the happiest of omens, a feeling apparently shared by Fleet Street, for when 9-year-old Joan Nott of North Finchley found nine four-leaf clovers near her home on 13 May 1953, the *Daily Express* considered the event important enough to merit a four-column headline.

*** Sir John Melton records in his *Astrologaster*, 1620, p. 46 (cited by Brand): 'If a man, walking in the fields, finde any foure-leaved grasse, he shall, in a small while after, finde some good thing.' It is not generally known that there is a cultivated form of White or Dutch Clover in which, the 'sport' being genetically fixed, leaves with four leaflets are fairly constant. These plants are sometimes cultivated by talisman-vendors, and the leaves are offered at half-a-crown each.

Coal. If a piece of coal is dropped in the road by a coalman 'the first person who comes along is supposed to pick it up and spit on it, then he or she must throw it over their left shoulder and wish. Whatever they wish for they are supposed to have sometime or other' (Girl, *c*. 12, Aberystwyth). A Pontypool girl adds that after throwing it over the left shoulder it must not be looked at. Spitting on a piece of coal for good luck is also referred to by children in Dublin and south-east Bedfordshire. A Knighton girl learnt the practice in a jingle:

> If you see a piece of coal, pick it up,
> And all the day you'll have good luck.

An Aberdeen girl adds that should one 'pass a piece of coal on the road it is said to bring bad luck'. (See further under Luck in Exams.)

Coins. In south-east Bedfordshire they say that any coin found should be spat upon; in the Potteries that it should be picked up 'only after you have trod on it'; and in Penrith that it is unlucky to spend a coin which has been found, it should be given away. Boys in Liverpool liked to find a farthing, for this augured good luck; and a Pontefract boy said: 'If a sixpence with the head of the king or queen who is the reigning sovereign is found, that is supposed to bring good luck.'

Feathers. 'If you find a black feather, and stick it in the ground you will have good luck' (Boy, 15, Felindre, Radnorshire). In Market Rasen the belief is expressed in the rhyme:

> Find a feather, stick it up,
> All the day you'll have good luck.

Horseshoes. Every self-respecting child knows that a horseshoe should not be passed by. 'When one sees a horseshoe lying on the ground one should pick it up, spit on it, and throw it over one's shoulder' (Girl, 14, Aberdeen). 'What to do with a horseshoe is throw it over your head and put your hands to your ears and wish' (Boy, 12, Aberystwyth). Several children stress that the shoe should be taken in the right hand and thrown over the left shoulder. Two dissenters (in Forfar and Letham) specify the left hand and the right shoulder. A few children make the point that the thrower should not see where the shoe drops, and some that he should not hear it drop, but should 'jam his fingers in his ears' and even run in the opposite direction lest he hear it fall. All say that the rite is meant to bring good luck, although one 13-year-old says, 'Every time I do it I end up in trouble'.

₊ Robert Boyle records the custom in his *Occasional Reflections upon Several Subjects*, 1665, p. 217: 'The common People of this Country have a Tradition, that 'tis a lucky thing to find a Horse-shoe. And, though 'twas to make myself merry with this fond conceit of the superstitious vulgar, I stooped to take this up.'

Pins. To find a pin, and in particular a bent pin, is lucky. 'Whenever I am walking and see a pin I always pick it up and say:

> See a pin and pick it up
> All the day you'll have good luck.
> See a pin and let it lay
> Bad luck you'll have all that day.

I have done this ever since I was little and I suppose I'll do it now till I leave school' (Girl, 14, Newbridge). The charm, variously stated, appears to be known everywhere (including the United States), and was recorded over a century ago.[1] Usually the pin is stuck into a coat lapel and worn for as long as possible. In Alton the rhyme is more imperious:

> Pin, pin, bring me luck,
> Because I stop to pick you up.

Rings. 'Finding a ring of any kind means someone you know very well is going to get married, though I know an old lady who keeps all the rings she finds and she is still a spinster' (Girl, *c.* 13, Forfar).

Sticks. 'If you get a green stake and spit on it and throw it over your left shoulder you have your luck' (Boy, 12, nr. Barnsley, Yorkshire).

Stones. Various kinds of stones are considered lucky. In Liverpool to pick up a duckstone is good luck, in Watford and elsewhere a stone with a hole in it, and London children look for round stones, 'the rounder the luckier'. A Pontefract boy says that for luck a pebble should be carried in the right-hand pocket, and in Alton, to bring luck, 10-year-olds spit on a pebble which takes their fancy and throw it over their left shoulder.

₊ P. H. Gosse, in his posthumously published essay 'A Country Day School 70 Years Ago' (*Longman's Magazine*, March 1889), wrote: 'In the gravel formations around Poole, perforated pebbles are not uncommon, and the occurrence of one of these was considered "lucky"; such a stone being denominated "a lucky stone". But in order to realize to the full the

1. J. O. Halliwell, *Nursery Rhymes of England*, 1842, p. 98.

felicitous results of such a find, it was important to go through the following ceremony. The stone was picked up, spat upon, and then thrown backward over the head of the fortunate finder, who accompanied the action with the following rhyme:

> Lucky stone! lucky stone! go over my head,
> And bring me some good luck before I go to bed.'

It will be noticed that to find any of the above objects is potentially beneficial. But there are three things which if found should never be picked up: a needle, a broken knife, and a flower dropped by somebody else. To meddle with these means ill luck, a quarrel, or even death It is unlucky, too, to find a dead bird (a boy from Stock in Essex particularizes 'a dead pigeon'). A girl in Canonbie, Dumfriesshire, says: 'When we see a dead bird lying on the road we spit on it so that we don't get it for our supper.'

Luck in Examinations

Naturally the approach of an examination makes children doubly conscious of omens. They become watchful for anything held to be significant, and take notice not only of the everyday prognostics, but of some auguries specifically belonging to the occasion. Thus at Ecclesfield a boy says: 'If you have a dream about a horse before the exams you will have bad luck.' At Hampstead, and doubtless elsewhere, children believe that to have an argument before an examination is bad luck. And at Lydney, by the river Severn, they consider it unlucky if, when going into examinations, there are no seagulls flying around outside. In some places children even take note of whether, when they enter the examination room, the master is smiling (a propitious sign), or who it is théy walk in behind (they like to walk near a prefect or an entrant of known ability). And they are as careful as possible about their choice of desk. (At one school, at least, when the desks are being set out number 13 is omitted, for no child would willingly sit at it.)

More actively they bring a piece of magic with them: a pet small toy or mascot, a woollen, wooden, glass, brass, or china likeness of a pig, elephant, frog, dog, owl, black cat, white horse, or silver horseshoe, a Jack o' Lantern, Joan the Wad (popular in Wales), or other lucky image such as fancy gift shops regularly sell, but perhaps purchased on some special occasion with happy or mystic associations, such as at a fair, or from a gipsy or Indian pedlar at the door. The mascots are set up in front of them on their desks (and tactfully ignored by the examiners), or are worn as brooches or pendants. Sometimes they wear a sprig of white heather, or holly, or an ivy leaf, or have steel pins stuck into the lapel edge of their coat or a safety pin fastened in the hem of their dress. Or they bring – secreted in grubby pockets – talismans of personal but no intrinsic value: prized round stones, polished stones, white stones, stones with holes in them, champagne corks, mother of pearl shells, pieces of coral (very common), treasured lumps of wood, rabbits' paws (surprisingly often),[1] and sharks' teeth. Also, very frequently, they have special coins: coins with holes in them, coins which have been much polished, halfpennies with ships on, farthings which are bent, and silver coins, particularly new ones.

'It is supposed to bring good luck during an examination to have in your pocket a piece of coal,[2] a silver threepenny bit, or something silver with the present year's date, e.g. 1952 if the examination was tried this year.'

Girl, 14, Aberdeen.

'I think a silver sixpence is very lucky. If you were going in for an examination you might keep a silver sixpence in your pocket so that you might pass the exam, but some people say the sixpences should be very new sixpences, they should not have been used and they should have been new from a bank. Then people think you will have a good chance of passing.'

Girl, 12, Aberystwyth.

They are particularly conscientious about bringing charms to the 11-plus examination, the 'scholarship' as they call it, which determines whether they shall go on to a grammar school or to a secondary modern; and it may, perhaps, be reflected that grammar school children (the children who were successful in the examination) are more likely to be superstitious than secondary modern school children, for children at grammar schools are children who have found that lucky charms work.

1. Reported from Aberystwyth, Camberwell, Croydon, Headington, and Luncarty.
2. The belief that carrying a lump of coal brings good luck to its owner is widespread, and is not only reserved for examinations. A Presteigne boy, for instance, asserts that coal in the pocket brings luck all the year round; and a schoolgirl at Aylesbury in May 1955 offered Sir Anthony Eden a lump of coal for luck in the General Election. Nor is the belief confined to children. The *Standard*, 17 October 1882, reports that amongst articles found on an arrested man was 'a piece of coal, used by professional thieves as a "charm"'; and the *Daily Mail*, 11 May 1899, following a case heard at the Mansion House, reported that 'burglars almost invariably carry a small piece of coal with them when they start out on an expedition'. Sir Philip Gibbs in *The Times*, 7 August 1954, recalls that before going under fire in the First World War an Irish officer handed him a piece of coal. And a Monmouthshire girl, November 1954, relates that her uncle and aunt carried pieces of coal with them when they took their driving tests.

'My mother has always treasured a little brass owl. On the day I went to sit the scholarship I took the little owl and wrapped it up in a handkerchief in my pocket for luck hoping it would bring me luck and when the results came I found it had proved its worth. I also wear other lucky charms such as a black and gold poodle or a lucky black cat.'

Girl, 11, about to go to a grammar school in the West Midlands.

'A lot of boys around our school place most of their luck on wearing small things of a girl friend they know, articles such as silk scarves, small lace handkerchiefs, or a ring or a charm. On Thursday the 11th of April I was not wearing my friend's ring (in which I place my luck) and at school in the morning I broke the school's gramophone.'

Boy, 15, at a northern grammar school.

'I have a circular piece of red glass which I think is lucky because I take it to exams with me. I took it to the scholarship exam for the grammar school and I passed. I also took it to the A.T.C. exams and I have passed them all. I think it must be lucky although I found it in a stream.'

Boy, 14, at a Yorkshire grammar school.

Even during the examination some children are not happy unless they can entice the correct answers on to their papers by means beyond the ordinary power of nature. They put their faith in new pencils which have never written a mistake; they clasp their thumbs ('this is very lucky', says a Brixton boy); they cross their fingers or touch wood that an answer they have written down is correct (there is prolonged finger-crossing and wood-touching while they wait to hear the examination results); and a trick some of them have is to keep their legs crossed during the examination. A teacher at Portsmouth, who was having considerable trouble with collapsible desks during an examination, says that when she at last demanded of a girl why she would keep sitting in such discomfort with her knees bumping up under the flap, was told that the girl did not think she could pass the examination unless she maintained this position.

⁎⁎ The illusion that it is a help to a pupil to have his legs crossed has lingered in classrooms for generations. Thomas Park, who was at grammar school at Heighington in Durham, *c.* 1769–75, records: 'To sit cross-legged I have always understood, was intended to produce good or fortunate consequences. Hence it was employed as a Charm at School, by one Boy who wished well for another, in order to deprecate some punishment which both might tremble to have incurred the expectation of. At a Card-Table, I have also caught some superstitious Players sitting cross-legged with a view of bringing good Luck' – see John Brand, *Popular Antiquities*, vol. ii, 1813, p. 568 n. The practice 'for women to offer to sit cross-legged, to procure luck at cards for their friends', is confirmed by Francis Grose in his *Provincial Glossary*, 1787, p. 60.

Luck in Games

In their games, as in their work, it sometimes seems to children that it is more necessary to have luck than to have skill. Young marbles players, in particular, who on one occasion are able to hit their opponent out of the ring every shot, and on another, for no reason which is rational, cannot 'knock a shottie' however hard they try, easily become prey to strange thoughts. 'I started on Monday and had two days of good luck,' reports a 14-year-old, then 'on Wednesday I played with a green marble and it proved itself very unlucky because I never won a game. Now I never play with a green marble because I think they are unlucky.'

In some places marble players are addicted to charms. At Stoke-on-Trent they call out:

> One, two, three,
> Lucky, lucky, lucky,
> Four, five, six;

and in East Orange, New Jersey:

> Roll, roll, tootsie roll,
> Roll marble, in the hole.

Very frequently they practise what, in the old days, would have been called witchcraft, and today is known to the sophisticated as 'Gamesmanship':

'If you are playing marbles and you want to win, you put a cross in front of the hole with red chark and shout "Bad Luck!" and the person who is playing with you gets confused and misis the hole.'

Boy, 10, Birmingham.

In Nottinghamshire, 'when another boy is near our marble and it is his shot we draw a ring round it' (Boy, 10). In Dumfriesshire, 'if you make marks with your heel round your marble the person is said to miss' (Boy, 12). And in Swansea when a child is losing at marbles he cries the disconcerting supplication: 'Black cat follow me, not you.'

Casting spells is not, however, confined to marbles players. 'In any game in which a ball is used,' says an 11-year-old, 'when a person is shooting and we want him to miss we say:

> "Abracadabra, wall come up!"

and somehow the ball seems to miss.' In Monmouthshire, when girls are playing hopscotch, if someone stands on a line of the scotch while another is hopping it brings her bad luck. In Swansea, when children reach the same point in a game as their rival, to bring themselves extra luck they say:

'Tippet – Good luck to me – Bad luck to you – No back answers.'

And if, in a game such as skipping, a girl is doing badly, to regain her luck she chants:

Touch wood, no good;
Touch iron, rely on.

In Essex, in similar pagan manner, if a boy has eventually achieved his object in a game, he spits on the ground, or on whatever has baulked him, in revenge for his past failures. In Essex, also, children spit behind an opponent's back as a method of bringing bad luck upon him.

In Newcastle to win a toss children call 'Lucky tails, never fails'. In Peterborough it is held that if a player counts his fagcards during a game he is bound to lose. At Knighton to bring luck in a race children customarily hold a piece of grass in their hand. And in Alton to obtain a three when dicing, or to bring luck when turning up a third playing card, one group of youngsters, well known to us, have taken to chanting, 'Lucky three, bring luck to me.'

Yet children's main efforts to affect a game by infernal means are concentrated on hockey and football. Mascot carrying is universal:

'At a football match each side has a mascot. The mascot can be a doll, an animal, a midget, or a young boy. This mascot is regarded as it might bring good luck.'

Boy, c. 13, Monk Fryston.

'If a football club has a lucky mascot and it is forgotten to be taken to a match I believe that they will lose, and I believe that the same thing will happen at school sports.'

Girl, 14, Tunstall.

'I know of a footballer who earned the name of "Corky" because he always carries a champagne cork in his pocket when playing.'

Girl, 15, Forfar.

Sometimes the charms are carried not only to ease the way to victory but for personal protection:

'When I go out to play football I always wear on my pants a little charm (an elephant). On my boots I put a piece of red cloth between my laces and I never get hurt.'

Boy, 13, Featherstone.

And sometimes more than totemistic methods are employed. It appears to be not uncommon in the changing-rooms before an important match to hear a captain, when briefing his team and wishing them luck, direct them to wear their stockings inside out to make victory more probable.

ₑ As long ago as 1659 James Howell in his *Paroemiographia*, p. 18, recorded the advice: 'Wear the inside of thy stockins outward to scare the witches.' Miss Prue's nurse in Congreve's *Love for Love* (II. ii), 1695, makes Foresight well pleased by exclaiming that he has 'put one stocking with the wrong side outward'; and the propitiousness of this happening has frequently been referred to in more recent times, for example, in Brand's *Popular Antiquities*, 1777, p. 94; Forby's *Vocabulary of East Anglia*, vol. ii, 1830, p. 415; Hone's *Year Book*, 1832, col. 252; *The Gentleman's Magazine*, vol. cii, pt. i, 1832, p. 591; *The London Saturday Journal*, vol. i, 1841, p. 134; and Addy's *Household Tales*, 1895, p. 100. The omen is widely observed by children today, as is also putting on any other garment inside out (see e.g. the quotation on p. 229).

It is also considered propitious to wear odd socks. A Pontefract boy states: 'Some boys when playing at football they sometimes wear two different coloured socks. This, they say brings them luck.'

The association of witches with ill-dressing is still maintained in France where a student informed one of our correspondents that any garment put on inside out was a sign that the person was afraid of witches.

Courage

In nothing is sound psychology and ancient superstition more inexplicably entangled than in their preparations for a daring deed. To give themselves guts when accepting a dare – tying-up door knockers, or standing on the parapet of a bridge as a train passes underneath – boys variously grit their teeth, clench their fists, kick themselves on the shins, put elastic bands around their wrists, or touch wood ('usually our heads'). Some boys recommend finger crossing. 'If you are going to do a daring act you cross your fingers for luck.' 'You cross your fingers,' says one boy, 'and cross them as much as possible.'

Very commonly they spit on their hands: the practice being either to spit on the finger tips, or on the palms and then rub the hands together. 'Spitting on the hands seems to give an attitude to courage,' observes a 12-year-old.

In Southwark they spit in ritual fashion three times on the ground.

In Barnsley, Yorkshire, 'To bring courage,' says a 12-year-old boy, 'find a lucky stone and spit on it and throw it over your head and do not watch it land. If you see it land it will bring cowardice.'[1]

'When performing something which takes courage,' reports a 14-year-old boy from Romford, 'one makes the "Lucky Wall's Sign" by touching together your thumbs, and forming a big W with your thumbs and forefingers.'[2]

A number of boys also recommend counting. 'You count up to ten, saying, "I am going to do it", and then on the last number you do it.' 'Close your eyes and count twenty.' 'Count twenty very slowly and stamp on left foot.' 'Count twenty very slowly and take two deep breaths.' 'Hold your breath and count twenty.'

One boy recommends giving somebody a cherished possession to hold 'which he can keep if you don't manage to do it'. Another recommends throwing a cap or coin over the wall first, so that it is essential to climb over to fetch it. A girl aged twelve says, 'Drink a glass of beer.'

Other boys, noticeably the more broadly educated, favour Coué principles, telling themselves: 'I've got to do it and I will do it', 'If he can do it I can do it', 'Come on old boy you must do it, think of your honour', or they pretend to themselves that it is simple and not daring. 'This makes me succeed sometimes,' remarks a Brentwood boy.

One lad says, 'Trust to the Lord that He will get you there.'

And before embarking on the rash act they exclaim: 'Here goes', 'Wish me luck', 'Thumbs up', 'Let's get it over', 'Plucky-lucky', 'One can only die once', or, 'I like dandelions on my grave'.

1. His teacher writes: 'Markin brought me a "lucky stone", a curious clinker from a blast furnace with smooth sage-green parts and an odd half-natural, half artefact look about it. I find that these are normal but not exceptionally common products of silicates in the furnace and their odd appearance would be enough to cast the glamourie over them for children.'
2. For the origin of 'Lucky Wall's Sign' see above, p. 186.

FOR as long as history has been recorded special wildness and exuberance has been tolerated, if not exactly encouraged, at certain festivals of the year; and if we want to see in the present day how the great mass of the people enjoyed themselves in past times, the best practices we can look at are the juvenile fooling on the first of April and the first of May, the disorder on mischief nights, and the guising at Hallowe'en. Except for the tide of goodwill which rises in all men at Christmas, these juvenile activities are the most *living* calendar celebrations in Britain, for they are the most spontaneous. The present calendar does not, therefore, include every annual rite with which children are associated. Well-dressing, for instance, and beating the bounds, and clipping the church, and the children's great Whit walks in Manchester and elsewhere, are undoubtedly exciting occasions in the lives of local youngsters, but they are proceedings which are conspicuously adult-organized. It is the spontaneous customs – however puerile they may be – which are anthropologically the most interesting; and it does not necessarily mean that they have become decadent if, as is sometimes the case, they involve begging. In former times, in the days of 'merry England', it was always appreciated that the seasonal ritualist was worthy of his hire; that if ceremonial was to be maintained it must be paid for in the street just as much as in the church. Juvenile song on these occasions has always castigated the parsimonious; and the truth is that the street-child today with his soot-blackened face and red-daubed nose, rattling a tin, is a much more demure creature than his predecessors.[1] It is

1. See, for instance, Dr White Kennett's account of gangs of boys and girls in Oxfordshire in the seventeenth century going round from house to house the week before Easter. If, after singing their song, no gift was forthcoming at a house they would cry out:

> Here sits a bad wife
> The devil take her life
> Set her upon a swivell
> And send her to ye Devill.

'And, in farther indignation, they commonly cut the latch of ye door, or stop the keyhole wth dirt, or leave some more nasty token of displeasure.' – Addition to Aubrey's *Remaines of Gentilisme and Judaisme* (Lansdowne MS. 231), printed 1881, pp. 161–2.

curious that in these days when parents are habitually indulgent to children in the way of gifts and pocket money, they should take it amiss when – in the hope of reward – children sing a traditional song. And any reader of the following pages who, from one year's end to the next, is never visited by a youngster announcing the arrival of a new season, may well, we think, begin to regret that in London and the Home Counties the police now chase off the streets even the simple waits singing Christmas carols.

New Year's Day: 1 January

The year should begin happily, they say, so that it will end happily, and on the first morning of the new year children in Scotland, Wales, and the English border counties rise early so that they may make the round of their friends and neighbours. 'On January 1st,' writes a 13-year-old Radnorshire girl, 'I always go New Year's Gifting with my sister and friends, about four of us. I get up about 7 o'clock and call for my friends and go round the houses and farms.' They sing (although Christmas is seven days old):

> I wish you a merry Christmas,
>   A happy New Year,
> A pocket full of money
>   And a cellar full of beer,
> A good fat pig
>   To last you all the year –
> Please to give me a New Year's Gift
>   For this New Year.

'We do not always get money, we sometimes have mincepies or apples.' Nevertheless they collect 'nine or ten shillings every year', although gifting must be finished by midday. 'You must be gone before twelve o'clock or they will call you a fool and the people won't give you anything, and when the people see you next time they will all shout fool at you.'[1] In the outlying villages, such as Bleddfa and Llangunllo, the girls save their gifting money and put it with the money they have collected by carol singing, and keep it for a special outing to Knighton.

Across the border in south-west Shropshire, in the neighbourhood of

---

1. This abrupt termination of a custom when the clock hands point upwards at midday also occurs on Ash Wednesday, April Fools' Day, May Day, and Royal Oak Day. It almost seems that to children the days of the year change at midday rather than midnight.

Clun, children also call at houses, visiting as many of the scattered home-steads as they can. On New Year's morning, 1951, a young lad, aged about 10, knocked at the door of Miss Lily F. Chitty, F.S.A., at Pontesbury, and when she opened it, recited:

Happy New Year! Happy New Year!
I've come to wish you a Happy New Year.
I've got a little pocket and it is very thin,
Please give me a penny to put some money in.
If you haven't got a penny, a halfpenny will do,
If you haven't got a halfpenny, well –
God Bless You!

Around Aberystwyth, at Cefnllwyd and Llangwyryfon, 12-year-olds recite the soulful verse:

Dydd Calan yw hi heddiw,
Rwy'n dyfod ar eich traws
I mofyn am y geiniog
Neu grwst o fara caws.
O dewch i'r drws yn siriol
Heb newid dim o'ch gwedd;
Cyn daw dydd Calan eto
Bydd llawer yn y bedd.[1]

And at Tenby, in Pembrokeshire, children go about the streets calling at houses to offer New Year's water which they bring with them in cups, with sprinklers of something green, such as sea spurge; and after they have sprinkled some drops they, too, hope to be rewarded.[2]

In Scotland, where New Year's Day is celebrated with a heartiness no-where surpassed, the children's expectation is roast chicken or turkey for dinner, and a New Year's cake at tea, although how much some of them, who have spent the morning visiting, are able to enjoy this fine fare is questionable. A 15-year-old Forfar girl says that after she has breakfasted and exchanged gifts with her friends Margaret and Muriel, she sets out with them on a tour of their neighbours. At their first call, the black-smith's wife, they are given currant wine and a piece of black bun; at their next call they are given a glass of ginger wine and a piece of 'shortie'; and

1. 'It's New Year's Day and I'm coming to ask you for a penny or bread and cheese. Come to the door smiling. Before next New Year's Day many will be in their graves.'
2. See an illustration in *Country Life*, 14 January 1944, p. 77. At Lincoln, in the 1920s, children took a piece of wood to friends and relatives, chanting:

I've brought you a piece of wood,
And I hope it will do you good,
And I wish you a happy New Year.

(*Correspondent*, 1952.)

at their third call (though not before Muriel and she have been made to play a duet), they receive a glass of sherry and a slice of New Year cake. In return for these comforts, they are particular to leave a piece of coal with each of their hosts (some children bring a herring), for on New Year's Day it is considered unlucky for anyone to enter the house of a friend empty-handed.

St Valentine's Day: 14 February

On this day the girls awake prepared. They believe (when it suits them to believe it) that the first boy they see on St Valentine's Day is the one they will eventually marry. The resolute amongst them keep their eyes closed when they go out, and have a friend lead them to school so that the first boy they see will be the right one.[1] London boys invoke good St Valentine and attempt to kiss their sweethearts. But in Street, Somerset, 'if one speaks to a person of the opposite sex before it has struck twelve o'clock it is said to bring ill luck.'

On the outskirts of Birmingham, in the neighbourhood of Acock's Green, the children run through the streets shouting:

> I'll be yours if you'll be mine,
> Please to give at Valentine.

'People stand by,' writes a 9-year-old, 'with shuttles [oval Valentine buns] and handfuls of sweets and money. If there is snow on the ground a snow-ball helps a lot. The children sometimes stand outside a baker's shop or a sweet shop shouting again and again,

> I'll be yours if you'll be mine,
> Please to give at Valentine.

Then there is a scramble.' In Norfolk villages, Ingoldisthorpe for instance, they chant:

> Good Mother Valentine,
> God bless the baker!
> Who'll be the giver?
> I'll be the taker.

1. In employing this deceit they follow a practice of Stuart times. Pepys recounts how, on 14 February 1662, his wife shaded her eyes with her hands all the morning 'that she might not see the paynters that were at work in gilding my chimney-piece and pictures' until Will Bowyer came to be her Valentine.

> The roads are very dirty,
> My boots are very clean,
> And I've got a pocket
> To put a penny in.

In a number of such villages, from Heydon and Stalham in the north-east of the county to Loddon in the south, the younger children play 'Jack Valentine' and knock on the doors or windows of houses and leave little gifts on the doorsteps. At Mundham they chant:

> Old Father Valentine
> Draw up your window blind;
> If you wish to hear us sing,
> Come down and let us in.

And at Tuttington, near Aylsham:

> Good morning, Father Valentine.
> Trim your hair as I do mine:
> Two to the fore and two behind,
> Good morning Father Valentine.

Then they run away and hide until people throw out oranges or sweets for them. And if the children are apt to be late to school this day, it is said no one scolds them. Sometimes, however, the older children take advantage of the gift-giving and play tricks. They attach a piece of string to a parcel and jerk it away from the doorstep when someone stoops to pick it up, or they lodge a broom or a bucket of water against the door before they knock, so that when the door is opened it falls into the house.[1]

In all parts of Britain the young and romantic have sent out Valentines (Valentine cards are definitely in fashion again), and they have written anonymous verses. In Aberdeen and elsewhere in Scotland boys follow the old convention of putting verses on the envelopes, addressed to the postman:

Postman, Postman, do your duty,	Postie, Postie, don't delay,
Take this to my loving beauty.	Do the rhumba all the way.

1. The custom of leaving presents at people's doors is an old one in Norfolk, and used to be observed by grown-ups as well as children. Even within living memory St Valentine's was more of a day for present giving than was Christmas, and no expense was spared on the gifts. For descriptions of the custom in the early nineteenth century see *Time's Telescope*, 1826, p. 41, and *Notes and Queries*, 1st ser., vol. i, 1850, p. 293. The song the children sing at Tuttington has long been sung on this day, and is noted in Hone's *Year Book* for 14 February 1831, col. 201.

Postie, Postie, dinna fa,
If *Irene*'s nae in, gie it tae her ma.

Postie, Postie, dinna dither,
If *Isobel*'s nae in, gie it tae her mither.[1]

And whether it is the boys writing to the girls, or the girls to the boys, the verses they write on their Valentines are seldom original. They may fancy that their emotions are rare but their verses are trite and familiar, almost always one of the following:

My pen is black,
My ink is pale,
My love for you
Shall never fail.

Roses red,
Violets blue,
Darling sweet
I love you.

Roses are red
Violets are blue
Carnations are sweet
And so are you.
And so are they
That send you this
And when we meet
We'll have a kiss.

Maureen for now,
Maureen for ever,
Ross for now
But not for ever.

Patricia Swan is her name,
Single is her station.
Can I be the little man
To make the alteration?

Plenty of love,
Tons of kisses,
Hope some day
To be your Mrs.

I would wash all the dishes,
If you'd let me be your Mrs.

My love is like a cabbage
Divided into two,
The leaves I give to others
But the heart I give to you.

And since the objects of their gallantry are supposed to be kept guessing about the sender's identity, they sign their cards, 'From me to you, guess

1. A hundred and fifty years ago Valentine letters used to be addressed with such inscriptions as:

Postman, postman, haste away
To . . . . . . without delay;
Miss R— F— there you'll find,
A nymph that's generous, true, and kind.
You'll ramble far to find a better,
So knock in haste, and leave this letter

(*Notes and Queries*, 4th ser., vol. viii, 1871, p. 271). These rhymes addressed to the postman are perhaps the last relics of the Tudor custom of drawing a gallows design on express letters, with the inscription:

 Hast, hast,
post hast
hast for lyfe
for lyfe hast.

who ?' or 'From an old flame that's still burning', or, very popular, 'From a devil to a devil, who the devil sent it ?' [1]

Shrove Tuesday

For centuries Shrove Tuesday has been a day of high festival for apprentices and schoolchildren. It has been a day of feasting, cock fighting, and throwing at cocks, a day for football, rowdiness, and rebellion.[2] And it is pleasing to find that it is still a special day for children in some parts of England, notably in Staffordshire and Derbyshire, where 'Pancake Day', as they call it, is kept as a school holiday.

A 13-year-old girl in Longton, one of Arnold Bennett's 'Five Towns', writes:

'My special day is Pancake Day, every child has a holiday. Sometimes a fair comes to Longton and I think that everyone goes. Some children make up rhymes about pancake day such as –

> Pancake Tuesday, mother's busy baking,
> We are helping, lovely pancakes making,
> Pancake Tuesday, mix them up and fry them,
> When they are done you can come and try them.'[3]

1. Typical comment: 'This year I received a Valentine's card. It was from a boy who I rather like. I also sent him one. I guessed it was from him as I noticed his writing, he told me he noticed mine.' (11-year-old girl, Alton.)
2. See, e.g., William Fitzstephen's account of medieval London, *Descriptio nobilissimae civitatis Londoniae*, printed in Stow's *Survey of London*. Fitzstephen, who died in 1191, was Thomas à Becket's secretary and biographer; the account appears as a preface to the biography.
'On the day which is called Shrovetide, the boys of the respective schools bring each a fighting cock to their master, and the whole of that forenoon is spent by the boys in seeing their cocks fight in the school-room. After dinner, all the young men of the city go out into the fields to play at the well-known game of foot-ball. The scholars belonging to the several schools have each their ball; and the city tradesmen, according to their respective crafts, have theirs. The more aged men, the fathers of the players, and the wealthy citizens, come on horseback to see the contests of the young men, with whom, after their manner, they participate, their natural heat seeming to be aroused by the sight of so much agility, and by their participation in the amusements of unrestrained youth.'
3. Alternative last couplet from Stoke-on-Trent:
> Watch us put them quickly in the pan now,
> Toss it up and catch it if you can now.

A 14-year-old girl in Tunstall, another of the 'Five Towns', writes:

'A day that I always remember is Shrove Tuesday. On this day as we all know we have pancakes. We have the whole day off from school and the thing I remember about it is that all the children sing –

> Pancake day is a very happy day,
> If we don't have a holiday we'll all run away,
> Where shall we run, up High Lane,
> And here comes the teacher with a great big cane.

All the streets are crowded with children, running, skipping, and jumping.'

Pancake Day is, indeed, a day of song and pandemonium. In Blackburn the day's approach is marked by 10-year-olds with the curious announcement:

> Pancake Tuesday's coming on,
> And I'll get wed to my Uncle John.

In Pontypool they cry:

> Pancake Day, Pancake Day,
> Don't let the pancakes frizzle away.

And in Aberystwyth:

> Toss the pancakes, toss the pancakes,
> Turn the pancakes over.

At Toddington in Bedfordshire when the traditional Pancake Bell is rung at twelve noon, the children rush out of school, as they have done for generations, and flock to Conger Hill to put their ears to the ground to hear 'the Old Woman frying her pancakes' underneath.[1]

At Scarborough where a Pancake Bell is also rung (as at many other places), the special joy to the young, and even to the not so young, is the mass-skipping on the Foreshore, an exercise which has been traditional at Scarborough on Shrove Tuesday for 200 years. By the afternoon, even in frosty or snowy weather, the Foreshore is alive with skippers and the road-way becomes utterly blocked to traffic. Townsmen and people from the surrounding villages bring great lengths of clothes-line with them, and skip ten and even fifteen abreast in each rope. It is traditional, too, that the boys should bring out their tops on this day, and that the girls should play shuttlecock, although shuttlecocks have not been seen for some years now.

1. *Folk-Lore*, vol. lxi, 1950, p. 167.

Away in the West Country in remote farmsteads on Exmoor and in the Brendon Hills children still give voice to the wistful entreaty:

> Tippety, tippety tin,
> Give me a pancake and I will come in.
> Tippety, tippety toe,
> Give me a pancake and I will go.

'If your doors are left open,' writes a correspondent, 'the children with blackened faces will creep in and throw a load of broken crocks all over the floor and try to decamp unseen. If the householders chase and catch them they further black their faces with soot, and then give them a cake before letting them go.'

Lent Crocking or Shroving, once prevalent in the southern counties, is, indeed, part of the traditional licence and mischief of Shrove Tuesday and the night before, which now, in most places, is manifest only in the empty rhythmical threat:

> Pancake Tuesday is a very happy day,
> If you don't give us a holiday we'll all run away.

But at Tideswell in the Peak of Derbyshire the custom renowned in literature of 'barring out' the schoolmaster was, in 1938, still being practised. On Shrove Tuesday morning the children rode to school on poles, taking turns to carry each other. They then rushed into the schoolhouse in a body and locked the door against the headmaster, shouting out at the tops of their voices:

> Barley, master, barley,
> Barley in a spoon!
> If you don't give us a holiday
> We'll bar you out till noon!

Their object, or so they supposed, was to force the headmaster to grant them a holiday in exchange for opening the door, and this he would at last reluctantly do. But since, in 1938, Shrove Tuesday was already a general holiday in the district, his reluctance was feigned. The barring-out had become a matter of form; the children at this one little village being apparently alone in maintaining a tradition once honoured by schoolboys throughout the length and breadth of England.[1]

1. Information about Tideswell from Christina Hole, author of *English Custom and Usage*, and from a Tideswell old boy. Unfortunately we have been unable to find out whether the custom still continues. Dr Johnson in his *Lives of the English Poets* describes Addison as the leader of a barring-out at Lichfield Grammar School about 1685. Maria Edgeworth has a story on barring-out in *The Parent's Assistant* (1796). John Graham in letters written 1804–8 from Dr Burney's school at Greenwich describes a barring-out

Ash Wednesday

In villages around Alton in Hampshire, and as far away as East Meon, near Petersfield, at Crowborough in Sussex, and doubtless in other places, children pick a black-budded twig of ash and put it in their pocket on this day. A child who does not remember to bring a piece of ash to school on Ash Wednesday can expect to have his feet trodden on by every child who possesses a twig, unless, that is, he or she is lucky enough to escape until midday. But if, as often happens, says one ill-used informant, the child is challenged in the bus on the way to school, 'there is no chance of escape'.

*** This misbegotten demand for an ash twig on Ash Wednesday is possibly a transference from Royal Oak Day (q.v.). On the twenty-ninth of May, in the nineteenth century, Wiltshire children used to carry a sprig of oak before midday, and change it for an even-ash in the afternoon (*Wiltshire Glossary*, 1893, *Shitsac*). Today this practice seems to have lapsed; and around Alton the custom of carrying oak leaves on Shik-shak day has disappeared likewise, although it continued to the 1930s.

Kissing Friday

A teacher writing to the *Yorkshire Post* (24 February 1955) tells how in the Dales after Collop Monday, Pancake Tuesday, Ash Wednesday, and

---

(Manuscripts sold at Sotheby's 13 December 1950). Not all barring-out was on Shrove Tuesday; in the north it was often at Christmas, and of course sometimes barring-out was open rebellion, not ritual. The curious may refer further to William Hutchinson, *History of Cumberland*, vol. ii, 1794, p. 322 (best Shrove-tide account); *Gentleman's Magazine*, November 1828, pp. 402–8; John Brand, *Popular Antiquities*, vol. i, 1849, pp. 441–54; M. A. Denham, *Folk Lore of the North of England*, 1850, pp. 8–9; *Notes and Queries*, 7th ser., vi, p. 484; 11th ser., viii, pp. 370, 417, 473, 515; xi, pp. 199, 271; 12th ser., ii, p. 111; 14th ser., clx, pp. 309, 327; Bracebridge Hemyng, *Jack Harkaway's Schooldays*, 1871, ch. xxxii; C. J. Billson, *County Folk-Lore: Leicestershire*, 1895, pp. 73–4; *English Dialect Dictionary*, vol. i, 1898, p. 173.

A correspondent who was at school in Aberdeenshire *c.* 1908 recalls that on Shrove Tuesday they used to chalk up on the blackboard:

> Beef-brose and bannock day,
> Please gie's a half-holiday.

Forty years ago engineering apprentices in Manchester used to take the afternoon off on Shrove Tuesday. In Cornwall the eve of Shrove Tuesday was a mischief night known as Nickanan or Nicky-Nan Night. See T. Q. Couch, *History of Polperro*, 1871, p. 151, and Angela Brazil, *A Fortunate Term*, ch. xiv.

Fritter Thursday, comes Kissing Friday. A few years before, when she arrived at a country school and was taking a mixed class of 13-year-old children in country dancing, she saw the leading boy suddenly lean across and kiss his partner, who showed no sign of embarrassment. When, as teacher, she expressed her surprise, the boy said, 'It's all right, Miss. You see, it's Kissing Friday', and explained that on the Friday following Shrove Tuesday any lad had the right to kiss any girl without being resisted. 'And so it proved. For at each break in lessons every girl was soundly kissed by any boy she encountered. It was useless for me to expostulate, so I did not try. But each year as Kissing Friday came round, the school was in turmoil.'

*** A Westmorland correspondent to the same paper (28 February 1955) recalled that when he was a boy in the Eden Valley he and his fellows used to call this day Nippy Lug Day, and they used to pinch each other's ears. A Yorkshireman broadcasting in January 1955 recalled that, when a boy, the Tuesday after Easter week (Hocktide) used to be Kissing Day, and the boys would challenge all comers, their girl friends in particular, by putting a rope across the road on the way to school and demanding either a kiss or a forfeit. This would seem to be a survival of Hoke Day, Hoc Tuesday, or Binding Tuesday, a festival (when certain dues were paid) celebrated with unbridled sport and merriment in the Middle Ages.

Mothering Sunday: Fourth Sunday in Lent

Today almost every schoolchild in Britain is conscious of the approach of Mothering Sunday, and prepares greeting cards and bunches of flowers, or purchases boxes of chocolates or other gifts. Yet the intense enthusiasm for this festival, which is now taken for granted, arose only at the beginning of the 1950s.

What seems to have happened is this. Three centuries ago Mid-Lent Sunday, the fourth Sunday in Lent, was recognized in country places as a day when apprentices and daughters in service were set at liberty to return home for the day, and customarily they brought home with them some small token of filial affection. Richard Symonds noted in his diary, 1644: 'Every Midlent Sunday is a great day at Worcester, when all the children and godchildren meet at the head and cheife of the family and have a feast. They call it Mothering-day.' But this custom, though deep-rooted, was, it seems, a quiet and provincial one. Writers in, for instance, *The Gentleman's Magazine* for 1784 confess their ignorance of it; and in the nineteenth century, and the first half of the twentieth century, although instances were reported by antiquarians and local historians, the custom seems to have been in decline. In 1936 the Folk-Lore Society reported that 'the observances of the mothering custom have become rare or have been discontinued'.[1]

In the United States, however, a Miss Anna Jarvis of Philadelphia, who lost her mother on 9 May 1906, determined that a day should be set aside in the American calendar to honour motherhood. By forming a league of supporters, by persistent lobbying, and by what amounted to emotional blackmail (anyone who opposed her did not love his mother) Miss Jarvis quickly had her way. After one year's campaign Philadelphia observed her day; and on 10 May 1913 the Senate and the House of Representatives solemnly passed a resolution making the second Sunday in May a national holiday, 'Mother's Day', dedicated to the memory of 'the best mother in the world, your mother'. This day, it may be noted, has (or had) no relation whatever to the English Mothering Sunday, a festival of which Miss Jarvis, who died in 1948, seems to have been unaware.

During the last war, however, with the arrival in Britain of American servicemen, to whom the second Sunday in May was precious, it seems that English people began to recall their own day, or, indeed (as is a common phenomenon in popular lore), confused the two celebrations and thought them to be one and the same.[2] Following the war, manufacturers seized on the idea that here was another occasion when presents should be given; and the day has grown in importance year by year. By 1956 the majority of High Street shops were displaying 'Mother's Day' gifts in their windows: confectioners had special purple-printed bands around their every-day tins of toffee, florists were accused of increasing their prices, and stationers who as little as three years before had ignored the occasion now offered for sale a glory of tinselled sentiments.

A boy, aged 9, Hanley, Staffordshire, writes:

'Every Mother's Day I buy my mother a present. This year I think I shall give her some money. Last year I bought her some clothes. They were a skirt, a belt, and a hat.'

1. A. R. Wright and T. E. Lones, *British Calendar Customs*, vol. i, 1936, p. 43. See also R. Symonds, *Diary of the Marches by the Royal Army*, printed by the Camden Society, 1859, p. 27; C. Wheatley, *Book of Common Prayer*, 1720, p. 225; W. Hone, *Every-Day Book*, vol. i, 1826, col. 359; A. E. Baker, *Northamptonshire Glossary*, vol. ii, 1854, p. 33; C. S. Burne, *Shropshire Folk-Lore*, 1883, pp. 323–7.
2. A similar confusion, not without happy results, seems to have taken place at Warrington in Lancashire where Walking Day (when hundreds of Sunday School children process through the streets) coincided with the Fourth of July celebrations at the huge American Air Force base near by.

The advertiser who, in the *Daily Telegraph* (17 May 1955), suggested that the ideal gift for 'Mother's Day' was an 'Infra-Red Table Griller with Automatic Revolving Spit' was not, it seems, impossibly wide of the mark.

Nevertheless the traditional gift on Mothering Sunday is a bunch of violets, and the traditional fare is Simnel Cake, a rich saffron-flavoured fruit cake with almond icing, mentioned by Herrick (*Hesperides*, 1648), and particularly popular in all counties adjoining the Welsh border where the custom of making it never seems to have quite died out. One teacher (Cheshire, 1953), remarking on the general notion amongst his boys that they must give a present and do the housework on this day, commented: 'to these depressed children the one ray of brightness is Simnel Cake.' And this cake is now acquiring a general sale for Simnel Sunday.

The posy of wild flowers – primroses where there are no violets – is a gift much fostered by the churches either in Sunday schools or at special afternoon family services, when children's posies are blessed, and, in some city churches, are actually distributed to the younger members of the congregation. In the United States the emblem of 'Mother's Day' is a white carnation.

April Fool's Day

The first day of April ranks amongst the most joyous days in the juvenile calendar.

'It is a day when you hoax friends of yours with jokes like sending them to the shop for some pigeon's milk, or telling them to dig a hole because the dog has died; when they come back and ask where is the dead dog you say "April fool" and laugh at them. There are some when you just say "Your shoe lace is undone" or "Your belt is hanging" or "Go and fetch that plate off the table", and of course their shoe lace is tied up right, and their belt is not hanging, and there is no plate on the table, so you say "Ever been had, April fool".'

Boy, 14, Knighton.[1]

1. The trick of saying 'your shoe lace is undone' is mentioned by children over and over again, and seems to have been played on more than 150 successive fools' days. William Hone, writing in 1825, noted: 'Thirty years ago, when buckles were worn in shoes, a boy would meet a person in the street with – "Sir, if you please, your shoe's unbuckled," and the moment the accosted individual looked towards his feet, the informant would cry – "Ah! you April fool!" Twenty years ago, when buckles were wholly disused, the urchin cry was – "Sir, your shoe's untied"; and if the shoe-wearer lowered his eyes, he was hailed, as his buckled predecessor had been, with the said – "Ah! you April fool." Now, when neither buckles nor strings are worn, because in the year 1825 no decent man "has a shoe to his foot", the waggery of the day is – "Sir, there's something out of your pocket." "Where?" "There!" "What?" "Your hand, sir – Ah! you April fool!"' (*The Every-Day Book*, vol. i, 1826, col. 410.)

'On April the first we try to trick people by saying things such as there is a gost behind you, or there's a spider up your slev and so on. We also say fings to friten peple by saying the bed has give way, or the pituer has fulen down and so on. If the people look you call them an April fool, if they do not look they sometimes call you an April fool.'

Girl, 9, Birmingham.

'On April Fools Day nealy all the time people fooled us. Last April I said to my brother "And so everyone must keep in till next January 27th." Then Brian said "Why Dave, because there's a disese going on?" and I said to him "No because it's April Fool to you." Then Dicky Riley said that he was looking for us to have our dinner. So off we set towards home and when we got there I told my mom what Dick had said, and mom said she had only just put the chips on. Suddenly Sailor our dog gave a low growl that was the sign that someone was at the door. I went to the door and who do you think was there, it was young Dicky Riley coming to say April Fool.'

Boy, 9, Birmingham.

Needless to say the people they most want to fool are the people who have just fooled them. 'Arriving at school,' writes a 12-year-old Longton girl:

'Elizabeth Arnold caught me with one of her witty jokes. "Ah, ah," I said. "You wait until I can think of one." At play time a grand idea had struck me. I went up to Liz and said, "Elizabeth, Miss Buxton wants you." "Alright," she said and ran into school. She walked all the way round the school and finally found Miss Buxton. Miss Buxton told her she did not want her. Liz was awfully sneapt [put out]. She came back to me, and so I said "April Fool".'

Teachers come in for their share of the fooling, and according to a 12-year-old girl from Usk, Monmouthshire, are the most exciting prey:

'The best joke I ever saw was in school when one of our girls brought another girl dressed as our new needlework mistress into the form room. She was introduced to the mistress who was taking us, and she was completely taken in. She even told us to stop laughing at the new mistress. Then we shouted "April Fool" to her and we all had a good laugh.'

And parents, of course, are not exempt. 'We have a lovely time,' says an 11-year-old Swansea girl, 'as there are so many jokes to play such as sewing up the bottom of Daddy's trousers.' And a 9-year-old Birmingham boy writes:

'Last year I fooled father by glue-ing a penny to the floor and saying "Dad you've dropped a penny on the floor." He couldn't get it off the ground because it was stuck firm, then I shouted "Yah, April Fool".'

In Scotland the day is generally known as 'Huntigowk Day'. Thus a 12-year-old girl in Edinburgh writes:

'Huntigowk is a day I love. I like to put a basin of water at the side of my sister's bed and hear her let out a yell when she puts her feet into it. I also put an empty eggshell in an eggcup so that when she opens it she finds that there is nothing inside it. I played a joke on my aunt once. She has a good sense of humour and can take any kind of a joke. When the butcher rang for the order I told my aunt that it was her boy-friend (my aunt is only in her twenties). So she rushed to the telephone and asked where he would meet her tonight. She did get a fright when the man said,
"Madam! What is the order for the butcher?"
"I'll go and ask," she stuttered, and when she walked into the kitchen to ask my mother I shouted "Huntigowk!"'

The name Huntigowk comes from the old joke of hunting the gowk or cuckoo another mile. 'You send someone with a message,' says an 11-year-old Elgin boy, 'and in it you have written,

> Don't you laugh, and don't you smile,
> Hunt the gowk another mile.

When the person reads this he says it has been brought to the wrong place, and that the message should be given to somebody else, and the fool takes it.'[1]

Equally traditional is the custom, already referred to by the Radnor-shire boy, of sending someone to purchase an urgent necessity such as 'pigeon's milk' or a 'long stand'. A 13-year-old Forfar girl writes:

'We played a trick on a boy aged about six. We told him to ask the man in the shop how much the long stand was and he said that he did not sell furniture "but if you would like a long stand you can stand there as long as you like".'

Other commodities in general demand on this day include:

strap oil	cooking glue
left-handed screwdrivers	smooth sandpaper
elbow grease	square rings

1. Hunting the gowk is referred to by Allan Ramsay in 1728 *Mercury in Quest of Peace*, 81). The trick has always been much the same as it is now. Thus Brand: 'In Scotland, upon April Day, they have a custom of "hunting the Gowk", as it is termed. This is done by sending silly people upon fools errands, from place to place, by means of a letter, in which is written:

> On the first day of April
> Hunt the Gowk another mile.'

(Popular Antiquities, vol. i, 1813, p. 121.)

boxes of straight hooks	striped paint ('with the stripes not less
buckets of blue steam	than half an inch wide')
reels of tartan cotton	whitewash for the Last Post.[1]

Another well-worn dodge is to write down a rhyme ending 'Whoever reads this is a big April fool', usually:

> A duck in the pond,
> A fish in the pool,
> Whoever reads this
> Is a big April fool.[2]

'Then,' says a 12-year-old, 'either put it on the teacher's desk or give it to him in a book. We did that to a certain teacher and all he said was, "You read it, I can't".'

Not all the fooling, however, has the traditional element of inducing a person to do something unnecessary to make a fool of himself. Some pranks degenerate into mere horseplay. 'We use stink bombs, itching powder, and sneezing powder,' says a Nottingham lad. Laughs are sought with piles of books balanced on half-open doors, and pepper sprinkled in people's handkerchiefs. But on one tradition every child is agreed. As on New Year's Day, and Shrove Tuesday, and Ash Wednesday, the licence only lasts until noon. Some of the young ones cannot at first believe it; they protest and cannot think why it should be: 'It's still April the first, isn't it?' But the rule is rigid and everywhere acknowledged. 'Anyone who tries to make a fool after mid-day is a bigger fool than he who has been fooled.' The tardy trickster is instantly rebuffed:

April Fool's Day's past and gone,	April Fool is past and gone,
You're the fool for making one.	And you're a noddy for thinking on.
Market Rasen.	*Welshpool.*

1. To send someone after these desiderata is one of the oldest of April pleasantries. In *Poor Robin's Almanack* for 1738 occur the lines:

> No sooner doth St. All-fools morn approach,
> But waggs, e'er *Phebus* mount his gilded coach,
> In sholes assemble to employ their sense,
> In sending fools to get intelligence;
> One seeks hen's teeth, in farthest part of th' town;
> Another pigeon's milk; a third a gown,
> From stroling coblers stall, left there by chance;
> Thus lead the giddy tribe a merry dance:
> And to reward them for their harmless toil,
> The cobler 'noints their limbs with stirrup oil.

Sleeveless errands are also of course traditional in some factories and business houses on all days of the year to the discomfiture of apprentices and office boys.
2. From Aberdeen and Birmingham. Also a familiar trick in New Zealand (*Western Folklore*, vol. xii, 1953, p. 17).

Huntigowk's past
And you're a silly ass,
Up the tree and down the tree
And you're a fool as well as me.

Edinburgh.

April's gone and May's a-coming,
You're the fool for being so cunning.

Market Harborough.

April Fool is up a tree,
You're a bigger fool than me.

Knighton.

April Fool's gone and past,
You're the biggest fool at last;
When April Fool's Day comes again,
You'll be the biggest fool then.

London.

'Only once,' says a 12-year-old girl, 'have I experienced this, for which I am devotedly thankful.'[1]

But in Stoke-on-Trent after midday they have an additional practice known as 'Tripping-up time'. 'After twelve o'clock when we come out of school,' says an 8-year-old boy, 'they say it is tripping up time and they try to trip us over, but I think it is silly because they might hurt themselves.' 'This year,' writes a 9-year-old boy, 'Peter tripped two people over. He nearly tripped me over. It is kissing time after four o'clock. If the girls trip you up they say you have got to kiss them after four o'clock. I did not kiss anybody, neither did Peter.'

'Tripping-up time' appears to be observed only in the Potteries, and we have found no previous record of it; but compare 'legging-down time' in Cheshire on 29 May.

Taily Day: 2nd April

At Kirkcaldy, Fife, the children have a kind of extension to April Fool's Day which, although of long standing, appears to be a purely local observance. On this day, which they call Taily Day, the tricks are of one kind only, played on people's backs or seats.

A girl at Kirkcaldy High School writes:

'April Fool's Day or Huntiegowk is followed, on the 2nd, by Taily Day. On Taily Day it is the custom to pin "tails" of paper on to other people's backs, without them knowing, of course. Sometimes "Kick me hard" is written on these pieces of paper, and the wearer suffers on account of this.'

1. In the United States, when the others chant:

> April Fool has come and passed
> You're the biggest fool at last,

the joker answers back:

> April Fool's again a-coming,
> You're the biggest fool a-running.

Another girl adds that while some tails 'are just pieces of paper with "Kick me hard for I am soft" or "Please kick me HARD" written on them', others are made from Christmas decorations. It is these tails which are particularly in favour on the following day, for on April the third at Kirkcaldy it is the custom to pin on a long tail and set fire to it.

⁎ The Woman Adviser at Kirkcaldy High School in 1952, Miss J. B. T. Christie, recalls that Taily Day was a flourishing institution when she was a girl at school there half a century ago, although she does not recollect that anything was written on the tails. 'They were long strips of paper about 1–2 inches wide which were pinned on at the nearest point to the coccyx, the pinner acting very surreptitiously and then moving quietly away; onlookers giggled and nudged each other, and enjoyed the quiet fun until it was too much for someone who gave the show away by calling "Taily, taily". The victim then tried to disburden himself of the tail or tails and part of the joke was to have pinned them on in spots which made removal by the wearer difficult or impossible. IIIA2a aver that they carried out the custom yesterday. They also say that the 3rd (today) is a kind of Taily day, when a long tail is set on fire. I have no knowledge whatever of this custom. Nor can I conjecture the origin of Taily day unless it goes back to a very old story. Tradition has it that the earliest inhabitants of Fife, which at that time was forested, lived in the trees and had tails like monkeys.'

It seems unlikely that Taily Day has ever been widely observed since no previous account of it has been found, although in the Wilkie MS., compiled about 1800 (cited by William Henderson, *Folk Lore of the Northern Counties*, 1866, p. 71), it is noted that on the Scottish border the second of April used to be a 'gowk day' as well as the first. Further it is curious that a man living in Christow, the other end of Britain (reported in the *Transactions of the Devonshire Association*, vol. lxxxiii, 1951, pp. 75–6) has recalled that when a boy he was told by an old man that the afternoon of April Fool's Day was Tail-pipe Day, and 'the ritual was to pin something incongruous to the victim's rear, such as a neat label "Please kick me", though originally it had been simply something white'. This term *tail-pipe* is confirmed in West Country word-books of the nineteenth century, but in reference to tying a tin to a dog's tail.

Good Friday

To the juvenile mind Good Friday possesses a medley of associations. 'Good Friday was when Jesus crist was crucified and we have hot cross buns,' writes an 8-year-old. 'Sometimes we sing:

> Hot cross buns, hot cross buns,
> One a penny, two a penny,
> Hot cross buns.
> If you haven't got a daughter
> Give it to your sons,

and sometimes we have fish.' Fish looms largely, and is the only topic a Stoke-on-Trent girl discusses. 'All the fishmongers are lined with people because the people always say that everyone should have some kind of fish. Before the fishmonger opens there's always some people outside waiting for the shop to open. My mother waits from about nine o'clock till about twelve o'clock. If some people do not like the fish which they get from the fishmongers they have a tin of salmon between them.' In Sussex Good Friday is sometimes known as 'Long Rope Day', and at Alciston and at South Heighton outside Newhaven – and, until recently, on Parker's Piece in Cambridge – adults as well as children skip in ropes long enough, sometimes, to stretch across the road. At Tinsley Green, just north of Three Bridges, a marbles championship (now, with American participation, assuming an international character) continues year after year despite attempts by the Church to defer the event to Easter Monday. In the West Riding, and to the north, preparations which have been afoot for weeks culminate in the rosetted foolery of the schoolboy Pace-Egg play.[1] But these customs are under adult sponsorship. The most curious Good Friday rite, the burning of Judas Iscariot, is wholly juvenile.

At the first sign of daylight in the densely populated, largely Roman Catholic neighbourhood of the docks, in the South End of Liverpool, children of all ages troop out into the streets, each group bearing an effigy called 'Judas', which has been carefully prepared, with comic mask for a face, and dressed in an old suit of clothes. As the sun rises the leader of a group hoists the Judas on a pole and knocks on bedroom windows while the rest of the children chant in chorus 'Judas is a penny short of his breakfast', and they give the householders no peace until some pennies have been thrown out to them. When they have called at as many houses in their

[1]. Children who annually perform the Pace-Egg play in the streets include those of Calder High School, Mytholmroyd, Settlebeck County Secondary School, and Brighouse Children's Theatre.

area as they can, the children bring out wood, straw, shavings, and other combustibles, which they have been collecting for weeks before, and begin the serious business of burning the Judas. According to the report published in *Folk-Lore*, April 1954, it is held that the burning of Judas must take place by eleven a.m. But since the fires are lit in the middle of the street 'amid scores of children whooping for joy and throwing wood and straw on them' the police soon intervene. 'To prevent accidents the police scatter the fires and seize the "Judases" and take them to the police station in Essex Street and destroy them there. It is comic to see a policeman with two or more "Judases" under his arm striding off to the Bridewell and thirty or forty children of all ages crowding after him shrieking "Judas", and by this time the youngest children are thinking the policeman is Judas . . . For a few days when a policeman is seen the cry of "Judas" is shouted after him, but it dies away after less than a week, only to be revived again next Good Friday.'

*** The practice of burning, hanging, blowing up, or tearing to pieces effigies of Judas Iscariot belong to Spain, Portugal, and Latin America. The tradition in Liverpool is that the custom originated in that city through the effigies being seen, during Holy Week, on board the old Spanish sailing ships which docked and discharged their cargoes of wines and citrus fruits in the South End docks. Tradition, for once, appears to be correct. A newspaper account of about 1810, quoted in Hone's *Year Book*, 1832, col. 357, tells of such effigies being seen on board Spanish and Portuguese men-of-war when berthed, at that time, at Plymouth; and an account in *The Times*, April 1874 (reprinted *Notes and Queries*, 5th ser., vol. i, p. 300), describes crowds watching effigies of the Betrayer being flogged on board Portuguese and South American vessels in the London Docks.

Easter

Easter, 'Queen of Festivals', is celebrated with a concourse of colourful and gracious children's customs. 'On Easter Day,' says a 14-year-old Knighton girl, 'I pick daffodils and give them to my mother, saying the rhyme:

> Daffodillies yellow,
> Daffodillies gay,
> To put upon the table
> On Easter Day.'

Despite the glittering show of manufactured eggs in the shop windows, in many households hens' and ducks' eggs are still decorated in the traditional manner. 'On an Easter morning,' says a 13-year-old Pontypool girl, 'it is great fun to ask Mother to boil eggs for breakfast. Before boiling we wrap each egg in a piece of colourful floral material and just tack it together. When the eggs have been boiled, and the material removed, the floral design is left on the egg.'

In the twenty-first century there will still, it seems, be many people who know how to colour eggs in the old ways; how to wax mottoes and designs on them before dyeing; how to engrave on them with a sharp steel point after dyeing (ducks' eggs are best for this); and how to tie them in onion skins which turn the eggs a pleasing brown, imprinting the vein pattern of the onion's structure. 'In Cumberland,' says a student, 'we take more notice of the pace eggs than chocolate eggs.'

Many families continue the tradition that the Easter hare or other fairy creature is responsible for the timely appearance of Easter eggs in the garden.

'On Easter Day my mother, or father, hides coloured and fancy eggs in the garden (if it is fine) or in the house (if it is wet). Then we follow a kind of set trail and following these clues we try to find the eggs. The one with the most eggs is given a special prize. Later on the eggs are distributed evenly.'

Girl, 13, Blaenavon.

'On Easter morning we, my brother, my sister, and myself, eagerly hunt the garden for Easter eggs which Daddy and Mummy have hidden among the flowers, bushes, grass and leaves. When we find them we set them in the middle of the table in a dish while we eat our breakfast. Afterwards we cut one of them into five portions and eat them before we drink our tea. This is just a little tradition. Daddy says he used to do it when he was small, and I enjoy doing it now.'

Girl, 13, Goytre.

'My small sister has every Easter from our Grandmother a black egg, which my gran says comes from a black hen which only lays eggs at Easter time and they are always black, but since I have grown older I have found out that she blacks them with blackett. Mother boils it for breakfast on Easter Sunday.'

Girl, 14, Tunstall.[1]

In the north-west of England, first thing in the morning, or on the days either side of Easter, children are out pace-egging or 'jollyboying',

1. As with Father Christmas, for five or six years the children believe the make-believe; for one year they are gloriously uncertain; and from then on (in our experience) they find it even more fun than before knowing that it is a pretence, and pretending that they do not know, and indeed pretending that they do not know that their parents know that they know that it is a pretence. And, curiously, in this quadruple make-believe the original feeling of magic continues to permeate the ritual.

visiting their relatives and friends, and begging for the brightly hued hard-boiled eggs which they know have been prepared in readiness for them.

> Please will you give me an Easter egg,
> Or a flitch of bacon,
> Or a little trundle cheese
> Of your own making.

Often the children dress up, or anyway have sooted and lipsticked faces. A contributor to *Folk-Lore* in 1951 gives a vivid description of a particular party of self-organized jollyboys (all of them, as it happened, girls) who belonged to the villages of Far and Near Sawrey, near Ambleside. They had a six-part song, opening:

> Now we're jolly pace eggers all in one round,
> We've come a-pace egging, we hope you'll prove kind:
> We hope you'll prove kind with your eggs and strong beer
> For we'll come no more near you until the next year.
> Fol de diddle ol, fol de dee, fol de diddle ol dum day.

Then the leading singer 'Old Betsy Brownbags' stepped forward with a verse of her own, then 'Jolly Jack Tar', then 'Lord Nelson', then 'Old Paddy from Cork', and lastly 'Old Tosspot'; each sang a different verse and each wore a costume appropriate to her part, with full accessories: a green and yellow Kate Greenaway bonnet for Betsy Brownbags, a sailor hat and blouse for Jack Tar, and a pig's tail for the seat of Tosspot's trousers. Their song ended, they enacted in the houses they visited a traditional version of the mummers' play, concluding with the begging verse:

> Now ladies and gentlemen who sit by the fire,
> Put your hands in your pockets, that's all we desire.
> Put your hands in your pocket and pull out your purse,
> And give us a trifle, you won't feel much worse.
> Fol de diddle ol, fol de dee, fol de diddle ol dum day.[1]

1. Mary Danielli, 'Jollyboys, or Pace Eggers, in Westmorland', *Folk-lore*, vol. lxii, 1951, pp. 463–7. Mrs Danielli noted that all the actors' parts were known to each of the performers, who did not necessarily take the same part year after year. The play had the character of a hereditary possession, the children concerned being jealous of who might and who might not take part each year. These children are probably the orally lineal descendants of the young pace-eggers Beatrix Potter used to welcome with smiles and shillings at Hill Top and Castle Cottage (*vide* Margaret Lane, *The Tale of Beatrix Potter*, 1946, p. 169).

Incongruous though the inclusion of Lord Nelson may seem, he has been calling at northern homesteads for above a hundred years In 1849 J. O. Halliwell (*Popular Rhymes*, pp. 244–5) printed an account of pace-eggers at York and gave this same entertainment, with the characters of a Captain, Old Tosspot, and Lords Nelson and Collingwood.

In Anglesey, similarly, though with less ritual, it is the custom for children to go round the farms at Eastertime begging eggs. This is known as 'Clapio wyau' The children clap two pieces of slate, held between their thumb and first two fingers, to give a castanet effect, and make out that they are in want, singing:

'Clap, clap, gofyn wy,
Bechgyn bach ar ben y plwy'.
('Clap, clap, ask for an egg, Small boys on the parish.')

In some places, notably in Cumberland, Northumberland, and Westmorland, children play an Easter game of conkers with their eggs known in Cumberland as 'dumping', and in Northumberland as 'jarping'. They hold a pace egg firmly in their fist and knock it against another person's egg to see whose is the strongest, and which egg can score the most victories. Sometimes the winner claims as his own any egg which he has succeeded in breaking.[1]

Somewhat similar, and very popular in the north, is the traditional Easter sport of egg-rolling, in Northumberland called 'booling'.

'On Easter Day we usually pack a picnic lunch, including a hard boiled egg. When we reach the picnic spot we sit down and play at games. Then we find a brae and roll our hard boiled egg down it until it is cracked. Then we pick it up and pick off the shell and eat it.'

Girl, 11, Perth.

'We celebrate Easter Sunday by having hard boiled eggs dyed in different colours. We go with our friends to a grassy hill and roll them down, and the person whose egg is the last to be broken is the winner.'

Girl, 13, nr. Pontypool.

As well as from Perth, contemporary Scottish accounts have been received from Edinburgh, where egg-rolling takes place on Arthur's Seat, from Glasgow, where the great place for it is Glasgow Green, and from Aberdeen, Golspie, Lairg, Newtonmore, Rothesay, Langholm, Eyemouth, Falkirk, Forfar, and Dundee. In Dundee the practice is so taken for granted that the publishers there of the nationally distributed comics

1. This game is referred to by Thomas Hyde (*De Ludis Orientalibus*, 1694, p. 237) as being played by Christian children in Mesopotamia on Easter Day and forty days afterwards. In England the game always appears to have been only a northern one for Hyde further observes: 'Hic Ludus non retinetur in mediis partibus Angliae ' An account of the game as played by schoolboys at Tudhoe, County Durham, in the eighteenth century may be found in Moore's edition of Charles Waterton's *Essays on Natural History*, 1871, pp. 11–12. In modified form it is a common Easter game or rite in Greece today, and apparently in some other European countries (*Sunday Times*, 26 December 1954, p. 2).

Beano and *Dandy* often depict the custom at Easter in their picture stories – to the profound mystification, it would seem, of scores of young cockney readers.

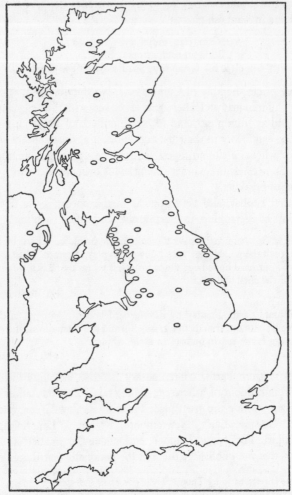

9   Districts where children customarily roll eggs at Easter

In England the custom is prevalent only north of the Trent (see Fig. 9). In some districts only a few children take part and the rolling is little more than a symbolic gesture before the feast: 'roll as hard as can and then eat as soon as possible.' In other parts the custom is far from fugitive. In a sample school in Cumberland fifty-four out of fifty-eight children were familiar with the sport. In the isolated dales between Scarborough and Pickering a traveller noticed (1957), 'there were signs of accomplished egg-rolling on the grass banks at the side of the road, even in Troutsdale.' Some townships have a special site where egg-rolling is traditional. At Preston egg-rolling takes place (on Easter Monday) on the steep slope in Avenham Park near the River Ribble; at Derby eggs are rolled on Bunker's Hill; at Penrith in the castle moat; in Manchester on Barney's Hill; and at Scarborough people go to 'the Valley'.

Egg-rolling is also traditional on the Isle of Man; and in Ulster it is as common as in Scotland, being reported, amongst other places, from Lisburn, Dundrum, and Kilkeel, the eggs first being coloured by boiling them with whin blossom, and sometimes having faces painted on them. It has not been possible to find how prevalent the custom is around Pontypool, but several children report it there.[1]

Mischief Night: 30 April

In the extreme West Riding, in an area around Halifax extending from Brighouse to Todmorden, the eve of May is still sometimes an occasion for mischief, and April, which began with a fools' day, ends with the devil's night. Window tapping, bottle breaking, gate removing, gutter blocking, and such-like diversions enliven the children's evening wanderings. But in general in Yorkshire less mischief is done on this night than on November 4 (q.v.).

₌ In the nineteenth century April the thirtieth was the chief occasion for mischief in the year, and it was recorded as the traditional Mischief Night in the following places: Barrowford (c. 1900), Bolton by Bowland (1856), Burnley (1867), Castleton (1895), Huddersfield (1883), Oldham

---

1. Egg-rolling is another sport referred to by Thomas Hyde in 1694. He says that boys in the north of England used to go round begging for eggs on Easter Eve, and having boiled the eggs hard and dyed them with the juice of herbs, took them out into the fields. 'Ovis hoc modo paratis, pueri in Campos exeuntes Ovorum Ludum exercent, magno cum gaudio, Ovis tinctis variè ludendo; scil. vel in aeremad instar Pilarum jaciendo, vel dando & excipiendo, vel ad instar Globulorum humi volvendo, plerumque ita ut sint obvia aliorum Ovis, & eis occurrentia frangant: & alia id genus factitando, quae à Borealibus hominibus meliùs inquirantur.'

Today the most vigorous exposition of egg-rolling takes place not in the United Kingdom but in Washington D.C. where on Easter Monday (since 1877) the President opens the White House grounds to anyone with a child, and an estimated 100,000 eggs are annually broken on the lawn.

(1896), Rochdale (1886), Sheffield (1890), Wakefield (*c.* 1835). How Mischief Night has, in general, come to be transferred to the other end of the year is one of the mysteries of the folklore calendar.

May Day: 1 May

On the first of May, in country districts, young maidens rise early and go out into the dawn, as they have done for centuries, to wash their faces in the May dew. In Somerset children call this 'kissing the dew'. In most places, for instance at Kirkcaldy and Alton, the girls do so to ensure that they shall have a beautiful complexion for the rest of the year. At Shrewsbury the girls pat the dew on their faces to rid themselves of pimples. At Llangunllo in Radnorshire the dew is thought a certain cure for freckles. A 13-year-old Aberdeenshire girl states that the rite is customary there because it is said to bring luck. And a Penrith 11-year-old says that it is believed that if, on the first of May, a girl washes her face in the morning dew she will marry the first man she meets thereafter.[1]

May Day is one of the days when half of England does not know what the other half is doing. At Workington in West Cumberland and to the East of the county at Penrith, at Topcliffe and throughout the area around Thirsk in the North Riding of Yorkshire, eastwards towards Scarborough, and south to York itself, children are not content with the fools they made or were made on the first day of April, but now attempt to make 'May Goslings'. In some places they are more in earnest about making fools on this day than on All Fools' Day, although the pranks they play – as here listed by Penrith boys and girls – are identical or indistinguishable from those played the previous month.

They say to their father: 'Dad, you still got your slippers on.' 'Your slippers are getting burnt by the fire.' 'Dad, it is already 8.30 you will be late for work.'

1. W. C. Hazlitt (*Faiths and Folklore*, vol. ii, 1905, p. 400) states that in 1515 Catherine of Aragon, accompanied by twenty-five of her ladies, sallied out on May Day to gather the dew for the purpose of preserving her complexion. James Howell in his *Familiar Letters*, under the date, Madrid, 10 July 1623, states that the Spanish Infanta Maria gathered May dew on more than one occasion in that year (ed. 1753, p. 139). Indeed, dew gathered on any day during the month seems to have been thought beneficial, for Pepys records, 28 May 1667: 'After dinner my wife away down with Jane and W. Hewer to Woolwich, in order to a little ayre and to lie there tonight, and so to gather May-dew tomorrow morning, which Mrs. Turner hath taught her as the only thing in the world to wash her face with.'

To their mother: 'You have laddered your nylons, Mam.' 'Your kettle is boiling over.' 'The fire is out.' 'The dog has made a mess on the carpet.' 'I have spilt some water on your cooker.' 'Mam, your bacon is burning.' 'It is raining and your washing is out.'

To a school mate: 'You have a beetle crawling over your coat, also you've torn your dress, also we're late for school and must run.' 'Look somebody is running away with your bike.' 'You haven't a coat and it's raining and thundering and lightning.' 'Look at that jet in the sky it is going to crash.' 'Tom, your shoe is loose.' – 'Ho! I'll have to fas'sen it. Why you joker it isn't!' – 'Ha, ha, ha, May Gosling!' One boy notes: 'The one were you say your shoe lase is loose is the most popular of the May Goslings but nearly everyone nosit.'

To their teacher: 'Please, sir, somebody has spilt an inkwell over the desk.' 'Please, sir, you haven't put the *e* on *Punctuate*.' 'It is somebody's birthday today shall we sing "Happy Birthday"?' 'Please, miss, why do you keep a pet frog in your desk?'

Amongst practical jokes: Stones are wrapped up to look like sweets. Letters are handed in bearing the message 'May Gosling'. Empty egg shells are served for breakfast as boiled eggs. The teacher's desk is turned round 'so that when she comes in the drawers go out the wrong way'. And notices are tied to the prongs of umbrellas so that 'when the person opens the umbrella they will find a paper with *May Gosling* on facing them'.

But, as on the first of April: 'If you say any of the jokes later than twelve o'clock the person who you said the joke to can say,

> May Gosling's dead and gone,
> You're the fool for thinking on.'

Or,

> 'You're the gosling for carrying on.'

Or, at Workington,

> 'May Gosling's past and gone,
> You're a fool for thinking wrong,
> Up a ladder, up a tree,
> You're a bigger fool than me!'[1]

---

1. Although this custom of making fools on the first of May is almost unknown to literature, its longevity is attested in *The Gentleman's Magazine*, April 1791, p. 327, where happily a correspondent observes: 'A May Gosling, on the first of May, is made with as much eagerness in the North of England, as an April noddy (noodle), or fool, on the first of April.'

More usual on this day, in fact common to a number of schools all over England, are the formal and rather pseudo-traditional May Day celebrations, such as here described by a 13-year-old Staffordshire girl:

'When I was at — School every May Day we chose a May Queen. The headmaster used to ask the chairman of the education committee to come to crown her. Before the queen was crowned each class in turn did a P.T. display. After that we had hurdle races and skipping and sack races and all sorts of races. There would of course be lots of people watching. Then the queen was crowned. After that the gay maypole was brought out and the dancers came skipping in. They performed in front of the queen many dances. The ribbons were red, white, and blue, each dancer took hold of one ribbon. There are many different maypole dances such as the plait, the twist, and the spiders web. That school repeated it every year.'[1]

Probably as a result of these organized activities, a number of the traditional practices which properly belong to this day are disappearing or are already forgotten. 'Fetching in the May', which used to be a universal custom, is now, according to a 9-year-old living on the outskirts of Birmingham, liable to be met with a frown:

'On May Day it is summer and some time I bring some may to school and then it decorates the class room. But mummy said it is unlucky, I do not know why. One day I picked some and gave it to my mother and she said "Take it out of the house it is unlucky". I said "Well I shall take it out side and put it in some water". When I came in mum said I was to have my dinner so when I had fineshed I got ready for school and I got one of my mother's papper bages to put the may in so that it dus not get my hands too derty. In class ICd Pat Smith, Hazel Riper, and Sheila Gilbert were chose for May Day [queen and maids of honour]. I cannot remember wether they were dressed up or not.'[2]

1. Such school celebrations and maypole dancing are becoming more common each year, yet the plaited maypole is no part of the English heritage, and does not belong to May Day. It is an importation from southern Europe where it is brought out for any local celebration. Violet Alford, the authority on the subject, writes: 'We do not yet know when the passion for plaiting the pole came to English schools – for it is they who are the prime culprits – but I suspect it was fancifully introduced by Ruskin (who may very likely have seen it in Italy) when he introduced the May Queen celebrations at Whitelands College. Pole and plaiting first appeared there in May, 1888, and from there it is likely to have been disseminated by College students into a thousand schools' (*Introduction to English Folklore*, 1952, p. 53). In the year following, 1889, the first congress of the Second Socialist International at Paris cunningly chose this day as Labour Day. It may be noted that by the mid-1950s May Day had become 'a very nice and happy day' (to an 8-year-old) while May 24, Empire Day, was allowed to pass unnoticed.
2. In 1648 Herrick could sing:

> There's not a budding Boy or Girle, this day,
> But is got up and gone to bring in May.

And in 1511 and 1515 even Henry VIII and Queen Catherine rode out a-Maying.

The traditional custom of shouldering little maypoles round the streets or visiting houses with may-garlands is still practised in some districts. At Shrewsbury an observer, Mr M. M. Rix, reports:

'On May 1, 1952, between 6 and 7 p.m., I visited the recent building estates in the Monkmoor area and found four separate groups of children performing a maypole dance . . .

'The Maypoles consisted of a pram wheel decorated with crepe paper and streamers, set on top of a pole so that it would revolve. The pole (varying from about 3 to about 5 feet high) was held in position by the Queen seated upon a wooden stool. The number of dancers (all girls) varied from four to ten. The dancing was accompanied by the following verse divided into four parts (the appropriate actions for each are noted below):

1. Round and round the maypole
     Merrily we go,
   Singing hip-a-cherry,
     Dancing as we go.
   All the happy children
     Upon the village green
   Sitting in the sunshine,
     Hurrah for the queen!

2. I'm the Queen don't you see
   I have come from a far country.
   If you wait a little while
   I will dance the maypole style.

3. Three cheers for the
     red, white, and blue,
   Three cheers for the red,
     white, and blue.
   The army, the navy, and
     the air force,
   Three cheers for the
     red, white, and blue.

4. Rule Britannia,
     Britannia rules the waves,
   Britains never, never,
     shall be slaves.

'At (1) the dancers sing and skip round the maypole in a clockwise direction holding the streamers. At (2) they stand still while the queen (sitting or standing) sings the four lines solo. At (3) the dancers take up the singing again and hop on one foot while tapping the toe of the other foot from side to side on the ground in front of them. At (4) they fall on one knee and sing with one hand at the salute, the other holding a streamer.

'A collection is made from the house outside which the performance takes place. In one case the tin was carried by an older girl of about fourteen, in another three small boys did the collecting from door to door. The performers seemed aged about 5–11 and were dressed in crepe paper finery, the queen usually wearing a crown of some sort. Each group had a following of small boys and girls (some in prams). One group had two mothers keeping an eye on a very young queen and maid of honour.'

In Oxfordshire, in villages such as Bampton, Wheatley, and Lower Heyford, children carry round garlands and sing traditional songs in much the same manner that they did in Flora Thompson's day, and long before. A teacher writes from Wheatley, near Oxford (1953):

'I have made enquiries among my children in school and I find that . . . little groups are formed and a May Queen is chosen. A small maypole is made and decorated with a garland a-top, and the Queen carries a stool upon which she sits for the ceremony, which is performed at intervals along the streets. She, by the way, wears a lace curtain and a ring on her finger, if possible. The rest of the company dance round her singing:

Round and round the maypole,
   Merrily we go,
Tripping, tripping lightly
   Singing as we go.

O, the happy pastime
   On the village green,
Dancing in the sunshine –
   Hurrah for the Queen!

Here they all kneel on one knee and the Queen stands up and sings:

I'm the Queen, don't you see,
Just come from the meadow green;
If you wait a little while
I will dance you the maypole style.

My hair is long, my dress is short,
My shoes are laced with silver,
A red rosette upon my breast
And a guinea gold ring on my finger.

Then all the company rises and, oddly enough, begins to hop round the may-pole singing:

Hop, hop, hop, to the butcher's shop,
I dare not stay any longer,
For if I do my ma will say
You naughty girl to disobey.'[1]

It will be noticed that these proceedings at Wheatley are closely akin to those at Shrewsbury eighty miles away. But at Bampton children custo-marily carry round a doll set in a beautifully decorated hoop-garland which two children carry between them on a pole.

In and around Great Paxton and Spaldwick in Huntingdonshire, the children have kept singing through the years one of the most picturesque of May songs:

This begins the merry month of May,
   The springtime of the year,
And now we've come into your house
   To taste of your strong beer.

And if you have got no strong beer
   We'll be content with small,
We'll take the goodwill of your house
   And return God thanks for all.

We have been travelling this long night
   And part of this long day,
And now we've come into your house
   To bring you a branch of May.

A branch of May we have brought you
   And at your door doth stand,
'Tis but a sprout but it's well budded out
   By the work of our Lord's hand.

The life of man is but a span
   And cut down in its flower;
We're here today, tomorrow gone,
   The creatures of an hour.

Instruct and teach your children well
   The while that you are here.
It will be better for your soul
   When your corpse lies on the bier.

1. This verse is also reported as part of a May Day song in Oldham, Lancashire.

Today you be alive and well,
    Worth many a thousand pound,
Tomorrow dead and cold as clay
    Your corpse laid underground.

With one turf at thy head, O man,
    And another at thy feet,
Thy good deeds and thy bad. O man,
    Will altogether meet.

Our song is done, we must be gone,
    No longer can we stay.
God bless you all, both great and small,
    And we wish you a happy May.[1]

In Ashford, Kent, the garland-carrying is less ostentatious. A correspondent writes on May Day, 1954:

'This morning three girls (looking the Marsh or Gipsy type) came to the door with a pole held between two girls with a thick navy cloth draped over it. – "Would you like to see the garland?"

'I was busy and refused. We have only been here three years, and it was only when they had gone that I remembered that it was May Day. I went to our neighbour next door and asked if it was a local custom. She said that in the old days and up to the last war children brought these wreaths or garlands to the door on May morning always covered. In answer to the question you lift the curtain and criticise the garland – saying if it is better or worse than the others you have seen; and if it is up to standard you reward with a copper or two.'

A further entertainment, and way of collecting coppers, appears to be peculiar to Blackburn and mid-Lancashire. One boy, who is supposed to be a monkey or a bear, is tied in a sack up to his armpits, and is led along the street on the end of a rope by one of the others, all of whom chant over and over again:

    Addy-addy-on-kon-kay,
    Addy-addy-on-kon-kay,
    Addy-addy-on-kon-kay.

The boy in the sack jigs up and down, his hands raised like a puppy dog begging, and when his master who holds the rope stops chanting, and calls out 'Tippy over' the sack-dancer responds with a somersault.

It will indeed be apparent to the reader that no custom, however rural seeming, necessarily has its vitality sapped merely because the countryside in which it once thrived has become overgrown with streets and supermarkets. An observer in Manchester reports that in parts of the city the May Day processions of young children are so numerous that their begging amounts to a racket. Yet even here the little gutter queens continue to pipe

1. This song is really a medley, the order and number of verses varying even in the same district. The 3rd, 4th and 5th verses above are quoted as the 2nd, 3rd, and 6th verses in a similar 'Mayer's Song' at Hitchin in Hertfordshire, recorded in Hone's *Every-Day Book*, vol. i, 1826, cols. 567–8.

traditional tunes, and improve their song with arcadian verses such as Mary Howitt's:

> Buttercups and daisies,
> Oh what pretty flowers,
> Coming in the springtime
> To tell of sunny hours . . .

And they make the age-old announcement:

> We come to greet you on the first of May,
> And we hope you will not send us away
> For we dance and sing our merry song on a Maypole Day.

While, in north Manchester, gangs of boys calling themselves 'Molly Dancers' wear old clothes, mostly women's, and make-up their faces, and go round singing:

> I'm a navvy by my trade,
> I can wield a pick and spade,
> I can shove a little barrow up a brew;
> I get thirty bob a week
> And my wife and kids to keep
> And that's what a navvy has to do.
>   – 'Spare a copper for the Molly dancers.'

*** John Brand, in his *Popular Antiquities*, vol. i, 1813, p. 184, records that on 1 May 1791, in a walk between Hounslow and Brentford, 'I was met by two distinct parties of girls with garlands of flowers, who begged money of me, saying, "Pray, Sir, remember the Garland".' And Robert Chambers in his *Book of Days*, vol. i, 1862, p. 573, suggests that it was the children alone who preserved the memory of May Day in the first half of the nineteenth century. 'The only relic of the custom [of having a Queen of the May] now surviving is to be found among the children of a few out-lying places, who, on May-day, go about with a finely-dressed doll, which they call "the Lady of the May", and with a few small semblances of Maypoles, modestly presenting these objects to the gentlefolks they meet, as a claim for halfpence, to be employed in purchasing sweetmeats.'

Thus the motley bands of urchins roaming the streets of villages and housing estates in their crêpe-paper finery are not, it will be appreciated, trivial imitators of the continental maypole dancers, but upholders of a native tradition; and the 'pretence' maypoles and home-made garlands they carry with them are objects which were familiar in the English countryside generations before the plaited maypole had reached our shore. It is ironic that in at least one village the police put an end to May garlanding in 1951, the year of the Festival of Britain.

Garland Day at Abbotsbury: 13 May

At Abbotsbury in Dorset 13 May has long been 'Garland Day'. The children customarily carry round a large flower garland on a pole, and show it at front doors, calling out 'Would you like to see my garland?' and collecting pennies. On this day wreaths used to be taken down to the beach, placed in boats, and carried out to sea where the floral offering was given to the waves to bring luck to the mackerel fishing. In 1954 the newly appointed village constable, seeing the procession for the first time, ordered it to stop, declaring that the thirty children taking part were breaking the law by begging. He impounded the money they had collected (£1. 1s. 7½d.), and within an hour found that he had the whole village against him. The next day there was an adult-sponsored procession in protest against the breaking of a 'thousand year tradition'. Outcome: the chief constable of Dorset apologized, the local constable asked for a transfer, and in 1955 the custom continued as usual.

Empire Day (now Commonwealth Day): 24 May

In contrast to May Day, this is a festival which most school authorities now ignore. Once, and not long ago, it was a day for a school outing in the most beautiful time of the year; a day on which more goodness was commemorated (future coloured historians will say) than on any other secular anniversary. A certain wistfulness is apparent in the commentary of even a 13-year-old:

'Empire day is a day which is very seldom kept now. But in some schools they still keep it. Some years ago it was an annual tradition, and all the children would take flags to school, and they would all assemble together and sing "Land of Hope and Glory" and all the different hymns. The streets would be decorated with flags, and hymns were sung everywhere.'

In England it now seems to be just a day of relics. A Bishop Auckland boy says: 'An old chant is,

Empire Day, Empire Day,
If you don't give us a holiday
We'll all run away.'

A teacher in north Staffordshire says that some of his children 'try to wear red, white, and blue, and a daisy' on this day.

But in Edinburgh the Monday nearest 24 May is a trades' holiday, known officially as 'Victoria Day', still sometimes referred to as 'the

Queen's Birthday', and hailed by the children as 'Bonfire Night'. In the centre and east of the city, in an area extending to Portobello and Musselburgh, almost every side-street has its bonfire with a crowd of excited children round it, and handsome fires burn in the closes off the Royal Mile and up the Pleasance and round about Tollcross, often to the alarm of the householders. In 1958 the city's firemen had to deal with 46 calls to bonfires, which was 'just a normal Bonfire Night' according to a senior officer. But 1958 was the last year of Edinburgh's street fires. The City Corporation, concerned by the damage to the tarmacadam of the road surfaces, has now used its powers to prohibit the fires from being lit anywhere but on approved sites.

Royal Oak Day: 29 May

Three centuries after Charles's adventure at Boscobel it can still be foolhardy for country children to come to school on 29 May unmindful that it is Royal Oak Day or, as they may call it, 'Oak Apple Day', 'Oak Ball Day', 'Nettle Day', 'Yak Bob Day' (Westmorland), or 'Shik-Shak Day'. Although the number of places where the day is remembered is dwindling, in parts of the north country, especially in Cumberland, Westmorland, Furness, and the North Riding, and also quite commonly in the north Midlands in a broad belt stretching from Shrewsbury to the Wash (see Fig. 10), children continue to commemorate old loyalty with a more painful history lesson than the severest of their masters ever gave them. A 9-year-old girl at Acock's Green in Warwickshire writes:

'In the rein of King Charles when he ran away the soldiers were after him and he hid in a very thick oak tree and by luck the soldiers went under the oak tree and past him. That is why we in the country have to have a piece of oak leaf or an oak apple in our button hole at school, for if we dont the people will sting you with a nettle.'

'The girls tell me,' reports a Welshpool teacher (29 May 1952), 'that if anyone does not wear an oak apple, the other children run after her with nettles and try to beat her on the legs, or try to push her into a patch of nettles. This is chiefly at the primary school, but I did also see attempts at doing it this morning among some of our juniors.'

In some places a sprig of oak is enough to give protection; in others it is essential that the twig bears an oak apple. In some places they call the rite 'nettle tickling', although the operation 'performed by the bigger boys

10   Districts where children wear oak leaves on Royal Oak Day

carrying large stinging nettles' is not necessarily delicately executed. In Ulverston, where the day is known as 'Bobby Ack Day', and hair-pulling is favoured rather than nettling, the following cry is traditional:

> Nob him once,
> Nob him twice,
> Nob him till he whistles twice.

Sometimes, when a child has once suffered, he is given an oak leaf by his tormentors so that he will not suffer again; and, as on other punitive days, it is customary for the persecution to cease at noon. A. W. Boyd, however, in *A Country Parish*, 1951, p. 79, while confirming the custom of nettling amongst the children of Antrobus and Great Budworth in Cheshire, reports an interesting extension. 'After twelve o'clock,' he says, 'it is "legging-down time" and when they reassemble it is "half-past legging time"; for the rest of the day it is the regular practice to trip up any who are careless enough to be caught unawares, for the possession of an oak-leaf is now no protection against assault.' [1]

In 1660, by Act of Parliament, Restoration Day was declared a day of annual thanksgiving (not discontinued until 1859), and in unconscious remembrance of this children, particularly in the north country, very commonly chant:

> Twenty-ninth of May,
> Royal Oak Day;
> If you don't give us a holiday
> We'll all run away.

'We never do get a holiday, and we never run away,' complained one child, rather perplexed.

Probably, however, there has been more than one case of pupils not arriving at school on this day. 'One time when it was Oakapple Day,' says an 8-year-old, 'my mother forgot to put an oakapple in her buttonhole and they stung her on the forehead and hand and she had two big lumps on her. She would not go to school because she looked so funny.'

⁎ John Brand, writing in Newcastle upon Tyne, 1776, says: 'The Boys here had formerly a taunting Rhime on the Occasion:

> Royal Oak
> The Whigs to provoke.

There is a Retort courteous by others, who contemptuously wore Plane-Tree Leaves, of the same homely Sort of Stuff:

> Plane-tree Leaves
> The Church folk are Thieves.'
> (*Popular Antiquities, 1777, p. 354.*)

P. H. Gosse, writing about his schooldays at Poole, Dorset, 1818–23, recalls that gilded oak leaves could be purchased against this day: 'The 29th of May, Oak-apple Day, was called Shicsack Day, when all loyal urchins were expected to display a bit of oak in their hats or caps. A mere twig of oak leaves was sufficient, but if an oak apple was attached it was better, while those who wished to be altogether "the cheese" wore leaves or apples on which a fragment of gold leaf was gummed. There was a con-

1. Cf. the practice at Stoke-on-Trent after midday on 1 April (p. 269).

siderable demand for gold leaf just before the day at the stationers' shops, and for boys whose "tin" was scarce there was an inferior kind of foil provided called Dutch gold, while in the little hucksters' shops bits of oak duly gilt could be obtained "for a consideration".' (*Longman's Magazine*, vol. xiii, 1889, p. 517.)

St James's Day: 25 July

Towards the end of July, in some of the poorer districts of London, the old custom of making grottoes at the wall-side edge of the pavement is even now not extinct, and this despite the fact that the oyster shells, with which the grottoes were traditionally made, are now almost unknown outside the West End. In 1953 a *John o' London*'s reader saw a little boy kneeling by his grotto with a cap out ready for pennies; and in 1954 a 12-year-old Camberwell boy gave this description of a grotto made by a group of his schoolfellows on a bomb-site:

'First a big pile of sand and earth was put on a board about 3′ × 2′. Then tunnels were burrowed into it. When the tunnels were finished, pieces of coloured china were stuck in the walls. Small rock-like stones were placed in it. In some places a small tin lid was filled with water, these were embedded in the tunnels also. Around the outside, pieces of moss and glass covered the earth and sand, and were studded with flowers.'

Today the usual request of the grotto-builders is 'Please, sir, remember the grotter' or 'Penny for the grotter'. But in districts such as Islington and Bermondsey older Londoners remember the song:

> Please remember the grotto,
> It's only once a year,
> My father's gone to sea,
> My mother's gone to fetch him back,
> So please remember me!
> A halfpenny won't hurt you,
> A penny won't kill you,
> Two pence won't put you in the workhouse.

According to a correspondent to *The Times* (26 November 1957) in Mitcham, Surrey, 'Grotter Day' not merely survives but flourishes. Each year home-going factory workers are besieged with requests to 'Please remember the grotter', and find themselves having to pick their way carefully along the pavement over structures of stones, shells, and flowers. Possibly due to the war-time evacuation grottoes have also, in the post-war period, been reported from as far afield as Waterlooville in Hampshire.

** According to an old proverb 'He who eats oysters on St James's Day will not want money' and on this day Londoners used to gorge themselves with the delicacy. 'The children of these gourmands, however,' says *Time's Telescope* for 1823, 'are contented with the shells, with which they erect grottos, illuminated by an inch of rushlight; and to defray the expenses of this infantine celebration, they do not cease to beg halfpence of the passengers. This fête of the oysters, although it is said to come but once a year, lasts for some weeks, to the great annoyance of those who pedestrianise in the streets of London in the months of August and September.' Joseph Blanco White considered that London children practising the custom, were representatives of some Catholic emblem which had had its day, and in his *Letters from Spain* (1822) he notes the similarity of their cry 'It is but once a year, sir' to:

> La Cruz de Mayo
> Que no come ni bebe
> En todo el ano.

('The Cross of May, remember pray, which fasts a year and feasts a day.')

Punkie Night

To children in south Somerset a punkie is a home-made mangel-wurzel lantern of more artistic manufacture than those commonly made elsewhere for Hallowe'en (q.v.). Laboriously executed designs, or floral patterns, or even scenes with houses, horses, dogs, or ships, are cut on the surface of the mangels, so that when the flesh has been carefully scooped out – leaving just a quarter of an inch to support the skin – and the stump of a candle has been lighted within, the designs become transparencies, and the lanterns 'glow in the dark with a warm golden light'. These lanterns (reported from Long Sutton and Hinton St George) are carried by a loop of string secured through two holes near the top just beneath the lid of the lantern. At Hinton St George, where Punkie Night is the fourth Thursday in October, some sixty children come out into the street with their lanterns, and parade through the village in rival bands, calling at houses and singing:

> It's Punkie Night tonight,   It's Punkie Night tonight,
> It's Punkie Night tonight,   It's Punkie Night tonight,
> Give us a candle, give us a light,   Adam and Eve wouldn't believe
> If you don't you'll get a fright.   It's Punkie Night tonight.

And this, incidentally, is another custom which the police have tried to stop.

Hallowe'en: 31 October

When darkness closes in on the vigil of All Saints' Day, Britain has the appearance of a land inhabited by two nations with completely different cultural backgrounds. While the young of one nation are employed upon their homework, the children of the other are wildly celebrating one of their major festivals. The difference is between children to whom Hallowe'en 'means nothing – absorbed in firework collecting' (Camberwell), and those to whom it is 'one of the most enjoyable days in the year' (Forfar), and 'the most special day I like best' (Longton, Stoke-on-Trent). The frontier between these two peoples appears, in the second half of the twentieth century, to run from somewhere around the mouth of the Humber south-west to Knighton, and then southwards along the Welsh border, counting Monmouthshire in with Wales, and then – although this line is less certain – south again through Dorset.[1] Further, it may be noted that the children of the north and west are kept company by children in Ireland, and in parts of the United States, in fact by most English-speaking children who do not, five nights later, rejoice over the death of Guy Fawkes.

Children who celebrate Hallowe'en almost always consider that a turnip or swede lantern is essential to the night's success. A 14-year-old girl at Griffithstown, Monmouthshire, writes:

'For this night we take a swede, cut it in half and scoop out the inside of both halves. Then cut two small holes in the top half and the bottom half, also two eyes, a hole for the nose and a mouth thus:

You then place a candle inside on the lower half and thread string in the holes and attach it to a pole. On the actual night you light the candle and go out into the street and if anyone comes along pop out from around a corner and frighten them.'

1. The celebration of Hallowe'en seems to be less general south of the Bristol Channel than north, but our coverage of the West Country has not been complete, and our information is conflicting.

A Knighton lad says that he and his mates tie their lantern on to a pole 'and lift it up to bedroom windows of some of the houses'. A boy at Castleford in the West Riding, where the lanterns are similarly carried, shows how in some places Hallowe'en and Guy Fawkes celebrations have become entangled. He says that the faces on the turnip lanterns 'represent the men who plotted to blow up the Houses of Parliament', and that after they have been carried about the streets, the heads are 'thrown on the Guy Fawkes fire'. A girl at Pontypool, where no such confusion arises, says that as soon as it is dark on Hallowe'en they take the lighted 'Jack-o-lanterns' and put them on their gate-posts 'to keep evil spirits away'; and this practice of putting turnip lanterns on gate-posts also prevails on Exmoor and the Brendon Hills in north Somerset. The most general use for the lanterns, however, particularly in Scotland (where they are often known as 'tumchie' or 'neep' lanterns), is to light the way of the guisers. 'On Hallowe'en,' writes a 14-year-old Forfar lad, 'young boys and girls dress up in old clothes and put on masks or blacken their faces with soot. They then go round the doors guising which means they dance and sing and recite poetry. They also carry turnips which are hollowed out, with holes for nose and eyes. A candle is placed inside which lights up the eyes and nose and makes it look ghostly.'

Guisers usually 'bunch up in groups of three or four', although a Canonbie lad remarks: 'Sometimes it is best to go in pairs because you get more money.' At Langholm as they 'go round the doors' they ask: 'Are ye wantin' ony guisers?' Usually they are invited in, and the house-holder tries to guess who they are. 'Then after the guisers have sung a song, they are given a gift of apples, oranges, nuts, or money. When leaving the householder is told who the guisers were if his guess was wrong.'

Throughout the Hallowe'en-observing territory the children seem to have a primeval urge to disguise themselves. 'Some dress themselves up beautifully, and others are just like tinkies,' remarks a 10-year-old. Usually the garments consist of anything fancy which can be found. Occasionally they wear witch costumes. Almost always they soot and paint their faces or wear weird masks. Coats and dresses are put on back to front or inside-out, and not infrequently they wear the clothes of the opposite sex. A university lecturer who used to help run a slum mission club in Bristol, about 1925, reports that on this night her girls always dressed up as boys, borrowing their brothers' clothes. She tried to keep them in the club house which was near the dock area but they longed to be roaming the streets.

In western Scotland the war cry of the street wanderers is 'Please help the guisers'. In Lanarkshire 'Please let the Gloshes in'. In Glasgow they call themselves 'Gloshins' and 'Please for my Hallowe'en' is contracted to 'Plessaleen'. In Radnorshire they cry 'A penny for the Gueyeer'. In Dublin, where the children's persistence in the pursuit of pence is said to outmatch that in any other Christian city, their plea is 'Help the Hallowe'en party' or 'Any apples and nuts?' In Alabama, and elsewhere in the United States, Hallowe'en is known as 'Trick or Treat' night from the children's threat to play a trick on the householder who does not treat them.

Threats also occur in the traditional songs sung by the guisers in Scotland. In several places besides Perth they sing:

> Tramp, tramp, tramp, the boys are marchin',
> We are the guisers at the door,
> If ye dinnae let us in
> We will bash yer windies in
> An' ye'll never see the guisers any more.

In Kirkcaldy, Fife, they chant:

> Please tae help the guisers, please tae ope' your door,
> Please tae gi'e the bairnies an aipple frae your store;
> Please tae help the guisers, please tae let us in,
> Please tae help the guisers, an' join oor merry din.

In two areas which could scarcely be farther apart, Exmoor, and Sutherland and Caithness, Hallowe'en is also Mischief Night, and garden gates and the gates of stubble fields are removed. The *Northern Times* (7 November 1952) reports that people are 'lucky if they see their garden gates still between their posts the next morning'. A 15-year-old Caithness boy says that at Wick on Hallowe'en there are more pranks than bonfires, and 'gates are set floating down the river'. And a 15-year-old Golspie boy, Forbes Munro, remarking that as far as he knew it had always been the custom 'for the youths of the district to go about changing the property of people around', exemplifies:

'If a man had a black horse in his stable he might find in the morning a white one, if he had a large pig he would very likely find a litter of small pigs in his sty in the morning. The story goes that one old man, wise to the tricks of the youths, tied a chain to his cart, led it through his window and tied the other end to his bed. When he awoke the chain and the wheel to which it was attached was still there but the rest of the cart had gone.'[1]

1. Similar mischief is reported as taking place at Golspie on Hallowe'en in the 1890s. But Forbes goes on to say that the best night for mischief is New Year's Eve 'when

Instead of guising, or in addition to it, many of the children of the north and west attend Hallowe'en parties. 'The best thing about the party,' says a Stoke-on-Trent girl, 'is that you should go in fancy dress. The most popular dress is a Witch's outfit, or something to do with lucky charms. It is said that one of the luckiest things at a Hallowe'en party is for a person to come in with a lump of coal (or Black Diamond as it is called). Lucky charms are worn by everyone.' A Monmouthshire girl says that as well as witches' cloaks and tall hats masks are sometimes worn to the parties. A Swansea girl says that in 1952 they had a street Hallowe'en party when the children wore their night clothes. An apple was hung from a drainpipe outside a house, then, with her back to the pipe, a girl would try to touch the apple with a pomegranate in her hand.

The games traditionally played at Hallowe'en are mostly peculiar to this night. They are in fact so much a part of the festival that in a number of places the local name for the night is derived from a game popular in the district. Thus in Liverpool Hallowe'en is known as 'Duck Apple', in Newcastle 'Dookie-Apple Night', in Swansea 'Apple and Candle Night', in Pontypool 'Bob Apple' or 'Crab Apple Night', and in Durham 'Nut Crack Night'. Sometimes the children only know the night by its local name. An 11-year-old Griffithstown girl felt it necessary to record the peculiarity that 'some people call crabapple night Hallowe'en'.

Like most old British games the games at Hallowe'en give the onlookers splendid entertainment, but demand fortitude on the part of the players.

Duck Apple. A large bowl or tub is filled with cold water (sometimes soapy water) and a number of apples floated in it. One or two players at a time get down on their knees and, with their hands behind their backs (not infrequently with their hands tied behind their backs), try to get hold of one of the apples with their teeth. 'When they have done this they must lift the apple out of the basin. If they do this they may eat it.' In Monmouthshire, as the game begins, the younger children shout gleefully:

> Crab Apple Night
> Is my delight.

---

every man has goodwill in his heart and a bottle in his pocket'. Compare a description of New Year's Eve written in Golspie sixty years previously by Forbes's namesake or fore-bear Willie Munro, aged 14: 'It is the custom of the boys to take all the portable property which is found lying about any house – such as carts, barrows, ploughs, window-shutters which are not lucky enough to have fastenings, and such-like – and place them at the doors of the houses, or carry them to a distance and leave them there to be brought back when found by the owners.' (E. W. B. Nicholson, *Golspie*, 1897, pp. 103–4.)

'If you take a bite of the apple nothing will happen to you, but,' exults an 11-year-old, 'if you miss, your head goes into the water with a splash.'

In variations of this game nuts – usually chestnuts or hazel nuts – are put in the water instead of apples, and sometimes coins. To pick a coin out with one's mouth means, of course, that the head has to go under water, but this is no deterrent: 'the money is allowed to be kept.' Further complications may be added when players are blindfolded, or when the water is constantly stirred round.

Forking for Apples. This is similar to Duck Apple but when the player's hands have been tied behind his back a fork is placed between his teeth. He has to kneel on or lean over a chair beside the tub, and must try to stab one of the floating apples and lift it out.

Bob Apple is also known as 'Snap Apple', or 'Apple on the Line'. 'First of all some sort of hook or nail must be available over a doorway. An apple is cored and the end of a length of string about a yard long is tied through the centre of the apple. The other end of the string is tied to the hook or nail. The string is twisted and the apple is sent spinning round on the end of the string, and people in turn try to catch the apple with their mouths and eat as big a mouthful as they can. This goes on until all the apple is eaten' (Girl, 12, Pontypool). Alternatively, the apple, or several apples at a time, are hung up from the rafters or from a wire or line stretched across the room. Occasionally the game becomes a contest to see who can take a bite out of his apple first. 'The enjoyable part of the game is that every time the apple is tried to be bitten it swings away from you or swings towards you and hits you in the face.' A player is given any apple which he manages to bite. As with Duck Apple, people 'bobbing for apples' are sometimes blindfolded, or have their hands tied behind their backs, and it is sometimes a rule that they must not move their feet. In Garndiffaith the children sing:

> Apple on the line
> On which we must dine.[1]

Apple and Candle. A short stick is hung horizontally from the ceiling at about nose-level, with an apple fixed at one end and a lighted candle at the other. The player, who may or may not be blindfolded, must grip the

1. 'When our parents were small,' reports a Caerleon girl, 'shops used to have their own tubs of water and everyone who wished to go and get an apple off a string or out of the water could do so.'

bobbing apple in his teeth while avoiding being scorched by the candle or anointed with its grease. Sometimes the stick is twirled before he begins, which does not facilitate the undertaking.[1]

Treacle Scones. A game highly rated in Scotland, it has also been reported from Devonshire. Scones spread with 'jeelie' or treacle are hung on strings from the 'ham cleeks', as a Perth boy says, and, as with Bob Apple, the player must try to 'scoff' the scones with his hands kept behind his back. 'If he uses his hands he is disqualified.' Sometimes the scones are hung just out of reach so that a person has to jump for them. 'Mostly, before we are finished, our faces are covered with treacle.'

Apple on the Mound. 'Another game,' says a Cwmbran, Monmouthshire girl, 'is you find a very small apple, or a nut, and set it on top of a large mound of flour on a dish in the middle of the table. Then you walk round the table in turn until you come to where a knife is.' Each person in turn has to scoop away some of the flour without dislodging the apple. 'When the apple or nut falls the unlucky person has to get it out with their mouths. If the apple is right in the flour you get your face covered with flour.' A child formerly living in Slough (where, in the new industrial area, there are congregations of families from Wales and other parts of Britain), describes the same game but with the apple balanced on soot. The game can also be played with an apple on a mound of salt.

In Scotland the last game they play in the evening is a form of divination. The children go out into the street, and come back into a darkened room. Often only a single candle is allowed, which by tradition stands in an apple from which the core has been removed. A large pot of steamed 'tatties' and 'neeps' is carried in, with lucky charms and silver coins mixed into the mash. Everybody is given a spoon and everybody either in turn or at the same time digs into the pot. When a child finds a lucky charm it tells him his fortune, and when a child finds a coin it assures him his fortune – he is allowed to keep it.[2] And while they crouch round the potato pot they

1. 'It is customary on this Night with young People in the North,' says Brand, 'to dive for Apples, catch at them when stuck on at one End of a Kind of hanging Beam, at the other Extremity of which is fixed a lighted Candle, and that with their Mouths only, having their Hands tied behind their Backs.' (*Popular Antiquities*, 1777, p. 343.)
2. A boy from the Orkney Islands confirms that a similar dish is traditional there: 'In Orkney on Hallowe'en they have a clapshot supper. Clapshot is made of potato mashed with turnip. You get a soup plate piled high with clapshot and sausages. This is how most Orkney people celebrate Hallowe'en instead of dooking for apples and trying to catch treacle scones in your mouth.'

tell thrilling stories of ghosts and eerie happenings, and repeat curious rhymes:

This is the nicht o' Hallowe'en
When the witches can be seen,
Some are black and some are green,
And some the colour o' a turkey
    bean.

Helensburgh.

Hallowe'en the nicht o' teen,
Three witches on the green,
Ane black an ane green,
And ane crying 'Hallowe'en'.

Airdrie.

Hallowe'en, they well know, is the night above all others when supernatural influences prevail, the night when divinations are most likely to succeed; and each new generation would be unscientific if it did not have an inclination to test for itself the age-old experiments.

'At Midnight,' says a 14-year-old in Aberdeen, 'all the girls line up in front of a mirror. One by one each girl brushes her hair three times. While she is doing this the man who is to be her husband is supposed to look over her shoulder. If this happens the girl will be married within a year.'[1]

'After they have done this,' continues the young Aberdonian, 'each girl peels an apple, the peel must be in one piece, then she throws the peel over her left shoulder with her right hand. This is supposed to form the initial of her husband-to-be.'[2]

Nuts are also in requisition. 'A person has to place two nuts side by side near the fire,' says a Golspie boy. 'One represents oneself and the other stands for the person one hopes to marry. If the nuts, when they catch fire, burn quietly beside each other, the two will be married; if they burn vigorously and jump apart, the two will have a row and part.'[3]

And snails, according to two Swansea girls, are still in demand, as they were a generation ago. 'From Hay in Breconshire,' recalls a spinster teacher, 'we brought a method of Hallowe'en divination with us. We caught snails and put them under a cover or box lid to prevent their crawling away. By the morning they were supposed to have traced out in

1. Burns, in a note on his *Halloween* (1785), states that an apple should be eaten before the glass. 'Take a candle and go alone to a looking-glass; eat an apple before it, and some traditions say, you should comb your hair all the time; the face of your conjugal companion, *to be*, will be seen in the glass, as if peeping over your shoulder.'
2. A form of divination described by Gay in 1714. See note on p. 362.
3. Burns said this was 'a favourite charm'; and Gay too gives the prescription in *The Shepherd's Week*, iv. 61–6. Turner in his *Tour in the Levant*, vol. iii, 1820, p. 517, reports that Greek women used the same test but with apple pips.

their slime the initials of our future husbands. But my snail always crawled up on to the underside of the lid and there it remained.'[1]

All Souls' Day: 2 November

Children living in rural parts of Cheshire, north Shropshire, and along the adjoining Staffordshire border, continue to go out Souling either on All Souls' Day, or on the preceding day, All Saints' Day. A. W. Boyd, writing about Great Budworth, near Northwich (*A Country Parish*, 1951), says that small children 'find Soul-caking a good excuse for wandering from farm to farm' singing 'traditional if somewhat tuneless songs'. A week after All Souls' Day they may still be heard chanting:

> My Souling Cap, my Souling Cap,
> It cost me many a shilling,
> My shoes are wore out through tramping about,
> And I can't get a pint of beer.

Soul-cakes are no longer made, and the children are usually rewarded with apples, biscuits, or coins which, however, they may stoutly refer to as 'soul-cakes'. Christina Hole (*English Custom and Usage*, 1943) quotes the following as one of the verses the children sing:

> Soul! Soul! for a soul-cake!
> I pray you, good missis, a soul-cake!
> An apple, a pear, a plum or a cherry,
> Or any good thing to make us all merry.
> One for Peter, two for Paul,
> Three for Them that made us all.

A 15-year-old girl attending school at Tunstall, north Staffordshire (1954) gives:

> Soul, Soul for an apple or two,
> If you've got no apples pears will do;
> If you've got no pears ha'pennies will do,
> If you've got no ha'pennies God bless you.

---

1. This is another charm described by John Gay (*The Shepherd's Week*, iv. 53–6) but according to his account the snail should be put in the ashes on the hearth on May Day:

> I seiz'd the vermine, home I quickly sped,
> And on the hearth the milk-white embers spread.
> Slow crawl'd the snail, and if I right can spell,
> In the soft ashes mark'd a curious L.

And a further relic of this custom is probably the 'Kay-kaying' that annually takes place at Stocksbridge, nine miles north of Sheffield. Here, during the first three days of November, the children regularly go round from door to door begging for money (which they use to buy fireworks for 5 November) and singing:

> Kay, kay, kay,
> Hole in my stocking, hole in my shoe,
> Please can you spare me a copper or two?
> If you haven't got a penny a ha'penny will do,
> If you haven't got a ha'penny God bless you.

And if money is not given they make a practice – despite the geniality of their verse – of returning the next night and doing mischief.

*** An array of references to Souling appears in *British Calendar Customs: England*, vol. iii, 1940, pp. 121–31 and 137–42. These references are mostly to the nineteenth century, but include West Felton, 1936, Llynclys and Porthywaen, 1937, and Tattenhall, 1938; to which may be added Whixall, near Whitchurch, 1952. It may be noted that although Soul-caking has been a custom among children for anyway 400 years, it never seems to have been a general practice. The area where the custom obtains today has apparently always been the centre of the Souling territory.

Mischief Night: 4 November

From coast to coast across northern England the eve of Guy Fawkes Day has become 'Mischief Night', a night of humour and hooliganism affecting most of Yorkshire, and parts of Lancashire, Cheshire, Derbyshire, Nottinghamshire, and Lincolnshire. On this night children are half under the impression that lawlessness is permissible. Householders' front doors are repeatedly assaulted with bogus calls, their gates removed, their dustbin lids hoisted up lamp posts, their window panes daubed with paint, their doorknobs coated with treacle or tied 'sneck to sneck', their evening newspapers (projecting from letter-boxes) exchanged, their milk bottles placed so that they will be tripped over, their house-numbers unscrewed and fixed on to other houses, their windows tapped, their backyards turned upside down and possibly ransacked for tomorrow's bonfires, their drainpipes stuffed with paper and set alight, and their porchlight bulbs considered legitimate targets for catapults. Both in villages and in great

11 Mischief Night. Places where it has become customary for children to play pranks on 4 November. Note, however, that in Manchester, for instance, Mischief Night is not general throughout the City. It has been reported from Levenshulme and Wythenshawe, within the City boundary, and from Trafford Park just without, but it is apparently unknown in some other districts.

industrial cities (see map) youngsters bent on mischief roam the streets in happy warfare with the adult world.[1]

1. 4 November seems to have become Mischief Night sometime during the last two decades of the nineteenth century, and in many places apparently even more recently. Nineteenth-century Yorkshire writers do not mention the day, speaking only of the Eve of May Day as Mischief Night (see p. 277).

'On Mischief Night,' writes a 12-year-old, 'my friends and I do many strange mischievous deeds. We knock at a door offering a woman cabbages, meanwhile somebody climbs on the roof with a bucket of water. If the person will not buy she gets wet through.'

'On Mischievous Night,'[1] writes another, 'one of our tricks is to collect some old tin cans, and tie them together with string. Then we fill them with ashes, tie a loop at the other end of the string, and put that on a door knob. Somebody knocks on the door and everybody hides. When the door is opened in flies the ashes, and then all sorts of language is heard.'

'A favourite trick,' say several lads, 'is to tie two door knobs together with a length of string, and knock at both doors at the same time.' The boys run and hide in a place where they can see both doors, and 'watch the occupants tugging against each other'. Sometimes, as the householders tug more and more strenuously, they creep out of their hiding places and cut the string, 'and both people' – so they hope – 'fly backwards as the doors fly open'. Alternatively, says a 12-year-old, 'a rope is tied to a door handle, and one of the boys knocks on the door. Some more boys hold the rope firmly, and when the man or woman attempts to open the door he cannot. Only when he pulls with all his strength do the boys let go of the rope. The man falls flat on his back.'

On this night they intensify their search for combustibles and uproot palings for their bonfire piles. They 'get even with bullies by firing their bonfire' or by taking as much of it as they can without getting caught. They 'give the milkman a hard time' (their own words) 'by smashing dozens of milk bottles on the walls of houses'. They go round and 'lift all the gates off the hinges and then', says a 13-year-lad, 'watch the faces of the people the next morning when they discover their gates off'.

'Fireworks,' as one of them needlessly points out, 'are available on Mischief Night.' 'You create a great disturbance by putting a firework that gives off a bright light on the edge of a window. It is then ignited. The people in the house get quite a scare,' says a 13-year-old. 'Other things that are rather more dangerous are pushing bangers through letter-boxes and knocking on the door. If it is timed rightly it explodes just as the occupant reaches the door.' Alternatively, bangers are thrown into the doorway when the door is opened, or a squib is inserted in the keyhole and lit, so that when the door is opened it rains sparks into the house. Bangers are let off, they say, 'behind girls and old men'. 'A jumping firework is fastened on to a dog's tail and lit, the firework explodes and the dog runs

1. So called, sometimes, in the West Riding. In Bootle the night is aptly known as 'Danger Night'.

yelping down the street.'[1] At Pontefract there is a fair on Mischief Night. Bangers are kicked under the openings of the stalls where the attendants stand. Then they take the gunpowder out of a large firework, light the dud, and toss it into the middle of the crowd. 'The people think it will go off and run away confusedly.'

The practice of hollowing out turnips 'making the ears, eyes, nose and mouth as horrible as possible' and scaring old women with them, is pursued on this night, and is considered by some children to be 'the best trick of all'. The face is 'held up at windows, poked round corners', and left suspended from people's door frames. 'The occupant opens the door to find the weird face of the turnip confronting him.' 'He thinks it is a ghost,' adds a 9-year-old.[2]

The occupants themselves seem to endure Mischief Night with admirable fortitude. Yorkshiremen are made of strong stuff; the realistic householder brings his dustbin indoors, secures his letter-box, bolts his door, and awaits the siege, sometimes preparing his hose in case hot youth in his front garden needs cooling. In 1948 the Chief Constable of Leeds advised: 'Take off your gate and hide it. It may seem a bother but it's less bother than picking it out of a pond later.' The wisdom of this advice is confirmed by a Scarborough correspondent (1954): 'My aunt who has just moved to a new house lost her front garden gate. Luckily it had only been removed to the end of the road. We hear it reported that up at Burniston (about five miles north of here) they not only removed farm gates but burnt them,' which, as she says, 'is going too far.' Her aunt, she continues, having retrieved her gate, went to see the house she had left and was much annoyed to find that the house-agent into whose hands she had put it had not got a notice up. 'She rang up to find out why, and the house-agent said sadly there had been a board up but they had lost about twenty boards on Mischief Night, and though the man had been round to replace them, they had been swiped again before the bonfires were lit "and they'll all be burnt by now".'

The local newspapers, the next day, are accustomed to issuing communiqués, not wholly indignant, on the ordeal which the district has been

1. Only two accounts of this practice have been received from present-day children. A couple of generations ago when today's old men were young it used to be not uncommon, being not always looked upon as pernicious by *their* elders. Today despite publicized lapses, boys and girls are undoubtedly more humane than they used to be. As adult thought on what is right and fitting in the treatment of animals becomes more stringent, juvenile practice follows not far behind.
2. This custom of bringing out turnip lanterns four nights after the traditional date is further evidence that Mischief Night is in origin a postponed celebration of Hallowe'en deranged by the newer and more robust commemoration of the Gunpowder Plot.

through. 'Mischief Night Damage in Gardens.' '20 Boys in Mischief Night Raid at Ayton.' 'Mischief Night Match Set Curtains, Paint on Fire.' So long as the children, girls as well as boys, do not go too far, the sport on this night seems to be recognized as traditional. A magistrate says: 'We all know of this mischief-night business. It is all right if you are reasonable and do things that do not injure anyone.' And, just occasionally the activities may not be without humour even to adults. On the morrow of Mischief Night, 1954, reports the *Yorkshire Post* (6 November 1954), a leading firm of estate agents in Leeds received a telephone call from a city councillor congratulating them on being instructed to deal with one of the biggest properties in the city. When one of the principals of the firm was summoned and asked him what he meant, the councillor replied: 'I see one of your boards is hanging on the main entrance gates to Roundhay Park.'

Guy Fawkes Day: 5 November

As the fifth of November approaches there is scarcely a cartoon in the children's comics which does not depict the excitement of Fireworks Day. For weeks the boys have been out 'chumping', as they call it in Yorkshire, or 'wooding' as it is sometimes termed, collecting branches, palings, straw, cardboard, and the boxes and debris begged from shopkeepers. Around Oldham in Lancashire they go 'cob-coaling', knocking at doors and singing:

> We come cob o' coaling for Bonfire time,
> Your coal and your money we hope you'll enjoy,
> Fol-di-day, fol-di-day, fol-di-diddle-i-do-day,
> Down in yon cellar, there's an old um-ber-ella,
> And in yonder corner there's an old pepper pot (or 'box'),
> Pepper pot, pepper pot, morning till neet,
> If you give us nowt, we'll steal nowt,
> But wish you good neet.

Preparations are usually well in hand by the third week in October. 'We are bound to have a wondrous bonfire in our street,' writes a mid-October correspondent. 'The pile already contains the clearings from twenty gardens, an ancient armchair, and a lorry tyre. Sundry fiery rehearsals do not seem in any way to have diminished the accumulation.' 'In our village,' says a Monmouthshire girl, 'we have started collecting wood for the bonfire already [14 October] and we have competitions between ourselves to see who gets the biggest bonfire.' It is not only an affair of building the biggest bonfire but of guarding it. Rival gangs are liable to steal from, or set fire to, neighbouring fuel stores. The *Yorkshire Post*, 28 September 1954, reported that in York City several fires had already been caused, and the corporation had had to order lorries to remove the bonfire piles which were accumulating in public places.

The guys vary in ambitiousness from the fifteen-foot effigy stuffed with rockets, Roman candles, and other whooshers, annually erected at Edenbridge in Kent where the celebration of the Fifth is adult-organized, and is almost a cult, to that of the humble penny-for-the-guy city child, with face as black as a piccaninny, who when asked 'Where's the guy?' replied 'I am.' Usually the guys are 'made very carefully and made to look as realistic as possible', or so the children say, and doubtless they are realistic in the eyes of their makers, whatever their shape and whatever strange garments they are stuffed into. As William Hone wrote in 1825 (and most of his long description might well be of the present day): 'It is not to be expected that poor boys should be well informed as to the Guy's history, or be particular about his costume.'[1] 'What's your guy's full name?' asked a *Times Educational Supplement* reporter in Chelsea in 1951. 'Charlie.' 'Why Charlie?' ''Cause that's what he looks like.' And so he did, 'sitting up in an old doll's pram on the pavement of the King's Road with an orange face of beardless innocence crowned with a blue knitted ear-comforter'. Indeed, during the war, the effigy was sometimes made to look like Hitler, and doubtless attracted further pennies in consequence.[2] In recent years, when the now variable Remembrance Day has clashed with Gunpowder Treason, small boys have been found sticking Flanders poppies on their guys 'for luck'. Only at St Peter's School, York, do they make a bonfire but burn no guy. Guy Fawkes went to school there, and it is not thought good form to burn the effigy of an old boy.

The following juvenile chants or 'nominies' (as they are called in Yorkshire) are repeated when begging with the guy, or when burning it:

Guy Fawkes, Guy,	Guy, Guy, Guy,
Stick him up on high,	Poke him in the eye,
Hang him on a lamp post	Put him on the fire
And there let him die.	And there let him die.

Numerous variations. In Folkestone they add: 'Burn his body from his head. Then you'll say Guy Fawkes is dead. Hip, Hip, Hooray!'

1. *The Every-Day Book*, vol. i, pt. ii, 1826, cols. 1429–30.
2. This transference is, in itself, in keeping with the past. Other figures which have been mortified on this day include: The Old Pretender, Napoleon, Cardinal Wiseman, Nana Sahib, Kruger, the Kaiser, Colonel Nasser (1956), and, of course, the Pope. Evelyn in his diary, 5 November 1673, wrote: 'This night the youths of the City burnt the Pope in effigie, after they had made procession with it.' Up to the beginning of the twentieth century the day was often known as 'Pope Day'.

Please to remember
The Fifth of November,
Gunpowder treason, and plot.
I see no reason
Why gunpowder treason
Should ever be forgot.

Very general. Occasionally with the additional verse:

Hurrah boys! Hurrah!
Make the bells ring.
Hurrah boys! Hurrah!
God save the Queen.

Please to remember
The Fifth of November,
The poor old guy
With a hole in his stocking
A hole in his shoe
A hole in his hat where his hair comes
  through.
If you haven't got a penny a halfpenny
  will do,
If you haven't got a halfpenny
  God bless you.

Market Rasen.

Guy Fawkes, Guy,
Hit him in the eye,
Hang him on a lamp-post
And leave him there to die.
Umbrella down the cellar
There I saw a naked fella
Burn his body, save his soul,
Please give me a lump of coal;
If a lump of coal won't do,
Please give me a ha'penny,
Then up and down the Drapery,
Round and round the Market Square,
Till I get to Marefair,
Where I'll spend my ha'penny,
Guy Fawkes, Guy.

Northampton.

A penny for the guy,
A penny for the guy,
A big umbrella
And a flashy tie.
The guy, the guy,
Pin him in the eye;
Stick him up a lamp post,
Don't let him die.

Aberdeen.

Such rhymes have a long and well-established tradition behind them.[1]

Each year adults complain about the early start children make collecting for the guys.[2] The children, however, point out that 'dosh' has to be

1. In an eighteenth-century book of days, *An Agreeable Companion*, 1742, p. 55, it is reported: 'This Day is called Gun-Powder-Treason, still kept in Remembrance. And the Boys have it recorded in the following lines, which they use to sing about this time.

> Don't you Remember,
> The fifth of November
> 'Twas Gun-Powder Treason Day,
> I let of my Gun,
> And made 'em all run.
> And stole all their Bonfire away.'

Other early recordings appear in *Juvenile Amusements*, 1797, no. 50, version similar to that most general today; *Popular Pastimes*, 1816, November; James Hogg, *The Jacobite Relics of Scotland*, vol. i, p. 127, parody, 'Let Whigs remember the fifth of November'; *The Children's Friend*, vol. ii, 1825, p. 251, 'Remember, remember, The fifth of November, The gunpowder treason and plot; The King and his train Had like to be slain, And I hope it will ne'er be forgot'; William Hone, *The Every-Day Book*, vol. i, pt. ii, 1826, col. 1431; William Howitt, *The Boy's Country-Book*, 1839, p. 81, verse entreating materials for the bonfire, 'Pray remember The Fifth of November! A stick or a stake For King George's sake, Timber or coal For the bonfire pole.'

2. 'I have just been asked "Any money for the guy?" Is this a record?' – Letter to *The Times*, written from the Reform Club, 18 September 1951.

found well before 5 November if they are to purchase their fireworks before the shops are sold out of the best ones. In the cities experienced youngsters take their guys outside the cinemas where fifteen shillings and more can be gathered in an evening. In the country they have to rely more on their own resources. 'I save my money for fireworks all the year through,' says an 11-year-old girl, 'and then in October I buy my choice.' They classify their fireworks as 'bangers', 'pretty ones', 'hoppers', and rockets; and even the manufacturers' names are poetry: Golden Rain, Daisy Fountains, Mighty Atoms, Boy Scout Rousers (banned after 1955), Mount Vesuvius, Fireflies, Serpents' Nests, Demon Cannons, and Witches' Cauldrons. Sometimes, to add to the effect, they explode the fireworks in milk bottles (a dangerous trick) or under tin cans (so that they make more noise).

To light the bonfire they have a sock 'and stuff old rags in it and tie it on the end of a middle-sized stick and just before we light the fire we dip it in oil'. 'The boys light the bonfire at about half past six in the evening,' says a young girl. 'It is always lovely when the fire is blazing, the sparks fly and the sky turns a lovely orange colour.' The grown-ups come out to watch the fire and set off their share of the fireworks or more than their share, and then go indoors again and this, the children say, is the nicest time. 'We make a ring and dance round the fire. We see who can collect the most used fireworks. We put potatoes on sticks and cook them in the burning embers.' And in parts of Wales, and away in the hills and on the moors in Yorkshire, and Lancashire, and Devonshire, places where they call this night 'Bonfire Night' rather than Guy Fawkes Night, children put on masks and join hands round the fire and dance and sing.

> Bonfire night, the stars are bright,
> Every little angel dressed in white.
> Can you eat a biscuit?
> Can you smoke a pipe?
> Can you go a-courting
> At ten o'clock at night?

> *Boy, 11, Blackburn, Lancs. 'Sung when dancing round bonfire.'*

The guy has long ago been burnt and forgotten. The last firework has been exploded. The bonfire becomes all-important, and somehow it seems to be a heathen Hallowe'en fire they are attending.

Christmas Coming

To the older generation preparations for Christmas, as for November the fifth, seem to start earlier each year, and the carol singers are said to become more and more commercial. One correspondent, remarking on their businesslike note, says that in her district 'innocent-eyed little girls (not boys)' have taken to ringing the doorbell before they start and asking politely 'Please may we carol?' 'If permission is refused they go away, still politely, but without having wasted time on an unprofitable venture.' If permission is granted, they know the householder will generally say 'Here's a penny for you. Just sing me one verse and go away.' Again they will have wasted the minimum of time. This practice can, however, largely be attributed to the general unwillingness of grown-ups today to give time to listening to what the children have to offer. The children themselves say that they want to give as good performances as possible; that they go carolling because they like singing and the fun of going out on a winter's night, and 'because Jesus was born on Christmas Day'. Their favourite carols are 'Good King Wenceslas', 'The First Nowell', 'We Three Kings', 'The Holly and the Ivy', and 'The Holly bears a berry'. A surprising number of children have a traditional rhyme to sing 'after we have sung our carols', the most usual verse being:

> Christmas is coming, the geese are getting fat,
> Please to put a penny in the old man's hat.
> If you haven't got a penny, a ha'penny will do,
> If you haven't got a ha'penny, God bless you.

The impudent say, 'If you haven't got a ha'penny, you're a skinny old Jew', or add, 'Skin a donkey, cut his tail off, put a carrot on, Amen'. In Tunstall, North Staffordshire (according to a 14-year-old girl), they continue:

> Slip down the cellar and see what you find me,
> An apple or a pear or a good strong beer,
> And we'll never come a-carolling till this time next year.

Other traditional chants still to be heard include:

Little Robin Redbreast	A hole in my stocking,
Sat upon a tree,	A hole in my shoe,
I wish you a merry Christmas	Please can you spare me
It's a greeting from me.	A copper or two.
With apples to eat,	If you haven't a penny,
Nuts to crack,	A ha'penny will do,
I wish you a merry Christmas	If you haven't a ha'penny,
With a big rat-a-tat.	God bless you.
Knighton and Manchester.	*Yorkshire.*

We wish you a merry Christmas,
We wish you a merry Christmas,
We wish you a merry Christmas,
And a happy New Year.

Knighton and Shrewsbury.

Now Christmas is here
Let's have a drop of beer
Bright celery, bright celery,
And a happy New Year.
Apples to eat, and nuts to crack
Here we come with our rat-tat-tat.

Dudley, Worcestershire.

The road is very dirty,
  My shoes are very clean,
I've got a little pocket
  To put a penny in.
If you haven't got a penny,
  A ha'penny will do,
If you haven't got a ha'penny,
  A mince pie will do,
If you haven't got a mince pie,
  A drink of wine will do,
If you haven't got a drink of wine,
  God bless you.

Shrewsbury and district.

In and around London there were, in 1951, signs of inflation:

Knock on the knocker, ring on the bell,
Give us a shilling for singing so well,
If not a shilling, a tanner will do,
If not a tanner, God bless you.

But in Great Driffield the lavish note in the children's song is traditional. According to the *Scarborough Mercury* (14 December 1956) boys and girls there assemble, as they have done for years, in one vast concourse and chant through the streets:

Here we are at oor toon end
A shoulder o' mutton, a croon ti spend,
  Hip! Hip! Hooray!

Christmas: 25 December

Christmas hardly qualifies for inclusion in this calendar since most of the activities on this day are family affairs; nevertheless some record of current practices may be of interest.

Children's belief in Father Christmas is liable to last until they are six, sometimes longer, and varying notions are entertained about him – Christmas mythology still being in a state of flux. Thus many children are told that he first comes around before Christmas to collect any messages; fairies, pixies, elves, golliwogs, and midgets are introduced into the legend as Father Christmas's helpers; and it is not uncommon for children to think that Father Christmas and Santa Claus are two different people. Disbelief in 'Daddy' Christmas comes when parents are spied at night filling the stockings, or when other children disabuse them. An 11-year-old writes:

'When I was younger I thought Father Christmas was a wonderful man. On Christmas Eve before I went to bed I would make my brother put out the fire. I was afraid that Father Christmas would get burnt when he climbed down the chimney. My sister would write out my Christmas list (because I couldn't write) and I would throw it up the chimney. When I went to town with my mother, I wondered how Father Christmas could be in all the stores at once. She told me that they were his brothers and the real one came on Christmas Eve. My sister would make a cup of tea and biscuits for him. But when I got to the age of six the older children called me silly because I believed in Father Christmas. When I got home I asked my mother and she said, "Of course there's a Father Christmas," but I did not believe her.'

The custom of leaving refreshment for Father Christmas is particularly common in the north, and its disappearance by the morning is counted additional proof that he really came. In Cumberland Father Christmas is sometimes left a glass of sherry, a cigarette, and half-a-crown. When the girl who said this was asked who got the spoils, she merely grinned, and reiterated that they always had disappeared by morning.

Christmas is everything that can be expected. To children in the south it is '*the* most special day'. 'When I wake up,' says a 9-year-old, 'I say,

> Christmas comes but once a year,
> But when it comes it brings good cheer.'[1]

It is a day of 'undoing presents and taking them round showing them to people'. But all children say it is their stockings they empty first, getting 'hold of the toe and shaking everything out', and leaving the rest of their presents until later. Everybody's house is decorated, and they say they have to wear their best clothes ('which', says a hoyden, 'I do not think is very exciting because you cannot go to play in the fields').

In and around Scarborough the boys go 'Christmas ceshing' (pronounced *Ch'is'mas keshin'*), which requires no equipment beyond a hard fist to knock on doors, and a strong voice to shout – in a special sing-song manner – 'Wish you Merry Christmas, mistress and master'. Their cry can be heard all the way along the street on Christmas morning, and they hope to gain pennies by it.

---

1. Thereby echoing the sentiment voiced by Tusser in 1573:

> At Christmas play and make good cheere,
> For Christmas comes but once a yeere.

Some children mention going to church, and that Christmas is 'a day of remembrance for our Lord Jesus Christ'. Rather more children merely speak of the pleasure of hearing church bells on Christmas morning.

One girl (Stoke-on-Trent) says that she goes to a farm and chants:

> Little turkey patter
> Be quick and get much fatter.

Then the farmer brings her back in his car with the turkey. At dinner a turkey or chicken with sausages and stuffing 'smells glorious', so that when a girl sits down to eat she is 'that full in a few minutes' she cannot possibly eat any more.

In the afternoon they listen to the Queen on the wireless, and to Wilfred Pickles at a children's hospital, or – possibly more often – go visiting. At Auntie's 'when you arrive they try to get you under the mistletoe'. 'It is good luck,' says a 14-year-old Lloyney girl, 'if the first man to kiss you under the mistletoe gives you a pair of gloves.'

When the evening closes in they usually have a party, inviting their friends to tea and playing 'all kinds of games' such as: The Grand Old Duke of York, The Farmer's in his Den, There was a Jolly Miller, Musical Chairs (or Musical Arms), Blindman's Buff, and Postman's Knock. Children in different parts of Britain name the same games over and over again. Half-way through tea (at Meir in Staffordshire) everyone starts singing:

> Bring out your mince pies,
> Bring out your mince pies,
> And share them all around,
> And share them all around.

And as the evening grows older and merrier they have trifle, nuts, toffees, lemonade, and crackers. The party ends with presents off the Christmas tree 'which is beautifully decorated with crackers and balloons and at the top of the tree there is a lovely fairy'. Sometimes Father Christmas comes to the party. 'My father dressed up as Father Christmas,' says an 11-year-old, 'and then the fun began. Dad came in wearing Mrs Evans's dressing gown and my hood. He started unloading presents off the tree. My young cousin Stuart who is five asked Dad had he got Rudolph the reindeer with him.[1] Dad said yes. He didn't quite know what to say. Then Stuart and

1. Rudolph is a new character on the Christmas scene, possibly come to stay. Despite a shiny nose which makes the other reindeer laugh at him he is chosen to pull Santa's sleigh in the Johnny Marks song 'Rudolph the Red-Nosed Reindeer', copyright St Nicholas Music Publishing Co., New York, 1949. A recording with vocal by Gene Autry has become an annual 'must' with teenagers.

Denise who is three wanted to see him. We told all sorts of things not for them to go out there. Mother had made an excuse for Dad by saying he had gone to Gran's. Then Dad went and as soon as he came back supposedly from Gran's the first thing Stuart told him was "You've missed all the fun, Uncle George. Santa's been here!".'

St Stephen's Day: 26 December

The custom of 'Hunting the Wren', or, anyway, of calling at houses and collecting on behalf of the wren, continues to be widely observed in southern Ireland, particularly in Cork and Kerry, but also in other places, including Dublin. Companies of young boys, sometimes dressed in girls' clothes, or with faces blackened so that nobody will recognize them, parade the streets on the morning of St Stephen (rarely known as Boxing Day). They carry a wren-bush of holly or gorse, dressed with ribbons and coloured papers, and in it is supposed to lie the body of a dead wren. Boys in Dublin hold out a hat urging, 'Give us a penny to bury the wren', and they have a song which was recited to us by a 10-year-old urchin in the heart of Dublin:

> The wran, the wran, the king of all birds,
> On Stephen's day was caught in the furze.
> We chased her up, we chased her down,
> Till one of our little boys knocked her down.
> We drowned her in a barrel of beer,
> A happy Christmas and a merry New Year.
> Up with the kettles and down with the pan,
> A penny or twopence to bury the wran.

The boys go round early for, naturally, the money is not to be used for burying the wren but to give themselves a treat later in the day. 'It is annoying to be roused so early after Christmas Day,' writes a correspondent who sends the following song from Cork, 'but they make such a din banging on the door that they are seldom refused':

> The wren, the wren, the king of all birds,
> St Stephen's Night was caught in the furze.
> Though he is small, his family is great,
> So rise up your honours and give us a treat.
> God bless the mistress of the house,
> A golden chain be around her neck,
> And if she is sick, or if she's sore,
> The Lord have mercy on her soul.
> Up with the kettle and down with the pan
> Give us our money and let's be gone!

Wren boys often make five shillings or more which they divide amongst them on the way home. Occasionally 'the bigger boys' have the body of a real wren in their bush, or, in County Kerry, they carry a live one in a glass jar, chanting at each house this fine example of a begging song:

> The wren, the wren, the king of all birds,
> St Stephen's Day he was caught in the furze.
> Although he be little his family's great,
> I pray you good lady give us a treat.
> My box would speak if it had but a tongue,
> And a penny or two would do it no wrong.
>
> Sing holly, sing ivy, sing ivy, sing holly,
> A drop just to drink would drown melancholy:
> And if you draw it of the best
> I hope to heaven your soul may rest,
> But if you draw it of the small
> It won't agree with the boys at all.

*_** Hunting the wren was formerly a practice in Wales, south-western England, and the Isle of Man, as well as southern Ireland. The whole population of some places used to turn out either in the first hours of Christmas morning or on St Stephen's Day, and when a wren had been killed it was hung on a pole and carried in procession, and everybody who gave money, when called upon, was presented with a feather which was looked upon as a talisman. In the first half of the nineteenth century the wren was also hunted in the south of France, and its capture was followed by similar but even more elaborate proceedings in which the Church took part. It seems indeed that the custom which today occupies occasional gangs of street boys (never girls), hawking some gorse in expectation of pennies, once had sacred significance. 'It is thus that the solemnity of ritual dwindles into the pastime of children,' remarks Frazer.[1]

New Year's Eve: Hogmanay

The merry spirit which prevails amongst the inhabitants of the northern half of this island on New Year's Eve is not overlooked by their children. From early evening youngsters with blackened faces parade the streets of Scarborough greeting passersby with the cry 'Happy New Year, mister', followed by an expectant pause for a New Year gift or copper.

1. Sir James Frazer, *The Golden Bough*, vol. viii, 1912, p. 319 n. For additional references to those given by Frazer and for texts of the song sung in the procession, see *The Oxford Dictionary of Nursery Rhymes*, 1951, pp. 367–70.

In Nelson, Lancashire, groups of children, usually three in a group, wearing old clothes and with faces blackened with soot, maintain a form of 'mumming', so called, in which, on being granted admittance, they slink into a house in Indian file and start to sweep the floor with a hand brush. While doing this they emit a high-pitched humming noise between their teeth (a cynic has suggested 'like a vacuum cleaner') and keep their faces strictly averted. Only when they have been given money do they become little human beings, and wish the householders a happy New Year.

Farther north, the greater the adult manifestations of seasonable good-will, the more elaborate are the children's exertions to benefit thereby. In almost all parts of Scotland it is customary for some children to go guising. 'At Hogmanay,' writes an 11-year-old Perth girl, 'we dress up in funny clothes and put soot on our faces. We knock at someone's door and sing:

> Please tae help the guisers, the guisers, the guisers,
> Please tae help the guisers, and we'll sing a bonnie song:
> New Year's coming, the pigs are growing fat,
> Please put a penny in the auld man's hat,
> If ye havena got a penny, a ha'penny will do,
> If ye havena got a ha'penny, God bless you.

They take us in and we sing a song, or say a piece of poetry. Then they give us something.' People commonly give them a 'piece', 'sweeties', an apple, or pennies.[1] In other places other songs are sung. Along the east coast (Kirkcaldy, Aberdeen, Golspie) a favourite is:

> Rise up, guid wife, an' shake yer feathers,
> Dinna think that we are beggars,
> We're juist bairns come oot tae play,
> Rise up an' gi'e's oor Hogmanay.[2]

1. A 'piece' usually means a piece of bread and butter but on this occasion something more fancy: black bun, shortbread, or oatcake.

The splendid hospitality traditionally afforded to children in Scotland on the last day of the year at one time played no small part in helping the needy through the first month of the coming year. Robert Chambers (born in Peebles 1802) recalled that in the first decade of the nineteenth century housewives used to busy themselves for several days beforehand preparing an excess of honest fare, and he adds that it was 'no unpleasing scene, during the forenoon, to see children going laden home, each with his large apron bellying out before him, stuffed full of cakes, and perhaps scarcely able to waddle under the load'. – *Popular Rhymes of Scotland*, 1869, p. 166.

2. This type of verse goes back to the time of Mary Queen of Scots. An obvious adaptation is printed in the early collection of sacred parodies of secular songs: *Ane Compendious Book of Godly and Spirituall Sangis*, 1567. See the *Journal of the English Folk Dance and Song Society*, vol. iii, 1938, p. 173.

A Forfar boy repeats a pleasing variation which, since it does not specify Hogmanay, he also recites on Guy Fawkes Night and other soliciting occasions:

> Rise up, auld wives, and shake yer feathers,
> We're no come here as tinks or beggars,
> We're only wee bairnies oot tae play,
> So see oor pennies and let's away.

A common verse in Fife, according to a Kirkcaldy girl, is the almost irresistible supplication:

> Ma feet's cauld, ma shin's [shoon] thin,
> Gie's ma cakes an' let me rin.

They also sing 'Tramp, tramp, tramp, the boys are marching' as they did at Hallowe'en, and a curious verse, half jocular, half threatening:

> A happy New Year, a bottle of beer,
> A slap on the ear that will do till next year.

In some places, such as Golspie, as the old year completes its cycle, the guising degenerates into mischief and the sharp-tongued or the 'dry-bags' (stingy people) against whom the boys have been waiting to work off a grudge must look to their carts and their gates if they are not to have a hunt for them in the morning. Another place at which Hogmanay is a mischief night is Kemnay in Aberdeenshire, and another is far away in north Pembrokeshire.

In Wales and in the north of Britain almost all children are allowed to stay up until midnight, or are woken up then, so that they can watch the customs which let the Old Year out and bring the New Year in. In Forfar, just before midnight, the ashes are cleared from the fireplace so that the year will be begun afresh. In several places, including parts of Monmouthshire, both the front door and the back door are opened to assist the Old Year's departure and the arrival of the New. Money, especially silver money, is placed outside the door (Monmouthshire and South Lincolnshire); and bread and a piece of coal are put out as well to ensure health, wealth, and happiness to the household when fetched in the next day (in south-west Devon). In many English homes, as well as Scottish, they await the first-footer who, when he arrives, is welcomed with the warmest hospitality. It augurs well, everywhere, if he is a man 'tall, dark-haired, and handsome'. He should 'cross the threshold with wood, coal, and silver coins in his hands to ensure the well-being of the household for the coming year' (Nottingham). He should have 'a glass of wine in one hand

and a lump of coal in the other' (north Staffordshire). In the North Riding and Durham, where he is known as the 'lucky bird', he should have a lump of coal and, if possible, a sprig of evergreen. It will not be taken amiss on Tyneside if his sprig is mistletoe, and if he offers each of the ladies in the family a seasonable salutation. In Sutherland, says a 15-year-old, 'Hogmanay is still spent in true Highland fashion.' 'A few minutes before twelve o'clock,' writes a 14-year-old Brora girl, 'all the doors of the houses are opened to allow the spirit of the old year to depart. Then the clock strikes twelve, the church bells ring, the siren of the local mill is sounded, and everyone wishes everyone else "A Guid New Year". Then toasts, kisses, handshakes, and usually "Auld Lang Syne" is sung. With the advent of the New Year groups of people go "first-footin'" armed with black bun, their "bottle", and perhaps a piece of coal. It is essential that the first man to cross the threshold in the New Year is tall and dark, to bring luck to the household. The rest of the night is spent in eating, drinking, singing, and dancing.'

MOST of the customs which follow occur at irregular intervals, usually more often than once a year. They have, however, been described less often than the annual customs: firstly because they do not fit into the calendrical framework in which folklorists commonly arrange their collectings; and secondly because most of the customs, such as those at the beginning and end of term, are exclusively juvenile and consequently seldom noticed. Not, be it said, that the mass of children feel there is much to celebrate at the beginning of term. A single couplet from Glasgow constitutes the poetry of this festival:

> Back to school, back to school,
> Pass your qualy and that's the rule.

A 12-year-old boy who remarked, 'We usually just say "Oh! We're back to the torture chamber. We're back to the murder house"', typifies his generation. Yet, as will be seen, even at the term's commencement tradition is often present, waiting within the gates to introduce itself to new-comers.

New Boys and Initiation Rites

'*I found by experience, what before I could not believe, that every young gentleman, at his first coming to a boarding school, is generally looked upon with a great deal of contempt by the upper Scholars, who sometimes think too much of themselves. I asked one a question, he turned from me without condescending to give me an answer; a second laughed at me; and a third even gave me a knock on the pate.*'
                    '*Master Michel Angelo*', *Juvenile Sports and Pastimes*, 1776.

The demeanour of 'upper scholars' today does not seem to have altered much since Master Angelo was at school. At day schools no less than boarding schools a 'new bug' still has to learn his place the hard way. 'When we are in the first year the seniors call us "little squirts" or look down on us and say "Huh! juniors!"' (Girl, 11, Kirkcaldy). 'When a child comes up to the big school from the small one, all the bigger children calls them "Teachie, Teachie, Mew, Mew" and lift them in the air'(Girl, 12, Langholm). 'The way we greet a new boy is this: we carry him to a big stone, put him over and we spank him. This is called "Putting over the stone" ' (Boy, 14, Liverpool). 'Custom at the beginning of term. Grassing the new kids. It means picking up grass in bunches, and putting it down their necks' (Boy, 12, Lydney).[1]

Other children tell of treatment, usually at their previous schools, even more likely to make an impression on new-comers.

'In my former school the favourite way of greeting a new boy was for most of the school to line up in the long corridor and to kick the new boy all the way to the bottom of the corridor.'

Boy, 14, Cumberland.

'At my old school we have a custom which every new boy has to go through, we take them into the hall and throw peas at them. Then they are taken into a school room and we hit their knuckles with blackboard rubbers. Then they are school members.'

Boy, 13, Yorkshire.

'At the old school when a new boy came to school, four boys gave him the "Yorkshire bumps". Four boys got hold of one arm and leg each and then asked the boy how old he was. Then they bumped him on the ground and let go of him at the time they counted to the year of his age.'

Boy, 14, Yorkshire.

'After the summer holidays new boys start at — School. Those that have been there for two or three years capture these new boys. They are taken onto the terrace in front of the school. They are rolled down a banking. When they have been rolled down it they are members of — School.'

Boy, 13, Yorkshire.

Since the war, disused air-raid shelters have provided further scope for initiation ceremonies.

'At our other school, boys passing up from the infants into the senior school were taken on a train (number of boys joined together) through an old air-raid shelter. All the air grates except one were stuffed with grass to make it darker. We fastened a piece of string through the grate that was not filled in to a can on the inside, the can was painted with luminous paint. When the train was getting near the leader of the train (who was the only boy who was not a new boy) would whistle, and the boys on the outside would pull the string and make a

1. This is an old custom in the Forest of Dean. Up to the nineteen-thirties, and the advent of buses, the forest remained largely isolated, and the foresters were inclined to pit themselves against strangers. People from outside were still 'turfed' on occasion, and new teachers certainly were, although perhaps more by custom than out of malice. Today, in child-to-child relations, the practice is far from obsolescent.

317

fearful noise. The party thus frightened would let go of one another, and the leader would depart leaving the new boys to find their own way out.'

'At the school I went to there were some air-raid shelters with water in the bottom, and we used to tell the new boys there was treasure in one of them and they had to find it. In the top of each shelter was a trap door and when they got to the middle of the shelter we closed the doors at either end and lowered a hollowed out turnip, with a face on it and a candle inside, through the trapdoor, and said, "Anyone who finds the treasure of this mask will not see daylight after dark." When they came out a basin full of water was tipped over them and a sack thrown over their eyes. They were then taken in school and locked in a dark room for about an hour.'

Further, the older children commonly strike terror into young hearts by telling of the greater dreadfulnesses which used to take place in initiation rites in times gone by, or which still take place at other schools where the new-comer may be sent if he does not behave himself. Tales are told of districts in Wales where schools have a custom known as 'bunking', forcing a new boy into a box or dustbin half-filled with fish-heads, potato peelings, ashes, and soot, and making him stay there for an hour. Rumours are spread that in Scotland, when a new-comer was receiving his ritual 'dookin', he was held under water too long and was drowned; and that at a rival school, not far away, when a boy was being bumped he was tossed too high, and, landing on hard ground, his spine was broken.

To the folklorist the most interesting initiation rites are those tricks, usually possessing a name, which follow carefully prescribed formulas, and which, as well as discomfiting the initiate, provide a certain entertainment for the spectators. A few of these tricks can also be classed as antiques.

The King and Queen of Sheba. The new boy or girl is led into a throne room where sit the king and queen somewhat apart on a makeshift couch. The royal pair ask questions, and express themselves satisfied with the answers. Indeed, they let it be known that they think so well of the new-comer that he may, as a special privilege, approach the throne and sit between them. As the proud one sits down the king and queen stand up, and since there has only been a tightly stretched rug between the chairs on which they have been sitting, he falls to the floor with a bump, or into a concealed tub of water.

⁎ Strutt, writing in 1801, describes this same trick as customary 'in some great Boarding Schools for the fair sex . . . upon the introduction of a novice'. And, under the name 'Ambassador', Grose described it in 1785 as a sailor's trick upon new hands.

The Court of Nebuchadnezzar. The uninitiated is brought into the room and told to kneel down on a rug in front of his majesty. After some formalities he is told to make obeisances to the king. Though he tries his best, he is informed that he is not being sufficiently servile, and that he must receive instruction. He is ordered to kneel in as upright a manner as he can and raise his arms to their fullest extent above his head. While in this position two courtiers behind him pull at the back of the rug on which he is kneeling, which prostrates him on his face before Nebuchadnezzar.

*** This trick, under the name 'Making Nuns' has previously been described as played by girls in Argyllshire in the nineteenth century. (*Folk-Lore*, vol. xvi, 1905, p. 443.)

Siamese National Anthem. The company of new-comers are informed that they are now to be taught the Siamese National Anthem, and are carefully rehearsed in the words, which are 'Oh wha ta na Siam' (or 'O ye Siam anas' or 'Owha tagoo Siam'). They are then instructed to sing the phrase over and over again to the tune of 'God save the Queen'. The special joy of this ceremony to the onlookers is that those new-comers who are most anxious to acquit themselves well will be heard the most clearly singing 'Oh what an ass I am'.

Submarines. This is a water trick. A boy is induced to take off his jacket, and lie down covering his head with it. A sleeve of the jacket, which someone holds up vertically, is said to be a periscope, and he is invited to peer up it. When he does so someone calls out 'Ship's sinking', and a jug of water is emptied down the sleeve.

Blind Bees or *Bees Bring Your Honey.* Another water trick. The new child is flattered by being appointed Queen Bee; and is told that he may give the orders to the worker bees to fetch honey, and deliver honey. The 'bees' run away out of sight when told to fetch honey, and fill their mouths with water. On being commanded to deliver their honey they run back and deliver it in the Queen Bee's face.

*** A nasty version of this trick, under the name 'Deliver Up Those Golden Jewels' is referred to by Norman Douglas in *London Street Games*, 1916. Compare also the experience of the young C. L. Dodgson when he was sent to Richmond Grammar School, Yorkshire, as told in his first letter home, 5 August 1844:

'The boys have played two tricks upon me which were these – they first proposed to play at "King of the Cobblers" and asked if I would be king, to which I agreed. Then they made me sit down and sat (on the ground) in a circle round me, and told me to say "Go to work" which I did, and they immediately began kicking me and knocking me on all sides. The next game they proposed was "Peter, the red lion", and they made a mark on a tombstone (for we were playing in the churchyard) and one of the boys walked with his eyes shut, holding out his finger, trying to touch the mark; then a little boy came forward to lead the rest and led a good many very near the mark; at last it was my turn; they told me to shut my eyes well, and the next minute I had my finger in the mouth of one of the boys, who had stood (I believe) before the tombstone with his mouth open.' (*The Diaries of Lewis Carroll*, vol. i, p. 12.)

Special Holidays

'At the Speech Days,' writes a knowing 12-year-old, 'we give the speaker loud applause and look as if we enjoyed his speech and he usually gives us an extra holiday.'

In Dublin exultant children rejoice:

> No school today, half holiday,
> When we get our holiday we'll all run away.
> Where will we run to? Down the slippy lane.
> Who will run after us? The teacher with the cane.

In Aberdeen they cry:

> Nae school the morn,
> Yer breeks are torn!

In Stoke-on-Trent and the west Midlands generally, when a holiday excursion has been arranged, the happy travellers chant:

> We're off, we're off,
> We're off in a motor car;
> Sixty cops are after us
> And we don't know where we are!

And throughout the coach journey a cheerful roar is maintained with the choruses of such songs as: 'Feet up, pat him on the bo-bo', 'Nick nack paddy-wack, give a dog a bone', 'We've got a lovely bunch of coconuts', and 'You can't go to heaven in an old Ford car'.

But if the children are merely to go home on the holiday, the elder girls mutter, with unwonted understanding, 'Teacher's rest, mother's pest'.

End of Term

'Towards the end of term the boys in my school seem to go mad because they will be having a holiday, and play tricks on prefects, and have riots in the yard,' observes a 14-year-old; and other boys concur: 'Games prevalent just now are "mobbing prefects" (always done at end of term) and "scragging toads" (also done at end of term),' states a 13-year-old; while a 14-year-old writes:

'On the last day of term we shout for the masters, rush around the playground after balloons, balls, tins, etc., boo the prefects, shout and make a general din, cheer all the popular masters, and crowd all the unpopular ones, ping pellets in class, and set booby traps, e.g. tie the master's chair under the table, rearrange the desks, put caps under the seats so that they explode on sitting down.'

Similarly, a 13-year-old girl in a girls' school reports:

'On the last day of term nearly everyone lets themselves go and the result is: clocks being turned back a couple of hours, doors shutting and getting "stuck" so that no one can open them, pictures in prominent places being turned round to face the walls, and a favourite one is to hide the bell which is used to mark the end of lessons. Also a very high pile of books suddenly (and apparently for no reason) will topple over crashing to the ground.'

And, in doggerel 'that is disrespectful to the point of being subversive', as a leader in *The Times* has expressed it, 'they enumerate the salient disadvantages of life at school':

This time tomorrow where shall I be?
Not in this academy.
No more Latin, no more French,
No more sitting on a hard board bench;
No more beetles in my tea
Making googly eyes at me;
No more spiders in my bath
Trying hard to make me laugh;
No more slugs in my dinner
Which the staff say make me thinner.
When the train goes puff, puff, puff,
I'll be in it sure enough;
If I'm not I'll curse and swear,
Knock old *Smithy* down the stair.
If a prefect asks me why,
Slap her seat and box her eye.
If a master interferes
Knock him down and box his ears.
One more day and we'll be free
From this place of misery.

Version from Worcestershire.

One more day and then we'll be
Out of the hands of – – –
No more Latin, no more French,
No more sitting on a hard board bench.
No more English, no more stick,
No more flipping arithmetic.
When we get to the old home station
We are met by a kind relation.
When we get to the old home door,
Out pops Mum and one or two more:
What will you have dear, what will you take?
A cup of tea, or a slice of cake.
Now the holidays are over
Back to the old school Straits of Dover.
When we get to the old school station,
We are met by *no* relation.
When we get to the old school door,
Out pops *Rātty* and one or two more:
What will you have, child, what will you take?
A cup of dishwater, or a plate to scrape.

Version from Kent.

On the whole these lengthy dissertations, often embellished, of course, with local colour,[1] describe the private fee-charging establishments. The children in the county schools normally favour shorter verses:

One more day of sin,
One more day of sorrow,
One more day in this old hole
We're staying home tomorrow.

No more pencils, no more books,
No more teacher's ugly looks,
No more things that bring us sorrow
'Cos we won't be here tomorrow.[2]

Hurray, hurray, it's the last day,
Tear up your books, burn your pens,
This is the day the term ends.

Kick up tables, kick up chairs,
Throw our homework down the stairs.

No more school, thank goodness for that,
Ha, ha, ha, I can go and slack.

'Take an axe.' 'What for?' 'School's breaking up today.' 'Goody! hurrah! out of the dungeon! yipee!' And as they slap-dash out of school at four o'clock on the last afternoon, shrill voices pipe over and over again:

> We break up, we break down,
> We don't care if the school breaks down.

'Quite a lot of people kick at the gatepost [as they leave] hoping to cause a minor breakage inside school,' observes a 12-year-old.

More solemnly, at Knighton, the superstitious-minded douse their eyes in water at the end of term – 'It brings luck.' At the City of London School those girls who are leaving for good throw their school hats into the River Thames from Blackfriars Bridge. Likewise, but less spectacularly, Scarborough High School girls on their last day bicycle to Valley Bridge, 'the bridge of sighs', and throw their berets away into the duck

---

1. Robert Graves, for instance, when at prep. school at Hillbrow, Rugby, in 1908, sang:

> No more mucky potted meat
> Scraped from dirty Tommy's feet.

'Tommy' was Thomas Eden, M.A., the headmaster.
2. American children have these rhymes too, albeit with linguistic differentiae, e.g. 'No more teacher's sassy looks'. And, not unexpectedly, French children sing verses expressing similar sentiments:

Vivent les vacances
Point de pénitences,
Les livres au feu,
Les maîtres au milieu.

Adieu les pommes de terre,
Les haricots pourris;
Je m'en vais chez mon père
Manger du bon rôti.

pond below. And everywhere, amongst the old girls, there are parting rhymes for those leaving:

I wish you luck, I wish you joy,
I wish you first a baby boy.
And when his hair begins to curl
I wish you next a baby girl.
And when you put her hair in pins
I wish you then a pair of twins.

Goodbye, *Margaret*, while you're away
Send me a letter every day,
And don't forget your old pal *Bella*.

Be a good girl, lead a good life,
Get a good husband, and be a good
    wife!

First of the Month

'On the first morning of the month,' notes a typical informant, 'before speaking to anyone else, one must say "White rabbits, white rabbits, white rabbits" for luck.' Subject to minor modifications the utterance of this spell appears to be the accepted routine throughout Britain. Some children feel it is enough just to cry 'Rabbits', as long as it is the first word they pronounce. Others, though not many, believe it is necessary to say 'Hares' last thing the previous night, as well as saying 'Rabbits' in the morning. In Romford a boy says that 'White Rabbits' must be intoned three times, 'after the first foot has touched the floor when getting out of bed, and not after the second foot has touched the floor or it will bring bad luck'. In Liverpool the first of the month is known as 'Bunny Rabbit Day'. In Luncarty, near Perth, it is considered especially lucky if 'Rabbits' is cried on the first of May. Others in Perthshire hold that it is important to say 'Rabbits' when there is an R in the month. Radnorshire children, or some of them, assert that 'Black rabbit' should be shouted on the eve of the new month, and 'White rabbit' shouted in the morning; and the same view appears to be held in parts of Devon, for a South Molton girl warns that while it is lucky to say 'White rabbit', 'if you say black rabbit on the first day of the month you have bad luck all the month.'

In some boarding schools, those for boys as well as for girls, it is the custom to walk downstairs backwards, and when the foot of the stairs is reached, to kiss the first person encountered. In apparently every day-school in Britain it is the practice on the first of the month for children to go up to each other, before noon, and say:

> A pinch and a punch (*here administered*)
> For the first of the month,
> And no returns.

'If you are crafty and say "No returns" quick enough that means the other person cannot return the pinch or punch.' But if he can, he replies,

> A pinch and a kick
> For being so quick,
> And no returns.

Then the first person may counter,

> A slap in the eye
> For being so sly,

or,

> A pinch and a blow
> For being so slow,

and one or other may continue with such makeshifts as 'Pull the ear for being so queer', or 'A slosh and a boot for being so cute', or 'A punch in the belly for eating my jelly', or 'A kick up the bot for being a clot', and the physical side to the repartee may not finally be closed by:

> Now don't be so fast
> Because I'm the last
> – to punch you!

In a few schools (reports from Cornwall, Essex, and Glamorganshire) this exercise also takes place on the last day of the month.

Birthdays

> Happy birthday to you!
> Squashed tomatoes and stew;
> Eggs and bacon for breakfast,
> Happy birthday to you!

There is painful uniformity about the greetings they offer each other on birthdays. A 14-year-old Kirkcaldy girl says: 'Nip the person concerned, kick her with your knee, and pull her hair according to age. Sometimes several girls lift her up and bang her on the floor.' A group of Swansea girls confess that their salutation, likewise, is to tug the hair of her whose special day it is, or pinch her once for each of her years, and then they turn her round and push her in the back 'once for luck'. A teacher in London, E. 8, reports that both boys and girls there bump the person who is celebrating his birthday. 'They take hold of arms and legs, lift him as high as they can and bump him on the ground, repeating it according to the number of years old he is.' And boys in Langholm confirm: 'On a person's birthday we give him the "dumps". Everybody chases him and when he is caught we slap him on the back the number of years he is, or some boys get him by the arms and some by the legs and he is swung up and down the number of years he is.'

The cardinal object of these operations, whether conducted by nipping, slapping, hair-pulling, or bumping ('dumping' in Scotland) is to remind the newly-aged exactly how old he or she has now become, and the birthday-child's friends rarely stint their self-appointed task. After repeating the operation 'once for each year he or she has been alive' they generally further manifest their goodwill by adding 'One for luck', or 'One for their birthday cake and one for their next birthday', or, in Lambeth,

> One for luck, two for pluck,
> Three for old man's coconut,

or, in Aberdeen, as a 14-year-old girl impassively puts it: 'The custom is for one's chums to pull one's hair the number of years old one is with additional tugs for different things, "One to make your hair grow", "One for your next birthday", "One for luck", "One to kiss your boy friend", and "One for a very happy birthday".' In Aberdeen, too, 'the girls in the class gather together and soak the unlucky person's head with cold water. This is called "dookin".' 'We pull her hair, mess it about and tie it in knots.' Sometimes 'we pull off her shoes and socks and make her walk about in the playground barefoot, or sometimes we will make up a parcel of papers and give them to her just for a joke'. In fact, they do everything in their power to make it a memorable day for her. And she knows she must bear it with fortitude. It is a belief widely held amongst them that 'if you cry on your birthday you'll cry the year round'.

New Clothes

The appearance of new clothes is another signal for pinches and derision. If a boy is under the necessity of coming to school in a new suit his fellows greet him with, 'Who's died?' 'Where's the fire been?' 'Has Grinley [the local junk merchant] gone bankrupt?' They call the boy a 'Spiv', 'Gaudy Georgey', 'Bobby Dazzler', 'Oh you dazzle me, you lucky boy', 'Swank pot', 'Posh guy'. At Chingford they chant:

> Ha! Ha! *Georgie King*'s all dolled up.
> Perhaps he's marrying his dog's young pup.

Then they remember that 'Pride must be pinched', for it is a custom about which they are punctilious (as Kenneth Grahame learned when he first wore 'tails' at St Edward's) that anything new, worn for the first time, must be pinched, and that this pinch should include a small portion of the tenderer flesh living underneath the new garment. They nip the person saying, 'A nip for new', or 'A nip for new, two for blue'. Or they nip the boy, asking, 'Is it good stuff?' They may splash water on the new clothes saying that it is to christen them. And some wit will run his finger down the crease of the trousers, and call out, 'Aw, I've cut my finger!'

The girls, too, admit that if someone comes to school in a new dress they are no less whole-hearted in expressing their admiration. They exclaim, 'Oh it's smashin. Pull your hair.' They call out to each other:

> Blue for true,
> Pink for stink,
> Yellow for jealous,
> Green for queen.

They point at the stuff and shriek, 'Pink for stink. You're a stinker!' And they count down the buttons of the offending garment to find out how it has been acquired: 'Bought, borrowed, stolen, given', hoping to learn that it has been borrowed or stolen, rather than purchased.

New shoes are commonly trodden on. 'When anybody receives a new pair of shoes the custom is to stand on her toes for luck', or 'Tread on her shoes and then cry "Christen them".' It is unlucky, they say, to put new shoes on a desk or table. And it is well known that should the shoes creak as the person walks 'the shoes are not paid for'.

At Weddings

> Here comes the bride
> Fair, fat, and wide,
> She cannot get in at the front door
> She has to get in at the side.[1]

Children continue to possess, as in Paul Dombey's time, 'an instinctive interest in nuptials'; and the girls, by the time they are fourteen, at latest, are in proper possession of the prognostics and impositions to be attended to on these occasions, for instance that on the wedding day the bride

---

1. Alternatively, 'See how she wobbles from side to side' (Bournemouth) and 'Six yards of muslin wrapped round her hide' (Bath).

should not meet the groom until she meets him in the church, that she should place a piece of silver in her shoe, that she should wear 'Something old, something new, something borrowed, something blue', that 'Happy is the bride that the sun shines on' (a Stoke-on-Trent child adds that a rainbow brings special luck), that it is lucky if a chimney sweep kisses the bride when she leaves the church, and that a boot 'and with the boot a toilet roll' should be tied to the back of the wedding car.

In some places, particularly it seems in the north, although also reported from Belvedere in Kent, a further inducement to children to cluster round the porch is the practice of the best man or the bride's parents throwing down coppers in the street as the bride makes her first appearance as a married woman. In Fife, children who think they may be disappointed in this custom, chant:

> Hard up, soor dook,
> Canna throw a ha'penny oot.

In Glasgow they cry 'Hard up, roosty pockets', to remind any wedding official who may be forgetful of his duty, and in Edinburgh they cry repeatedly 'Poor oot, poor oot' (pour out). Similarly on Tyneside, in the 1920s, the famous cry was 'Hi, canny man, hoi a ha'p'ny oot'. In Angus if 'baw' (ball) money is not given boys claim, or used to until recently, the right to cut the bride's gown. In *Summer Long Ago* (1954), William Glynne-Jones describes a gang of small boys in south Wales, about 1920, holding a rope across the road so that a wedding car was unable to pass until the groom had distributed such largesse as was considered necessary: in this instance thirteen pennies. And Daniel Parry-Jones in *A Welsh Country Upbringing* (1948) states that the custom is still observed in Carmarthenshire, the rope which obstructs the procession being known as a 'quinten'. At Hunmanby, on the Yorkshire coast, next to Butlin's Holiday Camp at Filey, boys still claim the right and practise it, of tying up the churchyard gates, barring the wedding party from the road until the bridegroom has paid toll. (A news report and photograph of this custom appeared in the Scarborough *Mercury*, 12 September 1957, p. 1.)

When Teeth Come Out

Inquiry into the manner in which children dispose of their milk teeth, when these come out, appears to show that three distinct practices are prevalent in Britain. In the north (generally speaking) the procedure, scrupulously observed, is to burn the shed tooth, usually after sprinkling it with salt. Thus a 14-year-old Tunstall girl writes:

'I tell everyone that I am not superstitious and I tell myself that I am not, but sometimes I wonder, because if one of my teeth came out I would not think of burning it without smothering it in salt first.'[1]

Likewise the excellent Aubrey, writing in 1686–7:

'When Children shaled their Teeth the women use to wrap, or put salt about the tooth, and so throw it into a good fire' (*Remaines*, published 1881, p. 11).

In Wales a common custom, possibly (according to our evidence) the general practice, is to carry the tooth out into the open and throw it hard backwards over the left shoulder, or over the head; and some say this brings luck, and some say that the person may then have a wish.

In the Swansea Valley they utter the charm:

> Giâr ddu, giâr wen,   (*Black hen, white hen,*
> Tafla' nant dros 'y mhen.   *I throw my tooth over my head.*)

And in Aberystwyth children stipulate that salt must first be sprinkled over the tooth before it is discarded.

The third means of disposal requires adult assistance. The tooth is carefully saved until nightfall and then placed under the child's pillow, or under a mat, or an egg cup, or on a clock, or in a glass of water, and during the night the fairies come and take it away and leave in its place a piece of silver: usually of the smallest denomination. Yet even when this commercial and apparently modern transaction takes place, the salt is sometimes attendant, for the egg cup may be covered with salt, and the glass of water is liable to be a glass of salt water.

---

1. It is worth noting that it is only putting the salt on the tooth that the girl considers superstitious; she seems to take burning the tooth for granted – that being the usual way of disposing of it in her part of England. Yet the origin of this practice too is superstitious; it was generally held in earlier times that unless the tooth was burnt a dog might find it and eat it, and then a dog's tooth would grow in the milk tooth's place; alternatively in Lancashire and Yorkshire it was thought that the penalty for not burning the tooth was that its owner would have to search for it after death in a pail of blood in hell.

IN this chapter appear some curiosities, preserved in juvenile tradition, which will perhaps be found to be the more curious when compared with old records and parallels from other parts of the world.

When Dr John Jamieson in 1825 came to the end of his great *Etymological Dictionary of the Scottish Tongue* the final subject he wrote about was juvenile lore. 'The terms and sports of children,' he said, 'although they may seem unworthy of attention, and any attempt to investigate their origin may provoke the sneer of fastidiousness, in various instances afford the sole vestiges of very ancient laws and customs.' And, proceeding two steps farther than Dr Arbuthnot, he continued: 'In proof of this, I beg leave to refer to the articles *Tappie-tousie* and *Thumb-licking*.'

Whereas too much meaning can be (and very often is) read into the formulas of children's games and customs, and restraint is a laudable practice when the desire is upon one to supply origins or interpretations, we do not think that the satchelful of comparisons offered here will be found to be far-fetched. It is also not without point to mention that whether or not the two customs cited by Jamieson, *Tappie-tousie* and *Thumb-licking*, are as venerable as he supposes (he takes the first back to the method of manumitting a bondman amongst the Romans, and the second to a practice among Iberian kings mentioned by Tacitus), both these rites continue to be practised by children today. Thus one more century and the slice of another can be added to the age they were when Jamieson remarked upon their antiquity. (For *Tappie-tousie* see p. 225, and for *Thumb-licking*, pp. 149–50.)

The Million Bus Tickets

Amongst the stranger stories children tell each other is the legend of the million bus tickets, a legend which has some of the qualities of a folktale, for the cupidity of 9-year-olds makes it altogether easy for them to believe in it. The details of the story vary, but its central feature is usually that an eccentric millionaire, defying the claims of wife and family, has left the whole of his vast fortune to anyone who has the time and persistence to collect a million bus tickets. The young imparter of this news is never quite certain to whom a person should apply for the reward, and is rarely able to name the precise amount of money involved – other than suggest that it is substantial – but, as Robert Lynd once remarked: 'The myth, nevertheless, persists, turning the children of towns into useful little scavengers, where otherwise they might have been brewers of mischief, an expense to their parents and a trouble to the State.' The moral which Lynd draws from the tale is that 'thus does Nature deceive her progeny into good works'. But we are able to add a footnote to the story.

It is not only bus tickets which are collected; sometimes it is a million used match sticks, sometimes a million used postage stamps, and sometimes a million cigarette cards – the word 'million' in itself has something magic about it – and this belief that a special reward awaits the diligent collector also takes some less ambitious forms. Some children believe that as long as the number on the ticket ends with a 'lucky' seven only a few need be collected – although others say it must be a million of these too (Croydon).[1] In some places it is believed that if all the figures of a ticket's number are the same the bus company will give a prize (Chelmsford and Ipswich). In 1953 there was a rumour in the juvenile world that if a person collected milk-bottle tops substantial rewards would follow: the Food Office was said to pay 10s. per 500 (Manchester). And in 1956 a son of ours came back from school with 300 carefully pressed Sharpe's toffee papers in happy expectation of reward (6d. for 50), and was at first incredulous when we told him that the story was a myth, similar to one other boys believed in about a million bus tickets, which we ourselves had heard and begun to act upon when we were young thirty years before. In fact, from a letter to *Notes and Queries* in 1883 (6th ser., vol. viii, p. 355), it appears that this story of a wonderful reward had been in circulation for more than seventy years. Under the heading '*Juvenile Pursuits*', a Brighton correspondent remarks: 'Another curious fashion is the collection of used

1. The *Yorkshire Post*, 27 June 1957, reported that in Bradford the collecting of these tickets had got out of hand. Investigation showed that the efforts of one collecting group 'ended at the home of a girl of 13, who, not knowing what to do with them, had thousands stored in her bedroom and more at the home of her grandmother'. It appeared that once a collector had built up an organization of helpers it was difficult to stop tickets from continuing to arrive. The belief was that in some way the tickets would help to provide guide dogs for the blind, or a wheelchair for a disabled person. For further about lucky tickets see pp. 353-7.

postage stamps. I have known a score of persons collect them, but none ever gave an intelligent reason for so doing. Some thought the Post Office authorities would pay something for a million.' Others, it appeared, thought that a poor person could be got into hospital if enough were collected; and the writer ends his letter: 'The subject is almost worthy of attention of folk-lore students as involving a wide-spread delusion.'

But the most unexpected feature of this legend is that it appears to be based on fact. Only a decade after the introduction of the prepaid postage stamp there really was, or so it seems, an urgent call for the collection of a million used stamps in order that a young lady in love might be saved from the whims of her father, a gentleman probably wealthy, and definitely eccentric. In the issue of the *Illustrated London News* for 18 May 1850, p. 349, we have come upon the following entry which is, we think, either the tallest story which has appeared in the pages of that respected journal, or one of its most remarkable:

'EXTRAORDINARY POSTAGE STAMPS CONTRIBUTION

'Some time since, there appeared in the public journals a statement to the effect that a certain young lady, under age, was to be placed in a convent, by her father, if she did not procure, before the 30th of April last, one million of used postage stamps. This caused numerous persons to forward stamps for the purpose of securing her liberty. In March last, a lady, a member of one of the first families in Derbyshire, residing not many miles from Derby, mentioned the conditions to her friends, and in a short time the lady began to receive packages by post and railway from every quarter, which poured in in such numbers, that, in ten days, during last April, she received parcels containing millions of stamps. The walking postman, who was in the habit of delivering a few letters daily at the mansion where the lady resides, became so loaded with letters and packages containing Queen's heads, that it was necessary to employ another man to assist him. On one morning between ninety and one hundred letters and packets arrived by post, and on another between 120 and 130. These were in addition to multitudes which arrived on other days. Boxes, bales, and packages also poured in by railway; and to such an extent that it became necessary to give public notice, by advertisements and printed circulars, that it was urgently desired no more stamps should be sent, as the young lady had procured the number she required. The accompanying Sketch [*an engraving measuring 3 × 6 ins.*] gives some idea of the packages. One of them is a large wine-hamper; another, a large wine-cooler; next, a large clothes-basket. The two latter were used to put the smaller packets in as they arrived, being, altogether, many bushels. Next is a packet from a great mercantile house in London, and containing 240,000 Queen's heads. There was, also, a tea-chest full, sent from another quarter. There were nine boxes between one and two feet long, a foot wide, and from four to ten inches deep; seven packages between one and two feet long, a foot wide, and about six inches deep. Smaller packets formed a heap two feet six inches long, one foot wide, and one foot six inches deep; and two baskets two feet long, one foot six inches wide, and one foot four inches deep were filled; besides which, many boxes full were not received, but sent back to the railway station. In addition to this accumulation, letters from all quarters arrived; many from persons of the highest rank, expressing the deepest sympathy and the most kindly feeling. Numbers of them stated that large collections of heads would still be sent if required.'

Levitation

Two witnesses may be quoted on this curiosity. The first is a correspondent, who was at school in Bath in the 1940s, writing 22 June 1952:

'The queerest happening I know of I have on my own memory. Some of my form-mates one day resolved to try a trick they had heard of, in which one person sat in a chair, and several others (I think four) stood round, with some part of their hands pressed on the victim's head – I think it was their thumbs. The idea was to continue this in an atmosphere of intense concentration by all (no talking or giggles) for a few minutes, after which it was supposed that the person sitting, contrary to all the laws of nature, would actually become *lighter* and could be lifted by the others as easily as if she were a cushion. This experiment was watched with keen interest by the form, and seemed to have a curiously uncanny effect. Whether by self-hypnotism or not I do not know, but the lifters, with a few fingers only under arm-pits and knees, certainly lifted the seated one with ease and grace into the air, and put her down in the same manner. It was more like real magic than anything else I have seen.'

The other is that 'good scholler and sober man' Mr Brisband, as reported by Pepys in his diary for 31 July 1665:

'This evening with Mr. Brisband, speaking of enchantments and spells, I telling him some of my charms; he told me this of his owne knowledge, at Bourdeaux in France. The words these:

> Voyci un Corps mort,
> Royde come un Baston,
> Froid comme Marbre,
> Leger come un esprit,
> Levons te au nom de Jesus Christ.

He saw four little girles, very young ones, all kneeling, each of them, upon one knee; and one begun the first line, whispering in the eare of the next, and the second to the third, and the third to the fourth, and she to the first. Then the first begun the second line, and so round quite through, and, putting each one finger only to a boy that lay flat upon his back on the ground, as if he was dead; at the end of the words, they did with their four fingers raise this boy as high as they could reach, and he [Mr. Brisband] being there, and wondering at it, as also being afeard to see it, for they would have had him to have bore a part in saying the words, in the roome of one of the little girles that was so young that they could hardly make her learn to repeat the words, did, for feare there might be some sleight used in it by the boy, or that the boy might be light, call the cook of the house, a very lusty fellow, as Sir G. Carteret's cook, who is very big, and they did raise him in just the same manner. This is one of the strangest things I ever heard, but he tells it me of his owne knowledge, and I do heartily believe it to be true. I enquired of him whether they were Protestant or Catholique girles; and he told me they were Protestant, which made it the more strange to me.'

We may add that when we were young we, too, practised this trick, three ways being known to us. In the first, the subject lay down and, if we recollect rightly, there were four raisers using one finger each; in the second, the subject was seated and there were two raisers using a finger of each hand; in the third, which was the most spectacular, the subject stood on a book with his heels and toes jutting over so that fingers could be placed underneath, and he went up vertically. In this last instance the child had to be smaller than the operators or they could not reach the top of his head to press upon. With us it was considered necessary for everyone taking part to hold his breath throughout the operation. One person counted to ten while all pressed downwards, then everyone swiftly changed to the lifting position.

Saying the Same Thing at Once

If two children accidentally say the same thing at once (it must be accidental), they instantly stop what they are doing and, without uttering a further word to each other or making any sound, glide into a set ritual which varies only according to the part of Britain or, for this is an international performance, the part of the world in which they live.

A 13-year-old girl in Pontnewydd, Monmouthshire, says: 'If by some coincidence you and a friend say the same thing at the same time you should link each other's little finger of the right hand and wish. Your wish should be granted.'

Twelve-year-olds from the villages around South Molton in north Devon replied variously when asked what they said: 'White rabbits', 'You'll get a letter tomorrow', 'That's my letter' (stamping foot), 'Shake hands', and 'Touch wood and whistle'.

The phrase 'Touch wood and whistle', according to one informant, also prevails in East Anglia; and a 15-year-old Ipswich girl elaborates: 'If two people say exactly the same, at exactly the same time, they "touch wood, touch knee, and whistle", and this is supposed to bring the first one to do so a letter.'

The idea that a letter will follow also obtains in Swansea, where the girls count the number of letters in the word or words which were spoken simultaneously, and by going through the alphabet that far, find the initial of the person from whom the letter can be expected.

In Alton, Hampshire, both parties touch wood, and say 'My letter in the post come quick', and then name a poet, usually Shakespeare.

In parts of London, if, when naming a poet, both children say 'Shakespeare' it is considered that there has been a second happy coincidence, and that each will be granted a second wish. More often it is considered unlucky to mention either of the two poets who most readily come to mind: Shakespeare and Burns. Each party must name a different poet, not Shakespeare because Shakespeare spears the wish; not Burns because he burns it. Sometimes if either mentions Shakespeare a third party must be called to unlink the fingers. The ban on Shakespeare and Burns also prevails in Edinburgh and the east of Scotland. Two poets are named (usually Keats and Shelley), and the silent wish is made while the 'pinkies' are still entwined. Sometimes the wish is allowed only to the first person who names a poet, and should both children name the same poet it is considered that the whole performance is invalidated.

Occasionally a goodwill chant is customary. At the Royal School, Bath, after making the wish, one girl says:

> I wish, I wish your wish comes true.

And the other replies:

> I wish, I wish the same to you.

In Southampton both chant:

> I wish, I wish this wish to you,
> I wish, I wish your dream come true.

In the back streets of Dublin little boys and girls shake their linked fingers up and down as they intone:

> I wish, I wish a very good wish,
> I wish, I wish I do;
> I wish, I wish a very good wish,
> I wish a very good wish to you.

And in Glasgow, E. 2, they link pinkies and press thumbs together, reassuring each other:

> Pinkety, pinkety, thumb to thumb,
> Wish a wish and it's sure to come.
> If yours comes true
> Mine will come true,
> Pinkety, pinkety, thumb to thumb.

But in Market Rasen, Lincolnshire, it is considered lucky if both go solemnly to the fireplace and, speaking together, call 'Shakespeare' up the chimney. This is interesting because children in Pennsylvania and Missouri and east Texas indulge in colloquies on this occasion in which the common factor is that one child says:

'What goes up the chimney?'

The other replies, 'Smoke.'

The first says, 'I hope this wish . . .'

And the second continues, 'May never be broke.'

In other parts of the United States the procedure seems to be more in line with the usual British practice. In Carbondale, Illinois, for instance, children lock the right-hand little fingers, wish silently, and then unlock simultaneously, each child giving the name of some animal or bird. In Iowa, children press thumbs together, or used to, uttering the word 'Philopena'.[1]

It appears, indeed, that the rite would bear detailed investigation in the United States, and possibly throughout the world, for the coincidence of two people accidentally saying the same thing at once is marked by some little ceremony in every country in which we have made inquiry, and almost invariably it aims at influencing or finding out about the future. In Italy children instantly put aside what they are doing, link their little fingers as in England, and shake their hands up and down three times, counting 'Uno, due, tre', whereupon they break their grasp exclaiming either 'Flic' or 'Floc', and if both choose the same expression both children are allowed a wish. The identical practice is general amongst youngsters in Vienna, and even sometimes amongst grown-ups, except that Austrian children after shaking their linked fingers three times choose

1. In France (Lyons) if a girl finds two kernels in an almond she gives one to a friend, and the first to cry 'Philippines' when they meet the next day demands a forfeit. A similar custom obtains in Norway. In Britain (Clun, Shropshire) a girl gives one kernel away; if she were to eat both she would have twins. Compare this with the Spanish superstition hereafter. There seems to be some connection between the beliefs and practices associated with unexpectedly finding a thing in duplicate, and those associated with accidentally duplicating the same words.

either Goethe or Schiller and may have a wish if both name the same poet simultaneously. Children also commonly invoke Goethe or Schiller in parts of Germany, for instance in Hamburg; but it is a general superstition in western Germany, if not elsewhere, that when two people say the same thing at once they are due to die, and to arrest this they shake hands, assuring each other that they will live together another year: 'Wir leben noch ein Jahr zusammen' (in Hanover); 'Wir beide sterben noch nicht' (in Krombach, Westphalia). The chant of three is heard again in Holland, at Amersfoort, east of Utrecht. After the coincidence has occurred the two children at once hook their right-hand little fingers and intone:

> Een, twee, drie,
> Rood, wit, blauw,
> Een, twee, drie.

They then simultaneously name one of the colours, red, white, or blue, and if they both name the same colour they both have a wish. In literary-minded Sweden each child has to name three authors. The two participants press their right thumbs together, name their authors, and, as long as they have not spoken since the coincidence, both may make a wish.[1] In Norway, where the occasion is also marked, it is three wishes which the children may have, always provided that they link little fingers, wish rapidly, and do not reveal what they are wishing for. In France (Lyons) girls believe that the event can be made the occasion of a wedding prognostication. Each maiden tries to pinch the other, and whoever succeeds in pinching first will be married first. In Spain, as in Bolivia, where the coincidence is remarked by adults even more than by children, women cross their fingers saying 'Que venga de allí' ('May you be the first to have a child'). And likewise in Egypt, although they do not give significance to the occasion with their fingers, it is customary to wish each other long life, 'عمرلم أطول سن عمرى' (literally 'Your life is longer than mine').

Curing Warts

When asked about the magic practices they knew, an unexpected number of children described folk remedies they had learned for the treatment of

[1]. Our Stockholm contributor states that when she was a child it was considered clever amongst her schoolmates to name the Brontë sisters, or the co-editors of one of their schoolbooks, as 'Möller, Larsson, och Lundahl' (maths), or 'Gummerus, Rosenqvist, och Johansson' (divinity).

minor ailments, as burdock root for bad blood, roast groundsel for boils, the brisk application of snow or holly leaves for chilblains, a red flannel bandage for a sore throat, mid-summer dew for scarlet fever, and salt in an old sock for toothache.

No specifics, however, were mentioned half so frequently as cures for that unpleasant affliction which seems to root on children in particular, the common wart. To their warts schoolchildren apply ink or castor oil, rusty water, egg yolk, 'first spittle', or the juice of the dandelion or sunspurge. They rub them with soda, or a piece of cheese, or raw potato, or with the inside of a bean pod, or with a slice of apple, or with brimstone, or with the head of a live match. 'If you have warts of any kind,' says an 11-year-old Pontypool girl, 'mix together lard and salt (you should not use any other fat than lard) then rub it on before you go to bed for two or three nights, and then gradually they will go.' 'Another way to remove them is to tie a horse hair round the wart' (Girl, c. 14, Ipswich; also Girl, 15, New-bridge). 'A rather repulsive way of ridding oneself of warts is to rub them with a snail' (Girl, 15, Lanark). 'Get a slug to crawl over your warts' (group of Alton 10-year-olds). In Swansea some girls recommend tying the slug to the wart. One child who used this method said that she had tied it on to the inside of her middle finger, where the wart was, for about two days. She kept it in place by a bandage which she did not remove during this time, but when she did look at the spot the wart had disappeared and the slug dried up.

This treatment, also reported from Portsmouth, is apparently based on the belief that the virus can be supernaturally transferred to an alien piece of flesh which should then be discarded and allowed to wither away, and no method is more commonly employed. 'To have a wart is a common enough complaint,' remarks a Suffolk schoolgirl, 'and a much practised way of removing it is to rub beef on it and then bury the meat in the garden. When the meat rots the wart will rot with it.' 'Rub a wart with pig's fat. Then bury the fat under a bush. This removes the wart,' says another East Anglian girl. 'I know a cure for warts, it is this,' says a Staffordshire girl, 'get a small piece of meat, rub it on the wart and then bury it in the garden.' 'Get a piece of raw meat and rub the meat on the wart and you bury the meat,' echoes a 10-year-old East Riding boy. And the same is reported in Huntingdonshire, only there it is specified that the meat must be stolen. And this method is also recommended in Monmouthshire, only there a piece of fat bacon rind is the usual specific which is sometimes buried, and sometimes 'put out on the clothes line until it rots'.

The practice seems to be known in all parts of England and Wales, as child after child vouches for its efficacy. 'The ways for curing warts,' writes a 14-year-old Radnorshire girl, 'are by getting a broad bean and rubbing it on the wart and then hiding it in the ground but don't tell anyone until it as gone. And you can do the same with a piece of fat bacon by rubbing it on and put it in the ground and when the bacon starts to rot the wart will go away. I have tried it with a broad bean and they turn out.'

These children of the supersonic age, who were not born when the last war began, are sharing an experience which astonished the young Francis Bacon a decade before the Spanish Armada set sail. In his *Sylva Sylvarvm*, 1627, p. 264, the philosopher recalls:

'I had, from my Childhood, a Wart vpon one of my Fingers: Afterwards when I was about Sixteene Yeeres old, being then at Paris, there grew vpon both my Hands a Number of Warts, (at the least an hundred,) in a Moneths Space. The English Embassadours Lady, who was a Woman farre from Superstition, told me, one day; She would helpe me away with my Warts: Whereupon she got a Peece of Lard, with the Skin on, and rubbed the Warts all ouer, with the Fat Side; And amongst the rest that Wart, which I had had from my Childhood; Then she nailed the Peece of Lard, with the Fat towards the Sunne, vpon a Poast of her Chamber Window, which was to the South. The Successe was, that within fiue weekes space, all the Warts went quite away: And that Wart, which I had so long endured, for Company. But at the rest I did little maruell, because they came in a Short time, and might goe away in a Short Time againe: But the Going away of that, which had staid so long, doth yet sticke with mee.'

In fact, it seems that children in the new Elizabethan age are more familiar with such matters, and take enchantment more for granted, than men did in the time of *Midsummer Night's Dream*. 'They say,' continues Francis Bacon, 'the like is done by rubbing of warts with a green elder stick, and burying the stick to rot in the muck.'

Today a number of children could instruct him in this practice, together with an up-to-date method of disposing of the wand. A 15-year-old girl, writing in 1954, says that her grandfather told her to pick a small twig of elderberry, touch her wart with it, chant the words,

> Wart, wart, on my knee,
> Please go, one, two, three,

and put it 'down the toilet'.

Herrick in his description of Oberon's Palace, printed in *Hesperides*, 1648, tells of 'Art's

> Wise hand enchasing here those warts,
> Which we to others (from our selves)
> Sell, and brought hither by the Elves.'

A Newbridge schoolgirl writes (1954):

'When I was about eight years old I had three warts on my finger. I tried many ways to get rid of them but I tried in vain. Then one day my cousin told me to go up to a certain lady's shop with a penny, and she would charm them away. I went up thinking it would still be there. She called me into the kitchen and rubbed my penny over the warts and said:

> "Warts, warts on your hand,
> I'll bury you in the sand."

She then buried my penny in the garden and told me it would go before long. I went out half-heartedly. I looked at my finger in the morning expecting to see it still there, but they had completely gone. I run down to tell my mother, we were all very astonished, but it is quite true.'

And if a charm has been proven for 400 years, it is not surprising to find that it has been part of man's knowledge for 2,000 years. Thus Pliny reported:

'The following is a method adopted for the cure of all kinds of warts: on the first day of the moon, each wart must be touched with a single chickpea, after which, the party must tie up the pease in a linen cloth, and throw it behind him; by adopting this plan, it is thought, the warts will be made to disappear.'[1]

And a Radnorshire boy writes (1953):

'Get a wheat and rub it on the wart and then wrap it up in a little parcle big enofe for someone to see and take it and drop it on a cross road when nobody is looking, and they say that will cure them.'

Neither Pliny nor the schoolboy 1,900 years later state in so many words that the parcel is for someone to find, and undo, and in consequence contract the warts himself and relieve the original sufferer. But that this is what is intended seems certain. The transference of evil to a material object as a step to foisting it upon some other living person is a practice known to distant corners of the earth. In Upper India scabs or scales from the body of a smallpox victim are placed in little piles of earth set up in the middle of the road and decorated with flowers in the hope that someone may touch them, and, touching them, catch the disease and relieve the patient. In Uganda, among the people of the Bahima tribe, attempts are made to cure abscesses by rubbing them with certain herbs, procured from the medicine-man, and then burying the herbs in a road where people continually pass. And among the Sena-speaking people to the north of the Zambezi, the doctor transfers a patient's sickness to a

1. *The Natural History of Pliny*, translated by John Bostock and H. T. Riley, 1890, vol. iv, pp. 450–51 (Book xxii, ch. 72). In Philemon Holland's translation, 1601, the quotation appears in vol. ii, pp. 142–3 (Book xxii, ch. 25).

little straw pig which is then placed where two paths meet on the chance that a passerby will kick it and thus absorb the illness and draw it away from the patient.[1] As if in confirmation that Pliny's informant intended that the infected parcel should be found by a stranger, Marcellus of Bordeaux, in the fourth century A.D., prescribed that a person should touch his warts with as many little stones as he had warts, wrap the stones in an ivy leaf, and throw them away in a thoroughfare. Whoever picked them up, he said, would acquire the warts, and he who worked the charm would be rid of them.[2] And this idea that evil can be transferred to a scapegoat by mystic means is still firmly held in parts of Britain, and continues to be practised. The following was written by a Presteigne schoolboy in 1953:

'MAGIC CURES. I had warts about five months ago and I was told to cut a hazel stick about half an inch thick, cut as many notches as you have warts. Then wrap the stick in brown paper, tie with string, go for a bycicle ride and drop it somewhere in the road. Do not tell anywhone aboute it. I have not told any-whone till now. The person who picks the parcle up will have your warts. About a fortnight after my warts disapeared.'

It appears that our children, or some of them, are successfully practising an enchantment worked by witch doctors in Africa, and have obtained this knowledge through having it orally handed down to them from men who were living in the days of Christ.

Cocking Snooks

Having shown that minor customs and practices tend, under children's propulsion, to spin on quietly from generation to generation, it is almost a greater curiosity when a practice, recently commonplace, and with a long tradition behind it, suddenly ceases. That peculiar form of recognition variously known as 'the five-finger salute', 'nose thumbing', 'making a long nose' or 'long bacon', 'cocking a snook', or 'taking a sight' used, between the wars, to be demonstrated by every child in the country, both in private and national schools. Today the gesture is no longer in fashion; indeed it is more often seen performed by obstreperous grown-ups than by children; and at most schools it has altogether fallen out of use.

1. For references to these and similar practices, see J. G. Frazer, *The Golden Bough*, pt. vi, 1913, pp. 6–7.
2. *Golden Bough*, pt. vi, p. 48.

Why this should be so is almost as much of a puzzle as when and where it began.

The gesture seems to be described in Urquhart's translation of Rabelais, book ii, 1653, ch. xix, pp. 134–5:

'Panurge suddenly lifted up in the aire his right hand, and put the thumb thereof into the nostril of the same side, holding his foure fingers streight out, and closed orderly in a parallel line to the point of his nose, shutting the left eye wholly, and making the other wink with a profound depression of the eye-brows and eye-lids. Then lifted he up his left hand, with hard wringing and stretching forth his foure fingers, and elevating his thumb, which he held in a line directly correspondent to the situation of his right hand, with the distance of a cubit and a halfe between them. This done, in the same forme he abased towards the ground, both the one and the other hand; Lastly, he held them in the midst, as aiming right at the English mans nose.'

Since Panurge is making fun of the Englishman it is possible that an insult, recognizable to the spectators, is here intended. And when the Englishman half copies him, applying his own thumb 'upon the gristle of his nose' the fun is enhanced by his unwitting adoption of a rude attitude. What is certain, or seems so, is that this derisive symbolism was familiar on the Continent at the end of the sixteenth century, for it is clearly depicted in the *Evangelicae Historiae Imagines* of Hieronymus Natalis, printed at Antwerp in 1593. Plate 67, which shows the undignified departure of the Prodigal Son from a tavern, has in the foreground a dwarf mocking him with both hands in position. But it is doubtful whether the gesture was established in England at this time. The gesture of contempt which Shakespeare knew was the fico, or biting the thumb, as in *Romeo and Juliet* (I. i) where Sampson says: 'I wil bite my Thumb at them, which is a disgrace to them, if they beare it.' Cotgrave describes this action in his French and English *Dictionary*, 1611:

'*Nique: Faire la nique.* To mocke by nodding, or lifting vp of the chinne; or more properly, to threaten or defie, by putting the thumbe naile into the mouth, and with a jerke (from th'vpper teeth) make it to knacke.'

In Italy, at this date, the term was *fare le fica* (Florio, 1611); and it may be noted that in London biting the thumb at policemen continued to be customary, in impolite circles, up to a hundred years ago (Mayhew, *Paved with Gold*, 1858, p. 115), as also in France, and also amongst children in Philadelphia, where the practice was known as 'breaking off', and employed when terminating a friendship (*Notes and Queries*, 6th ser., i, p. 426, and ii, p. 176). A possible relic of the gesture survives today in the expression 'Not to care a fig'.

Hone in his *Year Book* for 10 January 1831 states that the practice of placing the thumb of the left hand on the tip of the nose, and joining the thumb of the right hand to the little finger of the left, and then spreading out the fingers, forfex-like, to the utmost extent, was one which 'suddenly arose as a novelty within the last twenty years among the boys of the metropolis'. And, despite the frontispiece to *The English Theophrastus*, 1702, which appears to show satyrs making long noses, and the reference in the *Spectator*, 1712, to the apprentice speaking 'his disrespect by an extended finger', and the terms 'Queen Anne's fan' and 'Queen Anne's handshake', it is probable that Hone is correct. Anyway 'taking a sight' or 'a grinder' at someone, or 'cutting a snook' or 'working the coffee mill' became an accepted gesture in almost all classes of society in the middle decades of the nineteenth century. It is repeatedly portrayed in satirical prints, and in the pages of *Punch*, and even appears in the favourite children's book *Struwelpeter* which arrived in England in 1848.

The cocked snook (in France *un pied de nez*, in Germany *eine lange Nase*), carefully aimed at the person being insulted, was popularly supposed to have different meanings according to how it was performed. By the 1930s children had come to look upon some of the forms as definitely wicked; and it is possible that the significance these forms had acquired contributed to the gesture's disappearance. To hold up one hand wished a person in hell; to hold up two hands doubled the imprecation and meant that the person should go to hell and stay there; to hold up both hands and vibrate the fingers meant that the person should go to hell, stay there, and consort with the devil; and any exhibitionist who stuck out his tongue at the same time was looked upon as unspeakably rude.

Alternatively, particularly amongst girls, a child would raise one hand to her nose and say 'The moon came out', bring up her second hand and say 'The stars came out', and then, waggling her fingers, exclaim 'And they all began to twinkle'. More artfully, she would raise one closed fist to her nose, commenting 'The sun came out', fit a second fist in front 'The moon came out' (no offence being yet apparent), and then, quickly spreading the fingers and waggling them, declare 'The stars came out and twinkled'.

During and after the First World War some children had a joke in which they chanted:

> Salute the King
> Salute the Queen,
> Salute the German submarine,

honouring the king with a military salute, the queen with a naval one, and the German submarine with the thumb to the nose tip. Similarly, during the Second World War young 'barrack rats' would go through the performance: 'This is how the king salutes', bringing up their right hand with creditable smartness in a military salute; 'This is how Hitler salutes', raising their arm like a Nazi; 'And this', raising a leg, 'is how a dog salutes'. Occasionally they tried the trick, also known to American children:

> Salute the captain of the ship (*smart naval salute*),
> Sorry, sir, my finger slipped (*dropping the hand to the nose*).

At present rude gestures seem to be in a state of flux, the following being currently regarded as the most offensive:

1. The first and second fingers, extended and slightly parted, are jerked upwards, the back of the hand facing outwards.
2. The nose is pressed upwards with thumb, and the tongue put out.
3. Ears are twisted, or thumbs placed in ear-holes and fingers fluttered, a gesticulation known as 'elephant ears'.
4. The nose is held while an imaginary lavatory chain is pulled.
5. Air is forced through the pursed lips to make a juicy noise known as a 'raspberry'.

They also continue to make the well-known schoolboy 'face' by inserting their thumbs in the corners of their mouth and tugging sideways while simultaneously plucking downward the undersides of their eyes with their forefingers; and this, too, was an 'ill-favoured countenance' made by the jesting Panurge.

*** It should perhaps be mentioned that the engraving on a vase reproduced in Francesco Inghirami's *Pitture di Vasi Fittili*, vol. i, 1835, plate 13, showing a draped female figure called $\Phi\eta\mu\eta$, or 'Fame', fleeing from a young man, but with her head turned back at him cocking a fine snook, with the exclamation $E\kappa\alpha\varsigma\ \Pi\alpha\iota\ K\alpha\lambda\epsilon$, 'Be off, my fine fellow!' is a modern fabrication. The vase never existed except upon paper. The engraving was issued by Brønsted and Stackelberg, apparently in a fit of archaeological jealousy, and the credulous Inghirami, who was deceived by it, was too late in an endeavour to expunge it from his book.

Secret Languages

By using slang, local dialect, a multiplicity of technical terms, word-twistings, codes, and sign language, children communicate with each other in ways which outsiders are unable to understand, and thus satisfy an impulse common to all underdogs. In fact children use esoteric speech more commonly than is generally supposed. Rhyming slang, for instance, which they call 'Crooks' language': 'almond rocks' for socks, 'apples and pears' for stairs, 'turtle doves' for gloves, and so on, normally associated with cockneys, is neither confined to the metropolis, nor to the shift-for-a-living class. As far away as Newcastle respectable children can be heard saying they are 'going for a ball of chalk' when setting out for a walk, and accusing someone of being a 'tea-leaf' when they mean a thief.

Perhaps the most common secret vocabulary children use is a modification of back-slang, although 'Eggy-peggy' and 'Arague' language are also popular and seem to predominate in some areas, or it may be with some classes of children. Back-slang proper, sometimes employed by barrow-boys and hawkers, and indigenous to certain trades such as the greengrocer's and the butcher's, where it is spoken to ensure that the customer shall not understand what is being said ('Evig reh emos delo garcs dene' – Give her some old scrag end) consists simply of saying each word backwards, and when this is impossible saying the name of the letter instead of its sound, usually the first or last letter, thus: 'Uoy nac ees reh sreckin ginwosh' (You can see her knickers showing). An Enfield master reports that he found 'at least half a dozen boys who could talk it quickly'. But what most children colloquially refer to as 'back-slang' is either a simplification in which the final sound is moved to the front of the word, 'Shba uyo fi uyo tedon teshu aryou petray' (Bash you if you don't shut your trap), or a slightly more complicated and very popular form, sometimes known as 'pig Latin', in which the first consonant or double consonant (e.g. *br* and *th*) is transferred to the end of the word and *ay*, or less frequently *e*, is added thereafter, thus: 'Unejay ithsmay isay igpay' (June Smith is a pig); and the 'Bash you' threat becomes 'Ashbay ouyay ifay ouyay ontday utshay ouray aptray'. This has been spoken by children since before the First World War, and is sometimes given a high sounding name such as 'Sandy Hole Gaelic' (Wood Green, 1938).

In contrast to turning the words, they sometimes disguise what they are saying by inserting one syllable, or occasionally two, before each vowel. In Scarborough teenage girls are reported to have 'thageir agown pagattager' which they call pidgin English or double talk, putting *ag* before each vowel, a peculiarity said to have been first practised in that town at the beginning of the century, and then known as 'stage slang'.[1] In Watford, Hertfordshire, and Barry, Glamorganshire, girls report that *eg* is introduced before vowels.[2] In Worcester it is, or was, 'Aygo-paygo language'. In Chelmsford and Manchester boys use 'Arague Language'. Thus:

> Taragoo baraged, saragays slarageepy haragead,
> Taragarry ara wharagile, saragays slaragow,
> Paragut aragon tharage paragot, saragays grarageedy garagut,
> Waragell saragup baragefaragore warage garago,

which turns out to be:

> To bed, says sleepy head,
> Tarry a while, says slow,
> Put on the pot, says greedy gut,
> We'll sup before we go.

And this secret juvenile patter is another item which is not only old but adult in origin, for, by an ironic twist, it seems formerly to have been used when adults did not want children to know what they were talking about. The following passage appears in the privately printed autobiography of Elizabeth Grant of Rothiemurchus, and refers to the year 1808:

'There had been a great many mysterious conversations of late between my mother and aunt Mary, and as they had begun to suspect the old *how-vus do-vus* language was become in some degree comprehensible to us, they had substituted a more difficult style of disguised English. This took us a much longer time to translate into common sense. "Here*thegee* is*thegee* a*thegee* let*thegee* ter*thegee* from*thegee*," etc. I often wondered how with words of many syllables they managed to make out such a puzzle, or even to speak it, themselves. It baffled us for several days; at last we discovered the key, or the clue, and then we found a marriage was preparing – whose, never struck us – it was merely a marriage in which my mother and my aunts were interested.' (*Memoir of a Highland Lady*, reprint 1898, p. 73.)

1. *Scarborough Evening News*, 14, 25, and 28 October 1954; *Scarborough Mercury*, 5 November 1954.
2. This must be the most 'U' of secret languages, being spoken by members of high society in Miss Nancy Mitford's *Love in a Cold Climate*, 1949, ch. iii: 'Lady Montdore ... led me to the table and the starlings went on with their chatter about my mother in "eggy-peggy", a language I happened to know quite well. "Egg-is shegg-ee reggeal-leggy, pwegg-oor swegg-eet?"'

> I'll be your friend ever,
> Hers or his never.
>
> *Friendship oath. Girl, 11 Lydney.*

BOYS are definitely realists. The characteristic they most want in a friend is that he should like playing the same games that they do.

'My best friend is John Corbett and the reason why I like him is that he is so nise to me and we both draw space ships, and what's more he plays with me nearly every time in the playground. Another thing, he got by me when some other boys were tormenting me. Another thing about John is that he is sensible and nise. Whenever we are playing rocket ships he never starts laughing when we get to an awkward point.'

Boy, 9, Dulwich Hamlet.

A friend is colloquially referred to as 'my bud' or 'buddy', 'my butty', 'chum', 'crony', 'mate', 'my monkey', 'pardner', or 'pal'. They say a friend is one who always plays with them in the playground, who 'knocks' for them at 8.45 to go to school, and who goes home with them after school. A friend is also 'one who is a member of one's gang'.

In girls' friendships, presents and birthday cards, lending things, and sharing sweets, play no inconsiderable part.

'I have two friends called Carol and Brenda. I like Brenda because she is very funny and very small. I also like Carol because when she has any sweets she always gives me some, and she has lovely curly hair, and she is very nice. Carol, Brenda, and I nearly always go home together. Carol nearly always sends me a Christmas card and a birthday card, and she never forgets to send me a birthday present. Brenda has a nice face, and she has straight hair with a fringe.'

Girl, 9, Camberwell.

Little girls are highly conscious of their friends' appearance:

'Dulcie has got lovely hair, that's partly why I like her.'

Girl, 9, East Dulwich.

'My friend Barbara has fair hair and is very pretty and wears a Red Skirt and a Brown Sweater and she has brown eyes and Red Shoes and white Sokes.'

Girl, 11, Nunhead.

'I like Hazel because she is a nice girl who always wears school uniform if possible. She takes great care how she is dressed.'

Girl, 11, Camberwell.

'My best friend is Vera. She always dresses nicely and walks with her shoulders back. Sometimes she wears Brown slip-on shoes, a green cardigan and a dress. She wears white ankle socks.'

Girl, 12, Nunhead.

In none of the 340 essays on 'My Friends and Why I Like Them', from which these quotations are taken, did any *boy* think of describing the clothes or physical appearance of his friends.

They address their friends as: Old bean, old chap, old pal, old sop, and kiddo. 'Hi ya, old horsey.' 'Hi, chum.' And their greatest sign of approbation is to call a person 'a good sport' or 'sporty'. 'I like David,' remarks a typical 10-year-old, 'because he is a good sport and kind to animals. At games he never cheats, and he sits out if he is out.'

Making and Breaking Friends

In general children's friendships are far from placid. Perhaps because of the gregariousness of school life they make and break friends with a rapidity disconcerting to the adult spectator. Two girls will swear eternal friendship, arrange signs and passwords, exchange necklaces, walk home together from school, invite each other to tea, and have just settled down together, so it would seem, when suddenly they are very 'black' with one another and do not speak any more. They seek a new friend, and have no sooner found one than they are with their old pal again. And they may be well aware of their fickleness. 'I like Jean,' says a 9-year-old, 'because if we break friends it is only for a day or two.' 'Brian and I don't like each other now as he bosses me about and I boss him,' says another 9-year-old, 'but we will be friends again soon I hope.'

The finger of friendship is the little finger. They link the little fingers of their right hands and shake them up and down, declaring:

> Make friends, make friends,
> Never, never break friends.

They quarrel, and their friendship is ended with the formula,

> Break friends, break friends,
> Never, never make friends,

repeated in a like manner, but, in Croydon, with the little fingers moistened, and in Portsmouth with linked thumbs. They make up again, intoning,

> We've broken before,
> We break now –

and they separate their little fingers,

> We'll never break any more,

and they intertwine their little fingers again, squeezing tightly (Weston-super-Mare). Alternatively, in places as far apart as South Molton and Cleethorpes (and commonly in the London area), they say,

> Make up, make up, never row again,
> If we do we'll get the cane,

and thereupon they slap hands or smack each other. In Radnorshire they hook little fingers, touch thumbs, and then turn hands over and clap.

Sometimes the reunited friends merely shake hands with a formal expression of goodwill: 'Shake, bud', 'Always shake, never break', 'Let bygones be bygones', 'Put the quarrel down the drain'. In Glasgow when they shake hands they have a third person who brings his hand down between them, saying 'Cut cheese'. Romantically minded, some children solemnize the rite by pricking each other's fingers and mixing the blood so that they become 'blood brothers'. In Dublin girls employ an intermediary. She walks over to the person they are not talking to, and asks:

> Are you spin, spout, or blackout,
> Falling in or falling out?

Should the reply be 'blackout' it means the girl does not want to make up. 'Ahem to the dirt!' exclaims the rejected one. But if they make up they swear friendship: 'You're the lock and I've the key', and customarily, as a token of their restored friendship, they go out shopping together.

Attitudes to Opposite Sex

Even very young children sometimes have a special friend of the opposite sex, whom they unaffectedly designate their 'sweetheart':

'I like Eileen Williams because she is nice to me. I like Susan Hobbs because she likes me. I like Patricia Jones, she is my sweetheart.'

Boy, 7, Peckham.

'Anne Harris is very obliging and says "I love you" to all boys, but Pamela Williamson is my real sweetheart.'

Boy, 8, Dulwich.

Later their interest shows itself in rough play:

'After dark some boys like to try and frighten young girls on their way home by jumping in front of them and shouting.'

Boy, aged 12.

'At my junior school the boys had different doors from the girls and if a boy went through the girls' door he had a 100 lines to write out and visa versa. The girls used to play football it was smashing we used to run through to the boys' playground, take a ball and then run off with it.'

Girl, aged 13.

Thereafter may come curiosity. A 13-year-old girl writes:

'On Saturday night when my friend Joan and myself come out of the pictures we look at people and see if they speak different from local people. If they do we follow them but they have to be strangers to both of us first. It is mostly couples we follow. They usually go down dark streets as they can hold hands then without looking silly. Sometimes we follow girls about eighteen years old, they all have as we say their "war paint" on, and they stay on the main road, but sometimes boys of eighteen come and ask her, her name. She tells him and they go on speaking for a while and then they go off together to a dance or something like that.'

The following terms of endearment have been supplied by 13-year-olds: Ducky duck, my darling love, fruity sweetie, honey bun, honey bunch, and sweetie pie. The term 'B.G.' (Best Girl), popular in the thirties, seems to have become dated, and has been replaced by 'G.F.' (Girl Friend). 'G.P.' (Grand Passion) is usually reserved for hero-sweethearts, such as film stars and sports celebrities, thus they say: 'Elvis Presley is my G.P.'

It is fashionable to have a 'crush' on or a 'pash' for somebody. 'He's my pash', i.e. the one they are passionate about; while 'crush' is popularly supposed to convey the idea of someone to whom they would like to be crushed close.

Someone considered over-affectionate is said to be soppy, sloppy, gormless, a drip, or a clot. They jeer: 'If all the boys lived over the sea, what a good swimmer *Margaret* would be!'

> *Mavis Tate* was a very good girl,
> She went to church on Sunday,
> To pray to God to give her strength
> To kiss the boys on Monday.

Boy, 12, Portsmouth.

When *Ann* was little it was toys, toys, toys,
Now *Ann* is a big girl it is boys, boys, boys.

Boy, 13, Coventry.

If a couple they know are seen to be showing interest in each other, they call out across the street, 'When's the wedding going to be?'

A rhyme of general derision (Boy, 11, Birmingham):

> I say what a smasher,
> Pick it up and slosh it at her.
> If you miss
> Give her a kiss,
> I say what a smasher.

It should be noted that in the south of England a girl is often spoken of as a 'tart' (referred to as such by boys aged 11), and that no disrespect is implied by the word. A 'posh tart' is indeed a general term of admiration for a well-dressed, nice-looking girl.

Character Reading

Children are wonderful believers in their ability to tell a person's character or fortune by the singularities of his appearance; and the reliability of a favourite wise saw will be fondly supported with modern instances as if they were already in the fifth age of wisdom. Thus eyebrows which grow together are declared to be a sign of evil, and their possessor may end his life on the end of a rope. Bushy eyebrows mean that a person is superstitious. Much hair on arms and legs is said to denote strength, and golden hairs portend that the person will be wealthy. Long arms, they say, betray rapacity; long fingers disclose musical ability; and the white specks on finger-nails, known as 'gifts', are regarded as an augury of good fortune, probably the early arrival of a present – 'Gifts on your finger, one will linger,' affirms a Lincolnshire 12-year-old.

The significance of the colour of a person's eyes is summed up in the rhyme:

> Blue eyes, beauty,
> Do your mother's duty;
> Brown eyes, pick-a-pie,
> Run away and tell a lie;
> Grey eyes, greedy guts,
> Gobble all the world up.

Also green eyes are thought to reveal a jealous person, and light-coloured eyes that a person is a good shot. A turned-up nose means that a girl is cocky, a long nose indicates inquisitiveness, and a Roman nose denotes courage. Freckles are thought to distinguish the child with a merry nature, and are popularly believed to foreshadow beauty. Dimples are associated with obtaining a living:

> A dimple in your chin
> Your fortune will come in;
> A dimple in your cheek
> Your fortune's far to seek.

And moles are particularly inspected. 'A mole below your breath, you'll die rich before your death,' observes a Liverpool boy. Others assert that a mole on the lip is the emblem of a great talker, that a mole on the chin shows a man of wisdom, and that a mole on the back of the neck portends a life of hard work and sorrow.

A gap between the two front teeth, wide enough to take a sixpence, is considered a certain token that the person will become rich. Possession of a double crown signifies that a person is a wanderer and will not die in the country in which he was born. Bow legs are said to be a sign of greed; but hefty or plump legs are a sign of a placid disposition.

They say that cold hands mean a warm heart, and that moist hands, as Shakespeare noted, disclose 'an amorous constitution'.

Slanting shoulders, they think, suggest that a person will be a successful ballet dancer; and if a child's second toe is as long as or longer than his big toe it is a sure sign, they say, of a fast runner.

These and such-like significations are not looked upon as superstitions but as signs of nature, as certain as that a teacher's frown is a sign of trouble.

Love Tokens

The girls also know signs and omens which inform them about the progress of their romantic attachments. If a girl stumbles when going up stairs, if her apron comes undone, if an earring or hairclip falls from its place, or if her left ear burns, it is recognized that her sweetheart is thinking of her, probably affectionately. (They say of a tingling ear: 'Left for love, right for spite' or 'Left ear your lover, right ear your mother'.)

If a girl wears her belt twisted, or her nose becomes red, or if, when walking in a field, the burrs of the goose-grass (known as 'sweethearts') stick to her clothes, it is felt certain she is in love. In Alton, Hampshire, they say that the number of burrs sticking to her indicates the number of her sweethearts.

If a girl's fingers crack when they are pulled it reveals that she has a boy friend, and classmates will pull a child's finger to discover what she herself is unwilling to divulge.

If a girl finds a bright new pin, or if she accidentally makes the tea too strong, it means she is going to make a new and staunch friend. If two forks are crossed at her place at table it portends romance.

If a cluster of bubbles forms on a cup of tea or cocoa it represents a kiss,[1] and it is not unusual for girls to stir their cup vigorously in order to make froth, and then drink the bubbles to make sure of the kiss.

Equally there are ill omens, warning the girls that their friendships are in danger. If a girl finds that she has made the tea weaker than usual she knows that a friend is turning from her. If she loses her boy's picture it is evident that she is about to lose his affection. If two friends wash in the same water (and do not spit), or dry their hands on the same towel simultaneously, or are separated by a lamp post when walking out together, or allow themselves to be photographed together, it is generally conceded that they are in for a quarrel.

Knives are sharp with contention. To receive the present of a knife (or a pair of scissors, or a brooch) and not give a half-penny or other small coin in return is disastrous for it will sever the friendship. To find a table knife with the edge laid outwards, or two knives crossed, or to stir a drink with a knife, are recognized signs that there is going to be an argument. 'Stir with a knife, you stir for strife,' quote several youngsters. And to drop a knife is further intimation of a row, only to be avoided if the knife is trodden on before it is picked up, or if it is left for somebody else to pick up. Then, indeed, it may be lucky, it may mean 'a fellow is coming to see you'.

There are a number of signs, not without romantic implications, that a visitor can be expected. If a spoon is dropped it is propitious: 'Drop a spoon and your love will come soon.' If the coffee boils over, if a bumble bee comes into the house, if the cat is seen washing itself in the evening, or a stray teastalk rises to the top of a cup of tea, a visitor will soon be knocking at the door.

The floating teastalk (known as a 'stranger') can also show the type of visitor who may be expected. If the stalk feels hard the visitor will be a man, if soft a woman; if the stalk is long the visitor will be tall, if short he

1. This belief has been current at least since 1831, when it was noted by a correspondent to Hone's *Year Book* (29 February, col. 253).

will be dumpy. And the exact day when the visitor will arrive is ascertained by placing the stalk on the back of the left hand and hitting it with the back of the right, counting a day for each smack and noting at which smack the stalk is dislodged. In like manner, in Swansea, if a girl has dropped an eyelash, and she wants to know when her sweetheart will come to her, she places it on the back of her hand and hits it in the same singular manner, counting a day for each time she hits it.

Bus Tickets

Although some ancient auguries are now no longer heeded, it is probable that as many ways of foretelling the future are employed today as at any time in the past, for when old divinations become impracticable, new wonders, more in keeping with the times, arise to take their place. Thus a plurality of traditions concerning friendship and fortune have become attached to bus tickets. All over Britain the half-price community hold that the serial number of a ticket possesses intimate significance for the person to whom it is issued, and, since children probably predict the future more often with tickets than with anything else, it seems proper to describe this phenomenon in detail.

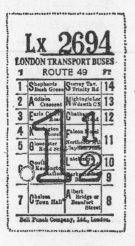

A lucky ticket.

The serial numbers most prized are those in which the sum of the digits is twenty-one, and tickets bearing such numbers are even thought to influence the future:

'If on getting on a bus and purchasing a bus ticket I find that the number of the issue of the ticket adds up to 21 then I always keep that ticket as a kind of charm that will bring me luck.'
Girl, 13, Pontypool.

'If the numbers on your ticket add up to 21 you are lucky.'
Girl, 11, Lydney.

'If the number on your bus ticket adds up to 21 you will be lucky all the month.'
Boy, 12, Wandsworth.

A Brixton boy adds that it is especially lucky if the letters in front of the serial number are the person's initials. A Brighton girl says that if the total comes to 21 it means 'one will get another boy friend'. A Watford girl says it means one will be married.

If the serial numbers add up to other totals they may also have significance, particularly multiples of seven:

'If the figures on your bus tickets add up to 7 or a denomination of 7 it is lucky.'

Boy, 13, Upminster.

'If the numbers add up to 7 it means a wish, 14 a kiss, 21 a letter, 28 a parcel.'
Girl, 15, Ipswich.

Inevitably:

'If the numbers on the bus ticket add up to 13 bad luck is forecast for the future.'

Boy, 12, Lambeth.

The actual figures in the serial number are also noted, the most auspicious again being the number seven.

'If the last number of ticket is a 7 you are going to have a lucky day.'
Boy, 12, Southwark.

Many south-east London boys confirm this, also children in the Home Counties and at Oxford. A number of boys at Croydon state that they collect such tickets. One boy says that he collects them for a blind person; and several say that a person should keep on collecting them until he has a million such tickets.[1]

An Upminster boy, aged 13, says: 'If the 7 is the second figure the owner will marry soon or has a secret lover.'

A girl, 14, from Cumberland, says that if a ticket has the figures 1, 2, 4, or 5 on it 'it means you are in love'. Twelve-year-olds in Sheffield say that if two figures are the same and next to each other 'you have a wish'. A North Weald boy says that it is lucky if all the figures are the same.

The general opinion, however, is that twenty-one is the important number, and in some cities the receipt of such a ticket gives, or is supposed to give, peculiar privileges. In Aberdeen for instance:

'If any girl receives a ticket on which the numbers add up to twenty-one she keeps it until she meets the boy she admires the most and gives it to him. This means she loves him.'

Girl, aged 15.

'If a person has a car ticket where the figures add up to twenty-one and she gives it to a person of the opposite sex, it means that she loves whomever she gave it to and she will be married at twenty-one.'

Girl, aged 14.

1. See pp. 329–30.

The significance of this token is sometimes taken a stage further, the response of the person to whom it is offered being of consequence.

'A well-known superstition is counting on tramcar tickets. If they amount to twenty-one we keep it and give it to a boy. If he throws it away he throws away one's love, but if he keeps it he keeps one's love.'

Girl, aged 14.

Other girls in Aberdeen say that if he tears it in half and 'returns half of it to her, that means he loves her'. But all emphasize that '*Twenty-one is the only number used for this*'. It is a practice which has also been reported from Bath, Brighton, Fife, Glasgow, Liverpool, London, Newcastle, Peterborough, Pontypool, and Swansea. Sometimes, particularly amongst boys, it is expected that the sign of reciprocated affection should be more explicit. A boy, aged 2, from Southwark declares:

'If you get a ticket with the numbers adding up to 21, you can get a kiss off your girl friend.'

This statement is confirmed by other London lads, thus: 'If get 21 G.F. will give kiss in exchange' – 'Every bus ticket adding up to 21 is worth one kiss' – 'Drop behind a girl and demand a kiss.' One lad says: 'If you have a bus ticket adding up to 21, then you should be allowed to kiss your girl, but it doesn't always work.'

In Swansea, the girls elaborate:

'If the number adds up to twenty-one and you give the ticket to your boy friend he must kiss you. If he likes you he gives it back to you and you then kiss him, and so on.'

They also say:

'If you have a ticket whose numbers add up to twenty-one your boy friend should take you to the pictures.'

'If you have twenty-one tickets adding up to twenty-one you ask him to come to your twenty-first birthday party.'

An Ealing girl states:

'If the total is 21 it means "I love you", but if it is 19 it means "I hate you". You give them to people you love or hate. Other totals also have meanings but these are the only two I know.'

In Aberdeen, Manchester, Oxford, and Swansea, it is also the custom to work out the initials of the well-beloved:

'If the number on the ticket does not add up to twenty-one it is usual to see which letter of the alphabet corresponds with the number on one's ticket and whichever letter it is will be the first in one's future husband's name.'

Girl, 14, Aberdeen.

In Swansea, where some buses use ribbon tickets, the girls examine the smaller code number to give them the initial of the boy friend's Christian name; and they use the route number on the ticket to give the initial of his surname.

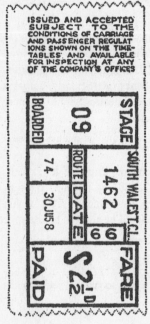

ISSUED AND ACCEPTED SUBJECT TO THE CONDITIONS OF CARRIAGE AND PASSENGER REGULATIONS SHOWN ON THE TIME-TABLES AND AVAILABLE FOR INSPECTION AT ANY OF THE COMPANY'S OFFICES

BOARDED
09
74
30JU58
STAGE
SOUTH WALES T.CL.
ROUTE
1462
DATE
66
FARE
PAID
S 2½D

Ticket issued by the South Wales Transport Company Ltd. The boy friend's initials are L.K.

In many cities (perhaps in most cities) bus tickets are further used for an even more comprehensive divination, two methods being predominant. In the first, the serial numbers are translated literally as they stand:

'The first two figures on the top is the age you will get married the third how much money you can earn a week and the forth how many children you will have.'

Boy, 12, Peckham.

Not all children agree with this. The usual formula is that the first two numbers on the ticket give the age when a person will be married, the third gives the number of children, and the fourth the weekly wage earned by self or husband. Thus the number 2158 means that a person will be married at 21, have five children, and earn £8 per week.[1]

Other such formulas, adopted by individualists, are liable to give more newsworthy predictions:

'5964 = 5 wives, 9 boys, 6 girls, and £4 a week' – *Boy, 12, Brixton.*

'6609 = marry when you are 6, have 6 wives, no children, and live 9 more years' – *Boy, 13, Croydon.*

'26406 = get married twice, have six children, live in forty different houses, earn £6 a week' – *Girl, 12, Ipswich.*

In the other method the future is worked out with the aid of an old folk rhyme, and the method affords an interesting example of the urbanization of a rural superstition, for the rhyme is one which country people

1. This can also be worked out with the dates on coins (described by girls in Oxford and Pontypool). We have also heard of it being applied to car numbers when, before the war, most number plates had four figures.

have long recited when a company of magpies is observed. A 10-year-old Birmingham girl writes:

'The way we tell our future is to keep our bus tickets and add up the numbers at the top, see how many times seven gos into the number, see how many you have over. Say this little ryhmn, and that is your furture. The ryhmn is –

> One for sorrow,
> Two for joy,
> Three for a letter,
> Four for a boy,
> Five for silver,
> Six for gold,
> Seven for a secret, that's never been told.'

This is the usual verse and procedure. Also reported from Bath, Bedford, Doncaster, Leicester, London, Oxford, Sheffield, Warwick, and from Hull, where children are said to have used this rhyme with tram tickets since about 1920.

Only a few variations have been found. In Coleraine, Ireland, they add up the numbers, and then add again (e.g. 6154, added together = 16, added together again = 7) and then recite:

> One for sorrow, two for joy,
> Three for a kiss and four for a boy,
> Five for silver, six for gold,
> Seven for a secret never to be told.
> Eight for a letter from over the sea,
> Nine for a lover as true as can be.

On the outskirts of Birmingham some children see how many times *five* goes into the number, and then recite the rhyme quoted by the 10-year-old above, with the addition:

> Eight for a bracelet, nine for a ring,
> Ten for a person that can sing.

And at a youth club in Ipswich teenagers have the sophisticated version:

> One for sorrow, two for joy,
> Three for a letter, four for a boy,
> Five for a sweetheart, six for a kiss,
> Seven for an evening full of bliss.

Thus do children in the twentieth century, many of whom have never seen a magpie in their lives, unwittingly sustain a rustic rhythm which was known in the days of Dr Johnson. And almost certainly the lines have greater currency today, in their new application, than they had in the pastoral days before the Industrial Revolution.[1]

Conveying, Ensuring, and Testing Affection

Possession of a lucky bus ticket is only one of the agreeable means by which a girl can make known her feelings, or a boy demand a kiss. There are symbols known only to the initiated; esoteric displacements such as postage stamps stuck crookedly on an envelope. There are the cryptic words penned on the backs of envelopes, SWANK, SWALK, BOLTOP, HOLLAND, and ITALY (standing for 'Sealed with a nice kiss', 'Sealed with a loving kiss', 'Better on lips than on paper', 'Hope our love lasts and never dies', and 'I trust and love you'). There are the erotic messages written in pictographs which can, with safety, be passed within the class-room itself (Their meaning, divulged by an 11-year-old, *I love you sweet, I long to kiss you, My heart is yours.*)

Even slapping a boy's face may have sly significance. 'If you slap a boy's face on the left cheek you love him, if you slap the right cheek you hate him,' say girls in Swansea; while girls in Aberdeen like to slap their boyfriend's face at twelve o'clock on New Year's Eve, for this, they believe, will make him faithful to them for the coming year. Some boys do not mind having their faces slapped at any time, they immediately reply 'A kiss for a blow', and act upon the saying.

Certain kisses, too, are held to be propitious. A kiss on a stile, especially if in the dark, is quite commonly thought to be lucky, and to ensure affec-

1. Cf. p. 238.

tion. Similarly, mistletoe not only gives permission for a kiss (sometimes as many kisses as there are berries on the sprig), but a kiss so gained is definitely auspicious. Unless a girl is kissed under the mistletoe at Christmas it is not thought likely that she will be married during the following twelve months.

Boys, when they want a kiss, propose a kissing game, notably 'Kiss Chase' or 'Truth, Dare, Promise, or Command', both games in which it is easy for the lad who is nimble-witted or nimble-limbed to kiss the special girl he wishes. Alternatively, at a party, they call for 'Postman's Knock', or 'Winkie', or 'Bottlie', or 'Shy Widow', or the curious and marvellously popular game 'Hyde Park Corner', in which, says a 12-year-old Londoner:

'Each boy gets a girl partner, and they all sit in a ring. The light is turned out, and the person in the middle of the room shines his torch round the room, if he catches anybody not kissing, he changes place with the boy. A girl can be in the middle, she then changes place with the girl.'

The locale of this game, despite its name, is by no means limited to the metropolis; accounts of it have been received from as far away as Ecclesfield, Kidderminster, Luton, Pontypool, and Wimborne. This despite the fact that not a few children have stated:

'If we kiss any person, boy or girl, it is supposed to be one minute off our life.'

In several places it is held that a person's love can be tested by inviting the claimant to span his sweetheart's wrist. If a boy can make a complete circle with his fingers around his girl's wrist it proves that he likes or loves her; if his fingers do not meet he cannot love her.[1] Some girls (Swansea) add that the degree of white pressure marks which show round the wrist after the operation indicate the strength of their mutual affection.

Likewise in Dorset it is said that if a hair is taken from a person's head and it remains straight after having a dampened thumb and forefinger

1. Accounts from Alton, Market Rasen, Portsmouth, and Swansea. In former times schoolboys used to be made to try this test on themselves. Robert Southey, in an autobiographical letter, 27 May 1824, concerning the schools he attended at Bristol in the 1780s, wrote: 'It was fully believed in both these schools, and at Corston, that no bastard could span his own wrist. And I have no doubt this superstition prevailed throughout that part of England.' The test is further referred to in *Notes and Queries*, 26 July 1851, and 1 September 1888, as practised at various schools, including the Royal Military College. S. O. Addy, *Household Tales*, 1895, p. 95, records the north country belief: 'A man who cannot span his own wrist is born to be hanged.'

pulled along its length the person is steadfast; if it curls the person is flirtatious.[1]

Other tests are mechanical rather than personal. In Glamorgan girls scratch their boy's initials on a leaf, place it in their shoe, and wear it all day long, leaving the leaf in the shoe overnight. If in the morning the initials are plainer than they were it is a sign that he will marry them; if they are fainter the friendship will fade.

Very popularly a banana is asked to decide whether a boy is being faithful. When the question has been asked, the lower tip of the fruit is cut off with a sharp knife, and the answer is found in the centre of the flesh, either a **Y** meaning 'Yes', or a dark blob ● meaning 'No'.

While counting cherry stones, apple pips, the seeds on a stalk of dog's-tail grass, petals on a moon daisy, or when jumping in a skipping rope, the following words are commonly recited:

> One I love, two I loathe,
> Three I cast away;
> Four I love with all my heart
> Five I love, I *say* (emphasis on 'say').
> Six he loves me, seven he don't,
> Eight he'll marry me, nine he won't,
> Ten he would if he could, but he can't,
> Eleven he comes, twelve he tarries,
> Thirteen he's waiting, fourteen he marries.[2]

To learn the prospects for two people who are interested in each other they write down the respective names one above the other:

JANE THOMAS

JOHN WILLIAMS

The letters which are common to both names are then cancelled ('like in fractions' comments one girl), and the formula 'Love, marry, hate, adore', is checked along the remaining letters of each name:

1. Reported only from Poole, but probably known elsewhere. A similar belief obtains in Glasgow, where it is asserted that the number of kinks found in a hair pulled from a girl's head denotes the number of husbands she will have.
2. For varia, and a note on the history of this verse, see *The Oxford Dictionary of Nursery Rhymes*, 1951, pp. 331–2.

This reveals that although Jane Thomas grows to hate John Williams, John will continue to love Jane.[1]

Lastly, several ways are known of carrying out the 'Nine Squares Test', here described by a 13-year-old Doncaster lad:

'Another charm is that we take a piece of paper, and draw four lines down and four lines across to make nine squares. At the side of the squares, or on any spare paper, mark 'L' for Love, 'E' for Engage, 'M' for Marry, 'H' for Hate, 'K' for Kiss, 'A' for Adore, and so on until you have nine. Then ask the person what names he would like put in the nine squares (i.e. the names of girl friends he is interested in, and wants to find out about). Then ask how old will he want to be when he marries, and count round the nine squares. When you come to the ninth square go back to the first again, and when you come to the number cross out the name in that square and put it against the first letter on the spare paper. Then count the number again starting at the following square and leaving out the one you have just marked off.'

Finding Sweetheart's Name or Identity

Equally pleasing to little misses, to those of them, that is, whose affections are as yet uncommitted, is the genteel occupation of making the acquaintance of their future lover by conjuration.

'In Lanarkshire,' relates a young informant, 'a girl wears a piece of ivy against her heart and repeats the rhyme:

> Ivy, ivy, I love you,
> In my bosom I put you.
> The first young man who speaks to me
> My future husband he shall be.

'I do not think,' she adds, 'that all people conform to this rule as it is rather risky.' The charm nevertheless appears to be popular, for it has also been found in use at Langholm in the Border Country, and has been collected from an infant class in Luncarty.

In the west country, reports our Bath correspondent, it is the custom, or anyway the hope, of young girls to count seven stars on seven successive nights, for following this, it is said, when they go to sleep on the seventh night they will dream of him whom they are to marry. In south Wales a similar but even more exacting belief is entertained, for Swansea girls

1. The reliability of this onomancy is easily demonstrated:

$$PETER\ \emptyset P\ell E\ = Marry$$
$$I\emptyset NA\ ARCHIBALD = Marry$$

Ceremony performed 2 September 1943.

assert that *nine* stars are to be counted on *nine* consecutive nights before the bridegroom is revealed.

In Swansea, also, it is said that if a girl runs round a holly tree seven times in one direction, and then seven times in the other direction, she will see her future husband in a dream.

Again, perhaps not believed in very seriously, but a common practice in the Millwall district of east London, girls look for ninety-nine policemen, then a postman, and then a bicycle. The next man they speak to after this, they declare, is the man whom they will marry. (According to our informant the working out of this prognostication goes on for days, a cumulative count being kept of the policemen.)

More old-fashioned, but nowise dying out, are the means of discovering a sweetheart's initial by apple-paring, ear-burning, and cotton thread.

If an apple is peeled in one continuous ribbon, without the skin breaking, and if the peel is then thrown over the left shoulder, it will fall, as every schoolgirl knows, in the initial of her future spouse.[1]

If a girl's left ear burns, which is the sign that her lover is thinking of her, and she does not know who he is, she can ask the first person she sees for a number, and counting through the alphabet learn the initial of her admirer.

If a piece of cotton is picked off a girl's dress and then wound round a finger, the number of times it goes round will likewise give the desired initial. (The same practice is also found among French children in the neighbourhood of Vichy.)

Some of the most frequently employed divinations are those with fruit stones, buttons, or beads, counted in the same manner as 'One I love', and here described by a Forfar schoolgirl:

'When you have prunes or something with stones in it at dinner, put the stones at the side of your plate and count them. As you are counting you find out what kind of man you are going to marry by saying,
 Tinker, tailor, soldier, sailor, rich man, poor man, beggar man, a thief, and whichever name you stop at you will marry.

---

1. Gay mockingly describes this spell in *The Shepherd's Week*, 1714, 'Thursday', ll. 91–4:

> I pare this pippin round and round again,
> My shepherd's name to flourish on the plain.
> I fling th' unbroken paring o'er my head
> Upon the grass a perfect L is read.

This and similar prognostics are, in the north country, powerfully employed at Hallowe'en, and the reader who has skipped our account of that festival is referred back to pp. 297–8.

After doing that you find out what you are going to be married in by saying,
  Silk, satin, muslin and raggs.
Then you know what kind of a house you are going to live in by saying,
  Big house, small house, pigsty and barn.'[1]

Lastly, much energy and calculation is devoted to skipping through the alphabet (the letter the skipper trips at being the significant initial), and since this mode of fact-finding has to be executed in public, it gives no small amusement to the onlookers who are ever ready to supply the names of well-known boys to suit the skipper and the initial arrived at.

The skipping formula usually begins either,

> Black currant, red currant, gooseberry jam,
> Tell me the name of your young man.
> A, B, C, D, ...

or,

> Rosy apple, lemon tart,
> Tell me the name of your sweetheart.
> A, B, C, D, ...

The performance then continues so that information about the young man's intentions and the wedding may be obtained; the following sequence being that used by an 11-year-old Portsmouth girl:

> Does he love me? Yes, no, yes, no ...
> Will he marry me? Yes, no, yes, no ...

If 'yes':

> When will he marry me? January, February, March ...
> What day will it be? Monday, Tuesday, Wednesday ...
> What shall I be married in? Silk, satin, cotton, rags.
> What colour will it be? White, blue, pink, yellow.

1. In 1823, 120 years before the Forfar girl was born, the delightful East Anglian, Edward Moor (who was at school in the 1770s) also described the procedure.
'We have a curious old *sortes fibularæ*, if such a phrase may be tolerated, by which the destiny of school-boys is fore-shadowed. On a first appearance with a new coat or waistcoat, a comrade predicts your fate by your buttons, thus:
Sowja, sailor, tinker, tailor, gentleman, apothecary, plow-boy, thief –
beginning at top, and touching a button, like dropping a bead at each epithet. That which applies to the lower button is your promised or threatened avocation in life. Another reading gives this course:
  Tinker, tailor, sowja, sailor, richman, poorman, plow-boy, poticarry, thief.
Young ladies gather similar results as to the station and character of their future husbands; by taking hold, in lack of buttons, of a bead of their own or school-fellow's necklace, touching and passing one onward to the end. The tallying of the last bead with the word, denotes that which "makes or mars them quite".' (*Suffolk Words*, 1823, pp. 377–8.)

How many bridesmaids? One, two, three, four . . .
How many page boys? One, two, three, four . . .
How many carriages? One, two, three, four . . .

Such formulas can be, and are, extended almost indefinitely, or until the school bell rings; and it is not considered extraordinary for a girl to devote from quarter to half an hour of hard skipping to working out her matrimonial prospects.

Telling Fortunes

The practice of telling fortunes is not of course confined to those who still have lengthy futures ahead of them; and the interest of the following five descriptions lies in their being child's-eye views of what are still primarily adult activities.

Playing-Cards. 'The way I tell fortunes is I have a pack of cards, and ask a person to take a card from the pack. If they have got Spades, it means hard work is coming. Diamonds means someone is going to give them some money. Clubs mean you are going to be ill. And Hearts mean good luck is coming.'

Girl, 11, Birmingham.

Palm Reading. 'I can read peoples hands and tell them how many children they'll have. It might not be true but it is fun. Sometimes I say to them "but there's a lot of water to flow under that bridge yet, and a lot of bottles to brake". I tell them by there thumbs first how long their life will be. Then I tell them who they will marry. Sometimes it can be true.'

Girl, 10, Hanley.

Tea Leaves. 'Fortune-telling by tea leaves is always popular. Leaves in the shape of a heart means future happiness. If there are dots round the side it means money. If two hearts appear there will be a marriage. Leaves in the shape of a letter means good news is coming. If a married person finds a shape of a flower it indicates that children will bring happiness. A sign of roads means happy days ahead. A ring at the bottom of the cup means separation.'

Girl, 14, Aberdeen.

Intuition. 'My sister is now seven but when she grows up she will be very rich and she will marry a very rich man. The reason why is because I have a feeling that she is going to be very rich. The feeling is like knowing that it is going to happen as soon as she grows up.'

Girl, 11, Stoke-on-Trent.

Spirit Spelling. 'Among the many ways of foretelling the future is one game which seems to be almost supernatural. This game is called "Spooks", and you need twenty-six small squares of cardboard and a glass tumbler. On each of the squares of cardboard print a letter of the alphabet (a different letter on each square) and laying them face upwards in a circle, with about two inches between each square, on some smooth, level, shiny surface, such as the top of a highly polished table, place the glass tumbler upsidedown in the centre. Next placing the forefinger of your left hand very lightly on the top of the tumbler, ask a question about your future. When playing this game it is essential that you must not guide the tumbler in any way, either by blowing or pushing. After the question has been asked the tumbler will very slowly move from letter to letter forming the answer to your question.'

Girl, 14, Forfar.

Further, there are three ways of telling fortunes which appear to be exclusive to the young.

Tape Measures. Shops have begun again to stock tape measures, for juvenile amusement, which have inches marked on one side, and proverbs and prophecies on the reverse, for example: 'You are born under a lucky star', 'At new moon time good news', 'Whoever rests rusts', and 'You will have children galore'. A person's head or chest or waist is measured, and the motto on the other side of the tape, corresponding to the measurement, is the one that applies.

Knife Spinning. An ordinary table knife is set spinning when there are a number of people present, usually at school dinner, and questions are asked, the most usual being: 'Which of us will be married first?' The answer is the person at whom the blade points when the knife stops spinning. (This popular diversion has been indulged in by anyway the past two or three generations. A reference to it appears in S. O. Addy's *Household Tales*, 1895, p. 82.)

Film Star Oracle. This fortune-telling device, illustrated on p. 366, of which specimens have been received from Cheshire, Derbyshire, Glamorgan, Hampshire, Lincolnshire, London, and Kent (where it is known as a 'saltcellar'), appears to be peculiar to children. Indeed it is easier for juvenile hands to operate than grown-up.

A sheet of clean paper about 7 inches square (usually torn from an exercise book) is folded diagonally both ways to mark the centre, and flattened out again. Each corner is then folded into the centre, and the whole paper is then turned over and laid on its face, and the four new corners are folded into the centre to make a $3\frac{1}{2}$-inch square. The paper is next turned face uppermost again, and the names of four or more film stars are inscribed across each of the four squares which have been made, while the name of a flower is written in each of the eight triangles which have been formed on the back of the oracle. It is then opened out by lifting up each of the four flaps, and eight predictions (such as those shown in the diagram) are written in each of the triangles corresponding to the names of the flowers written on the other side. The corners are then folded back again

to the centre. Next the paper is folded in half, and in half again, to make a
1¾-inch square. This is then slightly opened out with the points held
uppermost, and the first finger and thumb of each hand are inserted in the
pockets, under the flaps which bear the film stars' names, and the fingers
are brought together.

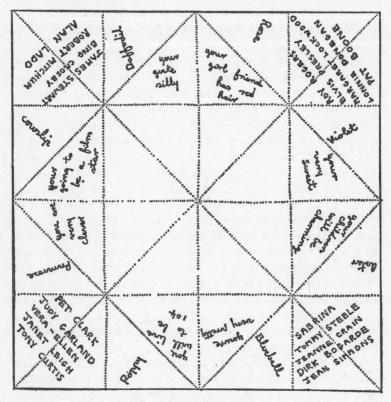

Film Star Oracle (unfolded).

The device is now ready to operate and is shown to somebody with the
invitation to choose one of the film stars inscribed on it. The operator spells
out the chosen star's name, and the device is opened and shut in an
alternate direction at each letter, stopping open at the last letter. The person who is having his fortune told is now presented with the four flower
names which have become visible, and has to choose one. The same opening and shutting takes place while the flower name is spelt. The person is

then presented with a second choice of flowers (which may, or may not, be the same four flowers as the first time), and this time the operator lifts up the flap bearing the name of the chosen flower, and reads out the inscription directly underneath. When operated by an expert the oracle can be worked with the fingers of just one hand, and the rapid opening and closing of the apparatus, first one way and then the other, can give the appearance of something marvellously like magic.

ALTHOUGH adult factions may have made peace with each other, their children on the way to school may continue sniping at each other for generations; and some of the battles of long ago are still being fought, verbally and otherwise, by children nurtured in the security of a Welfare State. In Liverpool, in Dundee, and in the heart of Glasgow, youngsters whose schoolroom attitude to history is apathetic, suddenly relive it in the streets, each July, when Orange boy and girl fall upon Catholic, and strangers are challenged, 'Are you Scots or Irish?'[1] In the green county of Kent, the Black Country around Birmingham, and in several other parts of Britain (see map, p. 287), bare legs are thrashed with stinging nettles on the twenty-ninth of May in recollection of Charles II taking refuge in an oak tree. And in Scotland children commonly show old contempt (and perhaps fear) of the Highlander, by jeering, when they see a kilt:

> Kiltie, Kiltie cauld doup (or 'dock' or 'bum'),
> Canna keep a warm doup.

Even if there was no evidence, one could be certain that street boys have always been actively partisan; and records show that in the past children's sympathies have been engaged not only in local rivalries, but in affairs of State. Thus Thomas Rugge, in his *Diurnal* for May 1660, records: 'The Rump Parliament was so hated and jeered at, that the butchers' boys would say, Will you buy any Parliament rumps and kidneys? And it was

---

1. This warfare extends to the other side of the world. In Melbourne and Sydney children used to gather round convent schools, and perhaps still do, on the anniversary of the Battle of the Boyne, chanting:

> The Irishmen ran down the hill,
> The Englishmen ran afther,
> And mony a Pat got a bullet in his back
> At the Battle of the Boy'an Wather.

> Up to me knees in shandygaff,
> Up to me knees in slauther,
> Up to me knees in Irish blood
> At the Battle of the Boy'an Wather.

a very ordinary thing to see little children make a fire in the streets, and burn rumps.' Two centuries later the village boys of Harrow-on-the-Hill, in unwitting memorial of this contention, were still shouting on the fifth of November:

> A stick and a stump
> For old Oliver's Rump.[1]

Sectarian Rhymes

In the present century sectarian oppugnancy is probably less evident amongst children in England than it is in countries such as the United States, Australia, South Africa, and Ireland, where the different communities are less assimilated. Our information here is not extensive, for it was not thought desirable to ask about sectarian matters in schools, but, for the record, in Lancashire Roman Catholics are known as 'Micks', and in Dundee as 'Left-footers'. In Glasgow a Catholic is 'Dan' and a Protestant 'Billy'. In Ireland, both north and south, Catholics are 'Cathies' and Protestants 'Proddy-woddys'. In Staines Catholics are 'Roman Candles', and R.C. children call the Protestants 'Old Proddy Dogs', or did so until very recently. They still call them 'Proddy Dogs' at Ilford, in Essex, and the 'Dogs' retaliate by dubbing the Catholics 'Cathy Cats'. This recalls the cry Flora Thompson's companions, at Fringford in north-east Oxfordshire, used to shout on their way to Sunday school, 'Old Catholics! Old lick the cats!' when they saw a horse and trap going to church in the other direction.

In Broken Hill, Northern Rhodesia, during the time of the Federation, the two schools that attracted each other's attention, inevitably, were the 'Government' School and the 'Convent'. Convent children would chant:

> Convent, Convent, ring the bell,
> Government, Government, go to hell.

This ditty is variable. In the 'Old Line State' of Maryland it is the Protestants who shout:

> Catholic, Catholic, ring the bell,
> When you die you'll go to hell.

1. *Notes and Queries*, 8th ser., vol. v, 1894, p. 55.

In mid-nineteenth-century England, November the Fifth celebrations still retained a distinctly partisan flavour; and to this day in Lewes, where seventeen Protestants were burnt alive in Queen Mary's time, four Bonfire Societies (adult) vie with each other in ensuring that the anniversary is not forgotten.

The Catholics reply with the charitable couplet:

> Protestant, Protestant, quack, quack, quack,
> Go to the devil and never come back.

It may be noted that sixty or seventy years ago both these cries were familiar currency in the streets of Victorian England.[1] In New South Wales they still have one of these verses, the Catholics shouting:

> Publics, Publics, go to hell
> While the Catholics pull the bell,

to which the Public School children respond in no uncertain manner:

> The Catholic brats, they don't like cats,
> They don't eat meat on Friday.

Similarly in New Zealand, in the 1920s, Protestant children would tease,

> Catholic dogs jump like frogs
> Don't eat meat on Fridays,

to which the rather lame reply was,

> Protestant dogs jump like frogs
> Do eat meat on Fridays.

In northern Ireland the Protestant children sing, or used to sing:

> Splitter splatter, holy watter,
> Sprinkle it where'er you can.

The Catholic children declare:

> The Pope he is a gentleman,
> He wears a watch and chain;
> King Billy is a beggarman
> And lives in dirty lane.

This, in turn, is roundly contradicted:

> *King Billy* is a gentleman,
> *He* wears a watch and chain;
> The Pope *he* is a beggarman
> And lives in dirty lane.

In Scotland Episcopalians come in for

> Pisky, Pisky, say 'Amen',
> Doon on yer knees (or 'hunkers') and up again,

1. See *Notes and Queries*, 7th ser., vol. xii, 1891, p. 367; and G. F. Northall, *English Folk Rhymes*, 1892, p. 312.

to which the response used to be:

> Presby, Presby, canna bend,
> Sit ye doon on man's chief end.

And in America, when there is a Quaker meeting, the facetious sometimes chant:

> Quaker meeting has begun,
> No more laughing, no more talking,
> No more chewing chewing gum.

In London, Jewish kids have long been harried by urchins running round them and shouting:

> Get a bit of pork,
> Stick it on a fork,
> And give it to a Jew boy, Jew.

This jeer which was current in 1875 and in 1914 (according to correspondents), probably runs back a further century, for Leigh Hunt, who went to Christ's Hospital in 1792, recalls in his *Autobiography* that there was a rhyme about pork upon a fork, concerning the Jews, chanted in his day. The Jewish child's traditional retaliation (London, 1892, and Eastbourne, *c.* 1914) was:

> Get a bit of beef,
> Stick it on a leaf,
> And give it to a Christian thief.

Today, children colloquially refer to a Jew as a Yid, Shylock, or Hooknose, and repeat the *jeu d'esprit*:

> Said Aaron to Moses,
> All Jews have long noses;
> Said Moses to Aaron,
> Not all, you've a square 'un.

This jingle may be compared with the tavern song, which was printed in *Vinculum Societatis, or the Tie of good Company*, 1688:

> Aron thus propos'd to Moses come let
>   us fuddle, fuddle our Noses:
> Moses reply'd again to Aron,
> 'Twill do us more harm than you are aware on.

371

Salvation Army

It is inevitable that the Salvation Army, often the sole attraction on the deserted Sunday streets, should come in for comment. It is possible, too, that some of the jeers at the Salvationists 'so free from sin' have an adult origin, for in its time the Army has had many opponents and many battles to fight. As an elementary schoolgirl wrote in Victorian days: 'The Army men and women is laught and whissled at by gentlemen standing at their doors and winders. My father says he is shamed to be called an Inglishman when he sees how the Salvation is knocked about and prossecuted. He says people will hold a drunken man up, but will knock a Salvation down. Mother says the polece is as bad as the uthers, cause they pitend not to see anythink of it.'[1] Few children in the English-speaking world do not know that:

> The Salvation Army, free from sin,
> Went to heaven in a cornbeef tin.

Some children say that the mode of conveyance was a 'sardine tin'; and in New Zealand children assert that they travelled in that important item of antipodean civilization, the kerosene tin. In Durham the youngsters cry:

> Salvation Army are a greedy lot.
> All go to heaven in an old jam pot.

In north Wales they are of the opinion that the 'Salvation Army all gone barmy' were unsuccessful in their attempt:

> The cornbeef tin it was too small,
> So Salvation Army couldn't go at all.

But the malice has gone; only the rhymes linger on as testimony of the Army's early struggle.

Boys' Brigade and Boy Scouts

Boys who band themselves together, who wear special uniforms, and who march along the street, cannot hope not to attract attention, and should not be surprised if this attention is derisive. At other times they sit in ordinary clothes in the same classroom. 'Ha, Jim, so you've joined the Brigade!

1. *Longman's Magazine*, February 1889, p. 407. The essay was written at some earlier date unspecified.

Afraid of getting your own clothes wet, are you?' Today, as half a century ago, the Brigade has to put up with other words to its special march.

> Here comes the Boys' Brigade
> All covered with marmalade,
> A tuppenny ha'penny pill-box,
> And a half a yard of braid.
>
> *Norwich, c. 1907. Eastbourne c. 1914.*

> Here comes the Boys' Brigade,
> All smothered in marmalade,
> The marmalade is mouldy,
> So is the Boys' Brigade.
>
> *Croydon, 1952. Peterborough, 1956.*

Likewise the Boy Scouts. Leslie Paul remembers, before the First World War, a mob of spitting youths around Aldgate jeering:

> Here come the Brussel Sprouts,
> The stinking, blinking louts.

That was in the days when a troop of boys with bare knees was a novelty.[1] Now, Scouts are a commonplace, but they are still known as 'Brussel Sprouts', and the kerbside spectators sing:

> Here come the *Claygate* Scouts,
> The dirty lot of louts,
> With tuppenny ha'penny broomsticks,
> Here come the *Claygate* Scouts.
>
> *Croydon, 1952.*

The Scouts, of course, are fully capable of looking after themselves. A Scout yell from Denton, Manchester, goes:

> Denton is the place for men,
> Always cheerful, always willing,
> Murder your mother-in-law for a shilling.
> DENTON! Hurrah!

Elections

Undoubtedly schoolchildren were more actively employed in nineteenth-century parliamentary elections than they are today. In the thin backstreets of the cities kids still hang around the beflagged committee rooms, but the most that is likely to be suggested to them is that after dark they tear down

1. Leslie Paul, *Angry Young Man*, 1951, p. 51.

a rival's posters. Election time which used to be, and still is in the United States, a period of high spirits as well as high words, is now dominated by the family television set. 'I remember how in the old days,' recalled Sir Anthony Eden in 1955, 'the boys used to go round singing in chorus:

> Vote, vote, vote for So-and-so;
> Punch old So-and-so in the eye;
> When he comes to the door,
> We will knock him on the floor,
> And he won't come a-voting any more!'

The children do still know this song, which is sung to the tune 'Tramp, tramp, tramp, the boys are marching', and was a favourite at elections as long ago as 1880, but today the words are more often heard in the playground than at the hustings. When the veteran Conservative candidate Tom Howard sought to revive the song at the West Islington by-election in August 1947, issuing a leaflet 'Special for girls and boys of Islington':

> Vote, vote, vote for Tommy Howard,
> Throw all the others on the floor;
> For Tommy is our man,
> We'll have him if we can,
> And we won't have the others any more. Oh lor!

he was slated for it by members of his own party. The *Evening Standard*, supposedly supporting him, came out with a feature deploring the childishness of the man. 'The Conservative Central Office will not be alone in echoing the last two words of that ditty with deep feeling.'[1] The days when a political squib could hound a government out of office appear to be over. The only juvenile verse caught in our net after the 1951 General Election was from Kirkcaldy:

> If you vote for Hubbard
> You'll have an empty cupboard.

Mr T. F. Hubbard was, nevertheless, returned with an increased majority.

Such verses are far more prevalent in the United States, the home of the campaign song, the following being among a number collected by Dr Howard:

One, two, three, four,	Roosevelt in the White House
Who are we for?	Talking to the ladies;
Roosevelt, Roosevelt,	Landon in the back yard
Rah, rah, rah.	Washing nigger babies.
Long Island, N.Y., 1936.	*New Jersey, 1936 Presidential election.*

1. *Evening Standard*, 27 August 1947, p. 6. The youthful reporter clearly believed that this 'remarkable spate of lyricism' had been concocted by Mr Howard himself.

Fried cats
And stewed rats
Are good enough
For the Democrats,

Maryland, 1940.

Roosevelt in the White House
Waiting to be elected;
Willkie in the garbage can
Waiting to be collected.

*Maryland, 1940 Presidential
election.*

Two of these rhymes may be compared with the Oxford and Cambridge
Boat-Race rhymes hereunder.

Sport

Perhaps interest in sport has taken the place of political partisanship, for it
is the spectator games which now produce a roar of songs, chants, and
slogans. Until the last war the event which most excited children's loyalties
was the Boat Race. Girls who had never seen the race, and were never
likely to, living a hundred miles away or more, yet made favours out of
twists of wool, little dark-blue or light-blue figures with eyes and mouths
carefully embroidered on the miniature heads. The boys spent their coppers on rosettes, or shiny tin buttons with the portrait of a man wearing a
cap of the chosen colour, or, most esteemed, little crossed oars of tin, their
glistening blades dipped in dark or light blue paint. From the beginning of
the century the race was a personal matter to the veriest gutter-snipe, and
there was something deep in a child's being about his love for the shade he
favoured, his contempt for the shade which opposed him. He defied the
cry of '*dirty* Oxford' with the cry '*dirty* Cambridge' and chanted:

Oxford the winner!
Cambridge the sinner!
Put them in a match-box
And throw them in the river.

Cambridge upstairs
Putting on their braces;
Oxford downstairs
Winning all the races.

Oxford upstairs
Eating bread and butter;
Cambridge downstairs
Playing in the gutter.

These rhymes, which are of course reversible, are still known and repeated; but the mid-century schoolchild's sporting enthusiasms are more
taken up with league football, ice hockey, and speedway matches. The girls
knit scarves, fishman caps, and even jerseys, both for themselves and for
their boy friends, in their team's colours. The boys collect portraits of
their champions printed on the backs of cigarette cartons and cereal boxes,

or given as 'free gifts' in comics or bubblegum packets. At these events an accepted form of ritual chant is common to all parts of England, Scotland, and Wales. The supporters bellow in unison:

Two, four, six, eight,
Who do we appreciate?

The name of the side they are 'sticking up for' is then spelt out, followed by a grand howl of the team's name:

P–R–E–S–T–O–N – PRESTON!

The cheer is taken up with the same enthusiasm whether at Wembley dirt track (coached by a loudspeaker), at Madison Square Gardens, New York, when a group of naval ratings are rooting for a British boxer, or at a girls' inter-school net-ball match. Probably, however, juvenile spectators at school matches ring more changes for their teams than can any crowd made up of the general public, and the following variations have been noted:

One, two, three, four,
Who do you think we are shouting for?
I–N–T–A–C–K – Intack!

One, two, three, four,
Who do we all adore?
L–O–W–E–R–F–O–U–R–T–H–S –
      Lower Fourths!

One, two, three, four,
Who do we despise the more?
D–E–L–T–A – Deltas!

Two, four, six, eight,
Rival Team's got the tummy ache.

Three, five, six, seven,
Here's a team from glorious Devon,
E–X–E–T–E–R – Exeter!

Five, six, seven, eight,
We should win at this rate,
C–A–I–S–T–O–R – Caistor!

One, two, three, four,
What do you think we've come here for?
Just to see old *Collins* score,
One, two, three, four.

One, three, five, seven,
Who d'you think the best eleven?
S–U–F–F–O–L–K–S – Suffolks!

One, two, three, four,
Who are we for?
P–O–W–I–S – Powis!
Five, six, seven, eight,
Who do we hate?
G–O–R–D–O–N–S – Gordons!

One, two, three, four,
Chuck *Berkhamsted* out the door.
One, two, three, who are we?
We are *Dunstable*, can't you see?

Four, three, two, one,
Look at *Whitgift* on the run.

Some of the chants are almost lyrical in their enthusiasm. The following pair are in support of Raith Rovers in Fife:

The Rovers fur me,
The Rovers fur me,
If you're no in Rovers,
Ye'r nae use tae me.
The East Fife are braw,
The Rangers an a',
But the cocky wee Rovers
The pride o' them a'.[1]

Come away the Rovers,
Dinnae be afraid
To show the dirty Celtic
How the game is played.
When Penman gets the ball
And raggies thro' them a'
And scores another goal
for the Rovers.

The following three come respectively from Ruthin, Kirkcaldy, and Birmingham:

Who are we, don't you know?
    We are the Clwydions.
We run and we sing,
We play games to win,
    We are the Clwydions.

Come away the High School
    Do not be afraid,
Show the slow coach Moderns
    How the game is played.

Now then *Putnam's* rally round the goal stumps,
Ready, steady, pass the ball along,
Now then half-backs pass it to your forwards,
Forwards bang it in the net once more.

The two following are from the dirt track and ice rink:

Two, four, six, eight,
Sydney's at the starting gate.
Will he win, Yes or No?
Go on *Sydney* have a go.

Oh! Hockey for me,
Oh! Hockey for me,
If you're no a hockey-player
You're no use to me.

A further set of chants or slogans are those in support of house or team colours, when the match is between children in the same school. In the changing rooms before going on to the field an exuberance of rude verses may pass back and forth between the contestants.

Greens, greens,
Kidney beans.

Yellows, yellows,
Dirty fellows.

Blues, blues,
Always lose.

Reds, reds,
Wet their beds.

If a person is himself a Green he says 'Greens, greens, top of the teams'. If he is a Blue he says 'Blues, blues, never lose'. If a Yellow, 'Yellows,

1. Very popular in Scotland. It is an adaptation of Robert Wilson's song 'A Gordon for me' published in 1950.

yellows, fastest fellows'. If a Red, 'Reds, reds, clever heads'.[1] If he is in a Red team playing the Blues, he may chant:

> Red, red, the bonnie red,
>   The red that should be worn;
> Blue, blue, the dirty blue,
>   The blue that should be torn.

And thereafter the collocution may degenerate into such exchanges as, 'Horrid old red, I'll chop off your head', 'Horrid old blue, you've got the flu'', and similar puerilities.

After the match the side which has lost may temporarily be silenced, while the winning team exults in its achievement:

> One, two, three, four,
> Who put Holy Souls on the floor?
> A-C-O-C-K-S – Acocks!
>
> Two, four, six, eight,
> We won, you ain't.

> We won,
> Three – one.
>
> Roses are red,
> Violets are blue.
> *Lackham's* none,
> *St Stephen's* two.

The following chant, with suitable adjustment in the place-name, is heard all over London, sung by victorious teams of under-fifteens as they travel home from the match:

> Rolling down the Old Kent Road
> All the windows open wide,
> Hi-tiddly-i-ti eat brown bread
> Ever seen a donkey fall down dead?
> We're the PECKHAM boys!

Some of the triumphal or consolatory songs sung by teams and their supporters while going home by coach may be thought of as being the modern equivalents of the old folk ballads. The following is from a Welsh school:

> Oh Maggie dear, a pint of beer,
>   A Woodbine and a match,
> A tuppenny ha'penny hockey stick
>   To see the hockey match.
> The ball was in the centre,
>   The referee's whistle blew,
> Fatty passed to Skinny,
>   And Skinny knocked it through.

1. These, or similar slogans, are common to many schools; and Dr Brian Sutton-Smith reports that they are also current in New Zealand. 'Green, green, you're the best ever seen. Red, red, you don't go to bed. Yellow, yellow, you dirty fellow. Black and white, you dirty skite.' *Western Folklore*, vol. xii, no. 1, January 1953, p. 17.

Oh! where was the goalie
    When the ball went through the net?
Sitting on the goal-post
    With his togs around his neck,
Shouting, Play up, play up,
    We can dribble, we can pass,
We can kick the ball straight at them,
    We can lay them on the grass.
– We're the *Wandering Wanderers*!

This one is from Enfield:

My old man's a dustman
    And wears a dustman's hat,
He bought a penny ticket
    To see a football match.
The ball was in the centre
    And when the whistle blew,
Fatty in a temper
    Down the field he flew.
Fatty passed to Skinny,
    Skinny passed it back,
Fatty took a flying leap
    And knocked poor Skinny flat.
They put him on a stretcher,
    They put him in a bed,
They rubbed his belly with a lump of jelly,
    And this is what they said:
Rule Britannia, two tanners make a bob,
Three make eighteen pence and four two bob.

Village Rivalry

Hostility between villages has caused broken bones before now, and in remote districts the rivalry was sometimes such that the inhabitants of one village, especially the boys, would regard those living in an adjacent village as foreigners. A northcountryman writing towards the end of the Victorian era instances a great rivalry which existed between the boys of two Derbyshire villages, Dore and Totley, who used to revile each other, the Dore boys shouting:

Totley bugs, water-clogs,
Water-porridge and hardly that,

the Totley boys replying:

> Dore bugs, water-clogs,
> Eating out o' swill tubs,
> Up a ladder and down a wall,
> A penny loaf will serve you all.

The girls of the two hamlets, he says, were equally hostile to each other, 'and used a set of verses, too coarse to quote, in which they imputed gross unchastity to each other'.[1]

Today village rivalry, even between children, is certainly tamer; but it is worth noting that in the one place where we asked for local rhymes, Golspie, the boys promptly came forward with:

Golspie is a bonny place,	Helmsdale is a dirty place,
A bonny set of people,	A dirty set of people,
A lump of gold at every door,	Herring heads at every door,
And a church without a steeple.[2]	And a church without a steeple.
Brora is a bonny place,	Brora bats,
A bonny set of people,	Dornoch rats,
Herring guts at every door,	Helmsdale cats,
And a church without a steeple.	Golspie, bonny boys.

It would be interesting to know to what extent village and local rhymes are bandied about elsewhere. Geographical rivalry does still continue, very outspokenly as will be seen, but it now seems to be more between the schools in the different villages than between the villages themselves. The village communities which were already, before the war, losing their identity through the workers being obliged to travel outside their village for employment, are now having the last remnants of their pride torn from them as the village schools are closed, and even the five-year-olds are taken into the town to be educated.

School Rivalry

Pride of school shows itself in two ways: in cheers for the school to which a child belongs, which is laudable; and in denigration of schools to which

1. Sydney Oldall Addy, *Household Tales*, 1895, pp. 130–31.
2. It will be remembered that in Golspie we were following a questionnaire which had been prepared for schoolchildren there sixty years previously (see p. 7). The milk-and-water version of the rhyme collected then, in 1892, incorrectly stated that Golspie had 'White stones at every door, And a church *with* a steeple'.

others belong, which is not laudable, but is, perhaps, the logical outcome of fostering a child's pride in his own establishment. We are more concerned here with denigration than with self-approbation, interesting though *Alma Mater* songs can be. For instance, at Powis Junior Secondary School in Aberdeen, where most of the children had been brought together through slum clearance, and little feeling of homogeneity had been expected, the girls chanted, with a pride which turned out to be justified (1952):

> We are the Powis School girls,
> We are the Powis School girls,
> We know our manners
> And how to spend our tanners,
> We are respected wherever we go.
>
> As we go marching along
> All the windows open wide,
> We're not afraid of Hitler's tommy guns,
> We're not afraid of Mussolini's sons,
> We are the Powis School girls,
> We are the Powis School girls.

On the whole the vituperation shot off at rivals is of pretty small calibre. Primary school children are called 'Primary Pigs' or 'Primary Peasants', modern school children are 'Modern Monkeys'. Constant use is made of the nomenclature: bats, rats, dogs, and duffers. Terms like 'College Cabbages', 'County Cabbage Stalks', 'Craft School Clots', 'Convent Cats', and 'Secondary Silly Sops', are typical. Uninspired though this invective may be it is doubtless much the same as small students were employing in 1744 when they evoked the entreaty:

If thou meetest the Scholars of any other School, jeer not nor affront them, but show them love and respect, and quietly let them pass along.

In recent times the sharpest feeling has been between the grammar schools and the secondary moderns, that is, between those who have gained a scholarship and those who have not in the eleven-plus examination. From the Grammarians it produces such poetry as:

Central School dunces	Modern School hams
Sitting on the wall;	Cannot pass exams,
Grammar School scholars	Makers of mascots
Laughing at them all.	Pushers of prams.

In return the home-work toilers are called 'Grammar grubs', 'Grammar-bugs stinking slugs, dirty little humbugs' 'Grammar School Slops',

'Grammar School Spivs', 'Grammar School Sissies', 'Filthy twerps', 'Saps'. One 13-year-old Modern boy almost falls over his pen in his abuse: 'Gramer Swabs with heads like logs, with there nose so flat and eyes aslit the look so daft when the stand on a stick.'

At Caistor, in Lincolnshire, the Moderns would chant:

> Grammar fleas, mucky knees,
> Hang them out to dry.

The grammar school pupils, without great originality made reply:

> Modern bugs, mucky lugs,
> Hang them out to dry.

Chants are, indeed, frequently turned about so that they make ammunition for either side, and sometimes the same squib is found doing service all over Britain. A chant which enjoins respectfulness in its hearers has been found as follows:

> Springfield cissies,
> Westbourne rats,
> When you see White House
> Raise your hats.
>
> *Ipswich.*

> Craft School blockheads,
> Council School cats,
> When they see the Grammar School
> Always raise their hats.
>
> *Lydney.*

> High School bulldogs,
> Convent cats,
> When you see Hinderwell
> Raise your hats.
>
> *Scarborough.*

> Come Coronation bugs
> Cock up your lugs
> While Cockton Hill laddies
> pass yer.
>
> *Bishop Auckland.*

> Bishop Blackall cats,
> When you come to our school
> Please raise your hats.
>
> *Exeter.*

> Ardwyn School rats,
> If you see Dinas School
> Please raise your hats.
>
> *Aberystwyth.*

Other chants advocate personal hygiene, 'Tech, Tech, wash your neck' (Lincoln), or isolation, 'County School snobs, County School dogs, Don't go near them' (Ruthin), or dwell upon the supposed pecuniary value, or lack of it, of their rivals:

> Grammarlogs, you dirty dogs,
> Tuppenny ha'penny goosygogs.

Or,

> Tom cats, penny rats,
> Two for tuppence ha'penny.

'We say this to St Thomas's when we are passing them,' says a Blackburn 10-year-old. Selhurst Grammar School boys warn their comrades 'Hold your noses, we're passing John Ruskin.'

> All the boys rotten and stinkin
> That do go to John Ruskin.

Purity of rhyme is not a strong point in these jeers. 'Grammar snobs, you dirty bogs' (Preston). 'Deacon Donkeys waddle wonkey' (Peterborough).

> Parkend is a rotten school,
> Bream is no better,
> Pillowell will beat the lot
> And throw them down the gutter.
> *West Dean.*

> Dinas School is no good,
> Chop it up for fire-wood,
> If they protest
> Call them a pest
> Dinas School is no good.
> *Aberystwyth.*

Sometimes nomenclature is inspired by a school's initials. S.F.S. of St Faith's School, Lincoln, is easily turned into 'Silly Fools' School'. M.F.S. of Milham Ford School, Headington, stands for either 'Mighty Fine Scholars' or 'Mouldy Fried Sausages' according to point of view.

Some names are puns. King Edward VI Grammar School, Southampton, is colloquially known as the Spud School. Mundella School in Nottingham is a challenge to the bards:

> Monkey-della, red and yellow,
> Can't afford an umbrella.

In Birmingham children at Acock's Green are known as 'Kidney beans', at Broad Road as 'Slimy toads', at English Martyrs as 'Squashed tomatoes', while the pupils at Holy Souls, another Roman Catholic school, are addressed:

> Holy Souls, sausage rolls,
> Put your heads in big round bowls.

At Sale, Manchester, the high school greet children of the primary school in Navigation Road:

> Navigation, Dictation,
> Three pigs in one basin.

In Forfar where the schools are 'North', 'South', 'East', and 'West', 'the Westies are pesties', 'Soothies are moosies', 'Northies are horsies', and 'Easties are the beasties'. Those attending the Academy are addressed:

> Academy kites, ye're no very nice,
> Ye bake yer bannocks wi' cats and mice.[1]

Sets of such names and calls exist in urban and rural districts alike. Thus in and around Portsmouth, according to a small feminine informant, Daley's School is known as 'Daley's Cow-shed', the Grammar School is the 'Glamour School' or 'School for Scandal', Kingston Modern is 'Kingston College for Clots', the High School is the 'Snob School' – those going there being 'High Snobs', while those going to Kentridge School are 'Kentridge Kids', and those going to the Southsea Modern are 'Southsea Scum'.

Similarly at Swansea. Boys attending Bishop Gore Grammar School are known as 'Grammar Goats', 'Grammar Grannies', or 'Grammar Grandpas'. Girls attending the High School for Girls are known as 'High School Snobs' – this despite the fact that the Education Committee has, for levelling purposes, rechristened the school Llyn-y Bryn Secondary Girls' School. Girls at Glanmor Girls' Secondary School refer to themselves as the 'Glanmor Glamour Girls', and have even been known to admirers as 'Glamour Buds', but are more often known as 'Glanmor Cow-sheds', which may be a reference to their wooden-hut type of building, but is more likely (since the term 'Cow-shed' occurs in other towns) to date back to the days when they were Glanmor Central School and had G.C.S. painted on the gate. And boys at Dynevor Boys' Secondary School, the remaining secondary school in the town (Swansea used to have six such schools, but two were destroyed in the blitz of 1941), have to put up with the jibes – Dynevor Dunces, Dynevor Dopes, and Dynevor Donkeys – for they are mostly boys who have failed to get into Bishop Gore – and they are taunted:

> Dynevor, Dynevor, dull as ever,
> Dynevor, Dynevor, stinks for ever.

1. Compare a Northumberland village rhyme of a hundred years ago:

> The Spittal wives are no' very nice,
> They bake their bread wi' bugs and lice:
> And after that they skin the cat,
> And put it into their kail-pat,
> That makes their broo' baith thick and fat.

M. A. Denham, *Folk-Lore of the Northern Counties*, 1858, p. 124.

In East Fife the verses are slightly more metrical. In and around Kirk-caldy children chant:

Dunnikier goats   Sinclairtown Susies
Can't eat oats.   Cannae tie their shoesies.

Bell-Baxter bugs   High Skael mugs
They're all thugs.   Cannae pu' the plugs.
                              They have to get the doctor
Viewforth hams   To punt them up.
Cannae pass exams.

High Skael mugs   Pathhead mugs
Cannae wash their lugs.   Have great big lugs.

They also have the verse, popular in other parts of Scotland, in northern England (Bishop Auckland), and in Dublin:

The West School's the best school,
It's made o' sticks an' plaister.
The only thing that's wrong with it
Is the baldy-headed maister.

Or as they say in self-deprecatory style in Aberdeen:

Our school's a rare school,
It's made o' stein and plaster.
The only thing I dinna like
Is the baldy-headed master.

At Welshpool, where a swarm of stinging names fly about, the senior Moderns call those at the County Grammar School: County Carrots, County Cats, County Cry-babies, County Custards, County Ducks or Quack-quacks, and Grammar Goofs or Grammar Grubs. The County children retaliate: Senior Sausages, Senior Senseless, Senior Slugs, Senior Snails, Modern Monkeys,

Modern Monkeys stuck in a pen
Can't get out for the County men.

Here, where bus-loads of youngsters come in from the surrounding villages to the central schools, village rivalry sticks out a juvenile tongue. Such calls are heard as: Arddleen Articles four a penny, Berriew Bleaters, Buttington Baa-lambs, Gungrog Golliwogs, Phenrôs Pups. And there is yet one more division between the children (a 12-year-old tells us), there is the division between those who leave the village each day and those who remain. Thus in the village of Forden the children call those who live in the village but who go to the grammar school in Welshpool 'County Cats', and those who go into Welshpool to the modern secondary school 'Senior Rats', 'and we,' she admits, 'call the Forden children who are left behind "Forden Frogs".'

THE teacher's lot, as every schoolboy knows, is an easy one:

> God made the bees,
>   The bees make honey;
> We do the work,
>   The teacher gets the money.

It is considered only right, if a teacher is uncongenial, to show disapproval. 'If a master has been beastly we put drawing pins on his chair, then we glue his books to the table, then we swing smelly sock in front of his nose by cotton looped through the window-catch and a boy operates the cotton.' Thus a 14-year-old, and a form-mate has written 'TRUE' beside the contribution; but the usual forms of retribution, pranks long prescribed by custom, tend to be safer for the perpetrators. There is the artful trick of 'filling the waste paper basket and fixing so that master knocks it over. Everybody scrambles to pick it up.' There is the old revenge of wetting the blackboard chalk. There is the room-evacuating stench produced when carbide is added to the ink; and the nice disruption caused by thistledown which mysteriously continues to fill the air after every window in the classroom has been shut. There is the ingenious but not always successful trick of throwing scraps of wet blotting-paper on to the ceiling, above where the teacher is to sit, in the hope that they will descend when class is in progress. There is the perpetual buzzing of a bluebottle which nobody can find because its match-box cage is pocketed when the teacher comes near. And there are the flies, delicately harnessed – in a secret manner handed down from one generation to the next – which circle round the classroom trailing insubstantial lengths of black cotton across the line of vision. Tradition (many teachers may feel) could be more discriminating in the skills it chooses to perpetuate.

Types of Teachers

A master who cannot be firm, as poor Mr Mell knew, can expect little compassion from his charges. 'Boys started in and out of their places, playing at puss-in-the-corner with other boys; there were laughing boys, singing boys, talking boys, dancing boys, howling boys; boys shuffled with their feet, boys whirled about him, grinning, making faces, mimicking him behind his back and before his eyes, mimicking his poverty, his boots, his coat, his mother, everything belonging to him that they should have had consideration for.

' "Silence!" cried Mr Mell, suddenly rising up, and striking his desk with the book. "What does this mean? It is impossible to bear it. It's maddening. How can you do it to me, boys?" '

But the boys with David Copperfield at Salem House were hardly more cruel than those over a century later who, noticing a particular habit of a master with a cockney accent, could chant in audible tones:

> Monday dinner time is very hi'sty
> But snot and salt pi'sties are very ti'sty.

Certain nicknames seem to be semi-traditional. The gardening master is commonly 'Spuds', the wood-work teacher is 'Chips', the gym teacher exposes himself to being called 'Hairy', and the divinity master is 'Holy Joe'. An 'Ikabod' is a really boring master (Manchester), a 'Boo teacher' is one who shouts and is strict (London, S.E.). The headmaster may be known as 'The Gaffer', 'The Guv'nor', or 'The Boss'; and, writes a 13-year-old boy: 'Our English teacher is very strong. Is Nick-kname is Sparky. Becase when he's caning The sparks do fly in the millions.'

Drawing masters, of course, are notoriously easy to torment. 'In Mr Trotter's drawing class,' wrote Dylan Thomas (*Portrait of the Artist as a Young Dog*, 1940), 'we drew naked girls inaccurately on sheets of paper under our drawings of a vase and passed them along under the desks. Some of the drawings were detailed strangely, others were tailed off like mermaids. Gilbert Rees drew the vase only.

"Sleep with your wife, sir?"

"What did you say?"

"Lend me your knife, sir?"

... Everybody liked the drawing class, except Mr Trotter.'

Songs About Teachers

There can be few teachers so respected (or so ignored) that they have not, at some time, been the subject of a little song, such as:

> Miss *Jonesy* bent to pick a rose,
> A rose so sweet and slender;
> Alas! Alack! She bent too far
> And bang went her suspender.

Or this, which is even more futile:

> Pounds, shillings, pence,
> Teacher has no sense,
> She came to school
> To act the fool,
> Pounds, shillings, pence.

The teacher can, however, rest assured that no matter how personal the lyric may appear, he or she is unlikely to be the original of its sentiments. Not a hundred miles from where we live there is a master who, on account of a prominent feature, is familiarly known as 'Barney Boko'. Of him the children sing:

> Barney Boko broke his nose,
> Without feet we can't have toes.

And in so doing, the children could claim they are merely singing a snatch of song popular in the days of the Prince Regent.[1] The probability is that any verse of this nature, in which the lines are worn smooth, is one which has been causing tutorial ears to tingle for a generation at least; and very probably it is known in a variety of forms. Thus the irreverent north London verse,

> Mr MacDonald is a good man,
> He goes to church on Sunday.
> He prays to God to give him strength
> To whip the boys on Monday,

[1]. The original words were:

> Barney Bodkin broke his nose,
> Want of money makes us sad,
> Without feet we can't have toes,
> Crazy folks are always mad.

The song was sung by Henry Johnston, and published 2 September 1811.

is also known as 'Mr Bewley is a very good man' (Bishop Auckland), 'Mr Adam is a very good man' (Kirkcaldy), 'Rhys Nicholas is a mighty man' (Carmarthen), 'Old Bruno is a good old soul' (Portsmouth), 'Miss Casson is a holy dame' (Dunfermline), 'Old Ma Baynes, she gives us pains '(St Mary Cray), and as 'Old Cock Nick, she makes us sick' (Blackpool). This is not to mention versions with anonymous or non-specific heroes, such as 'Our teacher is a nice old gel' (Market Rasen). And people with long memories declare that the song has been haunting school corridors and playgrounds since the nineteen-twenties.[1]

The following verse is even older and belongs to the eighteenth century, a fact which seems to show that modern children have a taste for the antiquarian, for the verse is one of the most popular anti-teacher rhymes of the present day (received from sixteen schools):

> Mr *Grainger* is a very good man
> He tries to teach us all he can:
> Reading, writing, arithmetic,
> And he doesn't forget to use the stick.
> When he does he makes us dance
> Out of England into France,
> Out of France into Spain,
> Over the hills and back again.[2]

There are, too, several rhymes which children commonly aim at each other, which, on occasion, they do not hesitate to level at larger game. 'Oh Judy, you're a funny 'un' (p. 191) sung to the tune 'The Ash Grove', becomes 'My teacher's got a bunion'. 'Doh, ray, me, fa, me' leads into 'Our teacher's barmy, she joined the army to get some grub'. In north Staffordshire an old game verse is adapted so that it sings:

> Down in the valley where the green grass grows
> There stands *Miss Hutchison* all on her own.
> She grows, she grows, she grows so sweet,
> The worst of it all, she's got sweaty feet.

1. Incidentally, Mr Bewley 'whacks the kids' and the others, respectively, 'belt' them, 'beat' them, 'cane' them, 'wallop' them, 'row' them, and 'whip' them.
2. A version appeared in *Infant Amusements*, 1797, song no. 11:

> Doctor Faustus was a good man,
> He whipt his scholars now and then.
> And when he whipt 'em made 'em dance,
> Out of Scotland into France,
> From France he whipt 'em into Spain,
> And then he whipt 'em back again.

The hoary scatological song concerning the Bishop of Winchester's daughter is easily adjusted to apply to a science mistress:

> Oh dear, what can the matter be?
> Old *Miss Proctor*'s locked in the laboratory
> She'll be there from Monday to Saturday.
> Nobody cares that she's there.

In Cumberland a one-time song hit has become:

> Put another nickel in
>   In old *Bodger*'s treacle tin,
> When he plays his violin
>   It's murder, murder, murder.

And in Kirkcaldy they sing to the well-known hymn tune:

> There is a happy land by the 'Red School'
> Where Miss *Macdonald* stands, preaching like a fool.
> Long legs and skinny jaws,
> She can fairly use the tawse
> On the wee bit bairnies' paws,
> Three times a day.

Even these senseless parodies may have general circulation. The following corruption of Mrs Heman's epic, involving three teachers at once, is thought sufficiently funny to be in vogue in several schools in north Wales, and has also been found in Lincolnshire:

> *Bella* stood on the burning deck,
>   *Miss Trix* blew the hooter,
> Who do you think came round the bend
>   But *Smithy* on her scooter.

The following is muttered under the breath during class:

> Sir is kind and sir is gentle,
> Sir is strong and sir is mental.

At a school near Doncaster children prick a drawing of an unpopular teacher with pins, threatening:

> Teacher, teacher, I don't like you,
> If you don't mark my sums right
> – I shall spike you.

And just as soldiers in barracks keep up their spirits by singing about the incompetence of their superiors, so schoolboys apparently find relief in thinking that their preceptors are unsuited for the positions they hold. In a famous grammar school they chorus:

> The *X.Y.Z.* is a wonderful place,
> The organization's a shocking disgrace.
> There's *Snowy*, and *Boco*, and *Dit Thomas* too,
> With their hands in their pockets and nothing to do.
> They stand on the field and they rave and they shout
> On subjects they know sweet nothing about;
> For all that I learn here I might as well be
> Where the mountains of Mourne sweep down to the sea.

Teachers' Jokes

Despite the eagerness of some of our junior contributors to make this section a lengthy one, we must agree with their mentors that anything like an extensive catalogue of the facetiae, however traditional it may be, which is sometimes allowed to emanate from the desk in front, is neither fair game nor within the scope of this inquiry. Nevertheless it cannot be denied that pedagogic wit may itself be one of the sources of the juvenile vernacular. 'Put your head in a bucket of water three times and pull it out twice', 'Take a running jump at yourself', 'Hi, you with a face, I'll introduce my bootmaker to your tailor', have the tortuous humour of donnish minds long exasperated by having to contend with lesser geniuses.

'Sir, my nib scratches.'

Pedagogue: 'Perhaps it's got an itch.'

'Sir, I can't think . . .'

Pedagogue: 'Stop scratching your head, boy, aren't you afraid of splinters?'

'Sir, can I go and fetch my book?'

Pedagogue: 'I don't know. How are your legs today?' 'Are you able to walk?' etc., etc.

Such shafts have always had a place in even the sternest teacher's armoury, and the rust on them is almost part of their humour: a teacher's joke is to be laughed at not because it is a funny joke but because it is a joke made by a teacher.

> Full well they laugh'd, with counterfeited glee,
> At all his jokes, for many a joke had he.

Latecomers

To everyone but the teacher, he who arrives behind time causes a welcome diversion. 'Ah! Here comes lightning!' 'Come on Christmas!' 'The Prodigal Son has returned at last.' 'Here comes the late Mr —.' 'Better late than never!' 'Better late than never, but better never late!' 'You're a budding late bird.' 'Well rolled up.' 'You're early, what kept you?' 'You want to wake up in the morning.' 'You'll be late for your own funeral.' 'You're too slow to catch a cold.'

He is a – Creepy crawler, Cow's tail ('You're like a cow's tail, always behind'), Dilly-day-dream, Guard's van, Idleback, Lardy, Lazy bird, Lazy bones, Lost Lawrence, Sleepy eyes, Sleepy head, Slowcoach, Slugabed,[1] Snail.

There are, as there have been for centuries, special chants to greet him:

You're late, you're late,
Your dinner's on the plate.
Ipswich.

Or, facetiously:
You're early, you're early,
Your hair's growing curly.
Manchester.

Sleepy head, sleepy head,
When do you get out of bed?
Kirkcaldy.

You're late, you're late,
The bobby's at the gate,
He won't let you in
Till half past eight.
Bootle, Liverpool.

A dillar, a dollar,
A ten o'clock scholar,
What makes you come so soon?
You used to come at ten o'clock
But now you come at noon.
Etton, Yorkshire.[2]

'If he is bigger than me I don't say anything,' says one boy. And the latecomer himself nearly always says, 'Please, our clock stopped.'

Late Teachers

This section is shorter. 'We had an easy-going headmaster,' recalls a correspondent who lived in Airdrie, Lanarkshire, 'and there were long

1. Lowsley's *Berkshire Words*, 1888, has: 'Sluck-a-bed, sluck-a-bed, Barley Butt, Yer yead be zo heavy 'e can't get up.' This was recorded earlier, and in cruder form, in *Tommy Thumb's Pretty Song Book*, vol. ii, 1744, p. 34. In Ray's *Proverbs*, 1670, appears a jeer: 'The sluggard's guise, loath to go to bed and loath to rise.'
2. William Howitt (b. 1792) records that this 'wise rhyme

> A miller, a mollar,
> A ten o'clock scholar'

was used to welcome latecomers when he was a boy attending a school, which, as it happens, was not very far from Etton where this rebuke is still employed.

times of waiting before the door was opened in the morning. I can still see some of the boys, noses red and fingers blue, one snowy morning kicking the door and chanting:

> Teacher, teacher, let me in,
> My feet's cauld, my shoes are din [done].
> If ye winna let me in,
> I'll no come back in the efternin.'

In the long ago the lines appear to have been strangely well known in Lanarkshire. In fact, the children there still know them today. But now, perhaps, it is only in their games that they recite:

> Teacher, teacher, let me in,
> My feet's cauld and my shaen's din
> If ye dinna let me in
> I'll knock yer windae ootside in.

Time to Go Home?

Country children out playing, and wondering whether it is time to go home, either count round the prickles of a holly leaf, or blow at a head of dandelion seed, intoning:

> Does – my – mother – want – me?
> Yes – no – yes – no – yes . . .
>
> *Sheffield.*

This practice is less common than it was a generation ago, when it appears to have been known all over Britain (recordings from Angus, Glamorgan, Sussex, and West Lothian).

*** Compare the custom described by J. O. Halliwell, *Popular Rhymes*, 1849, p. 111, in which a schoolboy, to know whether or not it was time for class to end, held a book between his knees, and measured along its length with the breadth of one forefinger after another, repeating:

> It's time, I believe,
> For us to get leave:
> The little dog says
> It isn't, it is; it 'tisnt, it is, etc.

The last finger to have enough space to rest on the book provided the answer. Similarly, John Aubrey in his manuscript *Remaines*, 1686–7 (printed 1881, p. 25), recorded that German schoolboys 'when the School-master stayes longer, than he useth to doe, they take a book and open it in the midst, at some part after the beginning or most at end, and then they begin with the first leaf of the book to say, he comes, with the second the schoolmaster comes not, with the third leaf again he comes, till they come to the last leaf, where they first opened the book, and thereby they believe he will come, or not at all'.

The Police

No matter with what awe a boy may privately regard the police, his vocal attitude is one of amiable derision. In juvenile song the upholder of the law has the worst of every encounter. The 'friendly policeman passing by' is inevitably the one who receives something unmentionable in his eye. He falls, in one song, into the corporation muck cart, and cannot swim; he falls, in another song, over a fence, improbably bursting his belly on a lump of jelly; and, in juvenile mythology, even the benign King Wenceslas is said to have knocked a Bobby senseless 'right in the middle of Marks and Spencer's'.

'We have all sorts of taunts and jeers for policemen,' says a 12-year-old in Edinburgh's Royal Mile. 'We are playing at football in the street when the old flatfoot comes striding down the road. His name is P.C. Wallace but we call him old Walrus. When he has gone round the corner we call names such as slop, natter knob, or flatfeet.' There are, in the London area, at least thirty nicknames current among boys, and any lad of wit seems to be able to recite a string of them. They include: Bobby, Blueboy, Boy in Blue, Bluebottle, Bluejacket, Blue Lamp Boy, Beetle, Beetle-crusher, Beat Basher, Bogey, Brass Bonce, Busy Bee, Cop, Copper or Coppernob, Creeper, Crook Catcher, Dick, Fly, Flatfoot or Flatty Kipperfoot, The Law, Nark or Narker, Nobby, Pavement Pounder, Peeler, Robert, Rozzer or Bozzer, Slop, Snobber, and Trapper. The only name which shows a trace of apprehension is Bogey, and this is quickly turned to ridicule, a new policeman being known as a 'Ha'penny Bogey'. 'Copper', 'Rozzer', 'Bobby' (occasionally, as a joke, 'Bobby-soxer'), and, surprisingly, 'Bluebottle', seem to be the commonest names. 'Bluebottle', which goes back to Elizabethan times,[1] gets amplified to 'Overgrown Bluebottle' when they want to be particularly disparaging. 'Slop', a modification of *ecilop*, back-slang for *police*, is still heard quite often, and is used in places as far from London as Manchester, Scarborough, and

1. Doll Tearsheet in *Henry the Fourth, Part II* (v. iv), shouts at a beadle: 'I will have you as soundly swindg'd for this, you blewbottle Rogue.'

Bishop Auckland. The historic names 'Robert' and 'Peeler', after the founder of the present police system, are perhaps heard more in the provinces than in London.[1] In Penrith children still commonly use the old northern name 'Scufty' or 'Scufter', a term which had been thought to be obsolete. In Manchester the names 'Penny' and 'Shilling' are sometimes used as 'comic' alternatives to 'Copper'. The popular name for a police station is 'Cop-shop'.

The standard joke that the amount of walking a policeman has to do affects his feet (a joke embalmed in such names as 'Flatfoot' and 'Kipperfoot') continues to give amusement, and the familiar cockney jeer:

> There's a copper on his beat,
> You can smell his cheesy feet,
> There's a copper on his beat over there!

has its Transatlantic counterpart:

> All policemen have big feet
> Specially on *Forty-Second* Street.

Other verses declaimed in Britain's alleyways include:

> I went down the lane to buy a penny whistle,
> A copper took it off of me, and gimme a lump of gristle.
> I asked him for it back, he said he hadn't got it.
> You fibber-tee, you fibber-tee, you got it in your pocket.

And,

> I wish I were a Bobby
> Dressed up in Bobby's clothes,
> With a big tall hat,
> And a belly full of fat,
> And a pancake in front for a nose.

As well as in London, this last chant has been heard in Aberdeen ('With a great big tarry hat'), Edinburgh ('With a tin and silver hat'), Swansea ('With a high pole hat'), and in Liverpool with two additional verses:

> I saw one on the corner
> Eating Christmas pie,
> I asked him for a skinny bit,
> And he hit me in the eye.

> I went and told my mother,
> My mother wouldn't come,
> So I went and got the rolling pin
> And broke it on his bum.

1. The children who reported these names had no idea of their derivation.

The 'high pole hat' is almost evidence in itself of the rhyme's vintage, and in *Candleford Green* Flora Thompson confirms that this is no modern composition. 'Small boys had a catch which at that time [*c.* 1885] they shouted from behind hedges at a respectful distance after a policeman had passed them:

> There goes the bobby with his black shiny hat
> And his belly full of fat
> And a pancake tied to his nose,

a relic, it is supposed, from the days before policemen wore helmets.'

The idea that policemen manage nicely in their job, and live on the fat of the land, is not only old (going back almost to the inception of the force) but is recurring. The rhyme,

> No wonder, no wonder, the coppers are so fat,
> They go around the market and eat up all the fat,
> And what they can't eat they puts in their 'at.
> No wonder, no wonder, the coppers are so fat,

has been found in several London districts (1950–53), and it is also an East End childhood memory of the author Mark Benny ('Ragamuffin Rag' in *Home and Away*, 1948). 'It is not wise to be too direct' when provoking policemen, he writes. 'But what can they do if, when they pass, solemn infant voices chant a little verse?' And the voices are sometimes surprisingly youthful. The following, to the tune 'Daisy Bell', has been picked up from an 8-year-old in Shrewsbury, a 7-year-old in Warwick, and from a kindergarten in west Sussex:

> Daisy, Daisy, the coppers are after you,
> If they catch you they'll give you a month or two,
> They'll tie you up with wi-er
> Behind the Black Mari-er,
> So ring your bell
> And pedal like hell
> On a bicycle made for two.

Playing Truant

The most general term for truancy seems to be 'to play hookey' (an Americanism which became naturalized around 1900), although very often, particularly in the north, young ne'er-do-wells use the older phrases 'playing wag', 'playing the wag', 'hopping the wag', 'wagging school', or 'wagging it', speaking with the same tongue boys used in the time of Dickens.[1]

There are also a fair number of local terms:

Bobbing. The chief term used in Hanley and Stoke-on-Trent, Staffordshire, usually in the phrase 'bobbing school', occasionally 'playing bob'.

Fagging off. Oldham, Lancashire. Possibly a twist on the slang: 'to hag off' (i.e. to clear off regardless of consequences).

Fanagin. 'He's fanagin' (never '*playing* fanagin'). Bilston, nr. Wolverhampton.

Jigging. 'Jigging it', 'jigging school', the truant being a 'jigger'. Current in the area of Barrow-in-Furness, Ulverston, and Millom in south Cumberland. Formerly common in parts of Yorkshire.

Jouking. Langholm, Dumfriesshire, and occasionally in Glasgow. The truant is a 'jouker', i.e. 'one who dodges'. The word is not used exclusively for truancy.

Kipp. 'Playing the kipp', a common alternative in Kirkcaldy to 'playing the tick'. The truant is a 'kipper' or a 'ticker'.

Lag. 'Playing lag.' Ulverston, Low Furness.

Miching or *mitching.* The general term in south Wales, Monmouthshire, Devon, and Cornwall. Also 'to play mitch' (Aberystwyth); and D. Parry-Jones *Welsh Children's Games* has 'to mitsho'. The truant himself is a 'mitcher'; thus the work-shy unwittingly glosses Shakespeare: 'Shall the blessed Sonne of Heauen proue a Micher, and eate Black-berryes?' – *Henry the Fourth, Part I* (II. IV). In Devonshire children used to speak of a 'blackberry michard', the following rhyme being repeated at North Molton:

> Blackberry michard,
> Blueberry snail,
> All the dogs in the town
> Hang to thy tail.

– *Devonshire Provincialisms*, 1895. Today, in Torquay and Penzance the term is pronounced *minch* rather than *mitch*. As well as being current in the west country the term 'mitch' is also used in Dublin.

Nick. 'Playing nick' or 'playing the nick'. This term, which in 1898 the *English Dialect Dictionary* stated to be obsolescent, is now the prevailing expression in Scarborough, and throughout County Durham from Teesside to Tyneside, and in east Cumberland. In West Hartlepool it is sometimes expressed as 'nicking out'.

1. 'My misfortunes all began in wagging, Sir; but what could I do, exceptin' wag?' 'Excepting what?' said Mr Carker. 'Wag, Sir. Wagging from school.' 'Do you mean pretending to go there, and not going?' said Mr Carker. 'Yes, Sir, that's wagging, Sir. I was chivvied through the streets, Sir, when I went there, and pounded when I got there. So I wagged and hid myself, and that began it.' – *Dombey and Son*, 1848, xxii. Subsequently, through the baleful influence of a popular boys' 'blood' *Charley Wag* 'the New Jack Sheppard', issued in penny numbers in 1861, children began to speak of 'playing the Charley Wag'. In 1900 'Playing the Charley Wag' or 'Playing the Charley' was described as the commonest expression of London Board School children.

Plunking. Alternatively 'to plunk the school', and the stay-away is a 'plunker'. In use in Glasgow and western Scotland. A contributor to the *Yorkshire Post* (22 December 1956) heard that year in the Isle of Mull: 'Are ye plunkin' the day? The school holidays dinna start till tomorrow.'

Sagging. This is definitely the prevailing term amongst delinquents in all parts of Liverpool. A student, however, adds 'scowing' as a Liverpudlian expression.

Skiving. Term in use in parts of Cheshire, and Staffordshire as far south as Brownhills, nr. Walsall. A few children in Kirkcaldy give 'sciver' as a name for a truant.

Ticking. 'Ticking school' is reported from Workington in Cumberland. In Kirkcaldy children speak of 'playing the tick', see under *kipp* above.

Twagging. East Riding, especially around Hull and Beverley. A correspondent to the *Yorkshire Post* (3 January 1957), writing from Hessle, states: 'I have been a School Board Man, School Attendance Officer and now School Welfare Officer for 28 years (to say nothing of Kidcatcher) and have always known it as "twag" or "twagging it".'

A truant may also, of course, be referred to as a 'school skipper', 'attendance spoiler', 'excuser', 'dirty dodger', or as 'trashy', and be said to be 'skipping school', 'stopping off', 'scarpering', 'hopping it' (in Rochdale 'going on the hop'), 'bunking out of it', 'taking French leave', or, in Shropshire, 'taking dog's leave'.

Keeping Lookout

'If some boys are going to clime over a fence that is Private property we have a lookout that we call "dickey-eye",' writes an Enfield lad. And whether the mischief is something serious, or merely ragging while the teacher is out of the room, there appears to be, almost everywhere, a special term for keeping watch or for the one who keeps watch. In parts of Durham and the North Riding the lookout is said to be 'keeping nix'. In Dublin he is either 'keeping nix' or 'keeping nicko'. In Liverpool he is 'keeping dixie' or 'dousy'; in Camberwell sometimes 'keeping Kate'; and in parts of Derbyshire 'keeping conk'. In the Midlands, in an area stretching from Birmingham to Lancaster, taking in Bolton, Manchester, and Derby, the usual name for the lookout is 'weany'. The common name in Wolverhampton, however, is 'dog-on-the-run', and in Sheffield 'dog-out'. It seems that in some places a dialect term prevails, in other places a slang term. In Levenshulme they appoint a 'scatterer' (his cry being 'scatter'), in Salford a 'dodger', and in Ecclesfield a 'spy-eye' or 'watch-eye'. In Glasgow he goes under the hopeful name 'Johnnie See-all'. The sentinel may also, of course, be called a guard, spotter, scout, spy, stoodge, or, very commonly, a watch-dog. In Kirkcaldy watch-dog becomes either 'watchie' or 'dog'. And in London districts the look-out functions under the names 'ween-eye', 'dog-eye', 'dig-eye', 'rookie', and 'crow boy'.[1] The term 'keeping cave', common in school stories, and well known in private schools (said to have been first used about 1750 at Eton), only rarely extends to boys who do not possess any Latin.

On the approach of danger the lookout in a grammar school 'keeping cave' may call just 'Cave!' (pronounced *kave* or *kay-ve*), and the north-country child calls 'Nix!'[2] or he may add the name of the authority approaching: 'Cave Smithson!' 'Cave Dragon' 'Nix Police!' or he (or she) may say 'Temper's coming!' 'Lama's on the prowl!' and so on. Or, anywhere, the cry may be: 'Scram boys!' 'Scarper!' 'Scoot!' 'Skedaddle!' 'Skip!' 'Allez bazook!' 'Bunk!' 'Bolt!' 'Buzz!' 'Fizz!' 'Vamoose!' 'Pack it!' 'Hop it!' or 'Beat it!' In Penrith they cry 'Nash!' or 'Nash for it!'

A gang, out on its own, very often has a secret signal which it fondly believes to be original, and which usually turns out to be nothing more enterprising than an owl hoot, or a low whistle, or the loud exclamation 'It's a nice night!' Nevertheless some peculiar and apparently traditional terms do exist – amongst them: 'A.B.C.' standing for 'A Bobby Coming!' (Ballingry, Edinburgh, and Langholm), 'B.B.C.' meaning 'Bolt, Boys, Copper' (Wandsworth), 'L.O.B.' meaning 'Look Out, Boys' (Dublin), and 'R.L.C.C.' meaning 'Run, Lads, Coppers Coming!' (Liverpool). In Alton they say 'Itma!' (It's That Man Again) after the radio programme. In Newcastle, 'Locker, locker, here comes the Bobby knocker'. In Shropshire, Cheshire, and Lancashire a recognized warning seems to be 'Eck-eck' (one Manchester boy says 'Aye-aye', and one Croydon boy ''ight-'ight'). In Ipswich the curious cry is 'Cooked pies are hot'; and in mid-Wales, when children are in a garden 'scrumping', it is traditional to call quickly 'Pigs in the garden' or, in full, 'Pigs in the garden, flies on the wall'.

1. 'Crow boy', a Southwark term, is possibly interesting because a crow boy used to be one who kept watch over the crops to keep away the birds. It is, of course, possible that the present term stems from, or has been kept alive by, the crow's-nest on a ship, but the fact that the term 'rookie' is also current in Southwark may point to a rural origin.
2. 'In the midst of the confusion a sentry at the door suddenly put his head in and shouted "Nix!" The signal had a magical effect on all but the uninitiated Stephen.' (Talbot Baines Reed, *The Fifth Form at St Dominic's*, 1887, iv.)

Beatings

Glory, glory Alleluiah,
Teacher hit me with a ruler.

*'This is a peace that we say to John
Browns Body lyes a Moldring in the
Grave.' Girl, 11, Market Rasen.*

There is no need here to digress on the advantages or otherwise of using a 'cosh' in schools, since a very thorough survey of both juvenile and pedagogic opinion on corporal punishment has already been made. We append merely some technicalities outside the scope of that report.[1]

Jeering cries for one about to face trouble: 'You'll cop it', 'You'll get the stick', 'You've had it', 'You're for the high jump', and, in Sale (Manchester), 'A-a-ah! Right for you!' The miscreant receives what is variously termed a bashing, beating, belting, biffing, bimming, birching, braying (Yorkshire), caning, clouting, coshing, dunting, flogging, hiding (usually 'good hiding'), lamming, larruping (a term once favoured by a Lord Chief Justice), a leathering (or 'taste of the leather'), a licking, mangling, pasting, slashing, slapping, splattering, swishing, tanning (or 'has his hide tanned'), a tawsing (Scotland), thrashing, walloping, whacking (satisfying to say, and common), welting, and whipping. He may say that he has had 'a dose of strap oil', or, when asked 'How many did you get?' reply 'Six of the best' or 'Six swishers' or 'Six stingers'. A 'stinger' is a hard blow, and the other may challenge: 'Let's see the marks then.' Alternatively a boy may say that a blow was 'not a stinger', boasting 'it was only a tickle'.

The problem with padding is to find a substance which is sufficiently insulating and yet not liable to immediate detection. The most common suggestion given, 'put a book in your trousers', seems hopeful rather than practical. Tradition has it that rashers of lean bacon (seldom available when required) are efficacious. The following advice is also proffered when the behind is to be caned: (i) tighten muscles, (ii) keep trousers loose, (iii) shut eyes.

---

1. *A Survey of Rewards and Punishments in Schools*, a report by the National Foundation for Educational Research in England and Wales (1952). The deterrents most disliked by boys were found to be, in order of disapprobation: (i) Unfavourable report for home; (ii) deprivation of games or some favourite lesson; (iii) to be regarded as a person to be closely watched by the staff; and only (iv) to be given the cane or strap. Girls rated the cane or strap the most disliked deterrent other than an unfavourable report being sent to their home. Not mentioned was that amongst children one of the most common names for the cane is 'the cosh', and that this term has been is use in schools since the nineteenth century.

Hand caning presents a more difficult problem. There seems to be fairly general agreement that if the hand is quickly licked, spat upon, or in any other way thoroughly moistened before the operation, it will mitigate the pain. Other recommendations are: rub onion on hand (many give this),[1] cover hand with vaseline, rub soap on, rub with a leaf (afterwards?), stick a clove in your hand, warm your hand. Afterwards, press it against a cold wall.

Alternatively it is said to hurt less if the hand is stiffened, if the hand is sloped, if the middle finger is raised, if the miscreant stands under the electric light (to give less room for the cane?), if he brings his hand down with the cane, or if he moves his hand away! Indeed, almost anything seems to be thought better than having the hand where it is, and in the condition that it is at the moment when the cane descends.

And the legend persists, so attractive that it will never apparently be wholly discredited, that a hair from the head (some specify a strand of horse hair) laid upon the palm of the hand will split the master's cane, and possibly even hurt the master instead.

₊ This belief has been current talk amongst schoolboys for over a century. Accounts recalling boyhood experiences in the 1850s and 60s both in Britain and the United States appear in *Notes and Queries*, 11th ser., vol. xi, 1915, pp. 277–8 and 347. A later account, including moistening the hand, occurs in William Glynne-Jones's novel *Summer Long Ago*, 1954, pp. 15–17.

Northamptonshire boys, as a charm to *prevent* flogging, used to place 'Briar Ball' or 'Robin's Pincushion' in their coat cuffs (A. E. Baker, *Northamptonshire Words*, 1854).

Condolence

Condolence is likely to be heartfelt. Juvenile commiserators are well aware that it may be their turn to suffer next. 'Bad luck, chum', 'It's a shame', 'Bad butter, old man', 'Bad eggs', 'Hard luck, dear bean', 'Hard buns', 'Hard cheese', 'Hard Cheddars' (terms of condolence seem to be much related to food), 'Hard going, old thing', 'You've had your chips', 'Hard lines', 'Rotten beans', 'Rotten eggs', 'Rotten luck, poor mite', 'What

---

1. Apparently an old and tried remedy. See S. O. Addy, *Household Tales*, 1895, p. 78, and *Notes and Queries*, 11th ser., vol. xi, 1915, pp. 409–10.

flipping rotten awful luck!', 'Oh, squashed eggs!', 'Tough luck', 'What a pity, old boy', 'You've had it, indeed', 'You're in the wars'.

It has, doubtless, been a 'raw deal'. And the 'poor blighter' is encouraged to face the world again with: 'Cheer up, chum', 'Chin up, old man, better luck next time', 'Buck up, old thing', 'Pull your socks up', 'Wakey, wakey', 'Don't cry over spilt milk'.

IT is an indication of the children's attitude to their acts of mischief that they do not refer to them as pranks, but as 'tricks' or 'games'. Almost any group of 12-year-olds, asked what are their favourite after-dark games, will name doorbell-ringing, and similar uncommendable activities, in the same breath as orthodox games like 'Kick the Can' and 'Jacky Shine a Light'. Indeed, minor lawlessness is sometimes an integral part of a game. In 'Kit Can', played around Manchester, the fun is to keep throwing a ball into someone's garden, taking turns to retrieve it, until one player is caught and has to talk himself out of the situation. In 'Truth, Dare, and Promise' each player has to agree either to tell the truth, accept a dare, or promise to do as he is told, and if he accepts the dare he is usually ordered to perform some mischief which it is a point of honour for him to carry out. Even when adult-teasing *per se* is the activity decided upon for the evening, the mischief usually has a traditional name and is played with rules as if it was a game. Thus a 14-year-old Forfar boy describes 'Chicky Melly':

'The way we start is we all chant a rhyme,

> Innerty fenerty fickety fage,
> El dell dominage,
> Urky burkey starry rock
> Black pudden white trout
> That shows your oot.

The body who is out has to go and fetch a milk bottle full of water and sand and place it on a high place, tie a piece of string round it and also to the door. Then we knock and shout in the door something to make them come so that the bottle will fall and make a terrible mess.'

A 12-year-old Pontypool girl writes:

'A good game for after dark is "Knock Out Ginger". A crowd of us stand with one foot towards the centre of a big circle. Someone stands in the middle and goes around the feet pointing and saying this rhyme:

Ip, dip, dip,
My little ship,
Sailing on the water
Like a cup and saucer,
But you are not on it.

The person whose foot is pointed to last changes her foot, the rhyme is repeated and then if the same person's foot is pointed to again she goes out and is not it. This goes on until everyone is out except one person, that person is IT.

Then a house is chosen. Everyone except the person who is It goes away to hide but always somewhere where they can watch the fun. Then this person goes to the house and gives a loud bang on the door, and then runs away to hide but she or he must hide with someone else. That someone is ON-IT next time.'

The unexpected and perhaps sociologically interesting fact which has emerged about this adult-baiting is that in many parts of Britain the pranks are carried out in prescribed forms; and, as in a traditional sport such as fox-hunting, almost as much attention is paid to technique as to results. The juvenile craft of tying-up doors or tapping at windows seems to be just as much an inherited skill, passed on from one age-group of children to the next, as the craft of the thatcher or the osier cutter. Accounts by old people show that the methods used by children today for agitating the television-bound householder are the same as those employed by their grandfathers and great-grandfathers in the days of zoetrope and musical box.

Door Knocking and Bell Ringing

Together with variants, there are more than sixty established names for the pursuit of illegally knocking at doors.[1] In London and the Home Counties it is generally known as 'Knock Down Ginger' or 'Knocking Down Ginger'. A boy will say, 'When we met at the lamp-post someone suggested we play "Knock Down Ginger",' or 'In "Knocking Down Ginger" the object is to knock or ring on a door and escape'.[2] Alternatively it may be known as 'Knock Up Ginger', a term common in Somerset

1. 'Wilfully and wantonly disturbing any inhabitant by pulling or ringing any door bell or knocking at any door', as also making a bonfire or throwing a firework to the obstruction, annoyance, or danger of residents or passengers, contravenes the Town Police Clauses Act, 1847, s. 28.
2. The term 'Knocking Down Ginger' goes back to the nineteenth century. A correspondent to *The Sunday Times*, 6 April 1947, quotes it as current around Islington and Barnsbury, c. 1902; and our own correspondents, with longer memories, confirm its use in other metropolitan districts. Similarly, Norman Douglas mentions it, along with 'Knocking Ginger out o' Bed', described as 'rough: played with door-knockers', in *London Street Games*, 1916, p. 143.

and the south-west; 'Knock Out Ginger', the usual term in Monmouthshire and sometimes south of the Severn; 'Knocking Out Ginger', general in and around Lydney; and 'Knock Off Ginger' at Brighton. But there is often more than one name current in a town. Thus an Oxford 12-year-old, noting this fact, cites the names 'Nanny', 'Nick Nock Nanny', and 'Knock Out Ginger'. A 12-year-old Edinburgh girl describing the same misdemeanour says it is called: 'Ring-Bell-Scoot or Chickydoory or Tap-Door-Run or Knock Down Ginger.' Of these Edinburgh names 'Ring-Bell-Scoot' and 'Tap-Door-Run' appear to be local slang names; 'Knock Down Ginger' has travelled from the south; and the indigenous term seems to be 'Chickydoory', which several Edinburgh children are careful to distinguish from 'Chickie Mellie', the name given to more elaborate pranks. It is usual, however, for one name to predominate in an area, and in the following list, in places where we have enough evidence to show which term predominates, we have marked the locality with an asterisk.

Bing Bang Skoosh. Glasgow*. Variant *Run Bang Skoosh* in Rothesay.

Black and White Rabbit. Throughout Manchester* and Sale. Alternatively, but less frequently, *Black Rabbit* and *Black Cat.*

Buzzing. Liverpool. Used especially of promiscuous bell-ringing on the way to school.

Bobby Knocker. Swansea*.

Catfeet. Bolton.

Cheeky Nellie. Perth. But the term is also used for more audacious tricks such as throwing stones on to roofs. Likewise *Cheeky Mellie* in Forfar. Both terms are probably rationalizations of *Chickie Mellie.*

Cherry Knock. Ebbw Vale, Monmouthshire. Alternatively, *Cherry Knocker* in Blackwood, and *Cherry Knocking* in the Vale of Berkeley.

Chickie Mellie. As already noted, this is really a term for an organized assault on a house, but it is sometimes used loosely for simple door-knocking. Aberdeen, Dundee, Edinburgh, Forfar, Glasgow, Luncarty, Inverness.

Chickydoory. Edinburgh*.

Dodger. Derby.

Ginger Knocking. Peterborough*.

Gingerbread. Brighton. Alternatively *Gingerbread Knocking*, Peterborough.

Jinksy Tat. Hemingbrough, near Selby, W. Yorkshire.

K.D.R.F. (*Kick Door Run Fast*). Isle of Bute. Cf. *R.B.R.F.*

Knock and Run. Aintree, Bacup, Barnsley, Bolton, Brighouse, Corwen (Merionethshire), Darwen, Doncaster, Hounslow, Inverness, Liverpool, Manchester, Ormskirk, Penrith*, Shepshed (Leicestershire), Stoke-on-Trent, Stourbridge, Torquay, Walkden. An obvious name, and one with no regional significance. Cf. *Ring and Run.*

Knock Down Ginger, or less commonly *Knocking Down Ginger*. Much the most common term in London and environs, e.g. in Camberwell*, Croydon*,

Dulwich*, Greenwich*, Peckham*, Putney*, Southgate*, Southwark*, Walworth*. Also the prevailing term in Barnet*, Bexleyheath*, Enfield*, Gillingham*, Hitchin*, Welling*. Only known to a few children farther afield, e.g. Edinburgh, Liverpool, Lydney, Sheffield.

Knock Door Bunk. Isle of Ely.

Knock Door Run. Langholm*.

Knock Go Run. Sale.

Knock-a-Down Ginger. Southwark, Preston.

Knock-a-Door Run. Bolton.

Knock Down Ginge. Guildford.

Knock Off Ginger. Brighton.

Knock Out Ginge. Gillingham (Kent).

Knock Out Ginger. Alton*, Caerleon, Cwmbran, Newbridge* (Monmouthshire), Oxford, Pontypool*, Portsmouth*, Plympton St Mary (near Plymouth), Varteg (near Pontypool).

Knock Up Ginger. Occasional alternative to *Knock Down Ginger* in London area. Apparently the usual term in Leighton Buzzard*, Luton*, and Watford*. Also common in the West Country: Bath*, Exeter, Lydney, Plympton St Mary.

Knock It And Fly. Rotherham.

Knock Knock. Blackburn. See also *Nick Nack*.

Knock Up. Shepshed (Leicestershire).

Knockers. Atherton.

Knockety Knock. Liverpool.

Knockie Door Neighbour. South Shields.

Knockie, Knockie, Run Awa'. Perth. Alternatively, *Ringie, Ringie, Run Awa'*.

Knocking. Lydney, Ockbrook (Derbyshire).

Knockng Doors. Ipswich.

Knocking Down Doors. Eccleshill, near Bradford.

Knocking Out Ginger. Lydney*.

Knocky Nine Doors. Much used in parts of Cumberland: Cleator Moor, Penrith, Whitehaven, and Workington*; and in County Durham: Birtley, South Shields*, and Sunderland*. Also in Newcastle upon Tyne*. Cf. *Nicky Nocky Nine Doors*.

Not Out Ginger. Street (Somerset). Probably a perversion of *Knock Out Ginger*.

Nanny. Oxford. Abbreviation of *Nick Nock Nanny*.

Napper. Liverpool.

Nick Nack. Blackburn*, Liverpool, Padiham*, Ulverston, Wigan.

Nick Nock. Glossop (Manchester), Liverpool (fairly common), Penzance. Also *Nick-Nocks* in Colby, Isle of Man.

Nick Nock Nanny. Lydney, Oxford.

Nicky Nocky Nine Doors. West Hartlepool*. Cf. *Knocky Nine Doors*.

Nicky Nocky Nino. Common alternative to *Knock and Run* in Penrith and district.

Rabbit Chase. Nelson (Lancashire).

R.B.R.F. (Ring Bell Run Fast). This and *K.D.R.F.* seem to be the usual terms on the Isle of Bute.

Rat Rat Rat. Widnes.

Rat Tat Tat. Abertillery and Newbridge in Monmouthshire, Barry in Glamorgan, Coventry*. A variant in Lydney is *Rat-a-Tat Ginger*.

Rat-a-Tat-Tat. Solihull, near Birmingham, and Grenoside, near Sheffield.

Rattling. Shrewsbury.

Red Apple. Upton Magna*, near Shrewsbury, and Wolverhampton*. Cf. *Rosy Apple*.

Ring and Run. Liverpool.

Ring-Bell-Scoot. Edinburgh.

Rip Rap. Derby.

Robbers' Knock. Salford.

Rosy Apple. Derby. Cf. *Red Apple*.

Rosy Knocking. Derby.

Run Away Spider. Swansea.

Slam and Knock. Salford.

Squashed Tomato. Wolverhampton.

Tap-Door-Run. Edinburgh.

Tappit and Skedaddle. Broughton Beck, near Ulverston.

Thunder and Lightning. Sale. A contraction of 'Knock like thunder, run like lightning'.

Tick Tack. Darwen. Cf. *Nick Nack* from the same area.

Tip Tap. Penrith.

Some children, particularly girls, mention the tactical side of doorknocking. A 10-year-old Caerleon girl writes of her favourite game:

'The game is called Knock out Ginger. It can be played by any number of children and is great fun. First of all you choose a person among the team who is the knocker. Next you find a house (the best kind are large ones) on which you play the trick. It is much safer for the knocker if there is an overhanging [porch] as it is not so likely that he or she will be recognized. The ideal night is very quiet with a minimum amount of wind. The team first creep around the house to make sure that all the inhabitants are safely indoors. When they have arrived back the "knocker" takes over; he or she steps up to a door (one nearest escape is best) and gives a loud and frightening knock – then runs out. The team and the knocker run to a safe hidingplace. When the noise has reached its destination and done its work the person comes out muttering in most cases "Alright leave the door on its hinges". The owner sees nobody and is very angry. Then the game is over and the victim now has very angrily slammed the door. The team chooses another knocker and the game is played again. It is necessary that the game should be played in the dark otherwise the game and its players might be discovered and banned.'

One girl (Birmingham) observes: 'We do not get a very big gang because when there are too many of us we usually get caught,' and adds 'we try to wear a scarf not to show much of us.' Another says: 'You have to be good runners to play the game and be good sports to take the blame if your caught and not tell on the others.'

Rudeness is not usual, but sometimes the pranks are deliberately played on 'cross-patches'. Occasionally they will continue knocking even after they have been seen: 'That will make them mad and it will make them chase you' (Boy, 13, Peterborough). And one Edinburgh boy, aged 12, says: 'When the person comes to the door we make faces, and shout names like you old haggis, you old ninkumpupe, you old gieser flatfoot soinso and sometimes we call them stued onion lugs or bawhead.' Elated with their sport, they sometimes run down the street, crying out like fairy fiends the nature of their activity, 'Cheeky Nellie! Cheeky Nellie!' or 'Knockie, Knockie, Run Awa'!' or 'Knock like thunder, run like lightning'. And a Middlesbrough teacher, who recalls that when she was young, about 1925, the children living in the poorer quarters of the town spent much of their time travelling to a well-to-do district to find a house with a bell, says that when they had rung the bell they used to chant:

> Me don't know, me can't tell,
> Me press a button and run like hell.

Prevalence of Pranks

Adult opinion about the pranks seems to be divided. There are those who deplore them, stating that, when they were young, children never got up to the devilry they do today. And there are those who, with a twinkle in their eye, assert that youngsters today are unadventurous and do not have the larks they used to in the old days. Both assumptions appear to be incorrect. The schoolboy's addiction to pranks seems, like his other characteristics, to remain constant through the years. The only change, possibly, is that today girls seem to take almost an equal part in these activities. Certainly almost as many accounts of pranks have been received from girls as from boys.

Nor does the variety of pranks diminish with the years. Some pranks, naturally, are no longer practicable. Street boys no longer have the opportunity to nail people's coat-tails to shop-window frames as they did in John Hone's time (*Every-Day Book*, 6 January 1825); and it is no longer a customary sport in country districts to block up chimney tops with turf, possibly because chimney stacks are generally higher now and less accessible But in new conditions new possibilities arise. The large tenement blocks, for instance, have their own temptations. Doormats can be collected even easier than turfs, and thrown over the banisters; and there is the trick they play on each other, at adult expense, called in Edinburgh 'Monkey Come Down':

'We get some people who don't know the trick to go up the stair and tell them when they reach the top flat we will hide and they will have to find us. But we ring all the bells of the downstairs flats and shout "Monkey come down" and the boys on the top run down and get blamed for ringing the bells.'

As will have been seen under Mischief Night (pp. 299–303), most of the traditional front-door tricks continue to be practised. Front-door handles are coated with treacle or grease so that when the owner returns from work his hands are messed up and he cannot turn the handle. Liquid soap is squirted under the door to make it stick, or in the keyhole to block it. (In the old days – Bermondsey, about 1870 – children used to squeeze hot pease pudding into the keyholes and the pudding would set like cement.) 'Bangers' and other explosive excitements are shoved through the letter boxes, or in a newspaper when delivery is expected. (A Lincoln correspondent states that about 1920 they used to catch shrews or field mice and pop them alive through letter-boxes.) Sometimes a door is knocked, and a motor tyre or old pram wheel is rolled into the doorway when the door is opened. Sometimes they ring at a door and do not run but play a game known in Liverpool as 'Any Answers'. They ask: 'Does Mrs Jones live here please?'

'If the person says yes you have to say anything you think of like Joan said she can't meet you tonight. After saying this they usually say I am sorry I don't know what you are talking about, I must be the wrong Mrs Jones' (Boy, 14).

Sometimes they creep round a house looking for a half-open window, and then see how many of them can throw a stone through the slit, a pursuit known in Camberwell as 'Knocking Down Jimmy'.

And they still possess the fiendish knowledge, bequeathed by tradition, of what happens when a dry drainpipe is stuffed with paper, or – even more exciting – with a paraffin rag, and set alight. The resulting conflagration is known appropriately as 'Devil in the Pipe' (Swansea), 'Devil up the Drainpipe' or 'Roaring Devil' (Newbridge), 'Bogie up the Drainpipe' (Featherstone), 'Pipe Alight' (Manchester), and 'The Bull Roar' (Pontefract). The flames are sucked up the water pipe (or 'roan pipe' as a young Aberdonian calls it) with an echoing roar matching Arthur O'Bower's progress up the land, or, as one lad admiringly exclaimed, 'like an underground train approaching'. It is a prank which will disrupt even a television party. Through the wall 'an eerie sound like a ghost wailing is heard inside the house. The people rush out to see what it is,' says a 14-year-old, 'but we have already bunked.'

Nevertheless the children do not always have everything their own way. 'If the people sees us coming they are prepared for us and tips water over us' (Girl, 14). 'Sometimes the man will answer the door quickly and catch you in the act' (Boy, 14). 'If one of the gang is caught then you get into terrible trouble because they will go and see your mother and father and then you have a row or a hiding' (Girl, 13). And these cardboard commandoes repeatedly urge the importance of a reconnaissance before a house is assaulted. 'Make certain,' says a 12-year-old girl, 'that the person is inside the house or he may come up the path and catch you.' 'A piece of advice to anyone who would like to try bell ringing,' writes a young Scotsman. 'Never ring the bell of a house whose owner has a dog.'

Pedestrian Duping

Duping pedestrians is one of their more tolerable amusements: it is the inquisitive or covetous passerby who suffers the most. An 11-year-old girl from Garndiffaith, near Pontypool, writes:

'When the nights draw in and it gets darker earlier I like to play tricks on people with some of my friends. One of the tricks we like is to get a piece of black cotton and tie it to a necklace, a coin, or anything that will show up and this we place somewhere [usually under a street lamp]. When someone comes along if they chance to see it they go to pick it up and before they can manage to get it we pull the cotton and the necklace or coin comes back to us.'

One 11-year-old boy (Pontefract) says that the coin they put out is an imitation one in which they can make a hole; another girl (Perth) says that they put out a 'bulgy purse', and do this on April Fool's Day so that when the purse 'vanishes behind a hedge, we all jump up and shout "April Fool"'. The most usual bait, reported from all parts of the country, is a carefully wrapped parcel. Sometimes it is placed on the highway to tempt the passing motorist, and the hidden spectators have the satisfaction of watching the car stop and the people get out and go back to see what it was lying in the road.[1] In Angus this prank is called 'Parcelie'. 'We also play another kind of "Parcelie" where we tie a string to the parcel and put it on someone's doorstep, knock at the door, and hide with the string.

[1]. 'I remember,' writes a Surrey correspondent, 'we went to investigate a parcel on the middle of the road one night, and my younger sister screamed with fright when it ran away from our outstretched hands. Of course some boys, out of sight, had it – and us – on a string.'

When someone comes to the door we pull the parcel away and run'
(Boy, 13, Eassie). Around Arbroath they make certain of their victim with
an even bolder ruse known as 'False Alarm':

'The most daring amongst us goes to the door, while someone else hides
round the corner. The person with the box taps at the door and when it is
answered he holds forward the box waiting for the person round the corner to do
his part. When the owner of the house is about to take the box the string tied to
the box is pulled tight and the box goes flying through the air out of reach. When
this happens everyone runs away' (Girl, 13).

There are further refinements on this trick which may catch even the
wide-awake. In one, when the passerby stoops for th parcel it is jerked
only a little way from him. The probability is that he will then make a
most determined grab for it and seize it, whereupon the parcel disinte-
grates in his hands, being filled with putrefying apples or fresh cow
manure. In another trick a parcel of rubbish is neatly tied up and a name
and address inscribed on it. This is left on the pathway for someone to find
and kindly take to the 'owner'. In another a parcel is made to look like a
crumpled up piece of paper or empty carton, but has a brick in it so, that
when somebody (as somebody inevitably will) has a good kick at it 'he
stubs his toe or scrapes his shoe'.

*** Fishing for pedestrians is no newfangled sport. In *The Misfortunes
of Toby Tickle-Pitcher*, a penny merriment printed about 1853, appear
the lines:

> Dame Cunning went out on a bit of a stroll
> To visit her neighbour, Miss Dorothy Droll,
> But as she arrived at Miss Dorothy's door,
> Her eyes they glanced down at a spoon on the floor.

> 'Oh dear!' said the dame 'I am lucky today,
> Only think now! to find such a prize in my way.
> Miss Dorothy's drop'd it – it's silver no doubt,
> If I hide it at once, I shall ne'er be found out.'

> But just as she stoop'd to the place where it lay,
> Toby T. pulled the string, and he snatched it away.
> 'Good lack!' scream'd the dame 'I am sorely afraid
> Those two saucy boys must have heard what I said.'

Booby Traps

All over Britain (Bedford, Derby, Edinburgh, Lydney, Manchester, and
Southwark) a 'favourite trick' is stretching a piece of cotton across a foot-

path to knock off a person's hat, a version of the guerrilla fighters' strata-gem of stretching piano wire across a road to decapitate motorbike dispatch riders. In the side streets off Edinburgh's Royal Mile boys aspire to topple even the coppernob's helmet. '*Trick on a policeman*,' writes a 12-year-old:

'Tie a rope from one tree to another a good bit higher than the policeman and when he walks under it lower it and knock his hat off. Then run away.'

Alternatively they stretch the thread across the path at ankle height, and hide behind a tree at a safe distance. 'Mostly the people stumble but don't fall,' remarks a 12-year-old Pontypool girl. 'Some take it as a joke but others get very cross, and tell us not to do such a wicked thing again.' In Peckham the boys go one further, stretching a thread across the pavement and attaching it to a milk bottle balanced on a wall, so that when the person walks into the thread the bottle smashes at his feet. And in Watford they tie a string across the road and then hide in a garden waiting for a car to break it and make an interesting 'ping' as if something had broken in the car.

Kicking Doors

No more than a variation on door-knocking is 'White Horse, One, Two, Three' or, 'White Horse Kick' (both Newbridge), or, the identical game, 'Kick, Horsey, Kick' (Forfar). In both corners of Britain the preliminaries are formal. A 14-year-old Forfar boy writes:

'The way that you play "Kick! Horsey, Kick!" is that at least six boys get together and one of the boys, usually the oldest, gets the others in a line with their arms out and their fists clenched and he goes down the line hitting the fists, and for every fist, he repeats one word of a rhyme. This rhyme is,

> Eachy, peachy, peary, plum,
> Throwin' tatties up the lum,
> Santa Claus got ane in the bum,
> Eachy, peachy, peary, plum.

The person at which he stops is out. This goes on until one person is left and then he gets the job of running to a house door and for every blow which rains on the door, he must shout "Kick! Horsey, Kick!" and run away as fast as he can.'

'This goes on,' he adds, 'until we all get fed up,' a feeling undoubtedly shared by the householders. The game, which is known in Derby as 'Kicking White Horses' and in Sheffield as 'Horse Kicking', is a hangover of a wretched trick they sometimes play on each other known as 'Kick,

Donkey, Kick' (London), 'Donkey Kick-Kick' (Enfield), 'Kick Bonny White Horse' (York), 'White Horse Backward Kick' (Luton), 'Shoeing a Blind Horse' (Bath), and in Forfar as 'Bread and Butter' or 'Rin, Horsey, Rin'. For this prank they induce a new-comer or unpopular lad to join them and take the principal part. They blindfold him, lead him along the road, and instruct him to kick various objects, in some places the test being to kick backwards like a donkey. They get him to kick a tin, a dustbin, a lamp post, and commend him on his vigour. Then, unknown to him, they lead him to somebody's front door, to which he may be tied, his ankle sometimes being attached to the door-knocker, and, as they begin to run, they instruct him as before 'Kick, donkey, kick', which he obligingly does as heartily as ever until the door is opened. Whereupon, if he has not been tied to the door, 'he turns to run, and trips over a rope stretched across the path by his "friends", and is usually pounced on by the irate housekeeper' (Boy, 14).

Mechanical Knocking

An improvement on 'Knocking Down Ginger' or 'Knock and Run', if the context admits the term 'improvement', is 'Hot Ginger', 'Knockety Knock Knock', or 'Devil on the Knocker', that is, rat-tatting with the aid of a length of wool or cotton. In a district where the houses have front gardens and it is not easy to get away quickly after assaulting the front door, a length of cotton is an acknowledged asset, and they equip themselves accordingly. A 13-year-old Lydney boy writes:

'When it is dark us kids get a few reels of black cotton. We then take it in turns to go up to peoples door knockers and tie on a long piece of this cotton. It must be long enough to stretch out of the peoples gardens on to the road where we hide. Then someone pulls the cotton about half a dozen times which will knock the door. Then we run for it leaving the cotton there tied to the door so that if no one dont come out we knob again.'

With the door-knocker dancing at their command on the end of a thread they can give themselves much cause for merriment. They do not necessarily run away. They 'climb up a tree and pull from there' (Girl, 13, Forfar), or 'lie in the pavement and pretend to be a dustbin' (Girl, 13, Newbridge).[1] 'When someone comes to open the door we let some cotton

1. This variation is known as 'Dustbins' or 'Ashbins'. A classmate writes that they bend down behind the bins and 'sometimes the people walk up and down the yard and you get terrified but usually they never see you'.

out so that it wont snap. Then when they go in we allow time for them to get back to what they were doing and knock again' (Boy, 15, Liverpool). Sometimes, wickedly brazen, they do not even trouble to hide themselves. 'If somebody saw you tearing down the street naturally they would know that you had knocked on their door. We don't play it like that,' states a smug-hussy, aged 11. 'We sit on the fence talking to each other. If the person whose door we knocked asks us if we saw anybody knocking we tell them that some boys knocked at the door but they have run away now.'

Again, doubly artful, they arrange that the door shall be knocked when they are not there, the deed being executed for them by an innocent passer-by who walks into their thread, stretched taut across the road and attached to a knocker. Or, in Brighton, they fix a twig under the knocker to prop it up, tie a thread to the twig, and then stretch the thread across the road so that when a car drives into it the twig is jerked away, letting the knocker fall. Or again, in the Berkeley district of Gloucestershire, they tie the cotton, 'black of course', to a door-knocker, so that when a person walks into the thread 'it automatically knocks at both doors'.[1] By a delicate operation they can also get the householders to knock up each other. In the Forest of Dean they tie together two opposite knockers, attach a small stone to the thread in the middle of the road, and bang on one of the doors.

Doors must open inwards

When this door is opened it lifts the stone, and the pull of the stone on the thread raises the knocker of the house opposite, so that when the first door is shut it releases the knocker on the other door. This device continues to make the door-knockers of each house bang alternately until one of the inmates realizes he is being imposed upon.

In a similar manner, in a neighbourhood which has bell-pulls that can be tied to the door-knobs of houses opposite, as in Edinburgh, where the prank rejoices in the name 'Ring the bell, Susie', the householders find

1. A Hampshire informant states that in his day, not so long ago, his mates would tie two strings to a cat and fasten one each to opposite doors. When the cat ran one way it pulled the knocker of one door, and as it could not go any farther it ran in the other direction and pulled the other knocker.

themselves pestering people with whom they are normally friendly. 'When you play "Ring the bell, Susie" you tie a piece of string to one woman's bell and the other end to another woman's door handle and then you ring the woman's bell that has the piece of string on the handle and then you hide,' says a 12-year-old, who beautifully conveys the confusion which follows:

'When she opens the door it rings the womans bell and when she opens her door she shuts the other womans door then she opens her door it rings the womans bell then she opens her door it shuts the other womans door and it goes on like that for a long time.'

'That is how you cause a row between two neighbours,' remarks a Newcastle 10-year-old.

Alternatively, where there is a row of crowded slum houses with front doors cheek by jowl, the bold and quick-fingered tie cotton from one knocker to the next linking together five or six front doors, with a lead from the last house to a safe place around the corner. When the cotton is pulled it raises the knocker on the nearest door. When the owner comes and opens the door the cotton tightens and pulls the knocker of the next door, and when this call is answered it awakens the knocker on the next house farther on, 'and so it happens that you bring a crowd of people to their doors,' observes a Headington, Oxford, 12-year-old. 'This game is exciting.'

Window Tapping

Another way to get a householder 'in two tempers', as a Pontefract boy puts it, is by window tapping, known as 'Window Tacking' (Bolton), 'Spirit Rapping' (Leicester), 'Button on the Window' (Lydney), 'Cotton and Button' (Pontefract), and 'Thief Knock' (Birmingham). In eastern Scotland it is generally referred to as 'Cheekie Melly' or 'Chickie Nelly', though also known as 'The Skeleton knockin' at the Windie' (Forfar).[1] All

1. Correspondents send the names 'Devil on the Window' (Swansea, c. 1930) and 'Devil on the Pane' (Llanelly, c. 1914), as well as 'Window Tapping' which was, and still is, the usual name. Names previously recorded include 'Pin-and-Button' (H. E. Bates, Kettering, c. 1916, in *Everybody's*, March 1954); 'Tick Tack' or 'Window Tacking' *Folk-Speech of South Lancashire*, 1901); 'The Button' (*Golspie*, 1897); 'Peter Dick' R. C. Maclagan, *Argyleshire*, 1901), and 'Clock Work', also Argyllshire (*Folk-Lore*, 1905).

that is needed for the trick is a long piece of dark cotton, something to fix the cotton with, such as a piece of chewing gum, soft wax, a pin ('strotpin' says a Birmingham lad), or nail, and a button or little stone, or 'skeillie' (Forfar), to make the rapping. 'A small round stone is best,' says a Forfar boy:

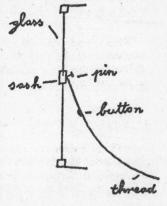

'The pin or chewing gum is fixed to one end of the thread and stuck in or on, as the case may be, the snib of someone's window. The stone or button must be fixed about a foot from the pin so that when the thread is loose it lies against the pane of glass. Take the other end of the thread and hide behind a bush or a wall. Pull the thread tight and then quickly let it loose. When it goes loose it taps against the window pane.'

The trick appears to be particularly successful when played on superstitious spinsters and irascible old gentlemen. The button 'emits an eerie tapping noise'. 'The aim of the game is for the people of the house to look out to see who is tapping the window and when they find no one there it gives them a scare.' 'Then when the window closes you begin tapping again.' This trick, which undoubtedly requires some skill for its successful operation, appears to be practised everywhere, accounts coming from places as distant from each other as Ipswich, Caerleon in Monmouthshire, and the remote village of Etton in the East Riding. The boy in Lydney who, unlike his classmates, describes 'Button on the Window' as getting a long piece of thread and a button and 'flinging it against the window and then running off as hard as you can' appears to be a faintheart.

Other window-pane pranks include sticking a rubber sucker to the window, pulling it off 'so it makes a funny noise', and then breaking a lemonade bottle 'so it sounds like a window breaking'; 'pinging' a little stone at the window and then breaking a bottle; firing peas or barley at the window through a pea-shooter; 'bobbing' an old hat on a stick, or 'a big ugly face' cut out of a turnip or mangel in front of the window; and fixing a piece of knotted string to the glass with a suction plug, pulling taut, and drawing the finger nail up the string so that 'inside the house it sounds like rrrrr'.

Door Tied to Movable Object

Not only do they lure householders to the street with their unwarrantable music on door and window pane, they may first tie some object to the door-knob so that when the door is opened it will add a jangle, clatter, or clash to the householder's confusion. They attach a dustbin or dustbin lid to the door 'making sure that when the door is opened the dustbin will clatter as much as possible', or string together a row of tins which make 'the sound of ghost's chains', or, most popular, they attach a jam jar or milk bottle placed on a nearby window sill. In Aberdeenshire this is known as 'Set the Bottle':

'An old bottle is raked out of the dump. Then it is tied to a piece of string. At a signal that the road is clear of people one boy who volentary said he would, ties it to the door handle. The bottle is then mounted upon a high piece of stonework somewhere near the door. Then the door bell or knocker is rung or chapped. "Run lads here's the wifie." The lights go on in the lobby and the door opens and "Crash!" down goes the bottle on the step. Next day down at the house some fragments of glass are lying on the doorstep.' – Boy, 14, Turriff.

This trick is also described as 'common' by children in Angus, Radnorshire, and Yorkshire. In Sale, Manchester, they sometimes attach the string to another movable object: a flower in the householder's garden.

Door Tied to Immovable Object

Still more boisterous fun is had by securing a person's door with stout string or cord so that it cannot be opened from within. 'It is a way to get your own back on an old nark who has spoilt a game,' declares an Edinburgh 12-year-old, and a Forfar girl seems to be stirred by similar animosity:

'The other night I went out to play with my friend and we decided to play Cheeky Melly. So we got a long piece of rope and tied it to the door of the grumfy ladys. Then we tied it to a post and knocked at the door and ran away and hid. The light went on and we heard the handle turn then a voise saying who's there, and we replied who do you think? She started to get angry and said, "I get the poliese to you and then you won't play that game again." Afterwards we cut the rope and ran away laughing. The next day I heard her telling some of her lady friends.'

More frequently they give themselves double-joy by involving two households at once. They tie the handles of two front doors together, either doors which are adjacent to each other, or doors which are opposite across the street. (Reported from Aberdeen, Alton, Croydon, Edinburgh, Exeter, Forfar, Oxford, Perth, and Pontefract; and doubtless practised everywhere.) The art of tying doors together appears to lie in being able to judge just how much slack rope should be left between the houses so that if both bells are rung at the same time, and if both householders come to their doors together, each is able to open his door just enough to feel that somebody is trying to prevent him from opening it, but not enough to let him see that nobody is there. 'Then there is a good tug a war match each person from each of the two houses trying to open the door' (Boy, 15, Pontefract). 'They pull until the handles come off' (Boy, 13, Forfar), or 'the bravest of us runs up and cuts the rope. At this both doors fly open and they fall on their backs' (Girl, 11, Edinburgh). Then 'once they get out it is best to run your fastest'.

₊ In *The Misfortunes of Toby Tickle-Pitcher*, c. 1853, already referred to, there is an illustration of boys 'Tying the Knockers' in which three lads have tied a rope to one knocker, passed it through the hoop of another across the way, and are now pulling on the end of the rope farther down the street. The result is that they can work both knockers simultaneously at a safe distance, and then, by heaving on the rope, can prevent the doors from being opened. One householder is, ineffectively, pouring a jug of water out of a bedroom window; the other has her hand caught in the door and – feeling much like her 1954 counterpart in Forfar – is crying:

> Lawk a daisy! Oh dear! we'll be murder'd I fear,
> When policemen are wanted, they never are near.

One of the boys is making a long nose. Fortunately for householders the ring or hoop type of knocker is rare now (is this the reason?) and Toby might find it difficult to reconstruct his mechanism today.

Geographical Index

This is an index to the places where the lore has been collected, when named in the text. As some of the lore is known almost everywhere, and the sources of some items were too numerous to specify in the text, it will be appreciated that the amount of material appearing in the book which comes from any one place is usually greater than is shown in this index.

A figure in a bracket following a page number shows that a place is named more than once on the page.

Index of First Lines

433

434

General Index

British Folktales and Legends, A Sampler £1.95 ☐
Katherine Briggs
A sample collection of Katherine Briggs' classic four-volume *Dictionary of British Folktales and Legends,* with a variety of stories, nursery tales, moral comments, magical remnants, wisdom and humour of the British people.

A Dictionary of British Folk Customs £2.50 ☐
Christina Hole
Every folk custom, both past and present, is described with its history, development and present-day usage. The book includes a nationwide calendar showing what happens, where and when.

The People of the Sea £1.50 ☐
David Thomson
The haunting record of a journey in search of the man-seal legends of the Celts. David Thomson has sensitively recorded the naturally gifted talk of the Gaelic people whose traditional association with the sea runs deep.

The Classic Fairy Tales £3.95 ☐
Iona and Peter Opie
Twenty-four of the best known stories in the English language are presented in the exact words of the earliest surviving text or English translation. Lavishly illustrated.

Witchcraft in Britain £1.50 ☐
Christina Hole
The classic history of British witchcraft, written by one of the country's leading folklorists and illustrated by one of the greatest fantasists, Mervyn Peake.

All these books are available at your local bookshop or newsagent, and can be ordered direct from the publisher or from Dial-A-Book Service.

To order direct from the publisher just tick the titles you want and fill in the form below:

Name _____

Address _____

_____

Send to:
Granada Cash Sales
PO Box 11, Falmouth, Cornwall TR10 9EN

Please enclose remittance to the value of the cover price plus:

UK 45p for the first book, 20p for the second book plus 14p per copy for each additional book ordered to a maximum charge of £1.63.

BFPO and Eire 45p for the first book, 20p for the second book plus 14p per copy for the next 7 books, thereafter 8p per book.

Overseas 75p for the first book and 21p for each additional book.

To order from Dial-A-Book Service, 24 hours a day, 7 days a week:

Telephone 01 836 2641 – give name, address, credit card number and title required. The books will be sent to you by post.

DIAL-A-BOOK

Granada Publishing reserve the right to show new retail prices on covers, which may differ from those previously advertised in the text or elsewhere.